WORLD ECONOMIC MELTDOWN

SUPERNOVA OF DEBT, CREDIT AND WEALTH INEQUALITY

KHAFRA K OM-RA-SETI

KMT PUBLICATIONS
SACRAMENTO

Copyright © 2018 by Khafra K Om-Ra-Zeti

All rights reserved. Without limiting the rights under copyright reserved above, no part of this publication may be reproduced, stored in or introduced into a retrieval system, or transmitted, in any form, or by any means (electronic, mechanical, photocopying, recording, or otherwise) without the prior written permission of both the copyright owner and the above publisher of this book.

First Edition
Published by KMT Publications
Printed in the United States of America
ISBN: 9781090892829

DISCLAIMER: No express or implied guarantees or warrantees have been made or are made by the author or publisher regarding certain incomes, earnings, profits or other financial claims. Individual results vary, in large part, due to an individual's initiative, activity, and capability as well as varying local market conditions and other factors. Also, this book cannot be an exhaustive and complete presentation on economic depression. While every effort has been made to make the information presented here as complete and accurate as possible, it may contain errors, omissions or information that was accurate as of its publication but subsequently has become outdated by the marketplace or industry changes or conditions, new laws or regulations, or other circumstances. Neither author nor publisher accepts any liability or responsibility to any person or entity with respect to any loss or damage alleged to have been caused, directly or indirectly, by the information, ideas, opinions or other content in this book. If you do not agree to these terms, you should immediately return this book for full refund. In no event will we be liable for any loss or damage including without limitation, indirect or consequential loss or damage, or any loss or damage whatsoever arising from loss of data or profits arising out of, or in connection with, the use of this book. The author and publisher do not warrant the performance, effectiveness or applicability of any sites listed or linked to in this book. All links are for information purposes only and are not warranted for content, accuracy or any other implied or explicit purpose.

Any trademarks, service marks, product names or named features are assumed to be the property of their respective owners and are used only for reference. There is no implied endorsement if we use one of these terms.Finally, use your head. Nothing in this book is intended to replace common sense and is meant to be a source of information to the reader. Therefore, if you wish to apply ideas contained in this book, you are taking full responsibility for your actions. You should not base investment decisions solely on this document.

In the Memory of My Father
Reverend James Lester Davis who never
lost his ability to expand his knowledge and
understanding of the secular world.
1918 - 2015

and

To the Millions of Americans who Lost Their
Homes During the *Meltdown of 2008* but
should have been provided a national
low fixed-rate mortgage solution.

"The Universe has Always Been, There Is No Beginning, There is No End."

             Khafra K Om-Ra-Seti

ALSO BY KHAFRA K OM-RA-SETI

World Economic Collapse:
The Last Decade and the Global Depression (1994)
Co-author: *Black Futurists in the Information Age:*
Vision of a 21st century Technological Renaissance (1997)
Capoeira, The Novel: A Tale of Martial Arts Mastery,
Mysticism and Love (2002)
Bubble Markets and Boom & Bust Cycles:
Paradigm Revolutions in the Information Age (2002)
Global Economic Boom & Bust Cycles:
The Great Depression and Recovery of the 21st Century (2012)

* * * * *

"Be greedy when others are fearful and fearful when others are greedy."

> Warren Buffett

"September and October 2008 was the worst financial crisis in global history."

> Fed Chairman Ben Bernanke

"If you're going through hell, keep going."

> Winston Churchill

* * * * *

CONTENTS

Tables   ix
Preface   x

PHASE I: THE OUTER LIMITS

Introduction   14

Chapter One
Reflections on the *Meltdown of 2008*   19

Chapter Two
President Barack Obama and the *Meltdown of 2008*   33

Chapter Three
Subprime Mortgage Crisis: No Massive Bailout for Homeowners   48

Chapter Four
The Extraordinary Power of the Federal Reserve System   62

Chapter Five
The GAO Audit Report and the Multi-Trillion Dollar Rescue Operations   101

Chapter Six
Derivatives: The Global Ticking Time Bomb   113

PHASE II: END OF AN ERA

Chapter Seven
Lessons from Japan's Lost Decades: Canary in the Coal Mine   126

Chapter Eight
Reflections on the European Union   144

Chapter Nine
Brexit: The EU Dilemma   167

Chapter Ten
President Trump and the Republicans: The Turning Point   173

PHASE III: THE GRAND CONVERGENCE

Chapter Eleven
Kondratieff and the K-Wave Cycles: Super-Long Economic Cycles   191

Chapter Twelve
Wealth Inequality and *Great Depressions*   200

Chapter Thirteen
The Singularity of the EPIC Global Super Bubble   218

Chapter Fourteen
Super Cycle of Debt and Credit   222

Chapter Fifteen
Harry Dent and Demographic Economic Turning Points   228

Chapter Sixteen
Richard Duncan and Creditism   237

Epilogue   258
Author Afterword on Surviving the Next Meltdown (Bonus)   260
Appendix A: Stock Analysis in *Tech Bubble*: 1995 to 2000   265
Appendix B: Stock Analysis in *Meltdown of 2008*: 2003 to 2008   270
Appendix C: Fukushima: An Economic X Factor   275
Glossary   288
Bibliography   304
About the Author   307
Index   309

TABLES

Table 1: Booming 80s Collectibles   212

Table 2: Post-2008 Collectibles   213

Table 3: Boom & Bust Historic Stock Prices: Dot-Com Era   269

Table 4: Boom & Bust Historic Stock Prices: Meltdown 2008   273

PREFACE

In my last book entitled *Global Economic Boom and Bust Cycles: The Great Depression and Recovery of the 21st Century* (2012), I presented a lengthy narrative on significant paradigm shifts and systemic disrupters, as well as a chronicle on some of the major boom and bust cycles of the 20th and 21st centuries. After nearly 600 pages of historical analysis, I concluded that the economic *Meltdown of 2008* was the First Phase of the Great Depression of the 21st Century. In that global episode, the global credit system froze and was literally in a state of shock. It was an epic event that would have quickly escalated to the status of a worldwide depression if not for the monetary actions of the Federal Reserve System (the Fed and other world central bankers) and the fiscal stimulus programs implemented by the U.S. government and other governmental bodies around the world.

Given the fact that there had been no deflationary depression in the U.S. since the 1930s (close to 90 years), most astute economic observers were well aware that we may have been fast approaching the advent of a new massive deflationary crisis. With the coming of the *Meltdown of 2008*, from Bear Sterns to Lehman Brothers, the tea leaves were indicating that we had entered a new zone of economic extremes. We were looking at the result of decades of overexpansion of the financial system (credit and debt expansion), a kind of economic, financial insanity that had become entirely uncontrollable. What we were witnessing was a multi-decade expansion of a fiat monetary system that had no gold-backing mechanism. The "Capitalistic System" was clearly in unchartered territory faced with some very tough monetary issues!

A gold-backed currency had been the standard for most of the time since the inception of the United States of America (between 1789 and 1971). The dollar's value remained stable during that period. For example, between 1934 and 1971, the parity value of the dollar to gold was $35/oz. The exchange rate was fixed, and this created a superior level of monetary discipline. However, since 1971, when the U.S. abandoned the gold standard and adopted a free-floating exchange rate system, the value of the dollar was greatly diminished, and a new monetary system became the dominating reality and a significant factor in creating our current global economic system.

We are now (in 2018) in the Second Phase of this epic economic drama, which is the primary focus of this current publication. Over-confident investors are fully aware that what has kept the global economic system from imploding has been the work of global central bankers using unconventional economic tools (QE, zero to near zero interest rates, negative interest rates, etc.), and that these institutions will not hesitate to use these tools again.

Over the past seven to eight years, trillions of dollars have been printed and deployed to prevent the advent of the next great depression. Successive quantitative easing programs (Q.E.) were implemented in the U.S. to delay the *Day of Reckoning*: (1) Q.E. 1: December 2008 to March 2010 (2) Q.E. 2: November 2010 to mid-2011 and (3) Q.E. 3: October 2012 to mid-2014. Also, in one of the most controversial financial agendas in the history of finance and central banks, from December 2007 to July 2010, the Fed provided massive loans and bailouts (trillions of dollars) to major banks, institutions and wealthy individuals in both Europe and America. Nothing like that had ever happened before, so this was a time of extreme political and economic desperation to keep the global economic system fully intact and functioning. Also, since the *Meltdown of 2008*, the overall global debt had expanded from roughly $140 trillion in 2007-2008 to $237 trillion by 2017. This meant that the entire worldwide system added a debt load of approximately $97 trillion in less than eight years. These numbers were staggering!

Given what the world experienced and witnessed in the *Meltdown of 2008*, absolutely no one can begin to explain what the fallout would be in a full collapse of the Second Phase. This phase is pregnant with a bust cycle much greater than what happened in 2008, and there is no desire to let this monster out of the cage. And let's be clear, this is not simply doom and gloom ranting (as this current publication will unveil); there is clear confirmation that since the bottom of the crisis in June 2009 and leading up to early 2018, greater global bubbles and extreme credit expansion journeyed into the outer limits.

We must never forget what has happened (and is happening) in Japan; it's not an isolated phenomenon, but a clear indication of what may be in store for the entire world. Japan's relative economic stability throughout its battle with deflation was (in part) mitigated by its ability to export into the flourishing markets around the world (i.e., the EU, China and the U.S.). External demand for its products and services, the massive use of unconventional monetary tools, and the resilience of its people kept this nation out of the death spiral.

As we shall see throughout this publication, the entire world (and the U.S. in particular) promoted the development of extreme economic distortions. Wealth inequality, the immense growth of "Too Big to Fail" banks, the astronomical growth of OTC derivatives and enormous sovereign and government debt are just some of the issues that are simmering in the global economic cauldron. Therefore, we can expect that the next meltdown will be much greater than the 2008 episode, occurring at a time when the entire world is knee deep in a vast swamp of credit and debt quicksand.

After following this story for nearly three decades, I'm convinced that we are faced with possibly the most significant economic depression in world history. I think the Fed and other central bankers around the world are entirely aware of the full implications of a global economic depression, and (as stated earlier) they are committed to keeping this "Global Bubble" alive and fully inflated for as long as they possibly can! Bottom line: most of the sovereign debt accumulated will never be repaid to its creditors. And that's the dilemma that will unfold in this current crisis: a deluge of debt that cannot be repaid!

For those of us who are involved in an in-depth study and analysis of this quagmire, it's understood that we cannot expect politicians, central bankers, and the super-rich to present the cold facts on this issue; they have no vested interest to do so (many of the people in their camp are looking to profit from the carnage). And despite this dire warning, this message is not just a prophecy of doom and gloom, but the sounding of an alarm to ALL of those enlightened spirits that are working on plans, strategies, and systems in preparation for a new day. We can expect, in the initial stages of this crisis that millions of jobs may be lost worldwide and global military confrontations might be imminent.

Perhaps it is no coincidence that we have entered this period of turmoil with the *Information Age Revolution* in full motion, humming seamlessly in the background. The tech revolution is going to be part of the solution for the economic recovery (and that too will come with a price), but we will first have to go through a period of financial and economic purgatory.

The world will have the means to overcome the destructive forces of this global depression, but the big question is, will our leaders pursue the right course of action or will they decide to continue to go to war over oil and other rapidly diminishing resources? The scarcity of natural resources is going to be a critical factor in driving many nations to the brink of economic insanity, and they will make bad decisions in the pursuit of governmental and regional survival.

At this moment in history, this world civilization has severe issues to contend with: global warming, population versus food production and water shortages, the massive threat of unemployment versus the technology revolution, and diminishing resources versus the rapid growth of emerging economic powers in the so-called developing world economies. With over seven billion people on the planet and massive distortions in the global financial and economic systems, this crisis has the full potential of bringing about a devastating implosion in the global capitalistic paradigm. A *Great Reckoning* is upon us!

What's at stake here is the continued existence of an entire civilization: barbarism or civilization. This is an economic crisis unlike any we have faced in all of human civilization on this planet. We have options, although many brilliant solutions will probably never be used. However, it will take unconventional solutions and a period of 21st century universal enlightenment to save our way of life on this planet.

PHASE I: THE OUTER LIMITS

INTRODUCTION

As of 2018, it had been ten years since the *Meltdown of 2008*, and for most people (particularly in the U.S.), the worldwide economy had recovered. By May 2018, the official unemployment rate in the U.S. hit 3.9 percent, which demonstrated a significant improvement over the past decade. And by May 2018, the bull market had not been derailed, and America had become the best investment market and safe haven in the world. However, much of the rest of the world was not booming.

Due to globalization and the marginal cost of labor, central banks in the West were able to print trillions of dollars (without generating significant levels of inflation or hyperinflation) and orchestrate the bailout of international banks, major corporations, and the wealthy elites. What we witnessed was the massive power of the global central banking cartel generating the conditions to re-inflate the massive credit bubble. The global economy was temporarily rescued from the destructive forces of a great deflationary depression, but this was not the end of the story.

After decades of double-digit growth rates, China's economic growth pattern was in the deceleration mode; Japan was still in an intense battle with deflation, Venezuela, one of the major oil producers in the world, had completely collapsed, with hundreds of thousands of Venezuelans fleeing their country. The EU was still struggling with a number of economic issues, from Brexit to major banking problems (particularly in Italy), and with anti-establishment groups (in several countries) seeking to break free of EU domination and euro restrictions. On the surface, much of this appeared to be manageable, but lurking in the shadows were a host of other issues that were never resolved after the *Great Recession*, some of which had been building up over a period of decades.

The massive debt and credit bubble that started to implode in 2008 is still with us. *This book is about that bubble* and the associated institutions, elements and instruments that have kept it alive and breathing. The global elite mantra is that it cannot be allowed to burst, for it might mean the end of civilization as we know it and the destruction of an enormous amount of wealth. It is the most massive economic and financial bubble ever devised in recorded history; there has never been anything like it! It took decades to create it; hopefully, it will not take decades to dismantle the massive destructive deflationary power embedded in its bowels.

The main narrative in this publication is that we will be confronted with a future meltdown (economic collapse) greater than the *Meltdown of 2008*. Major factors are converging that will generate a perfect storm.

Part One, "Phase I: The Outer Limits," examines the extraordinary events and critical issues of the *Meltdown of 2008*. I agree with former Fed Chairman Ben Bernanke when he stated that the *Meltdown of 2008* was the worst economic crisis in history. So an entire section of this book is devoted to examining that meltdown. In Chapter One, we reflect on some of the key issues and events of the crisis. We examine the issues of America's domestic decline and political gridlock in Washington versus its financial commitments to maintain an international presence and empire. We will also examine the collapse of America's middleclass and the era of deleveraging. In Chapter Two, the focus is on President Obama during the 2008 crisis. As president during the first phase of this massive collapse, what did he manage to accomplish and how much support did he receive from the Republican opposition, the banking industry and other critical institutions, such as the Federal Reserve System.

In Chapter Three, we take an unconventional look at the Subprime Mortgage Crisis and question why there was no massive bailout for the American homeowner. Trillions of dollars were deployed to rescue the global economy, however, for less than $1 trillion millions of homes could have been saved and America would have experienced a much stronger recovery. **In Chapter Four,** our attention will focus on the Federal Reserve System and its enormous power as an independent institution. A historical review of the Fed reveals some eye-opening facts and interesting aspects of this hybrid organization. It is the largest chapter in this book, and for a good reason.

In Chapter Five, we take a closer look at the double-digit trillion-dollar rescue operations that were put in place to bail out the top players in the banking industry, the wealthy elites, and major corporations in both America and the EU. It was an incredible display of massive financial power orchestrated by the Fed as the key player in bailing out the developed world. **In Chapter Six,** our focus will be on "Derivatives," the ticking time boom hiding in the shadows of an unregulated over-the-counter (OTC) derivatives industry. We will explore how this problem has grown much worst since the *Meltdown of 2008*.

Part Two, "Phase II: End of an Era," provides a detailed analysis of the political and economic issues impacting Japan, the EU, and America during the second phase of this crisis. **In Chapter Seven,** we reexamine the rise and fall of the Japanese bubble economy and its so-called *Great Recession*. Japan's battle with deflation over a period of decades is a living example of super boom and bust cycle developments. Understanding what has happened in Japan is a very important *study analysis* and will help us to better understand the fallout of the coming global crisis. Japan is a classic example of the destructive power of deflationary bust cycles.

Chapter Eight is a reflection on the European Union and the various problems and issues that have been ongoing since the *Meltdown of 2008*. We examine the Sovereign Debt Crisis and take a close look at the fate of the euro. The European Union (EU) has reached a critical impasse that will either be resolved in total political and economic union or collapse into economic disunion and political chaos.

In Chapter Nine, we briefly explore the issues that led to the historic vote in 2016 for the UK to leave the European Union (EU). The Brexit vote was unexpected and raised a lot of questions regarding the future of the EU. We question whether this historic vote will encourage other nations to decide to leave and quit the EU and the euro? **In Chapter Ten,** we swing back across the pond (the Atlantic Ocean) and examine the historic election of Donald Trump as the 45th president of the United States. The primary concerns in this publication are the economic policies President Trump, and the Republicans will pursue during the current downward wave. Major missteps and flawed policies (in the premier economy in the world) will prove to be very detrimental and lead to a collapse of the global economy. If America stumbles into the deflationary abyss, it will take the rest of the world with it.

Part Three, "The Grand Convergence," will examine the thoughts and ideas of three non-mainstream economists who have arrived at similar conclusions regarding the factors leading to periods of economic slowdowns, collapse, and downward waves. This section will also explore the collective force of several enormous factors that are destined to bring about a simultaneous shock to the global economic system. **In Chapter Eleven,** we examine Long-Wave Economic Cycles to determine whether this theory is still relevant in the modern era. Has the passage of time weakened the K-Wave theory; is it helping to define the current crisis? **Chapter Twelve** takes a look at wealth inequality and why this phenomenon will play a significant role in the next major global meltdown. The supermassive concentration of wealth in the hands of so few people is a significant indicator that is warning us that we are on the eve of a major economic depression. **In Chapter Thirteen,** the focus is on the super bubble or bubbles that are floating throughout the global economy, any one of which could ignite the next implosion of falling prices and deflation. In **Chapter Fourteen,** the subject is the enormous buildup of debt and credit, much of which will never be repaid. The global expansion of this mountain of debt will be another trigger in a domino effect that will have a severe impact on international banks, major corporations and entire nations. The focus in **Chapter Fifteen** is on the economic ideas of economist Harry Dent. Here we consider the significance of demographic trends and cycles, the massive impact of the *Baby Boom* generation and the economic seasons that repeat themselves over decades and centuries. **In Chapter Sixteen,** we examine the ideas and thesis of economist Richard Duncan. A central focus and analysis will be on his economic theory of "Creditism." Duncan sets forth the premise that "Capitalism" was replaced by "Creditism" decades ago, and that this is the system that is now in place in the global economy.

Introduction 17

In the Epilogue, I summarize the book's journey and bring into focus the key issues that are critical to understanding our current crisis and what technological, political and economic solutions the world needs to consider as we move forward in the 21st century. As a civilization and global economic system, we have traveled beyond the point where we can painlessly return to a place of safety: Economic and financial purgatory is unavoidable.

The Author's Afterword is a bonus section providing some basic recommendations on steps to consider in preparing for the next major meltdown. In conjunction with **Appendix A and Appendix B**, this section of the book is focused on investment ideas, strategies, preparation, and planning as well as options to consider as we move forward in the cycle. Observations of the data in Apendix A and B are designed to assist in understanding the actual impact of boom and bust cycles on stock market performance. I'm currently working on another book which will go into greater detail on how to survive and possibly profit from the chaos of a *Great Depression*.

In Appendix C, we take a hard look at the enormous natural disaster that struck Japan in March 2011. Of particular interest in this analysis is the Fukushima nuclear catastrophe that after seven years was still unresolved. As an *Economic X Factor* (an unexpected occurrence and unknown economic factor), Fukushima represents a significant turning point signaling the decline of a global energy vector. The issue of nuclear power is called into question as a very dangerous technology. As an industrial era technological development, its usefulness in the age of green energy is no longer viable.

What we are now about to experience in the West, which will provide the catalyst that will impact the entire world, is a grand collapse of an entire global economic system and the start of the second phase of the *Meltdown of 2008*. As governments and their central bankers struggle to avoid a major collapse in the global system, there is a strong probability that we will witness more frequent boom and bust cycles during the interim periods. It will mean that even during a long downward bear market, periods of *boom and bust* will continue to occur, just as they did during the Great Depression of the 1930s. These events will begin to happen in much shorter time frames.

Also, keep in mind that the financial markets in the U.S. may continue to move higher (before the grand finale) witnessing the Dow Jones soaring to possibly 30,000 and beyond. These events may play out over the next few years. However, it will be imperative not to lose sight of the central premise of this book: that at this point in the economic cycles, a major financial collapse is unavoidable.

This is the biggest story of the past half-century, and like so many economic thinkers and analysts, I have been examining a great deal of economic data wondering how this crisis might reach its final climax. Red alerts are all over the globe: Venezuela, Brazil, Turkey, Japan, the EU, China, etc. The perfect storm has arrived, but there is more to this story than meets the eye.

Breaking the link between money and gold should not have become the permanent monetary system. However, this cannot be undone painlessly without massive economic disruptions. But now that we are in this mess, how can we avoid the worse case scenarios? The Fed has been the ultimate backstop for decades. Should we be talking about limiting its power or expanding it in order to keep our civilization alive and functional? The stark reality is that we are not just facing a typical recession but something much more sinister: the *Greatest Economic Depression* is on the horizon which has the power to bring about the sudden evaporation of trillions of dollars of credit and wealth that will deal a blow so severe that it will be hard to imagine a recovery. The major downturn will witness panic and chaos, and collective insanity.

World Economic Meltdown is about coming to grips with this phenomenon; it's about markets, people, power, politicians, Wall Street, attitudes and beliefs, and about building a strategic plan for survival and success in the 21st century. We will have to live through the enormous challenges of what may become, the mother of all economic depressions: *The Great Depression of the 21st Century*. But this story does not simply end with a global economic collapse; as with all great boom and bust cycles, there will be a great recovery, and that will usher in a new era of prosperity. However, the world will have to go through a period of economic purgatory before the time of renewal.

CHAPTER ONE
REFLECTIONS ON THE AFTERMATH OF THE MELTDOWN OF 2008

Those who cannot remember the past are condemned to repeat it.

George Santayana

Sustained deflation can be highly destructive to a modern economy and should be strongly resisted. Prevention of deflation is preferable to cure.

Former Fed Chairman Ben Bernanke

The *Meltdown of 2008* will go down in history as one of the most devastating economic and financial catastrophes of all time; often cited as the most devastating economic crisis since the 1930s Great Depression. The global financial system was driven to extreme fragility, with systemic risk and leverage at all-time highs. It is fair to say that we (the U.S. and global economic system) came within hours of complete collapse and total economic disintegration! Stock exchanges plunged around the world, the global recession began quickly, unemployment skyrocketed, and market confidence fell through the floor. Worldwide, over 30 million people lost their jobs. This collapse witnessed a significant disruption to the global banking system and the rapid emergence of a freeze in credit markets.

By March 2009, Citigroup was trading below $3 per share; 95 percent of its value had been wiped out. After two bailouts, Bank of America had lost 85 percent of its stock market value. The meltdown generated a 17% decline in world trade and major disruptions to banks throughout the world. Over $11 trillion in household wealth was wiped out: retirement accounts, life savings, home equity, foreclosed properties, etc. In the 2008 crash, the Dow entered a death spiral, falling 2400 points over an eight-day period.

Mainstream economists tell us that the *Great Recession* covered the period from December 2007 to June 2009: an 18-month period that witnessed a 5.1 percent contraction in GDP and the S&P reaching a low of 666 and the Dow 6,547 in March

2009. The main actors in this drama were Lehman Brothers, AIG, Bear Stearns, Fannie Mae, Freddie Mac, Merrill Lynch, General Motors (GM) and other Wall Street financial titans.

Due to the impact on global trade and credit, by December 2008, 23 million people in Mainland China saw their jobs disappear as a result of the collapse in exports and factory closings. As the recession worsened, by early 2009, 800,000 jobs were being lost each month by American workers. *Given a similar set of circumstances, we can expect that this list of events will repeat itself or worse during the next significant downturn.*

The sharp declines and collapse had its most enormous impact on workers and their families throughout the world. In America, the foreclosure crisis heated up with one million foreclosures in 2008. In Iceland, unrestrained free market principles, privatization and a real estate boom, destroyed the economy: by the end of 2008, its banking system collapsed.

By 2010, the foreclosure crisis in America reached 6 million homes with another 9 million waiting in the wings. It was a global crisis of galactic proportions that in the end, would take trillions of dollars to prevent the onset of a Great Depression on a worldwide scale. It was the result of an unregulated economy - unfettered or unrestricted capitalism - and the development of a concentration of wealth and a widening gap between the ultra-rich and the rest of us. As a result of these developments, the biggest and most sensational financial bubble in history was created.

As we entered 2016, it was finally clear to most economic analysts that the aftershocks of the financial tsunami of 2008 were still with us. It had taken the radical, unconventional monetary tools and strategies to contain the most destructive elements of this epic economic event. In 2012, I argued in *Global Economic Boom & Bust Cycles* that the monetary policies of the Fed had *bought valuable time* in which Washington politicians could implement sound fiscal plans for economic growth and renewal. Some attempts at nation building (by the political establishment) were undertaken. However, the sad reality was that the Washington political system was broken, and as of 2018, is still broken.

The politics in Washington is more polarized than ever. It borders on pure hate and contempt, as well as strategies designed to orchestrate complete political disruption. It's clear, the only thing that will bring about any meaningful cooperation between the Democrats and the Republicans is a full-blown down-in-the-ditch economic global collapse. That would be the wake-up call and an inevitable call to action. And when that time comes, there can be no hesitation and no doubt as to what has to be implemented as a sound solution. It will be D-Day, for history tells us (and I will have much more to say about this in later chapters) that a severe economic crisis of this magnitude precedes civil unrest, war, and fascism. That's been the historical paradigm, and politicians should not underestimate the full implications of this lesson from history, especially in regards to the major economic disruptions in the 20th century.

In considering the collapse of Lehman Brothers (on September 15, 2008) as the final detonator of the 2008 meltdown, it was interesting to see the emergence, in July 2016, of a 214-page report written by Laurence M Ball, chairman of the economics department at Johns Hopkins University. In his report, Ball came to the conclusion that the Fed could have saved Lehman Brothers. Entitled "*The Fed and Lehman Brothers*", Professor Ball argued that the Fed should have acted more decisively with the Lehman crisis, stating that, "Fed officials have not been transparent about the Lehman crisis. Their explanations for their actions rest on flawed economic and legal reasoning and dubious factual claims."

Writing in *Global Economic Boom and Bust Cycles*, I often wondered why the Fed could not have saved Lehman Brothers. In Chapter Seven of that publication, I presented my analysis of this unfolding crisis. Opportunities were missed that would have prevented the escalation of events.

Even now it seems to me that they should have known about the systemic risk of a domino effect in the banking industry; it was their job to analyze such possibilities. Thus, the close examination by Professor Ball is significant, considering the amount of global economic damage that resulted from the demise of Lehman (the global *Great Recession*, the bailout of Wall Street, trillion dollar budget deficits, etc.). His report (and ultimately his new book) adds a further dramatic twist to this crisis as he confirms our doubts and suspicions when he states, "Lehman might have survived indefinitely as an independent firm; it might have been acquired by another institution, or eventually it might have been forced to wind down its business. Any of these outcomes, however, would likely have been less disruptive to the financial system than the bankruptcy that actually occurred."[1]

At that moment in history, policymakers were seemingly unaware that we would ultimately be staring into the abyss of a *Great Depression*. The Lehman crisis was grossly underestimated even in light of the devastating economic and financial events that had already occurred in 2008: the Bear Stearns bailout in March; and the massive Fannie and Freddie bailouts in September.

The stage was set for a finale, but the policy architects did not have a full scope of the unfolding crisis. No one had declared a recession in the U.S. economy and each previous bailout was viewed as singular events in crisis management; only unconventional thinkers and analysts understood the connections and knew what was unfolding.

When the deflationary death spiral began, there were desperate attempts by Washington and the Fed to ride to the rescue and prevent destruction (of ultimately) the global economic and financial system.

Without massive deficit spending by government - facilitated by central bank monetary policies - our world would have descended into a crisis far greater than anyone could have imagined. At that point, there was absolutely no capitalistic private sector solution.

The Fed was forced to initiate a new era of monetary policies which in part consisted of money creation (on a vast scale) to buy toxic assets: private sector debt was acquired and subsequently contracted, while government sector debt was increased with the additional expansion of the Fed's balance sheet. Government spending kept the economic show alive; without it, we would have gone down in flames.

Lehman's collapse exposed the real weaknesses of the investment banking industry. All of the major players at the time (Goldman, Bear, Morgan Stanley, Lehman, etc.) were over-leveraged 26 to 33 times in regards to the real equity held on their books versus total assets: $1 held for every $26 or $33 in total assets. Their vulnerabilities were fully exposed, and again, without the Fed bailouts, many companies and industries would not have survived.

In 2008, the debt and credit superstructure quite literally blew up! The financial system had been inflated with massive credit, and when the debt could not be repaid, the system went through an implosion, unlike anything that had ever happen before in the history of finance. The fallout was massive, with many state governments in America suffering a combined loss of $89 billion during the meltdown.

This massive meltdown also simultaneously exposed a lot of systemic economic weaknesses in the global economy, and events moved quickly as the collapse went into hyper-drive. Over-leveraged bets on derivatives in the inflated housing market was a major factor in the 2008 meltdown, with massive risk-taking by the Big Banks. What we witnessed was a grand convergence of a financial tidal wave of events that all centered around the Lehman Brothers demise.

And it's worth repeating so that there are no doubts about who and what was bailed out. The entire banking and investment banking industries would have been destroyed without the *welfare bailouts* generously supplied by Washington and the Fed (*remedies are always socialistic for the wealthy under the urgent requirement to save the economic system*). Many of the billionaires that were bailed out were spared the indignity of becoming refugees (with tin cups) on Wall Street. They benefitted immensely from the bailouts. Trillions of dollars of interest-free money put them back on their feet.

And you would think that in a crisis of that magnitude, policy architects would have expanded their bailout funds to include millions of American workers (and their families) that were upside down on their mortgages. It's interesting to note that it would have taken less than *one trillion dollars* to have bailed out the American people who were losing millions of homes. Since the American worker and consumer make up 70 percent of the nation's GDP, a critical factor not only for the American economy but also for global economic development, why was there not a massive emergency program made available for loan modifications and principal mortgage reductions? Not bailing out the American people at that point in the crisis was a huge and tragic policy failure and a primary reason why millions of people believe that the system is rigged in favor of the wealthy and their inner circles. That's what Senator

Bernie Sanders was really talking about during his historic 2016 presidential campaign; a political testament and campaign against gross inequality.

It's also interesting to note that during the initial stages of the meltdown, investment bankers, Goldman Sachs and Morgan Stanley (in a strategy designed to qualify for government support and bailout funds), decided that it was time to convert themselves into bank holding companies.

Close economic cooperation between the U.S. and Europe was instrumental in generating bailouts and recovery packages. The Fed provided loans and other financial resources for banks, institutions and some wealthy individuals not only in America but also for financial institutions in the EU. There was a joint effort to pull Western Civilization out of the spiral into the deflationary abyss.

Several years after the *Meltdown of 2008*, unprecedented spending by the three most significant global central bankers witnessed $7 trillion injected into the financial system: roughly one trillion by the ECB, two trillion by Japan, and four trillion by the United States. The global consensus is that this did little to raise worker's wages in developed economies or lift the prices of the cost of goods sold. The primary beneficiaries were wealthy investors and the rapid increase in asset prices, from stocks, to bonds, to real estate.

The U.S. government and the Fed engineered the contraction of over $4 trillion of financial sector debt during the period 2008 to 2016. History and technical analysis tells us that the bottom of the collapse was reached on March 16, 2009 (what I like to call the *wasteland* when the markets have been driven to their lowest levels) and was poised to begin the climb out of the abyss. From March 2009, the Dow soared from 6547 to over 18,000 by December 2014, a three-fold rise in just under 6 years. Also, the global financial system created $12 trillion in new money within that same eight-year period

DOWNFALL OF THE AMERICAN WORKER AND CONSUMER

The downfall of the American consumer was one of the great casualties of the 2008 meltdown. Since U.S. households make up 70 percent of the nation's GDP (a nearly $19 trillion economy), the health and well-being of this sector is a significant factor in determining the strength and virility of the entire economy. The enormous collective buying power of the American consumer played a significant role (over many decades) in the economic rise and development of many countries around the world, including such nations as Japan, China, and India. However, by 2008, this dynamic trend was shifting to a lower status, as purchasing power and economic well-being were decimated.

In the aftermath of the crushing impact of the 2008 meltdown, as stated earlier, millions of Americans lost their homes and most people were forced to focus on retrenching and getting out of or reducing their debt loads. Also, wages for the American worker had been declining for decades. Thus, the "70 percent household sector" was clearly pulling back and reducing consumption.

There has been a persistent 30-year decline in earnings of the American worker. And with this acknowledgment, some analysts began to make the connections, pointing to free trade, globalization, off-shoring, and outsourcing as the main culprits in the disappearance of jobs in America. It strikes deep into the heart of the American dream, with many people barely making it and living from paycheck to paycheck.

The U.S., as well as other advanced economies, was deleveraging from balance sheet excesses, and this would continue for several years. According to a report released by the Federal Reserve (in June of 2016) entitled *Report on the Economic Well-Being of U.S. Households in 2015*, 76 million Americans were struggling financially or only just getting by. In addition, half of Americans didn't have the savings to cover an emergency $400 bill. Food stamp use in America continued to expand since the 2008 meltdown, and by 2016 nearly 47 million Americans were on food stamps.

Mainstream economists finally woke up and began to understand that when the vast majority of the wealth, income and assets are transferred to a small minority of the wealthy elites, economic growth is unsustainable and a period of stagnation becomes the dominant economic theme. This then is the full implications of the slow but steady digression and deflation that occurs under the massive imbalances of wealth inequality.

The slow but steady decimation of the middle-class, particularly in reference to depressed incomes, exposed the negative impact and defects of globalization on western population groups. Globalization is a firmly entrenched economic system that has brought about the integration and interdependence of nations, economies, and markets throughout the entire world. After two to three decades of uninterrupted advances in this arena, the globalists succeeded in building this new paradigm. The primary negative impact on societies and nations in the West is the deflationary effects on wages and lower standards of living. Technological innovations, migration, trade and economic policies that are implemented to further the reach and designs of globalization, will continue to add more fuel to the fire of massive global discontent for the countless millions of people in the West that are not benefitting from these global developments. For the average middle-class American (as well as millions of people in Europe and elsewhere), the dream of retirement suffered a fatal blow.

As corporations went abroad for low-paying labor markets and a cheaper cost of operation, this drove growth and economic expansion in places like China, India, Mexico and other strong emerging markets. Good paying jobs in factories and heavy industries in America took a beating in the new era of the "internationalization of labor costs." As a billion or more people in the developing world entered the global industrial workforce, the price of labor continued to fall with significant deflationary consequences in the world's developed economies. Multinational corporations discovered that it was no longer necessary to pay the high labor costs in the West when a much cheaper alternative was available elsewhere. Off-shoring became the norm: why pay $160 to $200 a day for an auto worker in the state of Michigan when it became possible to pay $5 to $10 per day for a worker in China or India. According to a study conducted by *Forbes*, America had lost, on average between the period 2001 and 2012, 50,000 manufacturing jobs per month since China joined the World Trade Organization in 2001.

Labor unions in America lost their power to negotiate for higher wages and better benefits. Also, the power of the Internet, robotic manufacturing, and other technological advances increased productivity dramatically and shifted the spotlight away from the American worker. The first wave was the manufacturing base where automation has cut 5.6 million jobs since 2000; the second wave came in white-collar jobs: accounting, data entry, reading medical images and answering phones and virtual assistants for small and large business owners, are just some of the jobs that were sent offshore. Intense global competition is a driving force searching for higher productivity and lower wages. And this scenario will continue for decades as the world's massive excess capacity in labor will continue to drive down the price of labor. This movement has been on-going for decades and will only grow stronger in this era of globalization and the rapid adoption of new technologies.

Hundreds of former industries in the U.S. have been wiped out and millions of American jobs have been erased from our national ledger, never to be seen again. The majority of the jobs that have been lost will not be recovered. The industrial base is being decimated, piece by piece. Since 2001, more than 42,000 American factories have permanently closed their doors.

The impact has been severe, decimating the middle class in America. The ability to own a home, send the kids to college, go on a two-week vacation every year and eat out at least once a week is a thing of the past for many people. As defined by a federal government task force, the middle class is defined by these factors: (1) Homeownership; (2) Retirement security; (3) automobile ownership; (4) the ability to send the kids to college; (5) healthcare coverage; (6) family vacation. By these measures, many Americans have fallen out of this category and are struggling to make ends meet.

Middle-income jobs are disappearing. Sherle Schwenninger's report "The American Middle Class Under Stress," tells us that 17 million Americans with college degrees are doing jobs that require less than the skill levels associated with a bachelor's degree. The middle class is shrinking in America, it's being decimated. Schwenninger states, "I worry that we're becoming a barbell society - a lot of money, wealth, and power at the top, increasing hollowness at the center, which I think provides the stability and the heart and soul of the society...and then too many people in fear of falling down."[2] Some Americans have to rely on public assistance for the first time in their lives: middle-class people who have fallen financially into a hole. A *New York Times* article calls them "The New Poor." This destruction of the middle class and the rise of extreme wealth has generated a political and social firestorm in American politics and in population groups in other advanced economies:

> "Lower incomes mean less consumer spending and slower economic growth overall. The longer that persists, the longer it will take for the U.S. economy to create the kinds of well-paying jobs that allow the middle class to prosper. Meanwhile, more and more people will come up short on things such as education funding for their kids and retirement nest eggs."[3]

Government leaders and the elite in advanced economies all over the world are waking up to a new realization, that their people don't trust them and that economic policies are only benefitting the wealthy. Germany's finance minister, Wolfgang Schauble, made this observation on this issue at an IMF meeting in Washington in October 2016: "You can look all over at the advanced economies - the British referendum, the campaign in the United States...more and more people don't trust their elites. They don't trust their economic leaders, and they don't trust their political leaders."[4] Bank of England Governor Mark Carney shared his thoughts a few months after the Brexit vote: "Growth has been too low, but also sharing the fruits of growth has not been there."[5] Gross inequality and massive greed have gone beyond the limits, and millions of people are disillusioned and extremely angry about what is perceived as a broken and rigged global capitalistic system.

The deflationary impact of the marginal cost of labor, as well as the over-capacity of industries throughout the world, will continue to persist for years to come. The most significant factor here is the excess capacity that exists in China. This is the end result of globalization, and this new dynamic era will not be derailed or suddenly discontinued; our world has moved way past that point. A sudden reversal in this movement, or if the world's nations move into a period of trade wars or actual shooting wars, will drive the global economy into a period of economic and financial collapse. Thus, the prevailing trends of the deflationary push to lower the marginal cost of labor and the rapid adoption of new revolutionary technologies are destined to bring about dramatic economic changes across the globe in the 21st century.

SECOND PHASE OF THE GLOBAL DEPRESSION

The world is just not prepared to deal with a significant deflationary economic catastrophe on the scale of a "Great Depression," similar to or greater than the 1930s collapse. Billions of people are disconnected from the land and simply would not be in a position to feed themselves if there is a major breakdown in the supply chains and distribution networks that support major cities and metropolitan areas. Recent events in Venezuela is an example (or microcosm) of what that would look like on a global stage. Many nations would be faced with on-going riots, rebellions, wars, and civil disobedience and repressive political measures on all levels. And If various nations decide that erecting trade barriers as solutions for what ails their particular corner of the world, globalization will break down, followed by a collapse in the international banking system. That's why *"this time is different."*

Like millions of people in other countries, most Americans did not benefit from the so-called recovery. Thus, during America's 2016 presidential election cycle, the popularity of Senator Bernie Sanders and billionaire Donald Trump soared in the polls, due to a great extent to popular discontent and dissatisfaction with the status quo. Gross wealth inequality and globalization had hit a nerve that was demanding change. American politics descended to low levels of morality, decency and political responsibility. The system is broken, and there is de-facto political warfare between the Democrats and Republicans. No longer are many responsible politicians voting on the merits of political issues, but are merely voting along party lines. Dysfunction in Washington has grown deeper over the past 10 years, and the nation will continue to become more divisive if they and we cannot understand and fully appreciate the common good. In the event of an uncontrollable economic crisis, this can only mean chaos and mayhem in the streets, markets, and countryside.

As we navigate through the analysis of the *second phase* of this current crisis, the discussion will begin to illustrate how we are operating in unconventional economic territory unlike anything ever attempted in global economic history.

It is probably fair to say that following the advice of mainstream economists is useless. We are now operating outside of standard laissez-faire economic theories; this is a whole new ball game that includes massive governmental interventions. We have ventured too far from conventional economic theories, and cannot turn back. What the past ten years have shown is that low or negative interest rates, as well as quantitative easing (QE) and massive money printing, have failed to generate any significant economic growth. What has been accomplished is the prevention of the onset of a new *"Great Depression."* We have survived, and as of mid 2018, the world is not in complete chaos, spiraling into the deflationary abyss. That is the most crucial victory achieved during the period 2008 to 2018.

However, we are still faced with the fact that most of the factors and precursors that were in place before the 2008 meltdown, are prominent and still firmly in place in 2018, and in some cases, greater in potential destructive power. There is a minefield of unknowns and known critical issues in this current environment, unlike any period in the history of finance and economics.

THE STUDENT LOAN CRISIS

A massive problem for generations of Americans is the student loan crisis. According to Federal Reserve data, student loan debt had skyrocketed from $589 billion in 2007 to over $1.52 trillion in 2018.[6] Low-interest rates helped fuel this growth, and it had also created an enormous burden for over 40 million Americans that will be saddled with this crushing debt for many years to come. For a student graduating with a BA degree, the average debt load is over $37,000. For the millennial generation (individuals born between 1976 to 2004), it meant postponing the start of new households, marriage, and spending on durable and non-durable goods and services that usually takes place within this age group. All of this is detrimental to seasonal demographic and economic cycles, as the purchase of homes, washing machines, TVs, furniture and other big ticket items are significantly delayed or postponed. The data suggests that this is the first time in 130 years that adults ages 18 to 34 are not pursuing independent lifestyles away from their parents, with many still living at home due to limited financial resources.

Americans 60 and older owe about $66.7 billion in student loans, and more than 10 percent of those loans are delinquent. And in this category of student loans, social security checks are being garnished, as well as any other federal payments that the creditor can find. Some of these baby boomers went back to school to learn new skills, and in the process, took on student loan debt. Many others co-signed for their children and grandchildren, or are merely trying to pay off loans taken out decades ago. This is a nightmare for older Americans living on fixed income or limited financial resources. Thus, this is another significant level of debt choking American households. Interest accumulation, late fees, and missed payments all add up to a horrible nightmare for someone struggling to make ends meet. And to make matters worse, especially for a baby boomer, as of 2018, these loans are not dischargeable in bankruptcy. The 2005 legislation that extended this restriction to include loans made by banks and private financial institutions should be changed. Like child support, criminal fines, and unpaid income taxes, private student loans cannot be discharged in bankruptcy. An American citizen that has legitimate reasons for filing bankruptcy should be allowed to discharge private student loan debts.

Huge defaults on student loans are occurring and putting many people in dire straits. In many ways, this debt is worse than mortgage obligations; chief among them is the fact that creditors can garnish a borrower's wages, seize tax refunds, social security and other federal benefit payments. And consider the situation of garnishment of entry-level salaries on a student just entering the workforce; it's a huge burden that will only make matters a lot worse for the American worker and consumer for decades to come.

THE DOMINO EFFECT

There is no doubt that (in this *second phase*) we are poised to witness the most significant financial crisis in world history. With each passing week, month and year, the pressures will continue to intensify on all fronts: exasperating the geopolitical environment, currency wars and trade wars, accompanied by oil and commodity price deflationary or inflationary pressures. Once the dominoes begin to fall, all of the hidden fault lines in the "Too-Big-To-Fail" banks, Wall Street investment houses, OTC derivatives, sovereign funds, etc. will quickly fall apart much like the 2008 meltdown, but on a much larger scale. This is what the world's central bankers fear the most and are ultimately trying to prevent; the bursting of the greatest super-bubble of all time. As will be discussed in later chapters, it is best to avoid unleashing this narrative at all costs!

World economies are dependent on the creation of money and credit by financial institutions. Banks are highly leveraged. More turmoil is coming because there has been no profound changes in the system. Economic reforms have been weak: banks are bigger and more opaque. Derivative trades are much more significant and riskier than what they were before the 2008 meltdown. And again, unless there is some novel approach to remedy this global crisis, we can expect the next significant downturn to be worse than the 2008 collapse.

Ten years after the meltdown, long-term stagnation in Europe had been the norm while the U.S. experienced a period of slow growth, deleveraging and some measure of increased consumer demand. In fact, throughout the developed world, deleveraging consumer debt was a necessary economic and financial activity.

What the past ten years have demonstrated is that monetary policies alone, as well as austerity policies (as in the case of the IMF and EU measures in Europe), did not provide the ultimate solution of restarting the global economy. Many economists and analysts are now waking up to a reality that government fiscal policies are necessary for a slow growth global environment. There has been mainly no strategic coordination between monetary and fiscal policies. Thus, implementation of a novel "Fiscal New Deal" policy must include the real engines of economic growth, people, and infrastructure developments, as well as educational components. As will be discussed in a later chapter, this option is not only necessary for this current crisis, but is probably the only feasible solution we have of generating "escape velocity" out of the death throes of an impending deflationary abyss.

Acceptance of the collapse of globalization is really not an option at this point. In other words, the global community cannot afford to risk falling into the deflationary abyss with $700 trillion of derivatives and over $225 trillion of global debt on the table! Once the avalanche begins, there will be no way to stop it! There is no way we would come out of that scenario unscathed or with minimal damage, as in the case of a garden-variety recession. Those who advocate allowing the global economic capitalistic system to be taken off of central bank life-support stimulus and allowed to collapse into a free market resetting of asset prices, need to consider the dire global consequences at this point in the cycle. We are in an unconventional territory and following old economic textbooks and standard economic laissez-faire prescriptions, will not be adequate or suffice in this current global economic setting. There are far too many unknowns, and the consequences of such a collapse are most likely to be much worse than any of us could imagine.

This is the era of globalization and the intense interconnectedness of global economies. And as 2008 has demonstrated, any sequence of detrimental financial and economic events would be hard to predict. In 2018, what the global economic landscape is suggesting for the foreseeable future is economic contraction and not expansion. Central bankers will not be able to predict or prevent stock market corrections or a major global collapse. However, we can rest assured that they will respond with all available tools at their disposal to stop the descent into total global economic destruction. We can expect an intense battle to subdue the forces of global deflation or inflation (which will depend on the actions and policies of governments).

SUMMARY/ANALYSIS

As we observed in this chapter, the *Meltdown of 2008* offered us a glimpse of a nation almost wholly unprepared for the sudden demise of its financial system. The markets were in chaos and investors were totally confused concerning the moves and activities of the Fed. At one point Bear Stearns was rescued with a generous bailout package, in sheer panic, Fannie and Freddie were placed into conservatorship, then, in what appeared to the Treasury and the Fed that there were no more options, Lehman was allowed to collapse while AIG was bailed out. One has to wonder, what would have happened to Merrill Lynch if Bank of America had not committed to acquiring Merrill at that critical point in time? The Treasury Department and the Fed were reacting to a rapidly unfolding crisis with essentially piecemeal strategies and plans. However, the super-star investors during this devastating crisis that nearly sunk the entire global economy (John Paulson, Tricadia, Magnetar, and others), made billions of dollars betting against the sub-prime CDOs. It repeatedly happens, that in each significant boom and bust cycle there are winners and there are the losers.

The AIG rescue amounted to $180 billion in taxpayer money, and the world would later discover that AIG paid out $165 million in bonuses to executives and traders with some of this bailout money. Also, owners of the Credit Default Swaps at AIG were paid 100 cents on the dollar; the regulators didn't even try to negotiate a lower price in the face of the imminent collapse.

Looming on the horizon is the possibility of another credit crunch or a sudden rise in interest rates or oil could be the spark for the onset of an abrupt crisis. Financial

Weapons of Mass Destruction (derivatives) are in place and again represent a ticking time bomb. The chess pieces have reassembled; 2008 will happen again, but this time on a much larger scale. In 2008 it was mortgage-backed securities; at the center of the next significant downturn will be European sovereign debt. That debt cesspool is a lot bigger, and there will be enormous obstacles attempting to prevent any major bailouts.

In the next crisis and grand shock to the economic system, monetary policy will be the instrument of choice due to the political atmosphere against the use of effective fiscal policies. In 2018 and beyond, the financial titans (flying in on private jets) will not be able to go to the politicians with their begging cups, pleading for another handout.

Major banks have huge exposure to the derivatives that have been placed on European sovereign debt. There is no way of knowing who is set to go under until it actually happens. The derivatives market is still unregulated, and in 2018, there is nothing in place to alert the markets of who has derivative exposure to any particular asset or bond. Nobody knew about the cesspool of toxic waste in AIG until the weekend of the crisis. When the dominoes start to fall, there will be many unknown casualties emerging from the global financial battlefields. The power of Wall Street, the Federal Reserve System, and Big Banks have kept the derivatives market from any meaningful regulations. And when the *bubble burst*, we will begin to know who was indeed skating on thin ice. *In the 1920s stock manipulation was legal, and there were few or no controls; the modern equivalent is OTC derivatives.*

The underlining premise of this book is that we have yet to experience the full impact of this crisis. We must remain conscious of the fact that economic depressions have the potential of initiating political revolutions as the world continues to navigate through this period of vast uncertainties. In America (and to a lesser extent in other parts of the world), the gap between the extreme wealthy and everyone else (the 1% versus the 99%) is at a level reminiscent or worse than 1928, the year prior to the crash of 1929 and the advent of the 1930s Great Depression. History tells us that these types of extremes are not healthy and are unsustainable. I hope that we will not have to wait until everything is broken before we get full consensus on how to realistically deal with the economic crisis of our times.

As stated earlier in this chapter, I do not subscribe to the prevailing economic notion that we should, at this point in this huge crisis, follow the prescriptions of classical economic theories. We have traveled too far on this unconventional economic trajectory to suddenly reverse our course with the expectation of minimum pain and inconvenience. The next major downturn on the horizon will not be a garden variety recession or another so-called "Great Recession." We can expect something far worse, analogous to a Category 5 hurricane. Thus, the "example deflationary economic decline" we will focus on in this publication is the *Great Depression of the 1930s* and all of the enormous struggles that took place during that fabled decade. America (and most of the developed world) has not experienced a major deflationary depression in nearly 90 years!

NOTES

(1) James B. Stewart, "Pointing a Finger at the Fed in the Lehman Disaster," *New York Times*, July 21, 2016. Laurence M. Ball eventually published a book on his years of research on this issue: Laurence M. Ball, *The Fed and Lehman Brothers: Setting the Record Straight on a Financial Disaster*, Cambridge University Press, United Kingdom, June 2018.

(2) Peter Gorenstein, "America's Middle Class Crisis: The Sobering Facts," Yahoo! Finance, May 4, 2011.

(3) IBID, pp. 79-81.

(4) Patrick Gillespie, "World leaders get it: The public doesn't trust us," CNN Money, October 7, 2016.

(5) IBID., Patrick Gillespie, CNNMoney.

(6) Zack Friedman, "Student Loan Debt Statistics In 2018: A $1.5 Trillion Crisis, *Forbes*, June 13, 2018.

CHAPTER TWO

PRESIDENT BARACK H. OBAMA AND THE MELTDOWN OF 2008

If you look at the platforms, the economic platforms of the current Republican candidates for president, they don't simply defy logic and any known economic theories. They are fantasy. Slashing taxes, particularly for those at the very top, dismantling regulatory regimes that protect our air and our environment, and then projecting that this is going to lead to 5 percent or 7 percent growth, and claiming that they'll do all this while balancing the budget...Nobody would even, with the most rudimentary knowledge of economics, think that any of those things are plausible.

President Barack Obama
on Republicans running in the 2016 race.

It the midst of all of the economic calamity and turmoil of the year 2008, America was also preparing for a major presidential election in November. With the Republican Party in power under the Bush Administration, the economic crisis that was engulfing the entire world did not favor a continuation of the same policies of the ruling political party. The American people were ready for a change. After a long, grueling democratic primary season and billions of dollars of political contributions, the Democratic Party chose Barack H. Obama as its candidate for the president of the United States. In a year of unprecedented events, this represented yet another extraordinary development: the first African-American had won the Democratic race to become president of the United States. However, it would cost an enormous amount of money to put the first Black president of the United States into office.

With his unprecedented use of the Internet for donations supported by a dedicated nationwide political organization, Obama took his message of *change* to the

American people, and for the most part, the majority of the people agreed with that message. I like to refer to Obama as the $750 billion president because that's how much money it took to get him elected. On November 4, 2008, the American people went to the polls and elected Barack H. Obama as the next president of the United States. After two terms of Republican administrations (eight long years of President George W. Bush) and the near total collapse of the entire global economy, it was time for a *change*.

Obama came into the oval office at a time of extreme crisis. He joins the ranks of other presidents that walked into the oval office under similar circumstances: Harry S. Truman, Abraham Lincoln and Franklin Delano Roosevelt (FDR). On January 20, 2009, Barack H. Obama was inaugurated as America's 44th president and his administration had to hit the ground running with a new economic agenda. He ascended to the oval office inheriting over $10 trillion in national debt, the failed policies of the Bush Administration that had squandered the Clinton Administration's budget surplus with repeated tax cuts, two wars (which included the elusive *War on Terror*), and the worst global economic crisis since the Great Depression of the 1930s. At that point in history, America was right in choosing Obama in 2008 as its next president. With a Democratic majority in Congress, his mandate was set to take off. It was a historic moment, and Obama needed real solutions to solve some profound problems. It was going to be a tough job.

THE OBAMA ERA AND ECONOMIC RECOVERY

It is essential to understand what a new administration inherits from the policies of a previous era. First and foremost, eight years of the Bush-era squandered the budget surplus left by the Clinton years. It's worth repeating that in 2001, Congress approved a $1.35 trillion tax cut package, primarily for the wealthy. And this was followed by a second package of $350 billion in 2003. Bottom line, Bush-era policies wiped out nearly $6.3 trillion in expected revenue and generated more than $7 trillion in debt and, as the Pew Fiscal Analysis Initiative tells us, was the primary source of the enormous yearly deficit numbers. These were long-term economic consequences that needed to be acknowledged to understand what we were dealing with in 2009. This economic reality is one of the main reasons why the Obama era had to endure $1 trillion deficits each year to maintain stability and avoid a full-blown depression.

These economic realities cannot be ignored when we examine what transpired after the 2008 meltdown. The new Obama Administration had to contend with a host of deeply embedded issues: 30 years of deregulations, a powerful banking system entrenched in Washington, outsourcing and the internationalization of wage competition, two wars, and a massive sweep of productivity gains by information age technologies and job displacement.

Harvard University political philosopher, Michael Sandel, presented some insightful thoughts on the early stages of the Obama presidency, as he stated: "FDR did not run on the New Deal in 1932...He ran on balancing the budget. Like Obama, he did not take office with an articulated governing philosophy. He arrived with a confident, activist spirit and experimented. Not until 1936 did we have a presidential campaign about the New Deal. What Obama's equivalent will be, even he doesn't know."[1] Thus, it took years before FDR was able to fine-tune his approach to economic policies to deal with the enormity of the Great Depression. With history as a guide, it appeared that Obama was on the same trajectory regarding his administration finding a resounding path out of the massive economic ruin caused by decades of deregulations and unregulated markets.

Perhaps no one knew it at the time, but in 2008, President Obama was elected as a Depression-era president, similar to the election of Franklin Delano Roosevelt in 1933. However, it's important to note that FDR became president after America had gone through the first three years of the Great Depression; so Roosevelt had time to study the situation and carefully observe the failed policies and programs of his opponent. President Obama had to walk straight into the firestorm and the first phase of the *Great Depression of the 21st century*; and as stated earlier, his administration had to hit the ground running fast with new economic remedies.

When Obama stepped into the White House, he was confronted with the massive power of Wall Street and the big banks who had dominated the oval office for nearly three decades: a political establishment that was already profoundly influenced by these too-big-to-fail institutions. The big banks and Wall Street have tremendous influence in Washington: ample supplies of campaign money and an army of lobbyists.

With businesses and consumers pulling back due to the economic shock of 2008, President Obama's priority was to stabilize the economy and prevent the harsh reality of a global depression. The need for economic recovery was of supreme importance during the first year of his presidency. Under the Bush Administration, Congress, the support of President-elect Obama and the Federal Reserve System, the implementation of TARP and other monetary policies were already in operation, which had stopped the economic bleeding and slowed the pace of the downward spiral. In addition, Obama and his administration put together (in record time) a massive fiscal policy recovery plan in response to the *Meltdown of 2008*, to help jumpstart a deeply wounded economic system.

The coming of Barack Obama heralded the birth of a new era and a president who understood and appreciated the grand significance of the *Information Age Revolution* and the mission of *clean energy*: The birth of the Obama era in support of renewable energy followed the decline and collapse of the Bush era and the *Age of Oil*. He understood the reality of global warming and climate change, and that this civilization must now begin to break its addiction to oil and other fossil fuels. He was swept into office to begin a new era in the American economic journey; a dynamic era of change with substance and commitment to bold new economic, technological and social initiatives.

Against powerful entrenched forces of the *Industrial Age*, Republican opposition in Congress and the banking system, Obama tried to begin the process of moving America into a new era free from the overwhelming dominance of oil. He had the vision and conviction to get the job done, but the massive support he needed from various powerful entities in the United States, led to a *mission impossible*. As a nation, America has not taken bold steps (like Germany) towards making a full commitment to a nuclear-free and clean energy future. This nation was (and still is) deeply divided over that mission!

However, the crisis in early 2009 presented the new Obama Administration with an opportunity to do something *big*, something that would not have been possible under normal circumstances. This was Obama's audacious experiment in 2009; a fiscal plan with an initial value of $787 billion (an amount that by 2012 was increased to $840 billion). On Feb. 13, 2009 (a little over one month after Obama was sworn into office), Congress passed the American Recovery and Reinvestment Act of 2009 in response to the devastation and ferocity of the 2008 economic meltdown. Within a week the bill was signed into law by President Obama, and thus began what some observers have called the *New Deal* of the 21st Century. Franklin Delano Roosevelt's (FDR) *New Deal* of the 1930s Great Depression was the model, but on a much smaller scale in regards to broad-sweeping reforms. Author, Michael Grunwald, refers to the Recovery Act of 2009 as *The New New Deal: The Hidden Story of Change in the Obama Era*, which is the title of his book published in 2012.[2]

Passage of the 2009 Recovery Act was a very significant Obama era achievement that helped to implement many of his campaign promises of structural and dynamic change. However, Obama's team had to work fast, so this was not a comprehensive piece of legislation. Michael Grunwald's book, *The New New Deal*, is an excellent book for understanding the complexities, vision and politics that went into crafting this $787 billion piece of legislation, that will in time, be considered a major down payment on the *New Deal* of the 21st century. The *New Deal* investments in America's clean technology future were significant. Grunwald's analysis informs us of the following:

> "Obama and his aides thought a lot about the New Deal while assembling the Recovery Act, but in some ways it's an apple-to-bicycle comparison. While President Franklin D. Roosevelt forged the New Deal through a barrage of sometimes contradictory initiatives enacted and adjusted over several years, the stimulus was a single piece of legislation cobbled together and squeezed through Congress before most of Obama's appointees were even nominated. The New Deal was a journey, an era,

> an aura. The Recovery Act was just a bill on Capital Hill...But the Recovery Act did update the New Deal for a new era. It was Obama's one shot to spend boatloads of money pursuing his vision, a major down payment on his agenda of curbing fossil fuel dependence and carbon emissions, modernizing health care and education...building a sustainable, competitive twenty-first century economy. It's what he meant by reinvent the economy to seize the future.
>
> The Recovery Act's most critical long-term changes aimed to jump-start our shift to clean energy, reducing our carbon footprint, our electric bills, our vulnerability to oil shocks, and our subservience to petro-dictators while seeding green new industries...Overall, it pumped about $90 billion into green energy, when the United States previously spent a few billion a year."[3]

Grunwald's detailed behind-the-scenes analysis of the Recovery Act is an informative and highly readable account of the significance of this legislation. His investigative reporting provides a focused account of Obama's vision and the significant players that were brought together to implement that critical piece of New Deal legislation in record time.

With GDP contracting at an annual rate of nearly 9 percent and 800,000 jobs wiped out monthly, the initial mission of the Recovery Act was to "create new jobs and save existing ones." In addition, there was an urgency to generate economic activity and "invest in long-term growth." The immediate concern was to focus the stimulus on millions of working families and businesses by providing them with relief in tax cuts and benefits. Long-term unemployment benefits and entitlement programs received funding to keep individuals and families functioning and stable during the Great Recession. According to the Council of Economic Advisors (CEA), by the second quarter of 2011, the Recovery Act had "...raised employment relative to what it otherwise would have been by between 2.2 and 4.2 million people." It stopped the economic bleeding and rapid decline, however, the situation was still anemic.

The long-term reach of the Recovery Act of 2009 turned out to be what Grunwald describes as the "biggest and most transformative energy bill in U.S. history." The bill managed to include a substantial down payment on a clean energy and technology future for the American economy. Funding was made available for wind and solar energy, electric car production, advanced biofuels and refineries, energy efficient battery production, construction of a smarter grid and many other clean energy resources, research and jobs. Obama made use of this crisis to invest in a modern energy efficient society, preparing itself for the next stage in the *Information Age Revolution.* Here was a president attempting to implement a nationwide clean technology revolution that many futurists and progressive thinkers (including myself) dream about, however it was not fully appreciated, embraced or harnessed as a springboard for the beginning of a massive clean energy conversion and revolution (similar to what's happened in Germany) in America.

In education, healthcare, and national infrastructure projects, the Recovery Act again made a substantial down payment on the future of the American society. The Obama era set the stage for economic rebirth with the added mission of what's to come next in the technology revolution of the 21st century. Nations that do not seize the opportunity to make this transition now may find themselves at a distinct disadvantage at some point in the not-too-distant future. Political leaders who understand this and have the courage to act on their convictions and beliefs, are the kind of individuals that deserve our support. In January 2009, the Obama Administration was presented with a grand opportunity for structural and dynamic change, and that opportunity did not get wasted. That was the kind of leader we needed in this era of massive technological change.

Did the Obama era correct all of the massive problems generated by the *Meltdown of 2008*: the simple answer is no! And this is especially the case when observing the weak response to the American homeowner and the mortgage crisis (SEE Chapter Three). However, let us not forget that the deeply embedded economic and financial sins of the past three decades could not be rectified during the first four short years of his presidency. And as this publication will bring to light about job creation, the American worker is fully exposed to the internationalization of wage competition, robotic factories and workers, the Internet revolution and other factors that point to the birth of a new era. The advent of this era is similar in magnitude of when the *Industrial Age* emerged as the game changer in the 18th century. We are in the midst of a paradigm shift of profound significance, and many global leaders do not understand the full implications of this massive era of *change*!

Thus, the first few months of the Obama presidency focused on containing the crisis and the prevention of economic contagion by implementing massive fiscal programs. To achieve his administration's economic and financial goals, he chose as his top advisors many Wall Street types and insiders who, in previous years, could have implemented policies that would have prevented the crisis in the first place. Ben Bernanke was reappointed Federal Reserve Chairman in 2009 (a second four-year term), Timothy Geithner became Treasury Secretary, and Larry Summers became his Special Economic Advisor. Many dubbed his administration another Wall Street government. It represented a downside of the Obama Administration that the Wall Street cast had reassembled, and they did not bring *change*. But this was nothing new in the White House: Big business and Wall Street had been a permanent fixture in both Democratic and Republican administrations over the preceding 30 years, continuing the mission of deregulation and unfettered free market capitalism. What President Obama needed, and what the country desperately required, was an economic and financial team of *reformers*, not deregulators and people who got us into this mess in the first place.

As an astute and highly gifted politician, Obama was also given the enormous task of reforming the financial system that required help from the financial sector; however, he was locked into another *mission impossible*. The banks did not support Obama on any of the critical initiatives he put forth. Instead, they spent hundreds of millions of dollars lobbying Washington politicians (on both sides of the aisle) with campaign contributions pushing their case for deregulations. Also, his presidency was plagued in the beginning with hardcore Republican opposition, an intractable economic recession, and wars and rumors of war. And again, he needed a stronger team of economic and financial industry *reformers*, not the Wall Street people who were steadfastly against any significant reforms that would upset the status quo. Overall, during his first term as president, critics viewed the Obama Administration as having *banker-friendly policies*. One of his most vocal critics, Senator Elizabeth Warren (D-MA), was very fiery in her condemnation:

> "He picked his economic team, and when the going got tough, his economic team picked Wall Street...They protected Wall Street. Not families who were losing their homes. Not people who lost their jobs. Not young people who were struggling to get an education. And it happened over and over and over."[4]

In Ron Suskind's book, *Confidence Men: Wall Street, Washington and the Education of a President*, the author speaks to the difficulty the president had with his chosen economic team. The book tells us that Timothy Geithner and the Treasury Department ignored a March 2009 order to consider dissolving the over-bloated Citigroup while continuing stress tests on banks, which many were still burdened with toxic mortgage assets. Suskind writes "The Citibank incident, and others like it reflected a more pernicious and personal dilemma emerging from inside the administration: that the young president's authority was being systematically undermined or hedged by his seasoned advisers..."[5] In *Confidence Men*, we see Obama struggling with (individual members) of his chosen team that did not share his vision of *reforms* and other necessary policies to correct the evils of the past. His Wall Street team had a different agenda. Obama's economic and finance team *tinkered* with specific reform measures and gave the impression that something substantial was being done.

A case in point is "The Making Home Affordable Modification Program," a program that was supposed to help 3 million to 4 million borrowers. By September 2011, 720,612 mortgages had been permanently modified, falling short of its established goals. As stated earlier, there should have been a much stronger and dynamic program put in place to address the homeowner modification reform process. Millions of people did not have to lose their homes. In this regard, this economic team was a disaster and were not reformers.

According to CoreLogic (in 2011-2012), about 11 million Americans - approximately 1 in 4 homes with mortgages - were underwater. Confronted with a massive number of foreclosures and plunging house values, millions of American homeowners were searching and requesting novel solutions to this enormous nationwide problem. Simply sitting by and allowing massive foreclosures to take place would only plunge the nation into a broader economic crisis: this was an unprecedented situation that required a unique government/industry-wide solution. The Obama Administration's earlier attempts at resolving the housing, mortgage and foreclosure crisis in America did not bring about a measure of great success, much of that having to do with not having key *reform-policy architects* in his administration dedicated to the implementation of a *New Deal* for the housing industry. His economic and finance team, as well as the Federal Reserve System, *tinkered* with this problem and produced *Tinkerbell* results.

Critics make the point that Obama and his Democratic majority in Congress (the reality during his first full year in office) should have been more aggressive (during 2009) in passing legislation favorable to their agenda for *change*. Indeed, they had the *Power* to move mountains, but it was short-lived. After the Tea Party landslide victories in the mid-term 2010 elections, the Democrats lost their majority in Congress. The result of that political failure left Obama (with a decimated power base) extending Bush-era tax cuts for the wealthy (at the end of 2010) and not getting anything in return. His presidency now had to contend with a much stronger and powerful opposition: after 2010 it became gridlock in Washington on all fronts!

The first essential piece of legislation to emerge after the *Meltdown of 2008* was The Dodd-Frank Wall Street Reform and Consumer Protection Act (discussed in Chapter Five). This new legislation implemented financial regulatory reform and was strong on consumer protections but weak on the regulations required to prevent 2008 from happening again.

Simon Johnson and James Kwak, authors of *13 Bankers: Wall Street Takeover and the next Financial Meltdown*, pondered similar concerns in their book. Johnson and Kwak were recommending, among other things, the breakup of the megabanks. They were recommending a much stronger political response to the ongoing crisis, and they saw the likelihood of another global meltdown. Rather than bailing the megabanks out again, the political establishment should implement rock-solid banking reforms now:

> "The alternative is to reform the financial system now, to put in place a modern analog to the banking regulations of the 1930s that protected the financial system well for over fifty years. A central pillar of this reform must be breaking up the megabanks that dominate our financial system and have the ability to hold our entire economy hostage. This is the challenge that faces the Obama administration today. It is not a question of finance or economics. It is ultimately a question of politics - whether the long march of Wall Street on Washington can be halted and reversed."[6]

A significant observation here is that the new bill did not bring back Glass-Steagall nor did it mandate stringent regulations for the OTC derivatives market, the financial time bomb of this era.

OBAMA AND THE DEBT CEILING WAR OF 2011

The U.S. government hit its critically important debt ceiling on May 16, 2011, and it was announced that by August 2nd the final deadline date would be reached. A massive struggle in Congress took place by mid-2011 over the issue of raising the *Debt Ceiling*. An impasse emerged that threatened to plunge the country into an unprecedented debt default that left a bitter taste in the mouths of the American people and many nations around the world. It was an extraordinary spectacle of divisive politics that essentially held the American people and its government hostage to a political battlefield. Even the prospect of the United States losing its top-notch AAA credit rating did not stop fiscally conservative Tea Party-aligned Republicans from making a point of no new taxes, and other vows and pledges.

What was needed, and without delay, was to raise the $14.3 trillion debt ceiling to prevent a debt default by the number one economic and financial power in the world. It was a form of economic suicide to use this issue in a political battlefield and toy around with America's debt rating in the world. And each day that the battle continued (and this went on for many weeks) only made matters worse in the end. And amazingly, stock markets remained relatively calm while all of this was going on, patiently awaiting the outcome. This was a clear demonstration on center stage of how deeply polarized American politicians and lawmakers had become: we were witnessing hyper-partisan politics in Washington D.C.

Some interesting numbers began to surface, illustrating what would happen if the federal government could not pay all of the 80 million bills that would come due in early August 2011. An early bill due on August 3rd was $23 billion payments in Social Security benefits; on August 4th the government needed to pay $87 billion to retire maturing Treasury securities, and on August 15th $30 billion in interest payments were due. Federal employees, Medicare providers, defense contractors and others required payments of $5 to $10 billion daily.

World leaders were shocked by the dysfunction in Washington, and some began to wonder if America was going through some form of political insanity. The need to do something to stop the escalation of debt in America was something that required a national discourse. However, the venue to debate and resolve this issue should not have been at the time when the debt ceiling needed to be raised. Pushing the nation to the edge of a national default was irresponsible politics and a reckless display of partisan politics. According to Eugene Robinson of the *Washington Post*, the Republicans in Congress had three priorities: defeating President Obama, cutting taxes and reducing the size of government. That's it and, I guess by any means necessary. They chose the "debt ceiling" to make their stand.

What was interesting about this event was that since 1962 the United States had raised its debt ceiling 74 times. Also, in the recent years before 2011, the debt ceiling had been raised **NINE TIMES** during the presidency of George W. Bush (a Republican) which added over $4 trillion in debt. In essence, the government had to take on more debt to pay its bills because the tax cuts during the Bush era that were in place lowered the amount of tax revenue. The Bush Tax cuts and the Iraq War undoubtedly played a role in jacking up our overall debt. The following are some of the times when the debt ceiling was raised during the Bush Administration:

(1) September 2007 the Senate Finance Committee approved increasing the debt to $9.82 trillion.
(2) Housing and Economic Recovery Act of 2008: Debt Ceiling rose to $10.615 trillion.
(3) H.R. 24 2008: the debt ceiling was raised to $11.315 trillion.

World Bank president, Robert Zoellick, stated that the "United States was playing with fire." China, America's largest foreign creditor, stated that the United States had been "kidnapped by dangerously irresponsible politics." The fiscally conservative Republican majority in the House of Representatives had pledged to oppose any new bailouts and raise any new taxes. This meant that fiscal policy was going to be very limited in what it could accomplish in the future. Federal Reserve Chairman Ben Bernanke warned lawmakers that their failure to raise the debt ceiling could trigger a major financial crisis. He also stated that a United States default would send "shock waves through the entire financial system."

What was apparent to any business person looking at this situation, and to the majority of independent voters, was that spending needed to be cut and revenue (taxes) had to be raised in order to have a significant impact on the debt problem. A combination of tax increases and spending cuts had to be included in a solution to this problem. Instead, the American people received a plan with NO tax increases; the entire package consisted of spending cuts.

A deal on the debt ceiling was reached on D-Day (August 2, 2011) and signed in the 11th hour. The debt ceiling would expand by up to $2.7 trillion through a series of installment periods accompanied by a package of budget cuts. The American people would be spared another "debt ceiling" battle until early 2013, after the 2012 elections. Thus, we dodged the imminent American default on its national debt and the entire country breathed a collective sigh of relief: *"Thank God that's over!"*

After the drama and spectacle on Capitol Hill had concluded, global markets began to voice their disapproval: On August 4, 2011, panic swept through the markets with the Dow Jones Average diving 512.76 points (4.3 percent to 11,383.68), the S&P 500 lost 60.20 points (4.8 percent to 1,200.14), and the Nasdaq fell 136.68 points (5.1 percent to 2,556.39). It was the worse panic that had hit the markets since October 22, 2008. Observing that this date was President Obama's birthday, hardcore critics of his administration saw this as a birthday omen.

Fear was clearly beginning to manifest itself after the debt-ceiling battle in Washington. The fiasco in Washington demonstrated to traders and investors that the American political scene was in turmoil. Record high unemployment, diminishing consumer spending, fears of deepening economic troubles in Europe and political paralysis in Washington fed into a belief that the U.S. would probably stumble into a new recession or the dreaded double-dip recession.

Then, on Friday, August 5th (after the market had closed) for the first time in history, Standard & Poor's downgraded the sterling credit rating of the United States from AAA to AA+.[7] The other two major credit agencies, Moody's and Fitch, kept their AAA ratings on U.S. government debt. The title of the S&P statement of the downgrade was as follows:

"United States of America Long-Term Rating Lowered To 'AA+' On Political Risks And Rising Debt Burden"

The interpretation of this downgrade, and as most people came to understand, is that the U.S. was fully capable of paying its debts. However political gridlock in Washington placed the country in a possible position of not wanting or agreeing to pay its debts. Standard & Poor's concluded that this was a huge problem for the nation and that it would likely continue into the election year of 2012. S&P is the world's largest rating agency and is in the business of assessing the likelihood that debt will be repaid. Thus, the focus was on the political process and the rapidly rising debt overload by the federal government. As an independent observer, S&P played a powerful role in waking up the Washington political establishment to broader realities beyond the political battles in the halls of Congress. S&P emerged as an essential factor (an outside force) that brought sobriety to the drunken partisan crowd in Washington. Removing *Treasury Debt* from the list of nearly risk-free investments was a significant financial defeat for the American economic system and was something that could have been avoided, particularly at that point in history.

The agency had first warned the government about its concerns in April 2011 and that the U.S. needed to get its fiscal house in order to avoid a possible downgrade. I guess some people in Congress weren't listening or felt that the U.S. was immune to such an event by the credit agencies. But they were wrong!

Before the S&P downgrade on that fateful Friday, $2.5 trillion had already gone up in flames in global markets: This event dealt another severe blow to the nation and global stock markets.

The world absorbed and digested this event over the weekend and on Monday (August 8th) the global stock, currency and bond markets spoke loud and clear: there was a huge collapse. The Dow fell 634 points (5.5 percent) to 10,809, falling below the psychologically important 11,000 mark, an area the Dow had not seen since November 2010. The S&P 500 was down 79 (6.7 percent) at 1,119.46, and the NASDAQ fell 174.72 points (6.9 percent) to close at 2,357.69. Thus, political gridlocks in Washington lead to an S&P downgrade which sparked a major collapse in the stock market, wiping out trillions of dollars. This was a serious matter.

In a White House appearance, President Obama spoke to the nation as the markets were in a steep decline declaring that: "Markets will rise and fall, but this is the United States of America. No matter what some agency may say, we have always been and always will be a triple-A country." Obama blamed the downgrade of the U.S. credit rating to political gridlock in Washington and stated that our problems are "imminently solvable." Compromise in Washington was expected to become much more difficult especially since the majority of Republicans had signed Grover Norquist's (president of the tax payer's advocacy group, Americans for Tax Reform) "no new taxes" pledge (in the 112th Congress 238 Representatives and 41 senators signed the pledge). In light of this hardcore stance, many economists warn that a recovery would be virtually impossible without new revenues. In its report, S&P warned of a further downgrade if the U.S. was unable (or unwilling in political gridlock) to solve its debt problems.

Ultimately, fiscal policy decisions are political decisions, and that was one of the leading factors in the downgrade. John Chambers, head of S&P's debt-rating committee, was clear in his assessment that the political gridlock in Washington is something that could be a problem moving forward. Stock Market losses were brutal: From July 26, 2011, through August 8, 2011, $7.8 trillion in equity had gone up in smoke.

FOUR MORE YEARS OF THE OBAMA ERA

When America went to the polls on November 6, 2012, the majority of the people voted to keep President Barack Obama in the White House. This was a very important election for a lot of reasons however, regarding the various issues discussed in this publication (economic policies, climate change, economic and financial reforms, the green technology and the Information Age Revolution, etc.) this was, without a doubt, an astounding historical victory for the people of this great nation, and by extension, the entire world. With President Obama and the Democrats in power, the American people were given a fighting chance to build a strong coalition for economic justice and full development of the clean technology revolution. This victory was a grand opportunity to do great things! Either we would move forward and achieve massive change and revision of the global economy, or we would collapse into dysfunction and final creative destruction.

Billionaire investor George Soros stated in an article, in early February 2012, that President Barack Obama deserved a second term. In his words "The problems that he inherited, because he came in immediately after a financial crisis, were bigger than any president could have immediately remedied...So, whoever gets elected now has a much better chance of being successful than Obama had." I was hopeful that in his second term he would have had a much better chance of giving the American people a *New Deal* with much greater substantial change.

"The Nation We Need To Build Is Our Own" is what Obama stated in a campaign speech given in early May of 2012. This should have been the main driving force of his presidency throughout his final four-year term: the renewal of America. The vision I held for the second phase of his *21st Century New Deal* policy included some of the following reform measures: (1) Massive new infrastructure developments utilizing the genius of new technologies in various fields (2) A revolutionary plan for energy independence that would concentrate on phasing out the use of oil over the next 10 years and the implementation of a new energy vector and massive use of alternative energies (3) A comprehensive program to resolve the housing crisis and help families refinance their mortgages at lower interest rates (4) the use of novel strategies to put Americans back to work (5) A dynamic plan to deal with the $1 trillion plus student loan crisis and affordable higher education in America and (6) Resurrection of the Glass-Steagall Act with stronger reforms for the banking system and the over-the-counter derivatives market. These were some of the critical issues that many Americans wanted to see addressed, and many people wanted Obama to make the rebuilding of America the backbone of his push to redefine this nation's mission and power in the 21st century.

The expectation was that the next four years should have witnessed the implementation of a completely clean energy revolution. We were in the implementation stage of the *Information Age Revolution*, and the time for a significant transformation was utilizing the best technologies for economic growth and development. Perhaps if Obama had been fortunate to have secured greater support in Congress, his *21st century New Deal* might have been realized. Instead, he spent much of his second term in constant battles with his Republican opposition in Congress. The Republican Party was adamant in their opposition to the Obama Administration and its policies: obstructionism was the battle cry on all fronts!

SUMMARY/ANALYSIS

There were many challenges and powerful forces facing the new Obama Administration after his inauguration in January 2009. And after the 2010 mid-term elections, a deeply divided Congress paved the way for massive efforts to derail many of the Obama era economic solutions, and this epic political struggle resulted in half-measures and limited response, especially in regards to the pressing issues of the mortgage crisis.

Economic policies that fail to go to the heart and root of a severe systemic crisis will not produce the kind of results that could lead to a robust recovery. The prevalent economic thesis is that if you save the banking system and financial markets, this will stop the collapse and help pave the way for the beginning stages of recovery. That works well for a garden variety recession, however, when faced with something much more profound and destructive, a much broader stimulus approach is required.

In 2008, America embarked on a journey to print trillions of dollars to save the economic system from a deflationary collapse. Part of those resources should have been allocated to the people at the root of the mortgage crisis and not just given to the wealthy at the top. Where was the targeted bailout for the millions of American people who lost their homes? That's the question I have been asking for years!

While the big banks and the overall financial system was on their knees and backs, that was the time to make the *big changes and big demands of these institutions*! The government and the Federal Reserve System should have demanded concessions that would have benefitted the American people; instead, they received a blank check worth billions (and ultimately trillions) of dollars and a free ride. Big banks were given no conditions on the foreclosure crisis, no conditions on reforms, and no conditions on bonuses. The money came with no strings attached and no concerns about so-called *moral hazard*.

The year 2016 marked the final year of President Barack Obama's time in office, and Republicans were celebrating and delighted to see him go. GOP obstructionism had been a constant theme throughout Obama's presidency, and with the sudden death of Supreme Court Justice Antonin Scalia in February of 2016, it went into hyper-drive and panic mode. Justice Scalia represented the modern conservative wing on the Supreme Court, so his passing was of grave concern of who would fill his seat. With the Supreme Court evenly divided with four conservative justices nominated by Republican presidents and four liberal justices by Democrats, the issue immediately became contentious and would set the stage for a long battle.

As a requirement of the United States Constitution, President Obama began the process of deciding who would be the next Supreme Court Justice. In March, he nominated Judge Merrick Garland, an experienced federal appeals court judge, and that entire process ran into a Republican brick wall. Republican senators refused to hold hearings and issued their decree that since it was a presidential election year, the next president should be responsible for picking the next Supreme Court Justice. That was it, and the selection process was indeed put on the back burner until it was decided who would be the next president of the United States. This was a huge demonstration of the power of the Republican controlled Senate, and the lack of power on the part of Democratic Senators and the office of the President to orchestrate a plan to achieve their political goals.

After a public effort and outcry to move the nomination forward in spring 2016, the debate fell silent with the Republican obstructionism winning the day. Also, Republicans stated in October that if Democratic candidate Hillary Clinton were to win the election, they would block any person she nominated to fill the vacant court seat. The selection of Supreme Court Justices was clearly a political process that would decide whether the court would be conservative or liberal.

Shortly after the inauguration of Donald Trump (January 20, 2017) as the 45th president of the United States, Judge Neil Gorsuch was nominated to become the next Supreme Court Justice (January 31, 2017). Senate Democrats attempted a filibuster of the nomination but were out-manevered *again* when Republicans invoked the *nuclear option* (a parliamentary procedure that allows the United States Senate to override a rule). By April 4, 2017, Judge Neil Gorsuch was confirmed by a Republican majority rule of the Senate. Senate majority leader Mitch McConnell's obstructionist tactics in 2016 had worked like a charm.

In June of 2018, Justice Anthony M. Kennedy announced that he would be retiring from the Supreme Court by July 31, 2018. President Trump immediately announced his next Supreme Court nominee: Judge Brett Kavanaugh. Senate Democrats went on the offensive seeking to use Mitch McConnell's delay strategy, declaring that the Senate delay the Kavanaugh confirmation hearing until after the 2018 November mid-term elections. However, the Republican Senate majority essentially out-maneuvered the Democrats *again*. And after a fierce battle, and public outcry and rage regarding the Kavanaugh confirmation hearings, the Republicans ultimately succeeded in placing another conservative judge on the Supreme Court. On October 8, 2018, Supreme Court Justice Brett Kavanaugh was sworn in with less than 29 days left before the mid-term elections. The rush to consolidate political, judicial and economic power was on full display during this entire un-democratic process.

NOTES

(1) Thomas L. Friedman, "Finishing Our Work," *The New York Times*, November 4, 2008.
(2) Grunwald, Michael, *The New New Deal: The Hidden Story of Change in the Obama Era*, Simon & Schuster, New York, 2012.
(3) IBID., pp. 10, 12 and 17.
(4) Melanie Hicken, "Obama's economic team, chose Wall Street over 'families'," CNNMoney.com, October 13, 2014.
(5) Ron Suskind, *Confidence Men: Wall Street, Washington, and the Education of a President*, Harper Perennial, New York, 2012.
(6) Simon Johnson and James Kwak, *13 Bankers: The Wall Takeover and the Next Financial Meltdown*, Vintage Books (A Division of Random House, Inc.), New York, January 2011, pg. 1
(7) The United States first received its prized S&P rating in 1941.

CHAPTER THREE
THE SUBPRIME MORTGAGE CRISIS: NO MASSIVE BAILOUT FOR HOMEOWNERS

You remember the closed banks and the breadlines and the starvation wages; the foreclosures of homes and farms, and the bankruptcies of business; the "Hoovervilles," and the young men and women of the nation facing a hopeless, jobless future; the closed factories and mines and mills; the ruined and abandoned farms; the stalled railroads and the empty docks; the blank despair of a whole nation - and the utter impotence of the federal government.

Franklin D. Roosevelt, September 23, 1944.

THE HOUSING CRISIS

As of June 2010, 75 million Americans still owned a home. Of that number, 23 million owned their home free and clear. Another 37 million households were renters. However, by 2010, there were 4 million foreclosures. The states hardest hit were California, Nevada, Florida, and Arizona. They accounted for about 30 percent of the national economic activity. These states were also at the epicenter of the boom and bust of the housing crisis. Over-building and asset appreciation went to greater extremes in these markets.

Baby Boomers, who represent a significant amount of economic activity in America, were slammed to the mat by declining stock investments and home prices during the Great Recession. By January 2011, household net worth was still down by $9 trillion from peak levels of 2007 (pre-recession peak was $65.9 trillion). Home equity and stock market investments were the most significant casualties. Most baby boomers were placed in a difficult position of being poorly prepared for retirement. Industry analysts reported that many boomers did not have a guaranteed pension plan that they could count on anymore. Many boomers were forced to postpone any retirement plans and continued to work to survive. Baby boomers retiring with no savings may never be able to retire.

The sad legacy of the housing collapse will be that the Fed, White House, and banking community didn't push to the deep core of the mortgage crisis. They *tinkered* with the issue and got *Tinkerbell* results. People in power did not think outside the box; we were in a de-leveraging era, and the response needed to be a radical de-leveraging by the American people. In other words, instead of *just* bailing out the banks and their cronies, the focus should have *also* been to bail out the American homeowner with across the board loan modifications, debt reductions, and low fixed 30-year interest rates.

And here is a question: If the U.S. government indeed owns the Fed, and by extension, the American people, then why are there no provisions to bail out the people that pay the income tax and are called upon to bail out Big Banks and a host of other wealthy institutions and individuals in the time of extreme crisis? Their world was shattered; their lives were ruined, and yet there was no significant bailout package for the American homeowner. And if economic planners and the Fed wanted people to consume, borrow and spend, then the American homeowner needed to be bailed out! The American people, as a consumer base, represent 70% of GDP; if that base dries up and is completely tapped out, there would be no enduring and robust recovery for many years to come.

The Fed continued to tweak long-term interest rates as Ben Bernanke introduced Operation Twist on September 21, 2011, as another stimulus plan to lower the key mortgage rates. The policy involved selling $400 billion in short-term Treasuries in exchange for the same amount of longer-term bonds, starting in October 2011 and ending in June 2012. Many analysts considered this maneuver as a non-event; however, the Fed was signaling to the White House and Congress that it was doing its part in keeping interest rates low to revive the housing market. They also wanted to be seen as doing something to keep the markets calm and to help build confidence in a recovery scenario.

Washington needed to do the *unthinkable* as a depression era measure: the strategy or plan should have been to implement a novel plan to provide low-rate mortgages across the board to the American people, a bailout for the American homeowner. Politicians needed to wake up to the fact that the mortgage crisis had to be solved to regenerate the massive American economic system. One approach could have been to ask the banks, Freddie and Fannie to take a 50% haircut on the mortgage debt the way institutional investors were urged to take a 50% to 75% haircut on hundreds of billions of dollars of sovereign debt loans to Greece. We had reached a point where that type of a solution was necessary. Nearly 11 million people owed more than their home was worth, and that was a crisis that required a broad-based remedy.

BANKS AND FORECLOSURES: By the third quarter of 2010, a coalition of 50 state attorney generals and various federal agencies began investigating and probing the abusive foreclosure practices by major banking institutions on their use of robo-signing and other questionable tactics designed to foreclose on American homeowners. After news reports surfaced of widespread robo-signing, the issue that banks may have improperly foreclosed on troubled borrowers began to move to center stage. Problems of fraud, illegality, fabrication of missing documents and even the bundling of mortgages into marketable securities were starting to resonate with prosecutors, attorney generals and legal scholars throughout the 50 states. A critical showdown had finally come to challenge the banking industry on its practices and foreclosure procedures: the big guns had entered the arena on behalf of the American people. Five banks were targeted for the investigation: Bank of America, JPMorgan Chase, Wells Fargo, Citigroup, and Ally Financial. The stage was set to finally deal *with an industry that had received vast sums of* bailout *money but had done very little to alleviate the pain and suffering of the American homeowner.*

The 50 state attorney generals in negotiations with big banks insisted that debt forgiveness or principal reduction, reduced monthly payments and other relief for distressed homeowners be part of any settlement over the bank's faulty mortgage practices. In exchange for these settlement conditions the banks were seeking legal immunity and release from liability for past illegal actions and that there would be no further lawsuits stemming from the foreclosure crisis. Settlement amounts of between $20 and $30 billion were considered and would be divided among the 50 states. One proposed deal contemplated was to set aside $5 billion in cash penalties and a $20 billion fund for modifications and refinances of underwater mortgages.

Some participants pointed out that the settlement amounts were insufficient to cover the massive problem afflicting the American homeowner. And they were right. A settlement of even $30 billion would not have been sufficient for the state of California alone, especially when we were talking about debt forgiveness and across the board loan modifications. It was estimated that out of 2.2 million underwater homeowners in the state of California, only about 20,000 homeowners would have been given aid. And in exchange for this deal, the banks were to be granted broad immunity from any further legal actions.

The legal immunities that banks were seeking included the following: (1) release from any faulty practices covering loan origination (2) release from any issues regarding securitization and servicing practices (3) release from legalities of fair-lending procedures and (4) release in their use of the Mortgage Electronic Registration Systems (MERS).

Some of the state attorney generals and the Obama administration were eager to reach an early settlement with the banks to implement another solution for the crippling foreclosure crisis. On the other hand, there were state prosecutors that wanted to pursue a more comprehensive investigation, probing deeper into such legal issues of

Subprime Mortgage Crisis: No Bailout for Homeowners

whether banks followed the state's laws (in the case of New York) when bundling mortgages into securities; the question of whether mortgages were transferred correctly in the securitization process. A full investigation, including origination and securitization practices, was demanded before any settlement was contemplated. The banks wanted the coalition to give away too much immunity for alleged illegal conduct in the past. *Many felt that the banks needed to be held accountable for all of their actions in the same way that they were using an iron fist on the American homeowner, showing no mercy even for people who qualified for mortgage relief options.*

In the case of New York, Attorney General Eric Schneiderman took a more aggressive stance probing deep into the securitization process of mortgages and possible criminal charges against financial executives in the robo-signing scandal and other alleged wrong-doings. Early on in the negotiations, Schneiderman was adamantly against allowing the banks broad-sweeping immunity, freeing them from any future civil lawsuits. In addition to New York, Delaware, Massachusetts, Kentucky, Nevada, Minnesota, and California left the negotiation talks to pursue their own state investigations.

In October 2011, California Attorney General, Kamala Harris announced that she would no longer take part in the national multi-state foreclosure probe. She stated, "The relief contemplated would allow too few California homeowners to stay in their homes." In essence, California was saying that the contemplated settlement was not enough to deal with the size of the problem in the Golden State. In an interview with *The Times*, Kamala Harris stated that she removed herself from talks by a coalition of state attorney generals and federal agencies because the nation's five largest mortgage servicers "were not offering California homeowners relief commensurate to what people in the state had suffered...It has been a process of negotiating and sitting at a table in good faith, but ultimately I have decided that we have to go our own course and take an independent path. And that decision is because we need to bring relief to Californians that is equal to the pain California experienced, and what is being negotiated now is insufficient."[1] She also indicated (again) the issue that the banks were demanding to be granted overly broad immunity from legal claims. This was not the time to close the door on these investigations for this would bar any revelations regarding Wall Street's role in the mortgage meltdown. And that was the position that absolutely should have been taken!

After President Obama's State of the Union Address in January 2012, negotiations between the attorney generals and the banks quickly moved towards a resolution. As part of his speech and the stated mission to do more regarding the housing crisis, Obama said:

> "I'm asking my Attorney General to create a special unit of federal prosecutors and leading state attorney general to expand our investigations into the

abusive lending and packaging of risky mortgages that led to the housing crisis. This new unit will hold accountable those who broke the law, speed assistance to homeowners, and help turn the page on an era of recklessness that hurt so many Americans."[2]

New York Attorney General Eric Schneiderman was appointed by President Obama as the co-chairperson of the Unit on Mortgage Origination and Securitization Abuses. This was a welcome sign by many who considered Schneiderman a major factor in dealing effectively with the mortgage crisis and the abusive big banks. Schneiderman didn't waste much time in excising the power in his new position: In early February, he filed a lawsuit against Bank of America, Wells Fargo and JPMorgan Chase in New York State Supreme Court in Brooklyn. The focus of the lawsuit centered on the Mortgage Electronic Registration System (MERS) accusing the banks of fraud in their use of the electronic mortgage database which (as he stated) resulted in deceptive and illegal practices, including false documents in foreclosure proceedings. According to Schneiderman, "The mortgage industry created MERS to allow financial institutions to evade county recording fees, avoid the need to publicly record mortgage transfers and facilitate the rapid sale and securitization of mortgages en mass."[3] The lawsuit asserted that over 70 million mortgages had been registered in the MERS system, saving the banks over $2 billion in recording fees. Bank of America, Wells Fargo, Fannie Mae, Freddie Mac and other major financial institutions formed MERS in 1995 to effectively bypass county record offices to facilitate faster processing of their mortgage-backed securities business.

On February 9, 2012, the federal government announced that a $25 billion settlement had been reached between five of the nation's largest banks and 49 attorney generals. California Attorney General Kamala Harris, New York Attorney General Eric Schneiderman, Delaware Attorney General Beau Biden (son of Vice President Joe Biden) and Massachusetts Attorney General Martha Coakley (the attorney generals who had previously rejected or walked away from the negotiations) joined the final settlement agreement once it was understood that this settlement would not be the end of this matter and that the big banks would not be given absolute immunity. Thus, this deal did not release the banks from future criminal lawsuits by individual states. About one million homeowners would be helped under the settlement, and mortgages held by Fannie and Freddie would not be included in the process.

The rough estimates of how the money was allocated is as follows: (1) $17 billion would be used to reduce principal balances on loans that were underwater, with each homeowner receiving approximately a $20,000 reduction on their mortgage (2) $5 billion would be placed in reserves accounts for various state and federal programs. Some of this money would be used to make cash payments of between $1,800.00 and $2,000.00 to roughly 750,000 American homeowners who lost their homes due to the deceptive practices by the banks (3) roughly $3 billion would be set aside to help homeowners refinance their mortgages at 5.25 percent. This was not a great deal for the American people, and indeed, a lot more needed to be done. Following the multi-state settlement with the nation's biggest banks, California Attorney General Kamala Harris called on Freddie Mac and Fannie Mae to temporarily suspend all foreclosure sales in the state of California. Harris sent a letter to Edward DeMarco and requested "a good-faith pause." The state of California was scheduled to receive $18 billion in benefits over three years for homeowners. As part of the deal, Bank of America Corp., Citigroup, Wells Fargo, Ally Financial and JP Morgan Chase agreed to $12 billion in the form of principal reduction and short sales.

California was one of the hardest hit states in the nation's foreclosure crisis. The number of foreclosures in California was expected to reach 2 million before the end of 2012. This was a real catastrophe that needed to be stopped by any financial means necessary. It was an extraordinary crisis that required exceptional solutions. Fannie and Freddie guarantee about 60 percent of all mortgages in California, so these organizations were a vital part of the solution process.

On October 26, 2011, 19 Democrats in the House of Representatives met with the head of the Federal Housing Finance Agency (FHFA) Edward DeMarco, who was the overseer of Fannie Mae and Freddie Mac, to discuss a proposal that would allow bankruptcy judges to reduce principal amounts on loans. One suggestion by Representative Zoe Lofgren was to allow for a temporary reduction in the interest rates of those homeowners who filed for bankruptcy. The plan would allow homeowners to pay down loan principal and reduce negative equity during a five-year period with no interest. In exchange, borrowers would agree to settle claims against servicers which shield them from litigation. The push was to allow more underwater homeowners to refinance their mortgages at the then historically low-interest rates (30-year fixed rate mortgage hit 3.94 percent by early October 2011). The need for principal forgiveness was essential in the fight to stop the deepening foreclosure crisis.

Also, 34 Democrats in California's congressional delegation sent a letter to President Barack Obama on Oct. 11, 2011, urging him to take action on pushing Fannie Mae and Freddie Mac to implement new procedures to do refinancing of loans with principal reductions for underwater homeowners. They wrote, "Our current economic crisis began in the housing market. Until the housing market is stabilized, our economy will not be able to fully recover." And my thoughts at the time was that when Fannie and Freddie required additional assistance or another bailout (President Obama, Treasury Secretary Timothy Geithner, and Fed Chairman Ben Bernanke); tell them what they need to do: ***Bail Out the American People!*** As of November 2011 Fannie and Freddie guaranteed up to 70 percent of the country's home loans, and they had yet to approve of debt forgiveness.

Under conservatorship since 2008, Fannie Mae and Freddie Mac (tax-payer-funded companies) were not part of the multi-state deal and had not granted any principal reductions on their huge portfolio of mortgages. Fannie and Freddie had 3 million mortgages that were underwater, and of those, most were not delinquent. According to the acting director, Edward DeMarco, the cost of implementing principal reductions on all of the 3 million loans would cost taxpayers almost $100 billion. DeMarco presented a letter to Congress on January 20, 2012, stating his hard-line opposition to principal reduction. It's interesting to note that the U.S. government had spent $190 billion during and after the *Meltdown of 2008*, keeping Fannie and Freddie alive and kicking. And if the American taxpayer had to pay $100 billion for a principal reduction program, it should not have been a big deal! We spent trillions of dollars bailing out the big banks, and that was accepted without a lot of firestorm and hell raising!

Congress, the Federal Reserve, the Obama administration, MoveOn.org, several attorney generals, and Martin Feldstein, a chief economic advisor to the late President Ronald Reagan, all called for DeMarco to institute principal reduction. He clashed with members of Congress and the Obama administration who supported the idea that reducing the amount borrowers owe would be an essential component of the housing recovery. And again, the irony here is that the federal government bailed Fannie and Freddie out of its financial difficulties before the *Meltdown of 2008*, and now it could not play a key role in helping to bring about a housing recovery in the United States. This is the kind of crap that brings into focus deception, deceit and lack of economic compassion when it comes to the vast majority of Americans who were not part of the *wealthy elites*.

Democrats in Congress and some state attorney generals called for DeMarco's resignation. Attorney General Kamala Harris called on DeMarco to step down due to his response to the foreclosure crisis. Rep. Elijah Cummings (D-Md) stated of DeMarco, "...he and he alone stands in the way of hundreds of thousands of people, if not millions, being able to [literally] get a new lease on life." Several high profile observers called on the Obama administration to push harder to get a nominee to replace DeMarco. Shaun Donovan, the Secretary of Housing and Urban Development, stated, "Our goal is to get a good nominee and get someone in there who shares our view."

The Federal Reserve sent a report to Congress on January 4, 2012, that presented the case of 12 million borrowers being weighed down by $700 billion in aggregate negative equity. This was an interesting report coming from the Fed, especially when you consider the trillions of dollars spent bailing out the banks after the 2008 meltdown. Yet during these extraordinary times, no housing solution for less than $1 trillion could be found to help 12 million American borrowers - part of the backbone of this nation! Something was wrong with that picture, primarily because Fed Chairman Ben Bernanke was an expert on the Great Depression. He clearly could have established special facilities and programs to have bailed out millions of underwater American homeowners. Between the federal government in Washington and the Federal Reserve System, a solution could have been forged that didn't have to rely so heavily on the big banks, and Fannie or Freddie. Between 2008 and 2014, *seven million foreclosures took place. That's a lot of neighborhoods, families and extended families that were destroyed. And it was all preventable! And I can also say that, without a doubt, this was one of the main reasons why the Democrats lost the election in 2016. People were pissed off at how this system is rigged to benefit the wealthy during a time of extreme crisis.*

In March of 2012, U.S. Treasury Secretary Timothy Geithner began showing signs of interest (after years of silence) in resolving the U.S. housing crisis. In testimony before a U.S. Senate panel, he stated his belief that Fannie Mae and Freddie Mac should reduce the principal on some home mortgages held in their inventory. In his testimony, he said, "We've been encouraging Fannie and Freddie to take another look at the map, at the economics of the finance because we think there is a strong case in some circumstance to add principal reduction as part of their strategies to help maximize the return of the taxpayer."[5] Geithner had finally joined the party to find a solution to the crippling crisis. He indicated that they were now trying to "work on a credible national strategy." After nearly three years as Treasury Secretary, Timothy Geithner had proven that he was not an economic reformer dedicated to solving the housing crisis to the benefit of the American people. John Taylor, president of the National Community Reinvestment Corporation, presented a recommendation to the government that would have gone a long way in resolving this crisis with a proposal stating that, "The Treasury Department should also consider purchasing loans at a discount and mandating their modification...This does not require legislative approval, and could be done tomorrow."[6] This plan would have also considered principal reduction and reworking the loans, making them affordable for millions of distressed borrowers. This recommendation didn't produce any significant response from the Treasury Department

Since the start of the Great Recession in December 2007 until late 2011, nearly 5 million homes had been foreclosed upon in America. With nearly 11 million homes still underwater, the crisis demanded a solution of much greater scope and with a much broader base of power to move domestic and international banks to a comprehensive resolution. It was a huge transference of wealth and one of the main reasons why many Americans lost faith and trust in Washington and the Federal Reserve System. *And I repeat, people wonder why the Democrats lost heavily in the mid-term elections in 2010 and the presidential election in 2016; the housing crisis is a significant part of the anger, resentment, and betrayal that millions of American people felt as they went to the polls.* Allowing millions of homes to be foreclosed was a huge economic mistake in this depression era.

Debt forgiveness and loan modifications with historical low interest rates (while the rates were still low from 2012 to 2016) was, in my humble opinion, considered indispensable tools for fixing the housing problem. Smaller independent investor organizations that purchased non-performing notes and performing notes from banks at discounts, employed debt forgiveness as a tool to restructure their mortgage debt portfolios. This process had done a lot to help keep people in their homes.

One in five homeowners were underwater; total estimated negative equity was $700 to $800 billion. The banks and Fannie and Freddie could have taken this haircut. For less than a trillion dollars, the mortgage crisis could have been placed on stable ground, and that was a better solution than orchestrating another massive bailout for "Too Big To Fail" institutions that were doing very little to stabilize the housing crisis. We needed resolutions that were intended to go straight to the heart of the matter and not to some questionable banking institution that was not interested in solving the problem. *For the most part most of the big banks were simply trying to profit from this economic crisis.* The peak of home ownership in America was reached in 2005 with 70 percent of all occupied households owned by their residents. However, the good times had come to an end!

CoreLogic (a financial Analytics company) was another company that presented an analysis of 11 million homeowners underwater in their mortgages with lenders. A new and improved HARP program introduced by the Obama Administration in October 2011, offered little relief to millions of homeowners who were behind in payments on their mortgages. The new program stated that a homeowner could be underwater; *however, they had to be current on their mortgage payments to qualify for assistance.* This was a huge crisis and this kind of nonsense was tantamount to tinkering with a massive depression era disaster. It did absolutely nothing for people who were behind in their mortgage payments and required a loan modification reset; an opportunity to keep the roof over their heads and to get back on their feet similar to the bailouts for Bank of America, Citigroup, AIG, and others. Again, bail out the big institutions but no one else.

The track record for the HARP and HAMP programs was a disaster; people were required to fight tooth and nail to gain any benefit from banking institutions and their mortgage servicers. For instance, the HAMP program that came online in 2009 was supposed to help eight million homeowners to avoid foreclosure. By 2014, five years later, the program had only provided 1.3 million permanent mortgage modifications, and the vast majority of those loans were not 30-year fixed rate affordable mortgages. Most of these loan modifications came with fixed rates for short periods of time (two to five years) and then became adjustable rate mortgages. In 2014, some 350,000 loans were in danger of defaulting again due, in part, to the crappy deals these banks were handing out. The banking industry was littered with mortgage servicers, intermediaries, con games and outright fraud when it came to providing economic justice for the American people who are the American taxpayers that bailed out those untrustworthy institutions! Many banks and their servicers benefited from collecting structured fees, late fees, legal fees, profiting from keeping homeowners in default status, and at the end of the game, outright foreclosures. It was a racket during the *Great Recession*, and in 2018, it still is!

Many economists suggested writing down mortgages to market value. For example, consider the case where a family purchased a home in Sacramento in 2005 for $356,000, however, by October 2011, the value of the property had declined to $150,000. The solution was to write this mortgage down to market value. If the family was still in the home and still had sufficient income, then the bank should have worked with that family to make the mortgage affordable: principal reduction, a restructured loan program and provide this family with historically low-interest rates. Each home saved would have strengthened the American economy, helping families and extended families to survive the brutal period of collapse.

If a bank had to foreclose on a property (as in the above example) and take it back as a "Real estate owned property" (REO), it would have only been able to sell it at market value, $150,000. The question was: would the bank be made whole (not lose money) by any insurance they may have had on this mortgage (i.e., PMI or mortgage-backed security insurance), and if so, then there was no incentive to do loan modifications. Some banks had chosen to simply foreclose because they would suffer no significant loss due to their insurance coverage that paid for the deficiency in the foreclosure process.

Thus, the banks needed greater incentives (they needed to be paid more by federal government and Fed established programs) to be encouraged to do loan modifications that would have made them favorable (and in their best interest) in many ways. Enduring no foreclosure actions, avoidance of holding large inventories of REO properties, legal fees, and avoidance of future lawsuits, would have provided large banks much better solutions. The money was available to do this, especially since the Fed had handed out trillions of dollars during its bailout operations. Bottom line: the Obama Administration didn't do enough to stop this catastrophe, especially the Treasury Department under the direction of Timothy Geithner. When you put all of the pieces of the puzzle together, it was clear that the banking industry was looking to make huge profits from the massive foreclosure crisis.

A key victory by attorney Kathy Patrick, who won a lawsuit against Bank of America for $8.5 billion, was a crucial step in the right direction. This was the second largest such settlement in U.S. history. Backed by Blackrock, Pimco, and 21 other bond giants, this legal expert dealt a severe blow to the massive Bank of America. In an article appearing in *Forbes Magazine*, she stated "This group did not come together just to deal with Bank of America. They came together because they wanted a comprehensive industry-wide strategy and an industry-wide solution."[5]

During the third week of September 2011, a proposed plan surfaced that the U.S. government was considering bulk-selling the massive portfolio of foreclosed homes, that was owned by HUD, Fannie Mae, and Freddie Mac, to private investors, mainly Vulture funds and the wealthy elites. The transactions would involve huge discounts on the properties sold to private investor conglomerates. The plan included the stipulation that the buyers of these properties would turn around and rent the properties to the

American people who had been made homeless in the foreclosure crisis.

Under the pretense that neighborhoods would be stabilized and that there would be an increasing supply of rental properties at market rates, this plan was flawed from the beginning and was simply another strategy to increase the holdings of wealthy people. *Why did they not offer the American people pennies on the dollar for these properties instead of sovereign wealth funds, investment banks, vulture funds and wealthy individuals?* Billed as a "Rental Conversion" plan, it was nothing more than a colossal transfer of wealth. The American people didn't need or deserved *Billionaire Landlords*.

After the rollout of this program, I was further convinced that President Obama needed a new Treasury Secretary; Timothy Geithner was clearly not the right person for that job as a depression era cabinet member. He was simply not thinking like a reformer in the best interest of the American people, especially in regards to the housing crisis. His interest and allegiance were to the Big Banks and Wall Street, not the average American. In January 2012, Geithner indicated in an interview with Bloomberg Television, that Obama would probably not be asking him to remain as the Treasury Secretary for a second term if he was re-elected. Obama needed to clean house and begin setting up a complete cabinet of reformers and *New Deal* architects. And many people were aware of this issue as we entered 2012 and election-year politics.

By 2012, the housing crisis in America had been smoldering for five years and was the deepest U.S. housing crisis since the Great Depression of the 1930s. However, in the election year 2012, the stage was set for part two of the downturn with banks moving to wreak more havoc. However, the majority of the people still fighting for their homes in 2012 were hardworking, everyday Americans who had fallen on hard times due to a rough economy. And since this was a national crisis in extraordinary times, it would require national solutions with extraordinary remedies. Any politician running for the office of president who didn't recognize this problem as a national tragedy, especially since the crisis had been smoldering for over five years, should not have been voted into office.

ICELAND'S RECOVERY STORY: ECONOMIC JUSTICE

Iceland's banking and financial system collapsed in December 2008, a victim of global corruption and widespread greed of politicians and bankers. Iceland's experiment with a deregulated banking system proved fatal. With a GDP of $13 billion and a population of roughly 318,000 people, Iceland became one of the most severe cases of mismanagement and corporate greed in the *Meltdown of 2008*, after the country's three largest banks went broke and defaulted on $85 billion in debt. Over time their banking system swelled to over ten times the GDP, so this small nation could not bail out its megabanks in the time of severe crisis. Thus, these banks were simply allowed to collapse. In the wake of the collapse, the nation's currency, the krona, was severely devalued, losing half its value against the euro. Inflation soared to 20 percent, people lost jobs, were deeply in debt and the nation went thru a period of austerity.

After over three years of working on recovery measures and repairing their broken economic system, the country emerged in early 2012 in better economic health, illustrating to the world what can be achieved when a nation applies broad-based economic and financial solutions that benefit the majority of the people instead of a select few wealthy corporate CEOs and their cronies.

An agreement between the government and the banks paved the way towards providing relief for Iceland's struggling population. With the banks still partly owned by the state, *Bloomberg* reported that they "...forgave debt exceeding 110 percent of home values. On top of that, a Supreme Court ruling in June 2010 found loans indexed to foreign currencies were illegal, meaning households no longer need to cover krona losses."[7]

According to a report published by the Icelandic Financial Services Association, Iceland's banks have "forgiven loans equivalent to 13 percent of the gross domestic product, easing the debt burdens of more than a quarter of the population." The government of Iceland stepped up to the plate and put its people back on their feet as part of a broader plan to revive the national economic system. They bailed out the people that are the main drivers of the economic system and not just a few rich "Too Big To Fail" institutions that created the crisis in the first place. According to Lars Christensen, chief emerging markets economist at Danske Bank A/S in Copenhagen, "You could safely say that Iceland holds the world record in household debt relief...Iceland followed the textbook example of what is required in a crisis. Any economist would agree with that."[8]

When the people of a country are facing widespread insolvencies and bankruptcies, extraordinary measures and policies need to be implemented. Iceland didn't *tinker* with their problem as the U.S. had done over a four to five year period. Lars Christensen reminds us that "the bottom line is that if households are insolvent, then the banks have to go along with it, regardless of the interests of the banks." Iceland was bold enough to bring in the reformers to make the necessary changes. That's what the United States needed in 2012 and beyond. Our banks, along with many European banks, were given trillions of dollars during and after the *Meltdown of 2008*, yet it would have probably taken just $1 trillion (or less) to help stabilize the American housing crisis. *Bloomberg* made this very succinct statement in its article on Iceland, "Iceland's approach to dealing with the meltdown has put the needs of its population ahead of the markets at every turn." What happened in Iceland could not have been duplicated in the U.S., but the guiding principles and some measure of reforms could have been implemented to stabilize the housing crisis and other broken aspects of the U.S. economic system. This was indeed a success story for the people of Iceland!

SUMMARY/ANALYSIS

In regards to the individual American homeowner crisis, Federal Reserve Chairman Ben Bernanke (scholar on the Great Depression era) did not respond to the bust cycle with strong depression era strategies and structural initiatives. He should have known that our reform policies were weak (especially when it came to bailing out the individual homeowner) and that our economic initiatives were even weaker. The collapse in 2008 dealt a major financial blow to the American economic system, something that did not allow this nation to bounce back quickly in a few short years.

Chairman Bernanke and some of the other Federal Reserve officials did start to become more vocal and supportive in early 2012 of stronger remedies for the housing crisis. At a home builders' conference in Orlando, Florida, Bernanke stated "The state of housing has been an impediment to a faster recovery...We need to continue to develop and implement policies that will help the housing sector get back on its feet."[9] The Fed Chairman acknowledges that the housing recovery had been slow for several reasons which include: (1) overly tight credit by lenders that were holding back the origination of good mortgages, or simply unwilling to do loan modifications, and (2) a glut of vacant homes and foreclosures that continued to depress markets throughout the United States. In a special paper to Congress outlining possible remedies to the housing crisis, Bernanke argued that Fannie and Freddie could have played a significant role in the housing recovery if they were allowed to provide cheaper mortgages to a "broader pool of homeowners." I couldn't help but wonder why it had taken Chairman Ben Bernanke (the 1930s Great Depression scholar) over four years after the *Meltdown of 2008* to arrive at these conclusions!

President Obama was elected on a platform of *change*, and he had a similar role to fulfill in orchestrating one of the most significant governmental reform movements in the history of U.S. government. The Recovery Act of 2009, Obamacare, and his clean energy revolution began his *first New Deal*; he was given four more years to complete his journey. The hope was that he would find his mission and fulfill it just as FDR did in the 1930s.

NOTES

(1) Halah Touryalai, "No Deal: California Backs Out Of Nationwide Foreclosure Settlement," *Forbes*, September 30, 2011.
(2) Office of the Press Secretary, "Remarks by the President in State of the Union Address," The White House, January 24, 2012.
(3) Reuters Staff, "New York sues banks over electronic mortgage systems," Reuters Business News, February 3, 2012.
(4) Meera Louis and Clea Benson, "Geithner Says Fannie, Freddie Should Cut Some Principal," *Bloomberg*, March 28, 2012.
(5) James R. Hagerty, "Should Treasury Get Into the Mortgage Modification Business?," *The Wall Street Journal*, January 11, 2010.
(6) Nathan Vardi, "Wall Street's New Nightmare," *Forbes*, November 7, 2011, p. 113.
(7) Omar R. Valdimarsson, "Icelandic Anger Brings Debt Forgiveness in Best Recovery Story," *Bloomberg*, Feb. 19, 2012, Online pg. 1.
(8) IBID, pg. 1.
(9) Chairman Ben Bernanke, "Housing Markets in Transitions," Board of Governors of the Federal Reserve System, February 12, 2012.

CHAPTER FOUR
THE EXTRAORDINARY POWERS OF THE FEDERAL RESERVE SYSTEM

We came very, very close to a global financial meltdown, a situation in which many of the largest institutions in the world would have failed, where the financial system would have shut down, and...in which the economy would have fallen into a much deeper and much longer and more protracted recession.

Former Fed Chairman Ben Bernanke

Throughout my public life, I have supported all measures designed to take the Government out of the banking business. This bill puts the Government into the banking business as never before in our history. The powers vested in the Federal Reserve Board seem to me highly dangerous especially where there is political control of the Board...The bill as it stands seems to me to open the way to a vast inflation of the currency.

Senator Henry Cabot Lodge

THE FEDERAL RESERVE SYSTEM

The Federal Reserve System (the Fed) is America's central banker (the banker's bank) and has a massive controlling influence over the economic well-being of the nation. It is a very powerful organization that regulates the flow of credit and money, and when called upon, has the magical power of money creation. As the nation's central bank, the Fed has direct control over the money supply, interest rates, and credit creation. Also, it has the ability to influence the direction of inflation and, to some extent, levels of employment.

Before the establishment of the Fed, the last major central bank for the United States was the Bank of the United States, which was abolished in 1836 by President

Andrew Jackson. President Jackson, like others before him, had a deep distrust of the pervasive power of central bankers over the nation's money supply. He also felt that this centralizing power held a pernicious and overwhelming influence on the activities of the nation's economy. It would be 77 years before the next central bank was to be installed in the American economy.

Of interest here is the fact that the Federal Reserve System (in concert with other strategic reasons and plans) was initially put in place to control the severe boom and bust cycles in America that had been rampant in the banking industry during the 19th century and early years of the 20th century. The primary reason for its existence was to bring stability to the economy and prevent rampant inflation and major downturns, to the benefit of the American people. It was the Bank Panic of 1907 that finally provided the catalyst for the super-rich bankers to initiate a plan to establish the next central bank in the United States.

The Panic of 1907 occurred in October of that year and took place over the span of a three week period. The trigger for this crisis was the activities of a wealthy investor, F. Augustus Heinze, who was seeking to corner the stock of United Copper and the copper market. At the time, an economic recession was in progress and investors were taking their money out of trust companies, as well as, initiating bank runs on untrustworthy banks. What started as a New York City crisis eventually led to a nationwide panic. The stock market collapsed, and a vicious liquidity crisis fell on the finance and banking communities. Since there was no official lender of last resort (a central bank) to stabilize the situation and provide liquidity, the system needed a private sector solution. Financier, J. P. Morgan, along with other New York bankers, provided an intervention by pledging their own money to provide liquidity for the banking system. The pervasive threat of this event galvanized the thinking of the wealthy elites to finally spearhead a new era of banking reforms and, in effect, revive the central banking system in America.

G.. EDWARD GRIFFIN: CREATURE FROM JEKYLL ISLAND

In his book entitled, *The Creature from Jekyll Island: A Second Look at the Federal Reserve*, author G. Edward Griffin provides a scathing commentary on the early development of the Federal Reserve System that began with a highly secretive meeting on Jekyll Island, Georgia in 1910. Some of the world's most influential people in the banking industry and the federal government came together to forge the blueprint and working model for the next central bank in America. Up to that point, many people in the United States had a significant distrust of the *Money Trust* (the dominant banking entities, especially on Wall Street) and their secret designs to control the financial lifeblood of the nation. Hence, the need for secrecy was paramount, particularly in light of the fact, that at the end of nine days, these powerful bankers (as Griffin explains) came up with a plan to establish a *banking cartel* which they called the Federal Reserve System.

A unique partnership between the federal government and the private banking industry was envisioned, providing exclusive privileges and benefits to both parties to the deal. According to Griffin, on the surface, the Fed would appear as a government agency working on behalf of the American people. However, this is not the total reality of the Fed; it's a half-truth: the Fed's main (unwritten) mission is to represent the interests of the banking cartel, thereby improving their bottom line and power. Griffin explains why this group should be considered a cartel:

> The composition of the Jekyll Island meeting was a classic example of cartel structure. A cartel is a group of independent businesses which join together to coordinate the production, pricing, or marketing of their members. The purpose of a cartel is to reduce competition and thereby increase profitability. This is accomplished through a shared monopoly over their industry...Here were representatives of the world's leading banking consortia: Morgan, Rockefeller, Rothschild, Warburg, and Kuhn-Loeb...They were often competitors...But they were driven together by one overriding desire to fight their common enemy. The enemy was competition.[1]

President William Taft, the president in power from 1909 to 1913, was not in favor of a private central bank for America. He vowed to veto any legislation that was presented during his term in office. The next sitting president (President Woodrow Wilson) took a more accommodative approach to the central bank issue. In exchange for campaign support from those seeking the establishment of a central bank, Wilson had agreed to sign any new proposed central bank legislation.

During the same year Woodrow Wilson became president of the United States, the Federal Reserve Banking System came into existence on December 23, 1913, two days before Christmas while most of Congress was home with their families. The day before the passage, Minnesota Congressman Charles A. Lindbergh (1859-1924: father of the famous aviator Charles Lindbergh) argued against this legislation:

> When the President signs this act [Federal Reserve Act of 1913], the invisible government by the money power - proven to exist by the Monetary Trust Investigation - will be legalized. The new law will create inflation whenever the trusts want inflation. From now on, depressions will be scientifically created.[2]

Thus, The Federal Reserve Act of 1913 was enacted by Congress and signed into law by President Woodrow Wilson, who three years later, would regret that decision. It didn't take long before the president realized that it was a wrong decision to have a private banking system responsible for the entire monetary system of the nation:

> A great industrial nation is controlled by its system of credit. Our system of credit is concentrated in the hands of a few men... We have come to be one of the worst ruled, one of the most completely controlled and dominated governments in the civilized world - no longer a government by free opinion, no longer a government by conviction and the vote of the majority, but a government by the opinion and duress of a small group of dominant men.[3]

The year 1913 also witnessed the passing of another milestone piece of legislation, the passage of the Sixteenth Amendment (Amendment XVI) to the United States Constitution which allowed for Congress to levy a federal income tax "without apportioning it among the states or basing it on the United States Census." This amendment (where the U.S. Constitution was ratified) was adopted on February 3, 1913, authorizing Congress to impose a tax on income. Some historical analysts have reasoned that the new national income tax system (known then as the Bureau of Internal Revenue) was implemented in part to help pay for the many bailouts that would become the ultimate backstop for the new Federal Reserve System. In short, henceforth, the American people would be responsible for the bailouts (for the Bureau of Revenue Service which was renamed the Internal Revenue Service (IRS) in the 1950s), stimulus requirements and the payment of federal governmental debts.

THE EASY MONEY POLICIES OF THE ROARING 20S

Shortly after the birth of the Federal Reserve System, World War I began during the summer of 1914. To pay for this war, the warring European powers, due to their limited financial capabilities and gold supplies, were forced to abandon the gold standard. Central bank printing presses in Europe generated an expansion of fiat currencies, which according to economist Richard Duncan, was a major contributing factor to the emergence of the decade of the Roaring 20s in America. Also, between 1914 and 1919, the money supply was also substantially increased in America which, in part, lead to a major financial crisis in 1920.

Some historians and economists labeled this the *Great Depression of 1920* or the *Forgotten Depression* of that era. It was primarily a *sharp deflationary recession or mini-depression* that would last (according to historical records) from January 1920 to July 1921.

A major contributing factor to this crisis was the transition (in America) from a wartime to a peacetime economy. The surge of soldiers returning home from the war to a civilian labor market unprepared for the expansion was a major problem for the emerging American economy.

During the roughly 18-month downturn, unemployment skyrocketed from 4% to 12%; the stock market collapsed (losing half of its value), the Fed engineered a *credit contraction* throughout the monetary system, and the GDP went into a free fall. Bank runs, bankruptcies and systemic collapse led to sharp declines in economic activity throughout the nation. The failure of many independent banking institutions (some historians place the number at 5400 banks) that were not part of the federal reserve system became major candidates for acquisitions by the powerful financially stable banking cartel. These powerful bankers were also in a strategic position to acquire other financial assets and stock (shares) of major corporations at low prices.

This represented the first major crisis that confronted the newly installed 1913 Federal Reserve System, and as predicted by Congressman Lindbergh, it did not provide the promised stability to the nation's economy. In fact, the Fed didn't provide beneficial solutions during this crisis and essentially allowed the markets to work their will. It worked out to be a very lucrative crisis for those who were in a position to benefit from the economic failure of weaker businesses, banks, and institutions.

The cartel emerged a lot stronger from that brief mini-depression which set the stage for what history would come to identify as the *Roaring 20s*. And it is fascinating that this all happened about seven years after the birth of the Fed. Lindbergh was clear in his original assessment of the design, strategies, and plans of the *Money Trusts or banking cartel*:

> The new law will create inflation whenever the trusts want inflation...they can unload the stocks on the people at high prices during the excitement and then bring on a panic and buy them back at low prices...the day of reckoning is only a few years removed.[4]

Lindbergh was one of the most outspoken critics of the banking cartel and the Federal Reserve System, and his book, *Banking and Currency and The Money Trust*, is a testimony to his firm belief and knowledge that the cartel would manipulate the markets to the benefit of its members and owners. To Lindbergh, the 1920 deflationary recession was orchestrated by the *Money Trusts*. He died of brain cancer in 1924, and therefore, was not alive to witness the 1929 crash and the Great Depression. I'm sure, had he been alive, we would have a book today (written by Lindbergh from his perspective) that would have shed a great deal of light on the events and developments that led to the October 1929 crash and the subsequent depression.

Flight capital from Europe was a major contributing factor that gave rise to the stock market bubble in the U.S. during the *Roaring 20s*. During the devastating conflict of World War I that killed over 17 million people, America remained on the gold standard and was emerging as the premier nation in the free world.

In America, the decade of the 1920s was dominated by three Republican Administrations under Presidents Warren Harding, Calvin Coolidge, and Herbert Hoover. Big business and the wealthy thrived in this atmosphere, as each administration gave significant support to New York as the center of world economic activity. In fact, the status of the financial capital of the world moved from London to New York.

The Republican Administrations implemented major tax cuts in 1921, 1924, 1926 and 1928. This gave big business and the wealthy greater incentives and more money to build major enterprises. From the mid to late 1920s, the Federal Government and the Fed pursued an aggressive easy money policy which significantly expanded the money supply (a 60% increase in the money supply from 1921 to 1929).

Also, to add greater strength and control to the monetary system, in 1923, Congress approved a bill that authorized the Federal Reserve System to undertake *open market operations* (this would be the beginning of the FOMC. And according to Griffin's research, since 1913, the Federal Reserve Act has been amended nearly 100 times providing greater powers and resources for its operations). Besides making adjustments in the *discount rate*, the Fed would now be able to place or remove money from the banking system by selling or buying back Treasury bonds. It was a pro-business era, with each administration paving the way for the next.

Charles Mitchell, who was President of National City Bank, introduced the concept of mass marketing stock ownership to the small investor. The average American, in the pursuit of riches and following the lead of the wealthy, began to buy stock on *margin* the same way that he or she purchased consumer goods on credit. With the establishment of a 10 percent margin requirement, an investor could buy $1000.00 worth of stock with only $100.00. However, if the value of the stock fell below a certain threshold in the investor's account, a *margin call* would be given, and the investor had 24 hours to add the required additional funds or suffer the penalty of losing the entire holdings of that account or investment.

Another innovation was the introduction of financial trusts (the forerunner of mutual funds) which allowed the small investor to invest in professionally managed stock funds at low fees.

Low-interest rates and the easy money policies of the Federal Reserve and the Treasury helped to promote the speculative frenzy for all Wall Street investors. The 10 percent margin requirement lured many investors, especially in an atmosphere of an exciting *bull* market with prices continually going up. With the higher share prices, market capitalization went from $27 billion in 1925 to nearly $90 billion by 1929. Buying stock on margin would later prove to be a terrible strategy for many small investors who lost everything due to the massive margin calls that the banks enforced during the October 1929 crash.

Radio Corporation of America (RCA) was one of stocks that experienced tremendous growth during this period. In 1921, a share of RCA could be purchased for

$1.50 (near the close of the mini-depression), and by 1928 the stock had hit a high of $420 per share! And a month before the crash in 1929, RCA was trading at $505 per share (adjusted for stock splits and dividends). A very popular stock, RCA became the subject of many stock manipulation schemes that were controlled and operated by small groups of wealthy investors. Greed and power were at an all-time high, as investment pools manipulated stock values by buying low and selling high while generating a speculative frenzy around pre-selected stock issues. In some cases, millions of dollars were made in just a few days in these investment pools.

During the boom and bust of the 1920s, many stocks experienced tremendous valuations. By September 1929, the share price of General Motors had soared from $51 to $1,075; Dupont from $106 to $1,617 and General Electric from $168 to $1,612. And in those days, these were enormous valuations.

Mainstream economist Irving Fisher preached the gospel of permanent prosperity, and the speculation continued. The most popular dissenting voice that warned of a coming crash in the markets was economist Roger Babson. To the mainstreamers and power brokers, Babson was an intellectual troublemaker, but his theories on the economy would soon bear witness to the *Crash of 1929*.

Long Cycle theorist and Russian agricultural economist, Nikolai Dimitriyerick Kondratieff, began publishing his theories in economic journals during the 1920s, which brought together the central hypothesis and critical ideas of his belief in super-long economic cycles. He based his statistical data on the capitalistic free market system, which eventually got him into trouble with the ruling communist elite of the Soviet Union. He published *Long Economic Cycles* in 1928. Kondratieff's theories indicated that a *downward wave* was in progress during the late 1920s.

Also, to take some of the steam and speculation out of the markets (as well as to signal that the *boom* would soon be coming to an end), the Federal Reserve raised the discount rate three times in 1928. However, many people ignored these maneuvers, and the party kept going strong.

On October 29, 1929, the party came to an end. The stock market crashed, and over $50 billion in paper wealth vanished into thin air. The volume of shares traded that day reached 16.5 million, and the Dow plunged 30.5 points. The Dow collapsed on that fateful day from its peak of 381.17. To the millions of people that were, directly and indirectly, involved in the stock market, the blow was devastating. Some people gambled all the way up to the last minute and lost everything. Others bailed out early and waited for the crash. Historians tell us that Joseph Kennedy, Bernard Burach and other wealthy bankers had started getting out of the stock market as early as January of 1928, and in some cases, several months before the crash. As the acknowledged bear market strategist, Jesse Livermore shorted the market (strategic investments designed to profit when the market goes down) and made over $100 million in one week.

THE FED RESPONSE TO THE GREAT DEPRESSION

During the early stages of the Great Depression, the Fed didn't exercise the full power that it had to restore stability and confidence in the U.S. economic system. Some economic historians and analysts have argued that the main reason for this weak response was because the United States was still on the gold standard. Thus, the Fed and Washington's reaction was to protect the nation's financial position in gold by raising interest rates.

Also, President Hoover and his economic team thought that they were dealing with a regular *garden variety recession* (a typical business cycle downturn), but they were wrong. Hoover's conservative Republican prescription for the *bust cycle* stressed a business-oriented approach which consisted primarily of: (1) minimal governmental interference in the economy and (2) maintaining a balanced federal budget (in the face of a massive economic downturn) in order to restore confidence in the business community of the soundness of the U.S. economy.

Other historical commentators argue that the Fed was a young organization and that the 12 regional banks did not rely on a centralized authority in Washington, and that there were widespread disagreements among the various governors on how to address the crisis.

In Robert Sobel's book, *The Great Bull Market, Wall Street in the 1920s*, the author provides valuable insight into the events of that period. His comments on the banking system and of the early 1930s bring us closer to understanding some critical issues of that era. Sobel recounts the actions taken by Mr. George Harrison (the Governor of the New York Federal Reserve Bank) during the crisis of the great crash in October 1929. When the market fell, Mr. Harrison used the Open Market Investment Company to purchase short-term government notes, thus providing desperately needed liquidity for the markets. Low-interest rates were maintained to provide the economy with low-cost capital, keeping banks active. The rediscount rate fell from 4.5 percent to 3.5 percent from November 1929 to March 1930.

The New York Fed strategy of easy money and open market operations restored confidence in the system. The banks were saved in the early stages, but this would not last. Sobel's observation is important as he states, "The key to any financial crash is the banking system. If banks can remain solvent and retain public confidence, then recovery may take place." In short, a strong banking system was the primary engine that could have saved the economy from ultimate disaster. However, the lesson of the early 1930s tells us that the system was not saved. The prescription to provide liquidity should have been expanded for the entire national economy. However, the central authority in Washington decided against any further monetary easing, thinking (as some commentators reasoned) that this might have re-inflated the 1920s bubble mania.

Sobel tells us that, "By January 1, 1931, there was no doubt that the nation was in a depression. Corporate profits, which reached $9.6 billion in 1929, fell to $3.3 billion in 1930. American Corporations lost $800 million, and a further decline to a $3 billion loss followed in 1932...President Hoover was convinced as most that there would be no depression."[5]

Here is where I begin to seriously question the legitimacy and authenticity of the Fed. Congress had created the Fed in 1913 (sixteen years before the great crash) as the lender of last resort, and yet it did not prevent the *advent of the Great Depression* through the use of its monetary powers. Why? As we shall see, the Fed allowed the entire American banking system to collapse. And this presents a huge question: *Why was the American banking system allowed to collapse, especially when it was preventable?*

Protectionism dealt a further blow to the fragile world economy, particularly with the introduction of the *Smoot-Hawley Tariff Act of 1930* (signed into law on June 17, 1930) which closed American markets to foreign competition. Some 1,028 American economists urged President Hoover to veto the bill, but he refused. What happened after that is history, for the bill set off a chain reaction of retaliation throughout the world. Economist Charles P. Kindleberger tells us that: "The signing of this bill...made it clear that, in the world economy, no one was in charge."[6]

As the leading creditor nation, America did not provide the financial leadership for the world as conditions grew worse. In the final analysis, it was every nation for itself; the international economic order was in turmoil. Each country had to pursue the best route for survival.

THE BANKING SYSTEM

The total number of bank failures in 1929 was 659. In 1930, over 1,300 banks collapsed, leaving the overall banking system in serious trouble. Another 2,300 banks failed in 1931, and in 1932, 1,453 banks bit the dust. Between 1929 and 1933, 10,000 U.S. banks failed. *And in 1933, the entire banking system collapsed in America.* The unemployed in 1929 numbered 1,550,000 people, and by 1932, the number had swelled to 12,060,000.[7] Thus, as banks collapsed and corporations were forced to cut back or close down, unemployment figures skyrocketed.

As stated earlier, one of the main reasons why the Federal Reserve System was initially brought into existence, was to control the severe *boom and bust cycles* that were a source of great economic distress during the 19th century and early 20th century America. And I repeat this fact again, a central reason why Congress voted to create the Federal Reserve System is that it would be the lender of last resort. What happened to those basic mandates in the 1920 crisis and during the 1930s depression? These were back to back severe economic events that the Fed was suppose to respond with superior monetary powers.

Extraordinary Power of the Federal Reserve System

After observing the first three years of the Great Depression, the Fed stood by while the banking system and money supply collapsed, did very little to keep prices from falling, and basically allowed the *depression* and the dreaded *deflation* to take root in the American economy. Pennsylvania Republican Representative Louis McFadden, Chairman of the House Banking and Currency Committee (having served for more than 10 years), gave a speech before the House of Representatives on June 10, 1932. In that speech, he severely denounced the Federal Reserve System. The following are some of the opening remarks of that historic speech:

> Mr. Chairman, we have in this country one of the most corrupt institutions the world has ever known. I refer to the Federal Reserve Board and the Federal Reserve Banks. The Federal Reserve Board, a Government board, has cheated the Government of the United States and the people of the United States out of enough money to pay the national debt. The depredations and iniquities of the Federal Reserve Board has cost this country enough money to pay the national debt several times over. This evil institution has impoverished and ruined the people of the United States, has bankrupted itself, and has practically bankrupted our Government. It has done this through the defects of the law under which it operates, through the maladministration of that law by the Federal Reserve Board, and through the corrupt practices of the moneyed vultures who control it.
>
> Some people think the Federal Reserve banks are United States Government institutions. They are not Government institutions. They are private credit monopolies which prey upon the people of the United States for the benefit of themselves and their foreign customers; foreign and domestic speculators and swindlers; and rich and predatory money lenders. In that dark crew of financial pirates there are those who would cut a man's throat to get a dollar out of his pocket; there are those who send money into States to buy votes to control our legislation; and there are those who maintain international propaganda for the purpose of deceiving us and of wheedling us into the granting of new concessions which will permit them to cover up their past misdeeds and set again in motion their gigantic train of crime.[8]

Before becoming a congressman, McFadden had been a cashier and bank president for the First National Bank in Canton, Pennsylvania. Thus, armed with his intimate knowledge of the banking industry, he was well aware of what the Fed was capable of doing and became its most active opponent in the early 1930s. His attacks and condemnation were grounded in a firm belief that the Fed was indeed an instrument of a private banking cartel serving the interests of its owners, not those of the American people. His sense of indignation was so intense that in 1932 he called for the impeachment of President Herbert Hoover, and on May 23, 1933, brought formal charges against the Board of Governors of the Federal Reserve Bank system, The Comptroller of the Currency and the Secretary of United States Treasury. Some of the charges presented included treason, conspiracy, unlawful conversion, and fraud. His observations and searing comments on the deepening depression are seldom mentioned in mainstream books and media, particularly as he tells us:

> In 1930 while the speculating banks were getting out of the stock market at the expense of the general public, the Fed advanced them $13,022,782,000. This shows that when the banks were gambling on the public credit of these United States as represented by the Fed currency, they were subsidized to any amount they required by the Fed. When the swindle began to fall, the bankers knew it in advance and withdrew from the market. They got out with whole skins and left the people of these United States to pay the piper...
>
> Meanwhile and on account of it, we ourselves are in the midst of the greatest depression we have ever known. From the Atlantic to the Pacific, our Country has been ravaged and laid waste by the evil practices of the Fed and the interests which control them. At no time in our history, has the general welfare of the people been at a lower level or the minds of the people so full of despair.
>
> Recently in one of our States, 60,000 dwelling houses and farms were brought under the hammer in a single day. 71,000 houses and farms in Oakland County, Michigan, were sold and their erstwhile owners dispossessed. The people who have thus been driven out are the wastage of the Fed. They are the victims of the Fed...The United States has been ransacked and pillaged. Our structures have been gutted and only the walls are left standing.[9]

McFadden's testimony and observations of the early 1930s are reminiscent of the bailouts and foreclosures of the *Meltdown of 2008*; different era, but the same set of tactics, strategies and massive economic tragedies and misfortunes.

Scholars and academicians will continue to debate the pro and con issues on this matter for years to come, however, my final conclusion is that something else was apparently at work here, and I find it hard to believe the Fed could have been that inept and that dedicated to the *gold standard* and Republican ideology to have allowed the entire banking system to collapse without some other hidden agenda! However, what can be observed in some sense of clear thinking, is the fact that those who were fortunate enough to have ample liquid cash reserves and assets during the depression years, were able to buy financial and real assets for pennies on the dollar (conversion of conjured money into real and hard assets). As Griffin, Lindbergh, and McFadden remind us, the banking cartel was in that position. And we certainly should consider Griffin's precise assessment of the Fed's stated mission versus its ulterior motives:

> The accepted version of history is that the Federal Reserve was created to stabilize our economy...Even the most naive student must sense a grave contradiction between this cherished view and the System's actual performance. Since its inception it has presided over the crashes of 1921 and 1929; the Great Depression of '29 to '39; recessions in '53, '57, '69, '75 and '81; a stock market "Black Monday" in '87; and a 1000% inflation which has destroyed 90% of the dollar's purchasing power...That is the scorecard eighty years after the Federal Reserve was created supposedly to stabilize our economy! There can be no argument that the System has failed in its stated objectives.
>
> If an institution is incapable of achieving its objectives, there is no reason to preserve it - unless it can be altered in some way to change its capability. That leads to the question: why is the System incapable of achieving its stated objectives? The painful answer is: those were never its true objectives. When one realizes the circumstances under which it was created, when one contemplates the performance over the years, it becomes obvious that the System is merely a cartel with a government facade...when there is a conflict between the public interest and the private needs of the cartel...the public will be sacrificed. That is the nature of the beast. It is foolish to expect a cartel to act in any other way.[10]

Former Fed Chairman Ben Bernanke, who is a recognized scholar on the 1930s Great Depression, made this remark at a conference (in a November 2002 speech) honoring the 90th birthday of Milton Friedman, "Regarding the Great Depression...we did it. We're very sorry...We won't do it again." My interpretation of Bernanke's Fed confession for the entire organization (including those in power decades ago), is that the Fed essentially dropped the ball or fell asleep at the wheel at the beginning of the 1930s' crisis.

Before joining the Fed board in 2002, Ben Bernanke had been a tenured professor and former chairman of Princeton University's economics department. In his writings, Bernanke has been critical of Fed policies, particularly in the rate hikes that were major contributing factors in severe price deflation and the massive rise in unemployment during the Great Depression years. Bernanke tells us the following:

> "The U.S. central bank only compounded its mistake by failing to counter the collapse of the country's banking system in the early 1930s; bank failures both intensified the monetary squeeze (since bank deposits were liquidated) and sparked a credit crunch that hurt consumers and small firms in particular. Without these policy blunders by the Federal Reserve, there is little reason to believe that the 1929 crash would have been followed by more than a moderate dip in U.S. economic activity."[11]

According to Bernanke, if the Fed had been more aggressive in its policy prescriptions during the early stages of the crisis, the most damaging aspects of the *Great Depression* may have been avoided.

Bernanke's convictions about the failures of the Fed in the early 1930s crisis came alive in 2008. As Fed Chairman during the *Meltdown of 2008*, he kept his promise and conjured up more money and liquidity than any other Fed Chairman (including Alan Greenspan) in the history of the Fed. In the 2008 crisis, Chairman Bernanke literally *bailed out the world with trillions of dollars; it was a global bailout!*

Thus, the mistakes made by the young U.S. central bank in 1930 that led to the worse economic depression in American history, was not repeated in the modern era. In the early 1930s, the Fed essentially allowed weak and troubled financial institutions to fail. The end result of this policy (the liquidationist policy) was the total collapse of the entire banking system. President Herbert Hoover's Secretary of Treasury, Andrew Mellon, was a strong proponent of this approach.

In 1932, the American people voted for *change* and FDR and the Democrats came into power in January of 1933. The first order of business (the central mandate in his election) was to put in place policies and programs that would end the depression. Unlike Obama in the 2008-09 meltdown, FDR had three years to study the failed policies of the Hoover Administration and was better prepared to implement a new era of massive economic change.

Of major importance, and priorities in his administration's economic strategy was the rehabilitation of the banking system and devaluation of the currency. As a policy tool to fight the economic downturn, the push was to inflate the money supply and lower interest rates. Thus, FDR took America off the gold standard on June 5, 1933, a few months after he took office. Britain had already abandoned the gold standard in 1931, and FDR and the Fed were aware of the full implications of that move. The justification for this development was based on a Fed-driven policy stating that "increasing the amount of gold held by the Federal Reserve would, in turn, increase its power to inflate the money supply". However, the opposite reality was that people wanted to redeem their *gold-backed* dollars for physical gold through their banking institutions. The net result was that this was something that the *banking cartel* needed to prevent.

Not everyone agreed with this strategy, which probably did more harm than good, particularly as the American people were ordered to turn in their gold or risk penalties of a $10,000 fine and/or 10 years imprisonment. In effect, this was the wholesale confiscation of private property (the gold reserves of the American population) which amounted to another bold tactic by the Federal Reserve System.

For those who were fortunate enough to own any gold during the deepest period of the *Great Depression*, Roosevelt's Executive Oder 6102 (on April 5, 1933) and Executive Order 6260 (on August 28, 1933) dealt a severe blow to their survival plans. In essence, these laws made it illegal for American citizens to possess physical gold coins or bullion: the remaining hard currency wealth of the people was taken. All gold (nuggets, dust, coins in denominations of more than $100, but with the exception of jewelry and collector's coins) needed to be turned in to the Federal Reserve by May 1, 1933, for the set price of $20.67 per ounce. Through this process, the Fed was able to increase its gold reserves (by May 10th) to the tune of $470 million of gold certificates and $300 million in gold coins, courtesy of the American people.

Before 1933, the dollar was backed and redeemable in gold. The statement on the American currency was that the denomination would be payable *"in gold coin payable to the bearer on demand."* After the gold standard was abandoned, the dollar simply became legal tender Federal Reserve Notes, exchangeable on a dollar for dollar basis, with no hard currency backing.

On January 30, 1934, the Gold Reserve Act was passed which further solidified the power of the government and the Fed to seize gold in the United States. Also, to add injury to insult, in this new legislation the U.S. government increased the value of gold from $20.67 per ounce to $35.00 per ounce. This increased value in the price of gold would certainly have benefitted those who were forced to turn in their gold several months earlier. The Fed confiscated gold increased in value by 69 percent, and the Gold Reserve Act required that the gold and gold certificates held by the Fed be surrendered to the U.S. Department of Treasury.

Representative Louis McFadden was very critical of this FDR/Fed maneuver to confiscate wealth (from an already depressed population) in the name of new economic policies:

> At noon on the 4th of March, 1933, FDR with his hand on the Bible, took an oath to preserve, protect and defend the Constitution of the U.S. At midnight on the 5th of March, 1933, he confiscated the property of American citizens. He took the currency of the United States standard of value. He

repudiated the internal debt of the Government to its own citizens. He destroyed the value of the American dollar. He released or endeavored to release, the Fed from their contractual liability to redeem Fed currency in gold or lawful money on a parity with gold. He depreciated the value of the national currency.

The people of the U.S. are now using unredeemable paper slips for money. The Treasury cannot redeem that paper in gold or silver. The gold and silver of the Treasury has unlawfully been given to the corrupt and dishonest Fed. And the Administration has since had the effrontery to raid the country for more gold for the private interests by telling our patriotic citizens that their gold is needed to protect the currency.

It is not being used to protect the currency! It is being used to protect the corrupt and dishonest Fed. The directors of these institutions have committed criminal offense against the United States Government, including the offense of making false entries on their books, and the still more serious offense of unlawfully abstracting funds from the United States Treasury! Roosevelt's gold raid is intended to help them out of the pit they dug for themselves when they gambled away the wealth and savings of the American people.[12]

McFadden essentially denounced the initial thrust (gold confiscation) of the *new* FDR government as a strategic plan by the Fed and the *banking cartel* to avoid the "contractual liability to redeem Fed currency in gold or lawful money on a parity with gold." In his observations of that period, it was not necessary to drain the American people of their remaining financial resources.

It would be 40 years before U.S. citizens could begin to legally own gold again. On December 31, 1974, President Gerald R. Ford enacted Presidential Executive Order (11825) which granted Americans the freedom to use, exchange and transact in gold coins and bullion in a lawful manner. In 2018 and beyond, it is essential to understand that something like this could happen to affect the availability of gold when the government or the Fed deems it necessary to restrict its use. What happened during the Great Depression is an invaluable history lesson.

The *New Deal policies* of the Roosevelt era began to uplift and regenerate the American economic landscape: millions of Americans (not just a few big banks and businesses) experienced the benefits of this new economic approach. Fed policies accommodated this new Washington era, atoning for the sins of the deregulated 1920s. *New Deal* reforms coupled with Keynesian economic principles, struggled to revive the sluggish economy of the 1930s. But it was not until World War II that America began to truly climb out of the pit of depression and into a new period of economic growth and development. She would again emerge from a *Great War* with no major reconstruction problems and this time as a much more significant superpower.

Most of the financial safety-net programs designed to prevent a major collapse or bank runs were brought into existence during the early 1930s in response to the crippling effects of the *Great Depression*. The 1933 Banking Act gave us the FDIC, which President Roosevelt and Congress designed as a 100% federal deposit insurance program. The purpose of the program was to safeguard deposits and prevent a breakdown of the financial system. In 1934, Savings and Loans were provided with similar protection, the Federal Savings and Loan Insurance Corporation (FSLIC). Federal guidelines for the S&Ls restricted their lending to 30-year, fixed-rate home mortgages, and they were not allowed to pay more than a 5-1/2 percent interest rate. The 1930s also witnessed the establishment of the Glass-Steagall Act of 1933 which legislated the division between commercial banks and investment banks, setting up a *FireWall* between these entities. It was discovered that during the boom of the 1920s, banks took on too much risk with depositors' money which involved stock market activities and investments. Also, Roosevelt signed the Social Security Act in 1935, providing another vital base of financial security to the system.

JOHN MAYNARD KEYNES

In the midst of the Great Depression British economist, John Maynard Keynes, published *The General Theory of Employment, Interest and Money* in 1936. In his book, Keynes set forth his prescription for getting the forces of the capitalistic system moving again. A central concern on everyone's mind was how to regenerate a sluggish world economy. Keynes stepped forward with the first real idea of what had to be done.

According to Keynes' analysis, the classical economics of Adam Smith, J.B. Say and David Ricardo could not alone be expected to resolve the deep contraction in the capitalistic system. The theory of supply and demand (the driving force of classical economics) had broken down and required some type of boost or stimulus, for large numbers of businesses and households, were forced to cut back on expenditures and, hence, demand. He recommended that government provide the needed capital to accelerate demand by implementing a deliberate deficit spending program. By using this procedure- along with tax reductions - the system would begin to regenerate itself. Keynes' theory advocated that governments run budget deficits during economic downturns and budget surpluses during upswing periods of prosperity. The ideal system envisioned a situation of low growth inflation and a steady flow of output without steady increases in prices. Government intervention would be consistent with the theory and not counter-productive or ill-timed.

The Keynesian approach was applied in the United States, Britain, Germany, Japan and other countries in the Western world economic arena. Things began to move, but very slowly.

THE BRETTON WOODS AGREEMENT

The twenty years that elapsed between the two Great World Wars (1919-1939) were marked by boom and bust cycles that shook the foundation of the entire world. It was this period that led to the development of the Bretton Woods agreements, which was the first successful attempt by a large group of nations to control their economic relations. After the First World War, reparations and war debts had been a severe and continuous problem between the quarreling European nations. Hyperinflation knocked Germany to its knees in 1923, and in the aftermath of the stock market crash of 1929, the entire world was confronted with a major economic depression.

All over the world, millions of people lost their jobs, their savings and their standard of living. Confronted by these difficult realities, governments resorted to various methods of economic warfare. To prevent a repeat of the aftermath of the First World War and subsequent events, the victorious Western Allies decided to put in place global economic and monetary systems that would address the pressing problems of the post-WW II era.

Representatives from 44 nations gathered at Bretton Woods, New Hampshire in 1944-45 and established the blueprint and working models of the International Monetary Fund (IMF) and the International Bank for Reconstruction and Development (IBRD, the World Bank). In conjunction with other international programs, such as the Marshall Plan, these organizations would henceforth be at the center of major short-term currency stabilization problems, and long-term economic developmental projects for nations requiring substantial aid over long periods of time.

The centerpiece of these negotiations was the establishment of a new gold standard, with the American dollar serving as the primary link to gold, thereby positioning the U.S. currency as the reserve currency of the world. The world's remaining currencies would henceforth be linked to the dollar, and the price of gold would still be pegged at $35.00 per ounce (the price that had been in place since 1934): that parity made the dollar good as gold. America emerged from the great war (where 60 million people lost their lives) as the greatest nation on earth. Victory in WW II granted America with the honor of being the world's ruling financial superpower.

During the 1940s and 1950s, Fed policies facilitated a period of growth and prosperity. Enormous governmental spending to finance the war finally put an end to the Great Depression. After the war, American corporations and industry were at the center of post-war reconstruction in Europe and Asia, as well as promoting a period of prosperity for all Americans. New innovations and technologies generated the growth of new industrial developments and major corporations. The Bretton Woods accord held strong during those critical two decades of prosperity with no significant problems. All of this would change as we entered the 1960s.

During the 1960s and early 70s, America spent hundreds of billions of dollars on the Vietnam War and its Great Society programs, and deficit spending went beyond the limits. Unprecedented governmental deficit spending eventually led to the oil crisis of the 1970s. For the American dollar, it was a major turning point. This critical period weakened the dollar in world markets, despite the fact that America was also experiencing its longest economic expansion in history. With the Eurodollar and other currency markets flooded with American dollars, the price of gold had to be revised. With governments and major institutions redeeming their dollars for gold, it became uneconomical and too cheap to maintain the price of gold at $35.00 an ounce. The dramatic drop in America's gold supplies prior to 1971, set the stage for a series of major developments in international finance and economics. It simply became very tough to keep the American gold window open.

DEMISE OF THE GOLD STANDARD

The Bretton Woods agreement was backed up against the wall. Events in the 1960s just ran that arrangement over the cliff. Enormous deficit spending simply abused the dollar and led to an unprecedented inflation rate, and on August 15, 1971, America came off the gold standard in a move to devalue its currency. This led to the total breakdown of the gold standard in the West and the dissolution of Bretton Woods. The sudden removal of the gold standard was a major monetary paradigm shift in global economics. And since the start of this new paradigm shift, the U.S. has been running deficits every year since 1971

A new dollar standard was introduced which would be based on a system of free-floating exchange rates, where currency relationships would be determined by the law of supply and demand. Interest rates and inflation rose together in response to the falling dollar. The inflation rate in 1972 was approximately four percent; by 1974, it was in double digits and climbing.

This new fiat currency era witnessed the rapid growth in the world's major currencies and the consequent push towards double-digit inflation during the 1970s. Paul Erdman tells us in his book entitled *Paul Erdman's Money Book*, the results of a world awash in dollar bills. In his words: "the average expansion in domestic money was 45 percent between year-end 1970 and mid-1973, a compound annual rate of nearly 16 percent a year! The inflation that followed...in 1973 and 1974 was obviously fueled by this huge wave of money creation...the U.S. had spread the virus to Europe and Japan."[13] In Erdman's analysis, we see how inflation was fueled worldwide, with leading Western nations supporting the American dollar as the *world's reserve currency no longer backed by gold.* This clearly demonstrated the strong political clout of America, the result of its post-World War II economic strength.

Known as the *Nixon Shock*, President Nixon initiated a new era, one that would generate the most massive global fiat money printing expansion in world history. Gold prices were allowed to work their will, and they did to the tune of $875 per ounce by the first quarter of 1980. These arrangements did not please everyone in the global community, and the repercussions brought about many unpleasant results.

When America broke the Bretton Woods agreement and abandoned the gold standard, it unleashed the great inflationary recessions of the 1970s and early 1980s. Devaluation of the dollar led to huge price hikes in the price of the oil/energy markets. OPEC's response dealt a deadly blow to industrialized nations relying on oil imports. They continued to raise the price of oil throughout the 1970s. The first oil shock hit in 1973 (the price of oil went from $2 to $10 per barrel, and led to the steep American recession in 1973-1975. As inflation continued to escalate throughout the decade, the second oil shock hit in 1979 and led to the steep recession of 1981-82. In the last great recession of that period, the federal funds rate would ultimately rise to 20% to quell the raging inflation; it left some 12.5 million people unemployed and was recorded (up to that time) as the worst downturn since the 1930s.

Under Fed Chairman Paul Volcker, who was appointed by President Jimmy Carter in August 1979 to fight inflation, bold measures were implemented to bring price stability to the national economy. At that time, the inflation rate was hovering around 13% on an annual basis, so the primary Fed tool to address that problem was to raise interest rates dramatically. It was an unpopular display of Fed power, however, during his tenure, Volcker increased the federal funds rate from around 11% to as high as 20%. It was a painful economic surgery, but the results were significant: the rate of inflation fell from 14% in 1980 to under 3% by 1983. Volcker became known as the Fed Chairman that broke the back of inflation, but like President Carter, his popularity fell through the floor. Jimmy Carter became an unpopular president and was not re-elected in 1980, however his policies and those of Fed Chairman Volcker, set the stage for the Reaganomics era that would follow. Also, eight years of Volcker set the stage and paved the way for the colorful career of Fed Chairman Alan Greenspan.

THE GREAT BOOM AND THE BOOMING 80S

In 1981, President Ronald Reagan began his first term in office battling a recession and double-digit inflation. While Fed Chairman Volcker concentrated on breaking the back of inflation, Reagan and his planners instituted an economic program designed to bring about recovery and balance the budget by 1984.

Reaganomics attempted a revival by instituting a drastic reduction in tax rates. Reagan architects decided to provide the artificial stimulus to the supply-side of the supply and demand equation. This theory, known in the economic world as supply-side economics, advocates allowing a larger portion of earned income to be held by wealthier individuals and major business entities to provide investment capital to finance economic developments. The economic benefits from these investments would then *trickle down* to the other levels of society (hence, the term *trickle-down economics*). Thus, significant tax cuts provided substantial benefits for wealthy individuals and major corporations. The basic policies implemented by Reaganomics consisted of the following:

(1) Large-scale deregulation of many industries.
(2) Huge tax cuts in 1981 for large corporations and the upper-income tax brackets.
(3) Heavy defense spending and major cuts in select social programs.

By the fall of 1982, the tight money policies of the Federal Reserve were reversed, due primarily to the deepening of Mexico's debt problems.[14] With the money spigot open and the inflation rate decreasing, the American economy embarked on a new growth period that eventually transformed the 1980s into the *Booming 80s*.[15] It was the decade of the growth and influence of the global billionaire, as enormous concentrations of wealth characterized this period of the mega-rich. It would also become the decade of $200 billion-plus budget deficits; where $1.8 trillion was spent on a defense budget during peacetime; and where the federal government of America became the highest debtor nation in the world with over $3 trillion in total obligations.

A rapid military buildup (perhaps the most expensive in the history of this country) was financed by deficit spending. It was a hefty price to pay, but the strategy worked. America had spent nearly $10 trillion over a four-decade period (1945-1991) defeating the Soviets in the *bipolar era* (the sequel to WW II). The end result was that America won the *cold war* while the Soviet Union and its global empire collapsed.

CONVENTIONAL FEDERAL RESERVE TOOLS AND MANDATES

As stated in the mission statement of the Fed, the primary objective of monetary policy is to influence the performance of the economy as reflected in such factors as inflation, economic output, and employment. "*Monetary policy, as conducted by the Fed, influences demand in the economic system by raising and lowering short-term interest rates. Through managing the money supply and availability of credit, the Fed is working to maintain sustainable economic growth and stability, and to promote effectively the goals of maximum employment, stable prices, and moderate long-term interest rates.*" These maneuvers affect many kinds of economic and financial decisions people make in America - on whether to invest in the stock market, bonds, or place funds in a savings account, to acquire a loan to buy a house or new automobile, whether to expand a business by investing in new plant or equipment, and on whether to take a vacation or start a new business. And since consumer spending makes up roughly two-thirds of Gross Domestic Product (GDP), effective monetary policy has proven to be very beneficial in jump-starting the national economy. Also, given that the U.S. economy is the largest in the world (depending on which metrics are considered); significant changes here can produce major economic and financial effects in other countries. Some of the key tools employed by the Fed are as follows:

(1) **The federal funds rate:** this is the rate banks charge each other for overnight loans. When the Fed cut this rate, banks will tend to lower their prime interest rates; the rates they charge their best customers. Cuts in the Fed funds rate works through three primary channels: (a) lower borrowing costs; (b) stimulate the stock market; and (c) helps to make U.S. goods more competitive in world markets. Rates on credit cards, home-equity loans, car loans and other consumer rates are affected. It is the rate most cited by the media when reporting the latest rate activities of the Federal Reserve.

(2) **The discount rate:** this is the basic rate banks must pay when they borrow money from the Federal Reserve Bank. In essence, the Federal Reserve Bank is the banker's bank. This rate is generally lower than the federal funds rate.

(3) **Reserve requirements:** this is the proportion of deposits that banks and other depository institutions must maintain on reserve (generally 10% against specified deposit liabilities) in their vaults or at Federal Reserve banks.

(4) **Open Market Operations:** Under the authority of section 14 of the Federal Reserve Act, the Federal Open Market Committee (FOMC) administers the purchase and sale of securities in the open market as part of its system for implementing monetary policy. A Trading Desk handles open Market Operations (OMOs) at the Federal Reserve Bank of New York. These operations will increase or decrease the Fed's balance sheet with the intention of influencing the levels of currency in circulation throughout the economy. In regards to the 2008 meltdown, according to the Fed: "During and after the financial crisis, permanent OMOs were used to adjust the Federal Reserve's holdings of securities to put downward pressure on longer-term interest rates and to make financial conditions more accommodative. Currently, permanent OMOs are used to implement the FOMC's policy of reinvesting principal payments from its holdings of agency

debt and mortgage-backed securities (MBS) in agency MBS and of rolling over maturing Treasury securities at auction."

A significant part of the Federal Reserve System is the Federal Open Market Committee (FOMC), which establishes monetary policy decisions regarding interest rates. The FOMC meetings are closely watched events with significant implications regarding stock and bond markets, and consumer confidence levels. The committee consists of the seven Federal Reserve governors and five of the 12 presidents of the regional Reserve Banks. They usually meet once every six weeks to review interest rate policy. As stated earlier, this part of the Fed operating arm was created by Congress in 1923.

FACTIONAL RESERVE BANKING: This system of banking is prevalent in most capitalistic countries in the world today. Central banks set the reserve requirement for member banks, and that percentage requirement establishes how much actual cash a bank must keep on reserve. In the case of the Fed, American member banks are required to maintain 10% of their bank deposits on reserve, making available the other 90% for loans and other transactions.

In practice, this system is what allows for the expansion of the money supply and for banks to create money by establishing new loans or debt on their books: **money is loaned into existence, and thereby interest is charged on the creation of this new money.** As financial intermediaries, banks serve as the essential link between borrowers and savers, providing long-term loans to borrowers while making available immediate liquid funds to depositors. Banks pay depositors a specific rate of interest (a lower rate) and will lend money at higher rates of interest, making a profit on the spread between the two rates.

A great example of this process is the massive quantitative easing programs (QE) that were conducted all over the developed world after the 2008 meltdown. In the case of the U.S., at the beginning of the process, the Fed electronically created money and used it to purchase toxic mortgage-back securities that were on the books of insolvent banks. These banks then had a fresh infusion of capital to lend into circulation (if they chose to do so), keeping the 10 percent requirement on reserve and lending out the other 90 percent, thereby continuing the process of the creation of new money. **This new money decreases the value of existing money through a process of dilution which the economic system records and recognizes as inflation.** Author G. Edward Griffin calls this process a hidden tax which has devalued our currency by over 90 percent since the creation of the Federal Reserve System in 1913.

At the fundamental root of this process is the Fed creation of money out of thin air, which it loans to governments that issue bonds that pay interest on these debt obligations. The creation of a continuous flow of debt keeps the interest payments due and payable on money that was initially created out of nothing. It is the genie that supports the foundation of the international banking cartel.

WHO OWNS THE FED

There is a great deal of confusion and controversy over who owns the Federal Reserve System. Is it privately owned, and what about its independence to make decisions and execute monetary policies? This book will answer part of the question, but not all of it. Of course, the earlier comments in this chapter points to direct and indirect ownership by a banking cartel that has been institutionalized well over a century, ingrained in the fabric of our economic system. The official line, as presented by The Board of Governors of the Federal Reserve System, provides the following brief description of the central bank and who owns it:

> The Federal Reserve System is not "owned" by anyone. Although parts of the Federal Reserve System share some characteristics with private-sector entities, the Federal Reserve was established to serve the public interest. The Federal Reserve derives its authority from the Congress, which created the System in 1913 with the enactment of the Federal Reserve Act. This central banking "system" has three important features: (1) a central governing board - the Federal Reserve Board of Governors; (2) a decentralized operating structure of 12 Federal Reserve Banks; and (3) a blend of public and private characteristics.
>
> The Board of Governors in Washington, D.C., is an agency of the federal government. The Board - appointed by the President and confirmed by the Senate - provides general guidance for the Federal Reserve System and oversees the 12 Reserve Banks. The Board reports to and is directly accountable to the Congress but, unlike many other public agencies, it is not funded by congressional appropriations. In addition, though Congress sets the goals for monetary policy, decisions of the Board - and the Fed's monetary policy-setting body, the Federal Open Market Committee - about how to reach those goals do not require approval by the President or anyone else in the executive or legislative branches of government.
>
> Some observers mistakenly consider the Federal Reserve to be a private entity because the Reserve Banks are organized similarly to private corporations. For instance, each of the 12 Reserve Banks operates within its own particular geographic area, or District, of the United States, and each is separately incorporated and has its own board of directors. Commercial banks

that are members of the Federal Reserve System hold stock in their District's Reserve Bank. However, owning Reserve Bank stock is quite different from owning stock in a private company. The Reserve Banks are not operated for profit, and ownership of a certain amount of stock is, by law, a condition of membership in the System. In fact, the Reserve Banks are required by law to transfer net earnings to the U.S. Treasury, after providing for all necessary expenses of the Reserve Banks, legally required dividend payments, and maintaining a limited balance in a surplus fund.[16]

On the surface, each of the District Federal Reserve banks is privately owned by the commercial banks that are part of the system. As part of the ownership arrangement, these banks receive dividend payments of 6 percent per year and have the right to vote and elect each director that sits on the Reserve Bank's board of directors. Thus, each district Fed bank is owned by large privately owned commercial banks. However, these *share ownership rights* are not the same as owning shares in a corporation: the shares cannot be sold or transferred.

The Federal Board of Governors is based in Washington. Congress helps to shape policy directives, and the President appoints the Fed Chairman and board members, which are confirmed by the Senate. The official line is that "The Board of Governors in Washington, D.C., is an agency of the federal government." As overseer of the 12 district banks, the Board of Governors occupies the primary seat of power in the Fed. In addition, neither Congress or the President of the United States intervenes in the day-to-day decision-making processes of the Fed; there is no oversight on the Fed similar to the legislative, executive and judicial branches of the United States Government.

In its operations and primary mission, the Fed is primarily an independent organization and *not* a federal government agency similar to other department agencies (i.e., the Commerce Department).

However, it is of great importance to note that "the Reserve Banks are required by law to transfer net earnings to the U.S. Treasury, after providing for all necessary expenses of the Reserve Banks, legally required dividend payments, and maintaining a limited balance in a surplus fund." Quantitative easing programs orchestrated by the Fed provided the government an additional source of revenue, with the government essentially paying interest to itself. During the three rounds of Quantitative Easing (QE), the Fed returned over $596 billion to the U.S. Treasury.

Bottom line, the Fed, as G. Edward Griffin declares, is a hybrid organization (half government and half private), a partnership between the banks and the government. The Fed has the power and authority to issue money, without oversight and at its discretion. This is the *central power* that was granted by Congress to the Fed in December 1913.

When Griffin published, *The Creature from Jekyll Island: A Second Look at the Federal Reserve*, it indeed appears that he was seeking to identify a perfect version of a Dr. Jekyll and Mr. Hyde entity. And it certainly seems appropriate, in regards to his conclusion, that the Fed is mostly an extension and part of a massive *global banking cartel*.

CHAIRMAN BEN BERNANKE ERA AND THE BERNANKE PUT

Ben Bernanke (The Professor) became Federal Reserve Chairman in early 2006 with an agenda to continue the path and direction of the Greenspan era. However, a unique characteristic of Bernanke's appointment was the fact that (as mentioned earlier) he had spent most of his academic career studying deflation and the Great Depression of the 1930s, so he was in many respects, intellectually prepared for the devastating crisis that took place two years later. When the full force of the crisis struck in late 2008, Chairman Bernanke orchestrated some of the most daring Fed strategies in the history of this institution.

However, in 2006, Ben Bernanke and his fellow board members were not cognizant of an impending crisis in the housing industry (at least that's what we were led to believe). In a telling example of how the Fed misunderstood the severity of the impending crisis, the release of transcripts of Federal Open Market Committee (FOMC) meetings in 2006 revealed that most leaders in the Federal Reserve were entirely in the dark on what was going on in regards to falling housing prices. Full transcripts do not get released until five years after the year of the scheduled meetings, so it was very interesting to see what these financial experts and Fed officials were thinking in 2006 at the top of the bubble and the early stages of the collapse.

The transcripts cover the eight meetings of 2006 (the Fed meets every six weeks and on any additional special meetings that are convened due to extraordinary market conditions). In 2006, Greenspan's last meeting was in January, and Ben Bernanke's first meeting as Fed Chairman was in March of that year. Bernanke stated at the March meeting that "I agree with most of the commentary that the strong fundamentals support a relatively soft landing in housing... I think we are unlikely to see growth being derailed by the housing market, but I do want us to be prepared for some quarter-to-quarter fluctuations."[17] In September 2006, Timothy Geithner, then the president of the Federal Reserve Bank of New York, was not very concern about *collateral damage* from a housing slowdown. His observations were "We just don't see troubling signs yet of collateral damage, and we are not expecting much."[18] In December 2006, Geithner stated, "We think the fundamentals of the expansion going forward still look good."

Overall, the meetings in 2006 indicated that these overseers of our economic system did not foresee any danger on the horizon that could be triggered by the housing bubble. I don't think that they even recognized that there was a significant bubble in progress, and if so, as trained economists, bankers and experts in their fields, they should have known that bubbles do not last, that sooner or later they will collapse or burst. Bernanke and other Fed officials have stated that they failed to see the severity of the impending crisis, and these transcripts helped us to understand the extent of their limitations of managing the U.S. economy. The intimate connections between the housing market and Wall Street were not evident in their thinking.

In a July 2005 interview with Maria Bartiromo of CNBC, Ben Bernanke was questioned about whether a housing bubble was brewing in the U.S. economy. Bartiromo had stated that several economists had been on the airwaves voicing concerns about the bursting of the housing bubble and that it could ignite a recession. At that time, Bernanke was not concern about a housing bubble, as he stated, "Well, I guess I don't buy your premise. It's a pretty unlikely possibility. We've never had a decline in house prices on a nationwide basis. So, what I think is more likely is that house prices will slow, maybe stabilize, might slow consumption spending a bit. I don't think it's gonna drive the economy too far from its full employment path, though."[19]

Also, in writing for the *New York Times*, Binyamin Appelbaum made these remarks regarding the transcripts, "The transcripts of the 2006 meetings...clearly show some of the nation's pre-eminent economic minds did not fully understand the basic mechanics of the economy that they were charged with shepherding. The problem was not a lack of information; it was a lack of comprehension, born in part of their deep confidence in economic forecasting models that turned out to be broken."[20] It appears that all of these Fed officials were drinking the same Kool-Aid of deregulation and unrestricted free markets.

Despite all of his knowledge, writings, and research of the boom and bust cycles of the 1920s and 1930s, Bernanke was oblivious to the enormous bubble formation and exotic instruments employed to inflate the U.S. housing crisis. Before the *Meltdown of 2008*, Bernanke had studied Japan's ongoing deflationary crisis that had been in progress since 1990, and yet the warning signs were not considered imminent for the U.S. economy.

As the second largest economy in the world (at the time), Japan offered a first-hand observation and analysis of a developed economy that was conducting a fierce decade-plus battle to rebuild its economy and defeat deflation. Thus, in the early 2000s, Japan would be the first to experiment with "quantitative easing" (QE) (See Chapter Seven on Japan). With in-depth knowledge of Japan's collapse and the Great Depression, Bernanke was in a strong position to unleash the proper tools and economic medicine for the epic meltdown in 2008. After conventional Fed tools failed to stop the rapid descent of the meltdown, the U.S. began its first quantitative easing program in 2008 in response to the Lehman crisis.

UNCONVENTIONAL MONETARY TOOLS

In addition to the "Troubled Asset Relief Program" (TARP: discussed in Chapter One), Bernanke slashed interest rates to near zero and injected new money into the economy via a program of government bond purchases. Between December 2008 and March 2010 (QE1), the Fed loaded up on $1.7 trillion in government bonds in an effort to stop the downward deflationary spiral and stimulate the economy. This first round of QE didn't quite get the job done. Thus, Bernanke and the Fed decided to implement QE2 and QE3 to ensure that the U.S. would enter a recovery phase.

Known as "quantitative easing"- a procedure whereby the Fed prints money to buy assets - this financial and economic tool became the primary weapon of choice to restore order and stability. With the implementation of QE, central banks created electronic money (cash or money that did not exist before) and used that monetary resource to buy securities, such as government bonds and mortgage-back bonds, from banks. The stated goal was to bring solvency to the financial sector and improve the balance sheets of Too-Big-To-Fail institutions. This new source of money had the economic impact of increasing the level of bank reserves in the system, reducing leverage and increasing asset prices, particularly in the stock, bond and real estate markets. The official line is that the Fed was looking to encourage banks to make more loans. Since the Fed purchased bonds from the banks, these banks now had new money to generate additional assets via new loans, thus stimulating the economy. An additional benefit of QE was the fact that the federal government could finance large budget deficits at low-interest rates.

In the period December 2008 to mid-2014, trillions of dollars were printed and deployed to prevent the advent of the next great depression. The successive rounds of quantitative easing programs that were rolled out consisted of the following:

(1) QE 1: December 2008 to March 2010. This first program was designed to revitalize the mortgage lending sector and remove a lot of toxic waste from the system. Long-term government bonds, agency MBS (mortgage-backed securities) and GSE debt (government-sponsored enterprises) were the central focus of this campaign. Corporate borrowing rates were reduced by nearly one percentage point.

(2) QE 2: November 2010 to mid-2011. Here, the plan was to strategically lower long-term interest rates via the purchase of $600 billion in Treasury securities (notes, bills, and bonds). To further the interest rate operation, the Fed introduced the Maturity Extension Program, code name "Operation Twist." The Fed continued to tweak long-term interest rates as Ben Bernanke introduced Operation Twist on September 21st as another stimulus plan to lower the critical mortgage rates. The policy involved selling $400 billion in

short-term Treasuries in exchange for the same amount of longer-term bonds, starting in October 2011 and ending in June 2012. The primary goal of this operation was to flatten the yield curve (SEE Glossary), and this had no impact on the Fed's balance sheet.

(3) QE 3 - October 2012 to October-2014: The announcement by Fed Chairman Ben Bernanke (at the September 2012 FOMC meeting) to purchase $40 billion per month in mortgage-backed securities (from the banks) until the unemployment crisis in America had improved, and the real estate market was in a stable recovery stage. It was a clear indication that the country was experiencing an anemic recovery and that the Fed needed to pull out a monetary bazooka and blast out a new quantitative easing program (QE3). The new QE3 program was aggressive, open-ended and would continue until there was "sustained improvement in labor market conditions." The scope of this operation was to inject massive liquidity into the system by soaking up large amounts of agency MBS. Some observers began calling it *QE forever*. At the FOMC meeting in December 2012, the Fed announced that it would increase the open-ended purchases of bonds from $40 billion to $85 billion per month: $40 billion in mortgage-backed securities and $45 billion in Treasury securities. Again, this was seen as further efforts to hold interest rates down and jump-start the economy. However, with this next move, the global economy ventured deeper into unfamiliar territory, and no one (at the time) knew what the result would be.

The massive aftershocks and deflationary pressures generated by the Great Recession, required the Fed to orchestrate its QE operations for nearly six years. On October 29, 2014, the Fed put an end to QE3 after achieving the stated goals of reducing the unemployment rate and bringing stability to the real estate market. The Fed indicated in their policy announcement: "underutilization of labor resources is gradually diminishing." Thus, the Fed had reached its employment objective.

Compared to other developed nations in the world, the U.S. had achieved some measure of strength and stability and was on a path to recovery. Before the *Meltdown of 2008*, the Fed held between $700 to $800 billion worth of Treasury securities on its balance sheet. By the end of the QE operations, the balance was nearly $4.5 trillion. The price to stop the advent of the next Great Depression was considerable, but it worked. However, the overall crisis was not over!

MONEY PRINTING AND INFLATION

One of the core mandates of the Fed is to manage the rate and growth of inflation in the economy. Once the Fed started its massive money printing QE operations, many analysts and Fed watchers were extremely concerned that the U.S. would experience rapid growth in the rate of inflation or would even be threatened by hyperinflation. It was expected that the dollar would be devalued and the bond market crushed. None of this happened. In fact, after six years of QE and near-zero interest rates, the actual fear and threat was deflation, not inflation.

When the full force of the crisis struck in late 2008, the Fed's first line of defense was to lower the overnight interest rate to as far as it could go. When that operation failed to encourage banks to inject money into the economy, the Fed and other central banks (particularly the Bank of England) began to venture into the QE world that Japan had already implemented in the early 2000s.

After the Fed purchased bonds from the banks, the reserves of these banks were replenished and ready for new lending. According to the strategy, banks were supposed to make new loans available for the economy, buying new assets to replace the bonds that were sold to the Fed, but this did not happen for several reasons:

> (1) Instead of lending to the general public, banks began to hoard their resources, thereby preventing the general circulation of monetary resources in the system.
> (2) In the 2006 Financial Services Regulatory Relief Act, Congress voted to allow the Fed to pay interest on bank reserves held at the Fed: this policy was set to begin in 2011. In effect, this legislation allowed the Fed to pay interest on both the required reserves (IORR) and interest on excess reserves (IOER) held on deposit by member banks. Due to the Emergency Economic Stabilization Act of 2008, the Fed was granted the right to begin these interest payments at the beginning of October 2008. With the IOER rate set to be the same rate as the Fed funds rate, bank-to-bank lending experienced a dramatic decrease in activity. In this low-interest rate environment, banks received a competitive interest payment for taking no risk on their reserves. **The result was that banks were being paid not to lend money. Raising the rate of interest paid on excess reserves essentially made new bank loans less attractive, and brought about a decrease in overall credit creation.** It was yet another tool to keep runaway inflation at bay. Prior to 2008, banks didn't have any excess reserves on deposit. Fed records indicate that by 2014, excess reserves totaled approximately $2.7 trillion and required reserves were $75 billion. In 2014, the interest rate paid on these deposits was 0.25 percent, by the end of December 2015 (the Fed increase its Fed funds rate by 25 basis points in December 2015), the interest rate paid on these deposits increased to 0.50 percent. In May 2016, the comparable rate paid on Treasury T-bills was 0.28%. The risk-free IOER rate was a

better deal for the banks. And as the Fed continues its rate hiking program, the IOER and IORR rates will increase as well. As of March 22, 2018, the IORR rate was 1.75 percent, and the IOER rate was 1.75 percent. After over two years of rate hikes, the banks were being compensated generously for not taking any risk, again making new loans less attractive.
(3) The dollar's position as the world's leading reserve currency has also played a role in keeping inflation under control.
(4) Another point to consider about this issue on inflation is the fact that in the U.S. and the West, the impact of inflation gave rise to the dramatic increase in the price of assets, i.e., stocks, bonds, real estate, etc., inflating these markets into new economic bubbles. Thus, retail price inflation was not ignited to the same degree.
(5) Another factor which has not been clearly articulated by mainstream economists is the enormous impact of the globalization of wage deflation. I will have more to say on this issue in the chapter discussing economist Richard Duncan's thesis (Chapter Sixteen). The acceleration of this issue in the global arena has essentially made it possible for developed nations (where wages are much higher than in emerging economies) to print money and not experience runaway inflation. This factor had been particularly beneficial to the U.S. during its multi-trillion dollar money printing operations. The downside has been the multi-decade income depression that America's middleclass had been forced to endure.

If one of the Fed's goal was to boost equity, bond and real estate prices over the past ten years (generating the wealth effect), that mission was accomplished.

The significant impact of QE was to drive down the cost of money, e.g., interest rates. And it's doubtful that any of the central banks will ever sell their assets accumulated during the QE operations. Based on their money printing operations, the entire world is now hooked on Keynesian economics on a level that has never been seen before in global economics.

ZERO INTEREST RATE POLICY (ZIRP) and NEGATIVE INTEREST RATE POLICY (NIRP)

Japan's epic battle against deflation for over 26 years became the leading example of the use of QE, ZIRP, and NIRP following the enormous bursting of its stock and real estate markets in 1990. That historic implosion was a prime example of a massive boom cycle that led to a protracted bust cycle with extreme deflationary pressures. The near zero to zero interest rate policy was used extensively as the core tool to stimulate the economy. With much less than stellar results, the Bank of Japan (BOJ) went deeper into the rabbit hole and introduced QE, followed by NIRP, to resist the deepening impact of deflation. The results were dismal and underwhelming, with deflation firmly entrenched throughout its economic landscape.

With the coming of the *Meltdown of 2008*, ZIRP gain prominence in the U.S., and ZIRP and NIRP took root in many other nations in the West. Given the severity of the crisis, the Fed was persuaded to keep the U.S. on a near-zero to zero interest rate policy for over seven years, unleashing its first interest rate hike in December 2015. Similar to Japan, ZIRP did not ignite a significant recovery. And like Japan, the Fed realized what is firmly entrenched as the root cause of this era of stagnation and anemic growth: global deflation.

The systemic growth and widespread use of these unconventional monetary tools created distortions in the capitalistic paradigm, to the extent that movement towards normalization of interest rates had become a minefield of uncertain outcomes in the global arena. In other words, exiting ZIRP, QE and NIRP policies is likely to produce further distortions and lead to worldwide economic pandemonium: there will be no elegant departure from the ZIRP, QE and NIRP paradigm. A case in point is the position the Fed took after the Brexit vote in mid-2016. The scheduled rate hike had to be postponed due to the uncertainty of the impact on the European and global markets. Massive bubbles have been created, and they will have to unwind at some point in the future. However, the strategic plan is to allow for it to happen in an orderly, non-destructive fashion.

QUANTITATIVE TIGHTENING (QT)

In June 2017, the Fed announced that it would start reducing the size of its balance sheet and begin a process of normalization of its portfolio (taking the Fed's balance sheet back to more normal levels). Known as Quantitative Tightening (QT), this monetary tool is the reverse of Quantitative Easing. The stated plan was to begin this program in October 2017, unloading $10 billion ($6 billion in U.S. Treasuries and $4 billion in Mortgage-back Securities) per month for the first three months. Beginning in January 2018, the retirement of securities would increase to $20 billion per month for the next three month, then $30 billion per month from April through June, and $40 billion per month from July through September. And in October, the escalation called for $50 billion of securities to be removed from the system. After two to three years of QT, the Fed was looking at reducing its $4.5 trillion bond portfolio by 25 percent, or over $1 trillion. The end goal for the normalization process is to reduce the Fed's portfolio of bonds to roughly $2 trillion by 2020.

During the time of QE, the Fed continued its purchase of bonds by rolling over maturing issues and using the proceeds to buy new bonds. New money was electronically created to make the initial purchases. Under QT, maturing bonds would not be rolled over, and the bonds would stay on the Fed books. However, the money would be made to disappear from the monetary system (this is another demonstration of the extraordinary power of the Fed). Hence, this operation was scheduled to bring about a contraction in the money supply, substantially reducing the availability of credit. Thus, QE creates money and expands the monetary system, while QT destroys money and brings about a contraction in the monetary system.

The Fed was well aware that Quantitative Tightening (in that late stage in the cycle after nearly a decade of a boom period of asset inflation) was a delicate operation, particularly in conjunction with interest rate hikes and the approval by the Trump Administration and Congress (in December 2017) to provide tax cuts (mainly for the wealthy). The Fed emphasized the word "gradual" to acknowledge that it would be walking a tightrope while conducting the QT operation.

In addition, the Fed also needed to make preparations for a potential recession by reloading its interest rate tool (raising interest rates to higher levels, within the five percent range) and freeing up space on its balance sheet for future operations (another round of QE, etc.). The Fed made it known that if the economy encountered significant headwinds or setbacks, it was prepared to reverse its course and provide assistance (stimulus, lower rates, etc.) when required.

As interest rates rise and the Fed removes money (credit) from the economic system, the threat of a significant collapse followed by a deep recession is nearly guaranteed. The Fed has boxed itself into a corner where a financial crisis is unavoidable (at a minimum on a temporary basis) on the road to normalization. It was quantitative easing that prevented a great depression; quantitative tightening has a high probability of starting a *significant meltdown*. Make no mistake about it; these are dangerous waters to navigate with few or any safeguards. Observations by American attorney and economic commentator, Jim Rickards, provides a concise summary of the Fed predicament as he writes, "By raising rates and leaving open the possibility of further increases, all of the monetary actions being taken are tightening the economy. The Fed's QT policy that aims to tighten monetary conditions, reduce the money supply and increase interest rates will cause the economy to hit a wall."[21] That is the most likely scenario, given the objectives that the Fed hopes to achieve.

INTERNATIONAL CENTRAL BANKS AND QE

The vast majority of the world's population live in a country that has an established central banking system (approximately 99% of the world's population). All of the 187 member nations in the International Monetary Fund (IMF) have central banking systems. In essence, the leading nations in the West have convinced the entire world to adopt this system. In addition, an organization known as the Bank for International Settlements (BIS) is considered the central bank for the central banks in the system. Located in Basel, Switzerland, this super powerful organization has mechanisms to control the money supply of the entire world secretly. Thus, when a global economic crisis on the scale of the *Meltdown of 2008* strikes, the BIS goes on full alert, and we can assume that there are coordinated actions taken by many of the 58 central banks that are part of its core decision-making body.

Since 2008, most of the central banks in developed economies have followed a similar path towards recovery and the use of monetary tools. The massive struggle against the onset of global deflation witnessed global central bankers cutting interest rates 637 times, and (by April 2016) QE money printing operations added over $12.3 trillion to the global monetary system. To win the deflation war in the West, global central bankers declared a target inflation rate of 2% with a commitment to continue money printing and other growth strategies to increase asset prices and global demand. The top central bank players in the West are the Fed, Bank of England (BOE), Bank of Japan (BOJ) and the European Central Bank (ECB).

Like the proverbial canary in the coal mine, Japan's successive battles against deflation, extending well over two decades, had convinced most central bankers to avoid that plague at all costs. As stated earlier, former Fed Chairman Ben Bernanke, who had spent much of his academic career studying deflation in the 1930s, was clear in his pronouncement that, "Sustained deflation can be highly destructive to a modern economy and should be strongly resisted." His prescription for this deadly disease had been refined to the basics: slash interest rate to near zero and inject new money into the economy through a program of government bond purchases. The Japanese model was a living example of the use of these unconventional monetary tools.

Similar to taking prescription drugs that promise to provide relief from an illness but comes with a host of side effects, unconventional monetary tools (QE, ZIRP, and NIRP) created a host of economic side effects that generated dislocations, distortions and mal-investments in the global financial arena. As stated elsewhere, various asset bubbles manifested as a result of QE, ZIRP and NIRP; the extraordinary growth of the inequality of wealth became a manifestation throughout the entire world with enormous implications. Also, the over-expansion of investments generating over-capacity in such industry sectors as manufacturing, mining, transportation, and trade was a prime example of what mal-investments could do. This global disequilibrium, massive debt buildup and growing levels of insolvencies, will ultimately unwind with unfavorable results.

The distribution of QE monetary resources favored mainly the wealthy, who got bailed out and were given a new lease on life. When we examine the seven to eight years after 2008, we see that ZIRP and QE succeeded in keeping the developed world out of deflation and a *Great Depression*, but failed to revive substantial economic growth, decimating the middle class in America, Europe, Japan and elsewhere. The benefits were largely received by those at the top in major countries throughout the world.

Another side effect was the emergence of currency wars and the competitive fever among nations to devalue their currencies to maintain strong export markets. Downward pressure on such major currencies as the yen, euro and yuan revealed further vulnerabilities and vault lines in the global financial system, presenting a strategy to what some analysts referred to as a "race to the bottom." In the final phase of this crisis, each country will be forced to defend their competitive edge in the global marketplace.

HELICOPTER MONEY

As an unconventional monetary tool, the actual use of "helicopter money" would follow the unsuccessful application of the negative interest rate policy (NIRP): in other words, if all else fails, make money directly available to consumers to spend, thereby stimulating demand. Wall Street has labeled it *the nuclear option*, and due to his 2002 speech (given on deflation) before the National Economists Club, former Fed Chairman Ben Bernanke became known as *Helicopter Ben*. In fact, in a 2016 blog post, Bernanke stated, "Helicopter money could prove a valuable tool."[22] Fed Chair Janet Yellen was also considering this as a possible monetary tool during a serious crisis, "It is something that one might legitimately consider."[23] Economists, policy makers and analysts around the world have strongly debated the merits and economic benefits of a direct monetary injection to consumers. Critics and other commentary have likened helicopter money to a "Debt Jubilee," which links back to the old biblical idea of a historic celebration that would introduce a national (or international) cancellation of private debts. It suggests that our current civilization has reached a milestone of enormous debt and credit that will have to be dealt with in an extraordinary set of solutions. This is a very pivotal period in global economic affairs.

We can thank economist and monetarist Milton Friedman for his 1969 *helicopter parable*. His prescription has garnered a growing acceptance among Keynesian and Monetarist economic scholars, particularly after the ferocity of the 2008 crisis. It is now firmly in the toolbox of major central bankers around the world. The timing of the use of this tool will be carefully orchestrated (particularly in America), and will most likely occur in a deepening crisis or recession that is slipping into a deflationary spiral.

The world has already witnessed a form of helicopter money in the use of money printing quantitative easing (QE). In the QE paradigm, the Fed created electronic money (cash or money that did not exist before) and used that monetary resource to buy securities, such as government bonds and mortgage-back bonds from banks. Since the Fed is required by law to transfer its net earnings on these assets to the U.S. Treasury, this then represents helicopter money at the institutional financial level. The main problem here is that the economic benefits stayed primarily in the financial system (benefitting Wall Street, the wealthy, the well-connected and the U.S. government), and didn't provide maximum benefits for the consumers on Main Street. As stated earlier, by 2015, $596 billion in revenue had been transferred to the U.S. Treasury. The yearly Fed deposits to the Treasury were mainly used to pay down the budget deficits.

Under the original concept of helicopter money - people's QE - the plan would be for the Fed to create new money again for the U.S. government to distribute directly (no intermediaries, banks or other trickle-down theories) to consumers to spend or pay off debts, etc. The belief is that this type of stimulus would have a much stronger impact on economic demand thereby increasing inflation, generating growth, jobs, and new investments. Direct consumer spending is a central key in this proposition, and economists expect that there would be a much greater stimulus impact from this process. Fiscal and monetary policies will need to work closely together to bring about the desired results.

Macroeconomist Jordi Galli is a strong supporter of helicopter money, particularly as it relates to the on-going crisis in the Eurozone. His analysis reveals why this approach could be very effective in the current global crisis:

> The previous predictions contrast with the experience with quantitative easing and other unconventional monetary policies, which do not affect aggregate demand directly and which, as a result, have failed to jumpstart the depressed economies of many countries, especially in the Eurozone.
> An additional advantage of a money-financed fiscal stimulus, particularly relevant for a monetary union, is that the associated increase in government purchases may be targeted at the regions with higher unemployment and lower inflation (or higher risk of persistent deflation).
>
> The time may have come to leave old prejudices behind and come to terms with the urgent need to increase aggregate demand in a more fool proof way than tried up to now, especially in the Eurozone. The option of a money-financed fiscal stimulus should be considered seriously.[24]

Galli is indicating here that standard QE has not had enough of a direct impact on *aggregate demand*. As a Spanish economist based in Spain, he is well aware that the Eurozone is stuck in a severe crisis that previous options have not brought about a significant recovery in Europe. The EU is at the point where a much greater stimulus program is required.

An organization in the U.S. called "The Economic Security Project" unveiled a two-year mission to research and explore the idea of a universal basic income for the general population in America. Composed of more than 100 organizers, researchers, technologists, and activists, this group raised $10 million to fund their two-year research project. Their stated mission as presented on their website (www. http://economicsecurityproject.org/) shows deep concern about our current crisis and how their plan may be part of the solution:

The time has come to consider new, bold ways to make our economy work again for all Americans. In a time of immense wealth, no one should live in poverty, nor should the middle class be consigned to a future of permanent stagnation or anxiety. Automation, globalization, and financialization are changing the nature of work, and these shifts require us to rethink how to guarantee economic opportunity for all.

> A basic income is a bold idea with a long history and the potential to free people to pursue the work and life they choose. Now is the time to think seriously about how recurring, unconditional cash stipends could work, how to pay for them, and what the political path might be to make them a reality, even while many of us are engaged in protecting the existing safety net.[25]

As one of the organizers of this movement, Facebook co-founder, Chris Hughes, is very concern about the dire consequences of the exponential growth of inequality in the American economy. According to Hughes, "We know from research in the US and internationally that recurring, unconditional cash stipends are a shockingly effective way to encourage work, improve health and education outcomes, and create a ladder of economic opportunity."[26]

There are different variations on how the money would be made available to the public and under what conditions. Some proponents have suggested tax rebates or tax cuts; others are focused more on infrastructure developments, which to me doesn't get to the heart of the matter: Joe and Nancy on Main Street. During April of 2016, Fed Chair Bernanke offered his insights on what might be an excellent approach to this monetary procedure:

> A possible arrangement, set up in advance, might work as follows: Ask Congress to create, by statute, a special Treasury account at the Fed, and to give the Fed...the sole authority to "fill" the account, perhaps up to some pre-specified limit. At almost all times, the account would be empty; the Fed would use its authority to add funds to the account only when the [Fed] assessed that a [helicopter drop] of specified size was needed to achieve the Fed's employment and inflation goals.
>
> Should the Fed act, under this proposal, the next step would be for the Congress and the Administration - through the usual, but possibly expedited, legislative process - to determine how to spend the funds (for example, on a tax rebate or on public works). Importantly, the Congress and Administration

would have the option to leave the funds unspent. If the funds were not used within a specified time, the Fed would be empowered to withdraw them.[27]

Under Bernanke's plan, the Fed would establish the mega-account for the Treasury, and the government and Congress would need to decide and vote on how to allocate the funds to the specified population. However, the only way gridlock in Washington could be broken, and an agreement solidified on an unconventional plan of this type, would be a category five economic crisis, so deadly that politicians would cling to any solution that could save the country and prevent a *Great Depression*.

SUMMARY/ANALYSIS

The Fed needs to be nationalized and made to serve the interests of the American people. Most astute Fed observers are keenly aware that the long-term product of this central banking institution is debt. New money comes into existence by the issuance of loans and the collection of interest income. Thomas Jefferson stated a few centuries ago that "The issuing power should be restored to the people to whom it properly belong." It was true during his time, and it is just as relevant in the 21st century. When we examine the record of the Fed over a 100-year period, there are reasons to believe that it operates to serve the interest of the Big Banks that own it.

Fed Chairman Ben Bernanke stated that "September and October 2008 was the worst financial crisis in global history". Sitting at the helm of the Federal Reserve System during that historical meltdown must have been an extraordinary experience. So his statements on the crisis should not be taken lightly.

I believe that when economic and financial historians (in the not-too-distant future) finally complete a full historical analysis of this era, they will agree with Chairman Bernanke on the massive severity of this crisis. What we are witnessing is the result of a super-expansive experiment in fiat-money creation over a period of many decades. And the interesting thing about this experiment is that it will ultimately (as of 2018), take additional massive money printing to get us out of this mess.

As part of the overall global solution, it will take the intelligent use of fiat money printing to devise a strategy to escape the death throes of an impending *Great Depression*. Without ingenuity and unconventional ideas and procedures, we may be lost for decades with nations fighting like crabs in a barrel trying to escape the deflationary abyss. But all of this has to be figured out before the magic of the fiat money regime begins to lose its financial power. The West has a critical window of opportunity before the advent of the final big collapse. We have to recognize the uniqueness of this crisis and not waste the opportunities inherent in the bowels of deflation and stagnation.

And even after all the results of the devastating *Meltdown of 2008*, Ben Bernanke and Treasury Secretary Timothy Geithner, still didn't move to regulate the derivatives market. In 1998, Brooksley Born (head of the Commodity Futures Trading

Commission (CFTC)) did her best to warn Washington, the Fed, the SEC and the Treasury of what could happen, and they subsequently ran her out of office (See Chapter Five).

After the 2008 disaster, with its multiplicity of events, there should have been an urgency to establish reforms in this area (OTC Derivatives). It would have seemed appropriate for these actions to be taken in the aftermath of the most significant economic crisis since World War II. Even with all the damage that was done, our regulators were still allowing the world to go through the same downward spiral again.

The financial sector has now become a much more dominant and pervasive force in our society. *If the Fed is indeed an extension of a banking cartel, the 2008 meltdown provided clear evidence of their extensive power.*

One has to wonder, while in the eye of the storm, Helicopter Ben (Fed Chair Bernanke) didn't use helicopter money to bail out the American homeowner. It would have been perfect timing: the Democrats had a mandate and had control of the presidency and Congress. They didn't have to use the banks to implement a *people's bailout*; for less than $1 trillion that plan could have saved millions of homes and would have been the best down payment for stimulating demand within the American economy. And if the plan was to use banks in this novel people's *bailout strategy*, then the demands should have been made at the outset.

History has proven, that depending on the big banks as intermediaries was a huge mistake! Ten years later, everyone is now beginning to understand that the *nuclear option* is the best strategy when you are starring a deflationary depression dead in the face.

As stated elsewhere in this publication, the fact that the Fed and the Secretary of Treasury didn't establish a "Special Facility" and separate federal agency to address the devastating foreclosure crisis, was the worst absolute failure of the *Meltdown of 2008*. And as researchers and analysts continue to dig deeper into the details of Fed operations during the meltdown, the facts may indeed point to a conclusion that it was all orchestrated so that the majority of homeowners would not be bailed out.

NOTES

(1) G. Edward Griffin, *The Creature from Jekyll Island* (Fifth edition), Westlake Village, California: American Media, 2010) pp. 11-12.
(2) Charles A. Lindbergh, *Banking and Currency and The Money Trust*, Hawthorne, California: Omni Publications.
(3) Woodrow Wilson, *The New Freedom: A Call for the Emancipation of the Generous Energies of a People* (New York and Garden City: Doubleday, Page & Company, 1913)
(4) Ibid. Charles A. Lindbergh
(5) Robert Sobel, *The Great Bull Market*, (New York: W.W. Norton & Company, Inc., 1968) pp. 38-39.

(6) Charles Kindleberger, *The World In Depression 1929-1939*, (Berkeley: University of California Press, Berkeley, 1986) p.26.
(7) Charles P. Kindleberger, *Manias, Panics and Crashes*, (New York: Basic Books Inc. Publishers, 1978) p. 5.
(8) Louis McFadden, "Louis McFadden denouncing the Federal Reserve System," 1932-06-10, Congressional Record, June 1932, pg 12595-12603.
(9) Louis McFadden, "Congressman McFadden on the Federal Reserve Corporation Remarks in Congress, 1934 An Astounding Exposure," Reprinted by permission 1978 Arizona Caucus Club, http://home.hiwaay.net/becraft/mcfadden.html. This website contains extensive coverage of McFadden's views and bitter denouncements of the Fed.
(10) Ibid. G. Edward Griffin, pp. 20-21.
(11) Ben Bernanke, "A Crash Course for Central Bankers," Foreign Policy, September/October 2000.
(12) Ibid. Louis McFadden.
(13) Paul Erdman, *Paul Erdman's Money Book*, (New York: Random House, Inc., 1984) pp.53-54.
(14) Ibid, pp. 39-48
(15) The *Booming 80s* is a special term I coined to describe that remarkable decade. This decade would witness the birth of the microcomputer revolution and the beginning of the billionaire era.
(16) Board of Governors of the Federal Reserve System, "What are the Federal Reserve's objectives in conducting monetary policy?", The Federal Reserve Board, https://www.federalreserve gov/faqs/money_12848.htm
(17) Minutes of the Metting, "Meeting of the Federal Open Market Committee March 27-28, 2006," Washington, D.C., March 27-28, 2006.
(18) Minutes of the Metting, "Meeting of the Federal Open Market Committee September 20, 2006," Washington, D.C., September 20, 2006.
(19) Paul Zimnisky, "Is the Fed taper too little too late?," Futures (online publication), February 3, 2014.
(20) Binyamin Appelbaum, "Inside the Fed in 2006: A Coming Crisis," *New York Times*, 2012.
(21) Jim Rickards, "Get Ready for 'QT1' A First Look at the Federal Reserve's Hidden Policy", *The Daily Reckoning*, June 22, 2017.
(22) Steve Goldstein, "Bernanke says so-called helicopter money could work," MarketWatch, April 11, 2016.
(23) Patrick Gillespie, "Janet Yellen: Helicopter money is an option in extreme situations," CNN Money, June 16, 2016.
(24) Jordi Gali, "Thinking the Unthinkable: The effects of a money-financed fiscal stimulus," VOX Cerpr's Policy Portal, October 3, 2014.
(25) Catherine Clifford, "Facebook co-founder's new $10 million initiative to test if cash handouts will help fix America", CNBC.com, December 9, 2016.
(26) IBID., CNBC.com
(27) Chris Matthews, "Here's How Ben Bernanke's 'Helicopter Money' Plan Might Work," *Fortune*, April 12, 2016.

CHAPTER FIVE
THE GAO AUDIT REPORT AND MULTI-TRILLION DOLLAR RESCUE OPERATIONS

The Global Financial Crisis of 2007-2009 is remarkable for a number of reasons...it exposed the lengths to which central banks worldwide... would act to save the existing financial order, helping to preserve especially the largest and most powerful institutions...We will never know what might have happened had there not been such a strong intervention.

James Felkerson The Levy Economics Institute

The total amount of funding provided by the Fed to bailout the financial system in the *Meltdown of 2008* has been the subject of considerable debate and continued analysis. It took the combination of concerted efforts by powerful entities to finally force the Fed to divulge its secrets. The revelation that the Fed deployed trillions of dollars throughout the crisis was an eye-opener. A central point of contention is the way the various transactions were accumulated and assessed.

The leading organizations that have performed extensive work on this issue are *Bloomberg*, the Government Accountability Office (GAO), *The Financial Crisis Inquiry Report* and the Levy Economics Institute. What is hotly debated is the total bailout funding and loan estimates which range from a low of $1.2 trillion to a high of $29 trillion. What is not debated is the scope and size of the operation during the crisis, which, by most accounts, had an extensive global reach. This extraordinary crisis had the full potential of being the worse economic collapse of all times, had there not been a massive intervention by the Fed. In fact, during the *Meltdown of 2008*, the Fed became the global or international *Lender of Last Resort* (LOLR), essentially bailing out *Western civilization*.

In one of the most controversial financial agendas in the history of finance and central banks, from December 2007 to July 2010, the Fed provided massive loans and bailouts to major banks, institutions and wealthy individuals in Europe, America and other parts of the world.

BLOOMBERG

Many questions needed to be answered after the *Meltdown of 2008*, and *Bloomberg* was one of the news corporations searching for hard facts on the causes and the Federal Reserve's response to the massive crisis. Under the Freedom of Information Act (FOIA), *Bloomberg*, an American multinational financial news corporation, initiated a lengthy court battle to gain the release of documents that detailed the Fed's lending practices and operations during the crisis. It would take two years to break down the barriers, and it wasn't until March 2011, that the data was finally released. It took the firepower of *Bloomberg* to get this information; otherwise, it may have stayed buried for another decade. Also, in response to the Dodd-Frank Act, the Fed had to release 18 databases detailing its temporary emergency-lending programs. What the records revealed was that the $700 billion TARP operation was minor compared to the full-blown nearly interest-free trillion dollar operations.

Bloomberg sued in November 2008 when the Fed refused to release the names of the firms it lent to or disclose the number of assets it used as collateral under its lending programs. The lawsuit, handled by Willkie Farr & Gallagher LLP, was brought under the U.S. Freedom of Information Act (FOIA). Under FOIA, federal agencies are to make government documents available to the press and public. *Bloomberg* argued that the public had a right to know about the unprecedented use of public money. The Fed didn't want to release this information and fought hard during those two years to prevent releasing the identities of the borrowers and the terms of their loans. The fight went all the way to the Supreme Court.

The Fed's primary defense and overriding concerns for not providing disclosure was that it would "stigmatize banks," possibly leading to massive depositor withdrawals or bank runs, and ultimately would be harmful to their stock prices. For the most part, the banks kept quiet about these dealings with minimal disclosures in their quarterly and annual financial filings: these companies wanted to avoid the "stigma" of borrowing from Federal assistance programs. *Bloomberg* reported in August 2011 that "A group of the biggest commercial banks last year asked the U.S. Supreme Court to keep at least some borrowings secret. In March, the high court declined to hear that appeal, and the central bank made an unprecedented release of records."[1]

The lower court finally agreed with *Bloomberg*. Federal Judge Loretta Preska of the U.S. Court of Appeals in Manhattan decided to order the Federal Reserve to release documents related to the 2008 economic collapse. In her ruling regarding the central bank's concern about harm to the banks, Judge Preska states that this "speculates on how a borrower might enter a downward spiral of financial instability if its participation in the Federal Reserve lending programs were to be disclosed...Conjecture, without evidence of imminent harm, simply fails to meet the board's burden of proof."[2]

When the documents were finally released, *Bloomberg* was able to analyze 29,346 pages of documents in addition to 21,000 transactions from Federal Reserve databases. According to *Bloomberg*, these documents revealed "...for the first time how deeply the world's largest banks depended on the U.S. central bank to stave off cash shortfalls. Even as the firms asserted in news releases or earnings calls that they had ample cash, they drew funding in secret, avoiding the stigma of weakness."[3] The central bank documents highlight the fact that America's six largest banks, Bank of America, Citigroup, Goldman Sachs, JPMorgan Chase, Wells Fargo and Morgan Stanley, borrowed over $500 billion from the Fed. It appeared that out of this list of big banks, Citigroup was the most "chronic borrower." This bank was literally in *intensive economic care*, nursed back to life by the generosity and facilities of the Fed. The documents also revealed that as the crisis intensified in 2008, the Fed began to accept low-rated collateral for the loans that it was dishing out. The standard protocol was to allow only bonds with the highest credit grade; however, the Fed began accepting junk bonds and stocks as collateral.

Bloomberg makes the point that without federal money the *aristocracy of American finance* was going down the tubes. We were further informed:

> It wasn't just American finance. Almost half of the Fed's top 30 borrowers, measured by peak balances were European firms. They included Edinburgh-based Royal Bank of Scotland Plc, which took $84.5 billion ...and Zurich-based UBS AG, which got $77.2 billion. Germany's Hypo Real Estate Holding AG borrowed $28.7 billion, an average of $21 million for each of its 1,366 employees.[4] Other big European borrowers included Dexia SA, Belgium's largest bank by assets, Societe Generale SA, based in Paris, Barclays PLC (United Kingdom), Deutsche Bank AG (Germany), Credit Suisse Group AG (Switzerland), BNP Paribas SA (France), and Dresdner Bank AG (Germany).[5]

An interesting observation in the above statement is that Dexia SA had to be bailed out again in late 2011 as the European crisis intensified over the possible default of Greece and other PIIGS nations (moral hazard). According to the Fed, there were "no credit losses" on any of their emergency programs. Emergency loan activities from August 2007 through December 2009 are stated to have generated $13 billion in interest and fee income.

Overall, *Bloomberg* reported that by March 2009, the Fed had committed $7.7 trillion to "rescuing the banking system" from a devastating financial meltdown. According to Bob Ivry, who was part of the *Bloomberg* team of reporters that fought the Fed for disclosure, the $7.7 trillion total figure was "not money out the door, but...money that the Fed was willing to either guarantee or spend to get the banking system back on track."

Even as Congress debated the merits of the Dodd-Frank reform bill in 2010, legislators were utterly unaware of the Fed's trillion-dollar commitments and loans. Democratic Rep. Elijah Cummings, a member of the House Oversight and Government Reform Committee, made this observation:

> "Many Americans are struggling to understand why banks deserve such preferential treatment while millions of homeowners are being denied assistance and are at increasing risk of foreclosure."[6]

An interesting side note here is that it took a court order to force the Fed to release this information. By borrowing from the cheapest source, the *banking aristocracy of America* was able to survive the crisis, profit from the crisis and live to see another day. However, they did very little for the American homeowner in the foreclosure crisis. They were given a *secret* lifeline to survive, and then turned around and did the bare minimum to help the ongoing foreclosure crisis in America. The American people didn't receive any direct assistance in the form of foreclosure relief, loan modifications, etc. If the Fed purchased the majority of the toxic mortgage-back securities from the banks during its QE operations, then there could have been *special facilities and new agencies* established to address the foreclosure crisis. And after eight years of economic stagnation and a world economy that was still on the brink of a major collapse, the focus was always on maintaining the status quo.

DODD-FRANK: Enacted July 21, 2010:
The Dodd-Frank Reform and Consumer Protection Act.

The first major piece of legislation to emerge after the *Meltdown of 2008* was The Dodd-Frank Reform and Consumer Protection Act. This new legislation implemented financial regulatory reform and is strong on consumer protections but weak on the regulations required to prevent 2008 from happening again. Signed into law on July 21, 2010, by President Barack Obama, it mandated a GAO audit of the Federal Reserve System (discussed in another section). To many critics, Dodd-Frank was too weak and did not go far enough in preventing systemic risk. According to Kenneth Rogoff (in observing these developments), a former chief economist at the IMF and currently an economics professor at Harvard University, "Regulators are not going to go far enough to prevent this from happening again."[7] One critical observation is that the new bill did not bring back Glass-Steagall nor did it mandate stringent regulations for the OTC derivatives market, two key factors that ignited the 2008 collapse.

The sponsors of Dodd-Frank (U.S. Senator Christopher J. Dodd and U.S. Representative Barney Frank) were intent on providing legislation that would prevent the reoccurrence of a 2008 catastrophe. However, with the complex and lengthy body of law spanning over 2300 pages with over 225 new rules and 11 federal agencies, the purpose and intent got lost in much of the superfluous details. Large well-staffed organizations with an army of lawyers and CPAs developed workarounds and took full advantage of new loopholes in the voluminous paperwork. After several years of writing and implementation, the fear and grave concern for 2018 and beyond, is that this legislation would not prevent the next meltdown.

Even with the Volcker Rule (Title VI of the Act), the provisions limit the broader aspects of the Glass-Steagall Act of 1933. Granted, the Volcker Rule restricts the ways banks can engage the markets in regards to speculation, proprietary trading, and non-involvement with private equity firms and hedge funds, but even these regulations don't go far enough in creating the separation between commercial banks and investment institutions.

The Glass-Steagall Act didn't require a copious amount of paperwork to spell out its full intention to reform the banking industry in America; it took only 37 pages in straightforward language to get the job done. And for 65 years that legislation stood as a pillar of truth in the financial markets, providing a vital barrier prohibiting reckless abuse and mismanagement. This issue might be best described as 'simplicity versus complexity,' wherein Glass-Steagal is elegant, and Dodd-Frank is cumbersome and bulky.

The more regulations, the more regulators that will be required to enforce the various sections of the legislation. Simple rules are cheaper to administer and better to manage. In regards to derivatives, the Volcker Rule attempts to regulate the use of OTC trading and increase transparency, but too-big-to-fail institutions have found ways to maneuver within the complexity of the legislation. In short, Dodd-Frank is ineffective and burdensome in some key areas that are the most vulnerable: OTC derivatives, the separation of commercial banks and investment institutions, and stopping the massive growth of too-big-to-fail banking institutions.

GAO REPORT: $16 TRILLION DOLLAR GLOBAL RESCUE OPERATION

After three years of Senate hearings, investigative reporting and documentaries, a court-ordered release of Federal Reserve documents, and a special *Financial Crisis Inquiry Commission report*, in 2011 the American people were finally getting the total picture and corresponding events of what happened in the *Meltdown of 2008*. The shocking and disturbing truth is that an astronomical amount of money was spent to keep the entire world from falling into the next *Great Depression*. Trillions of dollars were spent preventing what would have been a devastating global meltdown.

Nothing on this scale had ever been contemplated or attempted in world economic history. Billions and trillions spent to save drowning financial institutions, but again nothing specifically targeted for the individual American homeowner.

As a result of an amendment by U.S. Senator Bernie Sanders to the *Dodd-Frank Reform and Consumer Protection Act*, the first major audit of the Federal Reserve System was mandated. The Government Accountability Office (GAO) was called upon to complete the audit of the Fed. The report uncovered an enormous level of conflicts of interest at the Fed during the financial crisis, as well as providing revelations of vast outlays in its emergency lending operations. The GAO covered the period between 2007 and 2010, when (by their analysis and methodology) the Federal Reserve System of the United States handed out nearly $16 trillion in virtually interest-free money to primarily *Big Banks* in America and Europe.

The GAO's $16 trillion massive figure is based on their methodology of accumulating a series of loan balances over time. An example would be of a bank having borrowed (at the Fed) $5 billion overnight for 50 days. The GAO calculation would state that $250 billion was lent during this time. The reality may have been something entirely different; a total loan amount over the 50 days of just $5 billion, overnight loans that were repaid the following day with an open line of credit.

In essence, the Fed made the strategic choice of who would win and who would lose in the global financial chess game. The broader period covered by this enormous outlay of financial resources is between December 1, 2007, and July 21, 2010, when the $16.1 trillion (the GAO conclusion) in secret loans were dispensed to financial institutions. Page 131 of the *GAO Audit Report* presents a list of the firms and the amount of money they received (See the complete report at: http://www.gao.gov/new.items/d11696.pdf).

While the Fed was passing out all of those trillions of dollars to bank executives and their cronies, at least one trillion dollars could have been allocated to bail out the American housing crisis. The American housing crisis was "Too Big To Fail," however this did not take center stage with a remedy to stabilize the industry, and as a result, there would be no strong recovery without supporting millions of people and their families that were hard hit by the American housing industry collapse. It took nearly five years for our leaders to finally understand that point. And it was very interesting to observe that when any mass solution was presented to help modify or refinance loans for the individual homeowner, pundits came out of the woodwork screaming the dangers of *moral hazard* (if the homeowner is given insurance or a deal, they were going to be less careful or prone to do something again). *Moral hazard* was massively pervasive in the financial industry when it came to big institutions and for those who accepted the bailout money during the economic crisis. This is what I identified as *moral hazard hypocrisy* or preferential treatment for *institutional moral hazard*.

During the meltdown crisis, the Fed primarily concentrated on stabilizing the global economy by bailing out prominent American and European banks. A quote by economist Nouriel Roubini concerning the bailout of big banks adequately describes this modern phenomenon: "We're essentially continuing a system where profits are privatized and...losses socialized."[8] De-facto socialism for the capitalistic banking system is what we witnessed.

Senator Bernie Sanders fought to have the Federal Reserve System serve the needs of the American people and not just the Big Banks. In his words, "To get this process started, I have asked some of the leading economists in this country to serve on an advisory committee to provide Congress with legislative options to reform the Federal Reserve." On a similar point regarding the Fed, the senator informed us that, "The Federal Reserve has a responsibility to ensure the safety and soundness of financial institutions and to contain systemic risks in financial markets. Given that the top six financial institutions in the country now have assets equivalent to 65 percent of our GDP, more than $9 trillion, is there any reason why this extraordinary concentration of ownership should not be broken up? Should a bank that is "too big to fail" be allowed to exist?"[9]

THE LEVY ECONOMICS INSTITUTE $29 TRILLION BAILOUT ASSESSMENT

In the continuing effort to uncover the full extent of the bailouts during the 2008 crisis, the research and analysis of two Ph.D. students (Nicola Matthews and James Felkerson) at the University of Missouri-Kansas City, brought to light a much broader scope of dealings than either *Bloomberg* or the *GAO Report*. Funded by a Ford Foundation grant, this report is entitled, *"A Research And Policy Dialogue Project On Improving Governance Of The Government Safety Net In Financial Crisis"*. In their thought-provoking analysis, the two researchers combed through the over 29,000 pages of raw data released by the Fed and arrived at some very startling conclusions. To provide greater clarity and purpose for the enormous bailout funding, the document informs us that:

> "In an attempt to counter the relative ineffectiveness of its conventional LOLR tools, the Fed designed and implemented a host of unconventional measures, unprecedented in terms of size or scope and of questionable legality. The goal of these unconventional measures was to explicitly improve financial market conditions and, by improving the intermediation process, to stabilize the U.S. economy as a whole."[10]

An interesting observation is the number of *special purpose facilities* the Fed created after the crisis began. In addition, we are provided greater insight into the various stages of the crisis, from a posture of providing emergency liquidity (identified as "Stage One: Short-Term Liquidity Provision") for the markets to outright purchase of financial assets (identified as "Stage Three: Purchases of Long-term Securities"); accordingly, "Each 'Stage' can be broadly viewed as a response to the evolution of the crisis as it proliferated through financial markets" (Felkerson 2011).

As various aspects of financial market operations failed, the Fed stepped in and restored order and liquidity as required. The sequential nature of the crisis witnessed the Fed putting out fires left and right to hold the global financial system together and functional. This was clear prima facie evidence that the Fed (as the lead central banker in the world: LORL) was determined not to allow the meltdown/bubbles to completely spiral into the abyss.

Perhaps the most instructive and beneficial aspects of the Levy economic report is the identification of the *special purpose facilities* and the various stages of the meltdown crisis. What is of considerable debate (10 years after 2008) is the actual amount of the bailout funding and how the Fed executed these transactions. The central purpose of this outline and discussion is to illustrate how creative, expansive and flexible the Fed can become in a time of enormous economic uncertainty. Bottom line: we should never underestimate the power of the Fed:

(1) The Term Auction Facility (TAF): This facility received its authorization under Section 10B of the Federal Reserve Act (FRA) and was brought into existence in December 2007. The central purpose of TAF was to alleviate financial pressures on depository institutions in their short-term funding operations in the markets. During the extreme chaos of 2007-08, the Fed created an option allowing financial institutions to acquire short-term funding "via an auction format." This program allowed banks to bypass the Fed's discount window and borrowing in the private markets, which had become over-heated with credit rationing, higher borrowing costs, and term restrictions. According to the Levy Economics document, "The adoption of an auction format allowed banks to borrow as a group and pledge a wider range of collateral than generally accepted at the discount window...Each auction was for a fixed amount of funds with the rate determined by the auction process...The TAF ran from December 20, 2007, to March 11, 2010. Both foreign and domestic depository institutions participated in the program. A total of 416 different banks borrowed from this facility...The Fed loaned $3,818 billion in total over the run of this program...All loans are said to have been repaid in full, with interest, in agreement with the terms of the facility"[11].

(2) The Central Bank Liquidity Swap Lines (CBLS): This facility received its authority under Section 14 of the FRA and first went into operation in December 2007. It was designed with a central focus to facilitate dollar liquidity swaps between the Fed and other central banks that had urgent requirements for dollars in their monetary systems. Structured as repo contracts or

agreements (See Glossary) with prearranged lines of credit, these arrangements sought again to relieve the "pressures in the short-term funding markets." The first phase of this facility was in operation from December 2007 to February 2010 and orchestrated a total of 569 loans with an enormous focus on the European market. Over $10 trillion was loaned through this facility, with the European Bank (ECB) alone, involved in over $8 trillion in transactions. And again, as with the majority of the special facilities, all transactions were repaid in full per the specified agreements.

(3) Maiden Lane, LLC (ML I-A Special Purpose Vehicle (SPV)): This facility received its authority under Section 13(3) of the FRA. The primary purpose of this facility was to facilitate the purchase of Bear Stearns' assets (by J.P. Morgan) for the negotiated amount of $30 billion. The Fed (through the assistance of the Federal Reserve Bank of New York- FRBNY) essentially arranged and primarily financed the shot-gun marriage of Bear Stearns and J.P. Morgan in March of 2008.

(4) Primary Dealer Credit Facility (PDCF): Authorized under Section 13(3) of the FRA, this facility was created to function as a discount window, providing overnight reserves to primary dealers upon their request. This program began in March 2008 and extended to February 1, 2010. It facilitated 1,376 loans that came to a total of nearly $9 trillion.

(5) The extraordinary bailout of American Insurance Group (AIG): A great deal of focus was given to this specific institution due to its size and global reach. A total of *four* special facilities and vehicles were created to stop the enormous collapse of this organization. This special series of operations was authorized under Section 13(3) of the FRA. On September 16, 2008, the Fed created the Revolving Credit Facility (RCF) which initially provided a line of credit of $85 billion for AIG. To stabilize AIG's domestic insurance operations, the Fed brought into existence the securities borrowing facility (SBF). Levy Economics reported that $802.316 billion was provided in "direct credit in the form of repos against AIG collateral." Then under the direction of the FRBNY, Maiden Lane II, LLC (ML II - SPV) was created to "purchase residential MBS from AIG's securities lending portfolio" (Felkerson 2011). The total amount of loans provided here was $19.5 billion. And finally, Maiden Lane III, LLC (ML III - SPV) was created to purchase $24.3 billion of AIG's credit default swaps (CDO) portfolio. And again, the FRBNY provided the funding for these loans.

Other facilities that were created during the liquidity stage (not detailed above) consisted of the following: (1) Series of Term Repurchase Transactions (ST OMO): total loans of $855 billion (2) Term Securities Lending Facility (TSLF): Total amount lent, over $1.9 trillion (3) TSLF Options Program (TOP): Total of $62.3 billion. There were also other facilities created during this stage but were not used or called into action. At this point, it is essential to come to some recognition that the Fed did not operate under any known restrictions or limitations during the 2008 crisis. There were tremendous opportunities and flexibility to expand its balance sheet (or the balance sheets of member reserve banks such as the FRBNY) when required to do so. The unconventional dimension of the Fed came out of the shadows in the *Meltdown of 2008*.

STAGE THREE: PURCHASES OF LONG-TERM SECURITIES

Most Fed watchers are familiar with the developments in this stage: the direct purchase of mortgage-backed securities and U.S. Treasury securities. During this final stage, the Fed goal (through the purchase of long-term securities) was to provide greater support to the overall credit markets. As stated elsewhere in this publication, the Fed implemented three rounds of "Quantitative Easing" (QE) over a period of several years. Authorized under Section 14 of the FRA, this program was created to stabilize the price of agency mortgage-backed securities (MBS). Also, according to the Fed, the direct purchase of these bonds was designed to "increase the availability of credit for the purchase of houses." The housing market was expected to be given more significant support by the banks with measurable improvements in the financial markets. The categories for MBS transactions focused on three scheduled maturities: 15, 20 and 30-year mortgages, with 30-year maturities comprising the majority of transactions.

To arrive at the roughly $29 trillion total that this Levy Economics report support, the analysts/authors took the individual sums of all of the various facilities and came up with a grand total (See Levy Economics Institute Working Paper No. 698 - December 2011: $29,000,000,000,000: A Detailed Look at the Fed's Bailout by Funding Facility and Recipient). This total is radically different from what either *Bloomberg* or the *GAO Report* present in their analysis. Levy's approach was to record the number of institutions involved in each facility and to examine each separate transaction they initiated throughout the life of each individual program.

This publication takes the position that this debate regarding the actual total amount of funding and loans is not over. The main purpose of this brief chapter is to highlight some of the key issues and organizations that have worked diligently to provide an accurate picture of Fed activities during the worse economic meltdown in modern history.

SUMMARY/ANALYSIS

For many observers and analysts who paid close attention to the central bank's (Fed) operations during and after the *Meltdown of 2008*, we are now aware of the many unconventional tools and clandestine strategies that have never been revealed, discussed or studied in university settings. And it is clear that this organization has the power to expand far beyond any pre-designed limits and boundaries established in the original charter. Much of these expanded powers were put to the test during the most severe financial crisis in history. The Fed now has a blueprint, and battle-tested tools to employ during the next *global meltdown*. I'll be curious to see what else they will pull out of their magical hat during the *second phase* of this massive crisis.

Further analysis of the 29,000 plus pages of transactions that the Fed was forced to release, will continue to shed more light on the enormous interventions conducted during the great 2008 collapse. Identification of the various stages of the crisis, in addition to the sequential nature of the breakdown in the financial markets and the facilities employed, has moved us closer towards understanding what the Fed had to do to hold the system together each step into the rapidly escalating crisis.

The total amount of monetary resources the Fed employed will continue to be debated. However, what is not debatable is the massive global response by the Fed to bail out a significant portion of the global economy. We know that it took trillions of dollars to achieve that goal, but there is still some mystery as to how many trillions.

The ability to create successive unconventional facilities to solve liquidity and financial support system problems, illustrated the dynamic powers of a major central bank in the heat of a devastating historical crisis. What I fell to understand was why a more direct approach to the American housing crisis was not placed into operation. Given the recognition of the severity of the crisis and the fact that the global financial *super-bubble* could not be allowed to go through a complete meltdown, why did they not go directly to the heart of the matter, the *American homeowner*? A facility could have been created (in conjunction with a "Special Purpose Vehicle" and a newly crafted federal program) to actively bailout the American homeowner. The American homeowner was at the root of the crisis and should have been given top priority or at least very significant assistance. And if we take the high estimate of $29 trillion as the total global bailout, then the homeowner bailout figure of less than $1 trillion would have been a significant factor in supporting the economic foundation of the American economy.

It was primarily a false assumption to rely on the banking system to do what it steadfastly refused to do on a grand scale (it's happened before, and it will very likely happen again if no structural changes are made to how the Fed operates). The expectation is that by bailing out the key financial institutions and the wealthy at the top of the system, the benefits and financial resources would *trickle down* to those in need in the lower levels of society. *This is a blatantly false and wasteful assumption that leads to deeply fractured solutions.*

The flawed design of the Fed is that it is set up to accommodate and bailout the wealthy and their banking institutions, ensuring that they remain on top in good or bad times. If there is ever a movement to reform the Federal Reserve System, then it should begin with making this system much more responsive to the majority of the people that it is presumably established to serve. *It is currently an elitist organization with the ultimate mission of serving the financial interest of banking institutions and the super wealthy elites.*

NOTES

(1) Phil Kuntz and Bob Ivry, "Fed's Once-Secret Data Compiled by Bloomberg Released to Public," *Bloomberg*, December 22, 2011.

(2) "Bloomberg L.P. v. Board of Governors of the Federal Reserve System," Wikipedia, August 24, 2009.

(3) David Glovin and Thom Weidlich, "Federal Reserve Seeks to Protect U.S. Bailout Secrets," *Bloomberg*, January 11, 2009, online news, pg. 2.

(4) Bradley Keoun and Phil Kuntz, "Aristocracy Got $1.2 Trillion From ," *Bloomberg*, August 22, 2011, online news, pg. 2

(5) Bradley Keoun and Phil Kuntz, "Wall Street aristocracy got $1.2 trillion in secret loans," BDN Business, August 23, 2011.

(6) Vishal Ganesan, "Congress was unaware of $7.77 trillion in secret loans ahead of TARP vote", *The Daily Caller*, December 01, 2011.

(7) Kenneth Rogoff, "Financial regulations isn't fixed, it's just more complicated,"*The Guardian*, September 10, 2012.

(8) John Cochrane, Paola Sapienza and Luigi Zingales, "my losing battle against the leviathan," The University of Chicago Booth School of Business, 2010.

(9) Senator Sanders Bernie Sanders, U.S. Senator from Vermont, "The Veil of Secrecy at the Fed Has Been Lifted, Now It's Time for Change," "http://www.sanders.senate.gov" "The Sanders Report on the GAO Audit on Major Conflicts of Interest at the Federal Reserve", Washington, DC, October 19, 2011.

(10) James Felkerson, "Working Paper No. 698: $29,000,000,000,000: "A Detailed Look at the Fed's Bailout by Funding Facility and Recipient", University of Missouri-Kansas City, Levy Economics Institute of Bard College, New York, December 2011.

(11) IBID., Fed's Bailout by Funding Facility.

CHAPTER SIX
DERIVATIVES: THE GLOBAL TICKING TIME BOMB

More than $600 trillion-worth of derivatives contracts are still being traded in an unregulated, completely opaque over-the-counter market. That market's size has made all its major participants too big to fail.

Economist Richard Duncan

A financial market deregulated is like a zoo without bars.

Henry Kaufmann

Multiple trillions of dollars of Over-the-Counter (OTC) derivatives are massively destructive instruments that are destined to play a supporting role in derailing the global economy on a scale much more severe than the *Meltdown of 2008*. Warren Buffett labeled them *financial weapons of mass destruction,* and for a good reason; they were a vital component of the colossal collapse of 2008. We now have clear evidence of the destructive nature of these instruments, what happens when there is contagion, and how the dominoes fall in rapid succession when the trigger is pulled.

OTC derivatives will undoubtedly be one of the most important triggers of the next financial collapse that is very likely to occur sometime between 2017 and 2020. The American people and the entire global population should fear the developments taking place in this arena. It is deadly, sinister and secretive, with very few people knowing what the actual numbers are, and all of the critical aspects of this massive global casino. It is our modern-day *Ponzi Scheme*, involving enormous speculation and betting on all manner of financial assets and global economic events. It also occupies the same area of market risk as stock market manipulations did in the 1920s;

undercover operations designed to generate massive profit opportunities in short periods of time.

Big Banks are the dominant players in this arena, responsible for nearly 96 percent of all the trading action. Over 90 percent of derivatives are traded in the OTC arena, unregulated and off the radar screen of most organized systems of regulation. Thus we have a derivatives market that is opaque with virtually no mechanism to determine the inherent risks these markets present to the entire global economy. A highly dangerous example is derivative types that harbor substantial levels of leverage that permeate throughout layers upon layers of synthetic derivatives that represent bets on the success or failure of other investor's bets. The system is riddled with potholes and explosives. However, the players are determined to carry on as if there are no problems and that there is nothing here to be concerned or worried about.

LONG-TERM CAPITAL MANAGEMENT (LTCM)

In the aftermath of the Russia sovereign debt default in 1998, investors dumped higher-risk securities and fled to the safety of U.S. Treasury Bills and FDIC-insured deposits. To calm the markets and restore stability, the Federal Reserve lowered short-term interest rates three times in seven weeks. Increased commercial bank lending in September and October (to the tune of $30 billion assisting corporations to roll over their short-term paper) helped to avert a hard landing during the early stages of this crisis. However, there was another major problem that emerged from the turmoil: Long-Term Capital Management (LTCM).

As a result of deep losses on its $125 billion portfolios of high-risk debt securities that included junk bonds and emerging market debt that investors were unloading, LTCM (a large U.S. hedge fund) was on the brink of total collapse. In normal business circumstances, it would have been a simple matter just to have allowed this high-roller hedge fund to move quickly into bankruptcy and dissolve its operations. However, the central problem here, and why LTCM became a prominent footnote in financial and economic history, was its use of leverage. To purchase its high-risk $125 billion portfolios, it was necessary to borrow vast amounts of money from several major investment banking institutions, maintaining a leverage ratio of 24:1: LTCM could borrow $24 for every $1 of investors' equity. Also, and this was probably more significant, the firm had further leveraged itself by entering into derivative obligations (mostly interest rate and equity derivatives) with a notional value of $1.3 trillion. The lenders included some of the most prominent names in the industry: Lehman Brothers, Goldman Sachs, Merrill Lynch, JP Morgan, Chase Manhattan and Morgan Stanley.

LCTM ran into a brick wall one month after the Russian partial default; the fund lost more than $4 billion, which was more than 80% of its $5 billion in equity. With a debt of approximately $120 billion, the company was facing a crisis of default and insolvency, not only with its primary lenders but also on its obligations to its derivatives counterparties, which included many of the prominent investment and commercial banks in America.

In the deregulated derivatives arena, there was no requirement to maintain reserves or collateral for these positions, and LTCM had posted very little collateral. An LTCM collapse, at this point, would have had some pretty severe consequences for all of these institutions, so something had to be done to prevent a major financial crisis.

It became necessary for the Federal Reserve to step in with a solution because in the opaque over-the-counter derivatives market (OTC) no one knew the full extent and size of the LTCM derivative positions. As we have seen in our discussion on the *Meltdown of 2008*, this type of *setup* can cascade and spin entirely out of control very quickly as counterparties across the board rush to liquidate their positions simultaneously. And as we have further witnessed in the 2008 crisis, credit markets froze, and fear and suspicions were permeating throughout the global financial system. In retrospect, the LTCM debacle was a prelude of things to come; a significant warning of what could happen in a deregulated derivatives universe.

The Federal Reserve System, under the leadership of Alan Greenspan, orchestrated a rescue effort to resolve what could have resulted in a significant economic catastrophe. It would not be a federal government bailout using taxpayer money, but an orderly "banker's gentlemen's agreement" to clean up this mess. In the end, the bankers were convinced to pay for the bailout of LTCM.

The Fed called an emergency meeting of the major banks that had significant exposures to LTCM's debts and derivatives, and they were encouraged to resolve this problem by any means necessary. On September 23, 1998, 14 institutions agreed to "organize a consortium to inject $3.6 to $4.0 billion into LTCM in return for 90% of its stock. The firms contributed between $100 million and $300 million each...An orderly liquidation of LTCM's securities and derivatives followed." According to James Rickards, author and economics advisor, and a central player in the negotiation of this historic deal, "It was a 4 billion dollar all-cash deal, which we put together in 72 hours with no due diligence." Having a front row seat in this LTCM crisis provided Rickards with a unique perspective. In his new book, *The Road To Ruin: The Global Elites' Secret Plan for the Next Financial Crisis*, he makes the case that the devastation of the 1998 collapse was very similar to the *Meltdown of 2008*. Rickards informs his readers of the following:

> "My point is that in 1998, we came within hours of shutting every market in the world. There were a set of lessons that should've been learned from that, but they were not learned. The government went out and did the opposite of what you would do if you were trying to prevent it from happening again...Then Basel 2, coming out of the Bank for International Settlements in Basel, Switzerland, changed the bank capital rules so they could use these flawed value-

at-risk models to increase their leverage. Everything, if you had a list of things that you should've done to prevent crises from happening again, they did the opposite. They let banks act like hedge funds. They let everybody trade more derivatives. They allowed more leverage, less regulation, bad models, etc."[1]

Like Brooksley Born, James Rickards was alarmed that the Fed and other regulatory bodies didn't take greater actions to prevent the repeat of 1998. But this was the era of deregulation and everyone, including President Clinton, was trying to keep the great boom that began in the mid-1990s, alive and well. No one wanted to create obstacles or tamper with the goose that was laying the Dot Com era golden eggs.

BROOKSLEY BORN AND THE ERA OF DEREGULATION

During the great boom cycle of the mid-1990s to the year 2000, Brooksley Born was head of the Commodity Futures Trading Commission (CFTC) under the Clinton Administration from August 1996 to June 1999. This agency and the independent department is responsible for the supervision of derivative contracts. While the whole world was on fire and running hard during the explosive years of the dot-com boom of the late 1990s, Born was deeply concerned about the over-the-counter (OTC) derivatives market that was rapidly building up momentum. Before the CFTC, Born had spent 20 years in derivatives law and was a first class financial regulator. Having observed and studied the fallout of the Orange County debacle in 1994, she was convinced that over-expansion in OTC derivatives in a deregulated environment was a disaster waiting to happen.

In the Orange County case, the investment fund of $7.4 billion was facing losses of $1.5 billion due to derivatives and enormous leverage. To increase the returns for the fund, fund management employed the use of interest rate-sensitive derivative contracts. The County Treasurer borrowed $14 billion to help facilitate these operations. When interest rates went up, Orange County was facing massive losses on its derivatives contracts. In the end, Orange County had to file for bankruptcy.

Brooksley Born, in the hostile deregulatory environment of the late 1990s boom period, decided it was time to regulate the OTC derivatives market. That set the stage for some very tense and often brutal confrontations with other regulatory agencies and federal administrative departments in Washington. To say that her proposals were not well received is an understatement. After all, it was the deregulated markets that gave us the boom times. It was a pro-business, anti-regulation economy, and no one wanted to stop that! It was an era of deregulations, unfettered free markets, and unrestricted capitalism. However, Born was pro-government regulations, especially in the high-risk game of derivatives.

On Wall Street OTC derivatives were known as the *Black Box*: big banks could operate in secrecy with no transparency, and best of all, the government didn't know what was happening. Born was not happy with this clandestine arrangement and felt that sooner or later these instruments would be the center of a major collapse in the economy. As a dedicated public servant, Born wanted to protect the America people from a disaster in the markets. She wrote that she was "really terribly worried" that a major financial crisis was coming.

Her opposition was some of the most powerful men in Washington: Fed Chairman Alan Greenspan, Larry Summers, Co-chair of the SEC, Treasury Secretary Robert Rubin, Arthur Levitt, Chairman of the SEC, Timothy Geithner, Undersecretary for International Affairs of the United States Department of Treasury, and even some senators in Congress. These were the people that ultimately stopped Born from regulating the OTC market.

As one writer put it, these people were looking to "shut her up and shut her down." Indeed, an article in *The Wall Street Journal* stated: "the nation's top financial regulators wish Brooksley Born would just shut up." She was utterly out-of-step with the order of things, and they wanted her silenced. With few or no supporters, Born stood her ground and maintained strong convictions that OTC derivatives were a *ticking time bomb* waiting to explode.

The fireworks started when Born announced that she was to release a "Concept Paper," which solicits input on regulation and is the first step in the process of establishing a regulatory model. Upon hearing about the paper, Larry Summers, Co-chair of the SEC, told Born (in his now famous 13 banker quote) **"I have 13 bankers in my office, and they say if you go forward with this you will cause the worst financial crisis since World War II."**[2]

At a meeting with President Clinton's Working Group, a gathering of top financial regulators that met at the Treasury Department, Born was informed not to release the "Concept Paper." She acknowledged the request, however, two weeks later the paper was released.

Now considered a "rogue regulator," Born would be forced to deal next with Congress and a series of hearings. Congress was confronted by Greenspan, Rubin, and Levitt urging that a moratorium is passed on the CFTC on regulating OTC derivatives. Born testified in Congressional hearings four times during the summer of 1998. After these hearings, Congress agreed with the urgings of the "Oracle," Fed Chairman Greenspan.

A few short months later, Long-Term Capital Management (LTCM) collapsed. It was a *perfect* example of what Born had foretold would happen in an unregulated OTC derivatives market. The thing she had been predicting had come to pass, but it did not sink in, it did not register high enough on the Richter scale for the free marketers. This single hedge fund nearly destroyed the economy and temporarily derailed the boom of the 1990s. And Chairman Greenspan and the Fed orchestrated the bailout, but they refused to consider any regulations of the OTC market.

Even in the wake of the massive problems that LTCM presented, Congress passed the moratorium to stop the CFTC. Born would later state that they were "muzzling an independent agency." She left office in April-June 1999.

About 18 months after Born left the CFTC, very significant legislation was put in place to deregulate the over-the-counter derivatives market. On December 21, 2000, President Bill Clinton signed into law *The Commodity Futures Modernization Act of 2000* (CFMA). It became America's official federal legislation that issued a license to a modernized regulation of over-the-counter derivatives (OTC). "It clarified the law so that most over-the-counter (OTC) derivatives transactions between "sophisticated parties" would not be regulated as "futures" under the Commodity Exchange Act of 1936 (CEA) or as "securities" under the federal securities laws." Since banks and securities firms were the dominant players in this arena, the passing of this law was another disaster that gave *Big Banks* and *Wall Street* the opportunity to conduct trillion dollar speculative operations without any formal oversight and governmental restrictions. It opened the floodgates for all manner of reckless behavior that eventually led to the *Meltdown of 2008*.

ERA OF DEREGULATIONS

After more than 30 years of deregulation and reliance on self-regulation by the financial sector, the core and lifeblood of the financial system finally got nuked. For decades, no one wanted regulations in the financial industry, and the game of leverage was allowed to increase beyond reason. All of this was akin to skating on thin ice or walking a tightrope over Manhattan. Many regulatory bodies had ample power in several areas, but they chose not to use it. And the power of money and political influence played a significant role in prolonging the *deregulation era*: From 1999 to 2008, the financial sector spent $2.7 billion on its lobbying machine in Washington. In the markets, traders and managers were encouraged to make the big bets and take on the enormous risks; this was the time to score that quick deal, and for the most part, the focus was for short-term gains without regard for any long-term consequences.

We need to understand as much as we can before entering the next downward phase of a systemic global decline. From the late 1990s to 2008, a series of legislative and political maneuvers helped to fuel the bubbles of this period:

(1) Passage of the Gramm-Leach-Bliley Act on November 12, 1999 that destroyed the economic safeguards of the Glass-Steagall Act of the 1930s. It happened during the Clinton Administration who was not watching how far the pendulum had swung. Financial markets were zooming, and the Clinton

Administration went with the flow of the *Roaring 1990s*. In response to the passage of Gramm-Leach-Bliley, bank analyst Lawrence Cohn at Ryan, Beck & Co. stated in an article in *Time Magazine*, Nov. 8, 1999: "This is horrible legislation...It creates a huge potential obligation for the U.S. taxpayers." He said the bill (the destruction of Glass-Steagall) "would encourage concentration of financial power in a few hands, any one of which could topple the system if it failed - forcing a government bailout."[4] That is precisely what happened in 2008!

(2) The decision in early 1998 to stop and silence a proposal by Brooksley E. Born, head of the Commodity Futures Trading Commission, to regulate derivatives.

(3) With the passage of the Commodity Futures Modernization Act of 2000, the political establishment and regulators had decided not to have federal oversight over this area of the derivatives markets (OTC derivatives). Indeed, the Federal Reserve did not take responsibility for regulating derivatives. In the FCIC report they noted: "Within the financial ystem, the dangers of this debt were magnified because transparency was not required or desired. Massive, short-term borrowing, combined with obligations unseen by others in the market, heightened the chance the system could rapidly unravel."[5] There are far too many unknowns with OTC derivatives.

(4) Bush tax cuts of 2001 and 2003.

(5) With the Securities and Exchange Commission's decision in April of 2004, large investment banks were allowed to increase their debt-to-capital ratio from 12 to 1 to 30 to 1, or higher. Since the *Meltdown of 2008*, the Securities and Exchange Commission Chairman began leading the call for increased regulation of derivatives.

DERIVATIVES AND NOTIONAL VALUE

Since the *Meltdown of 2008*, the derivatives market has increased in value year after year, which means that the level of real risk in the financial markets has soared. However, we must come to grips with the fact that it took decades of debt accumulation, mismanagement, over-speculative markets, and several boom and bust cycles to arrive at this place in history. And not surprisingly, Wall Street is at the center of this global derivatives casino.

The bets are getting larger, and leverage is being stretched to regions beyond reason and comprehension. The players will push on to the point where leverage will cease to work, and then it will stop working, initiating a stampede for the exits. It is the kind of sudden hysteria and panic in the markets that a collapsing derivatives pyramid can create.

Notational Value represents the underlying market value or amount of derivative contracts. It reflects the value of the trades in the system; however, it is not an accurate value of the amount of money at risk among the participants. That number is determined by the actual performance of the assets underlying the contracts: stocks, bonds, currencies, commodities, stock indices, etc. The creditworthiness of the trading counterparties is also considered in the valuation process. Thus, the high valuation numbers may be overstating the problem. However, the risks and collateral damages are still astronomical even when considered at lower valuations.

The entire global economic system is inundated with debt, risk and unsustainable derivative leverage that has mushroomed into a much broader problem than what was attributed to the *Meltdown of 2008*. The Comptroller of Currency reported in 2008 that the total notational value of derivatives in the largest 25 banks in the U.S. was about $180 trillion.[5]

In 2011, the Options Clearing Corporation (OCC) reported that "The notational value of derivatives held by U.S. commercial banks increased $12.8 trillion, or 5.5%, from the fourth quarter of 2010 to $244 trillion."[6] From 1999 to 2012, there was a 473% increase in the notational value of derivatives at the top 25 banks in America.

When the bubble began to burst in December 2007, the global notional value of derivative contracts was sitting around $500 trillion. According to a report published by the Bank of International Settlements, as of June 2011, the *global notational value* of outstanding over-the-counter derivatives rose 18% in the first half of 2011 to the astronomical level of $708 trillion![7] Thus, in late 2011 we were looking at a situation far worse than what was present in 2008! Given the massive uncertainties of the European crisis and the ongoing debt crisis in the U.S., banks and other wealthy institutional investors were loading up on hedge positions and gambling on the outcomes of all types of financial events: the direction of interest rates, movements in the bond markets, student loan debts, etc. Economist Richard Duncan invites us to explore why the exponential growth of the notional value of derivatives is not just about hedging financial asset positions:

> "Consequently, there is no greater transparency or oversight of this $600 trillion OTC can of worms than before the crisis began. Exchange trading would have provided transparency as to who undertook the trades and perhaps shed light on the rationale behind the transactions... One thing is certain: $669 trillion of transactions is too large of an amount to have been entered into for hedging purposes alone. It is equivalent to roughly $100,000 per person on earth - or, more or less, the value of everything produced on this planet during the last 20 years combined. There simply aren't $669 trillion worth of things in the world to hedge.[8]

Non-transparency means no one is allowed to understand what Duncan describes as the "rationale behind the transactions." Only the insiders know what is indeed going on behind the scenes. Only when there is a significant problem will we find out what has been hiding in the shadows. And once again, central bankers and governments will be called in to bail out the gamblers in order to save the world.

According to the Bank for International Settlements, by 2016 the global marketplace was accommodating derivatives with the notional value of roughly $710 trillion. The OCC released a quarterly report in 2016 identifying the largest derivative contract positions held by the top five too-big-to-fail banks. The following is their findings:

JPMorgan Chase: Nearly $68 trillion
CitiBank: Nearly $60 trillion
Goldman Sachs: Nearly $55.5 trillion
Bank Of America: Approximately $54.5 trillion
Morgan Stanley: Nearly $45 trillion.

In addition to the above, we were informed by Zero Hedge that Deutsche Bank (the German global powerhouse) had a massive derivatives exposure of roughly $75 trillion, larger than any of the top five U.S. banking institutions. [9]

The White House and Congress refused to regulate the over-the-counter *Derivatives Industry*, and now it is set to explode in our face once again when everyone starts running for the exits all at the same time. Most Americans will be caught completely off guard when this avalanche breaks; the speculators are pushing the limits in the pursuit of billions in profits in short periods of time.

TOO BIG TO FAIL BANKS: TO BE OR NOT TO BE!

During the second decade of the 21st century several major global banking institutions (Deutsche Bank, UBS, Barclays, JP Morgan Chase, and Bank of America) were accused of manipulation of the London Interbank Offered Rate (LIBOR), an important and often used baseline for various types of interest rates for trillions of dollars of loans and investments. Money laundering for Mexican drug cartels (HSBC), rampant mortgage fraud during and after the *Meltdown of 2008*, and other blatant misleading lending practices are just some of the things that remind us of how nefarious our banking institutions can be.[10]

And when we examine the practices and procedures in what the Big Banks are doing with derivative contracts and how they are traded, we can observe that very little has changed from the period leading up to the 2008 meltdown, with Big Banks still conducting the bulk of derivative trading.

These banking institutions are now more opaque, are much larger and more willing to take on much more risk ten years after the great meltdown. Within these institutions, the expectations are that the gain or loss on derivatives will be much smaller than the massive notional amounts that are often quoted. And in the case of Wells Fargo, they support the notion and risk assessment that "many of its derivatives offset each other." As was observed in the 2008 collapse, once the dominoes begin to fall, a chain reaction occurs that is much more dynamic than just the initial hedging or gambling bets placed by the originating institutions. In other words, the impact is entirely unknowable.

NEEL KASHKARI AND THE FEDERAL RESERVE BANK OF MINNEAPOLIS

One of the most prominent voices calling for significant reforms in the banking industry is Neel Kashkari. The contributions of Kashkari are substantial and noteworthy. During the *Meltdown of 2008*, he served as the chief manager of the U.S. Treasury Department's $700 billion Troubled Asset Relief Program (TARP). Kashkari was on the front line battling to prevent the next great depression. Working under Treasury Secretary, Henry Paulson, Kashkari witnessed a lot of deal-making and was deeply involved in the strategic planning and execution of TARP. In that position he learned a very valuable lesson concerning how to handle a major crisis; the best approach is to go in with "overwhelming force" and not to tinker with the problem with incremental solutions.

On January 1, 2016, Neel Kashkari became president and chief executive officer of the Federal Reserve Bank of Minneapolis. In this new role as a Federal Reserve Regional Bank president, Kashkari, along with other officials within this regional bank, began immediately to start thinking outside the box. By February, they had announced that it was time for a national transformative solution to the major problem of "too big to fail" banks (TBTF), and for nearly one year, called on people from all walks of life to submit their views and recommendations on how to tackle the ever-threatening menace of TBTF. Kashkari put forth an agenda and stated the following:

> "I believe the biggest banks are still too big to fail and continue to pose a significant, ongoing risk to our economy...Now is the right time for Congress to consider going further than Dodd-Frank with bold, transformational solutions to solve this problem once and for all...The Federal Reserve Bank of Minneapolis is launching a major initiative to develop an actionable plan to end TBTF, and we will deliver our plan to the public by the end of the year."[11]

By mid-November, a document entitled, *The Minneapolis Plan To End Too Big To Fail*, was made available to the public. The 53-page report set the stage for a national dialogue on addressing this issue before the start of a new crisis. A copy of this document can be obtained from the regional bank's website.[12]

Reactions to Kashkari's initiatives and plan were mixed and raised eyebrows, given that the source of these bold recommendations is from an insider. Vermont Senator Bernie Sanders was pleased to hear this call for change, especially coming from a Fed official: "I am delighted that the new president of the Minneapolis Federal Reserve believes that we need to break up too big to fail banks." Others were more skeptical, particularly those in banking circles holding conservative views on how the Fed should operate. Some considered Kashkari's views too radical, while others don't believe they, in fact, go far enough to halt the madness of TBTF.

SUMMARY/ANALYSIS

The primary mission of this chapter was to highlight the destructive power of multi-trillion derivative trading that threatens, once again, to derail the global economy in ways that no one can predict. Given that OTC derivatives operate in the netherworld of non-transparency, they are mostly *ticking time bombs*, where the failure of even a small percentage of contracts can do enormous global economic damage. No one can assess this kind of enormous risk; it's entirely unpredictable.

And we don't have to guess about this, it all came to light in the *Meltdown of 2008*. In fact, that's why it was called a *meltdown*; the massive global system of credit and debt froze, and the entire system came to a halt. The only large-scale deflationary crisis that comes close to this type of shutdown is the *Great Depression of the 1930s*. And even in that massive event, the initial collapse did not carry the mega-force of the *Meltdown of 2008*.

The 1970s inflationary recessions didn't cause a major systemic meltdown. The *Crash of '87* was a minor event compared to 2008. The enormous deflationary bubble bursting in *Japan in 1990* (where trillions of dollars of the stock market and real estate wealth were lost) didn't bring down the global economy. The *Dot-Com collapse of 2000*, which witnessed $5 to $7 trillion of equity losses, did not derail the global economy. So what was it that set 2008 apart from all of these other economic catastrophes? And from the perspective of 2018, why has this problem grown larger?

As of 2017, the six largest banks in America controlled 67 percent of all banking assets. Many of these banks were bailed out in the 2008 collapse, and many of these same banks did a bare minimum to stop millions of people from losing their homes. And it is these banks that carry on the global derivatives trading with the notional value of over $700 trillion. Thus, for the most part, financial reform (the Dodd-Frank Act of 2010) didn't work. These banks are much larger, and their trading activities are more opaque than ten years after 2008.

In a nutshell; this is the massive problem we face as a nation and as a world community. We are at the mercy of these colossal banks; if they go down, we go down with them! It is not speculation or hyperbole, it is a dangerous game these banks are playing, and they know it!

NOTES

(1) James Rickards, "The Next Financial Crisis," *The Daily Reckoning*, October 25, 2016.
(2) Simon Johnson and James Kwak, *13 Bankers: The Wall Street Takeover and the Next Financial Meltdown*, Vintage Books (2010,2011), NY, p 9.
(3) Financial Crisis Inquiry Commission, *The Financial Crisis Inquiry Report*, January 2011, pg. xxi.
(4) Daniel Kadlec, "Bank On Change," *Time Magazine* (Vol. 154 - No. 19), Nov. 8, 1999.
(5) "OCC's Quarterly Report on Bank Trading and Derivatives Activities First Quarter 2011," Comptroller of the Currency Administration of National Banks, First Quarter 2011 Report.
(6) IBID,. OCC Quarterly Report.
(7) Katy Burne, "Swaps market tops $700 Trillion," T*he Wall Street Journal*, Digital Network, November 16, 2011.
(8) Richard Duncan, *The New Depression*, John Wiley & Sons, (Singapore: 2012) pg. 99.
(9) Tyler Durden, "The Elephant In The Room : Deutsche Bank's $75 Trillion In Derivatives," ZeroHedge, April 28, 2014.
(10) Steve Denning, "Big Banks and Derivatives:Why Another Financial Crisis Is Inevitable", *Forbes*, January 8, 2013.
(11) The website for the Minneapolis Federal Reserve is as follows: www.minneapolisfed.org.
(12) IBID., Minneapolis Federal Reserve.

PHASE II: END OF AN ERA

CHAPTER SEVEN
LESSONS ON JAPAN'S LOST DECADES: CANARY IN THE COAL MINE

The balance sheet recession concept has been developed on the back of the Japanese people's suffering and sacrifices during the past fifteen years ...this concept should be of great assistance to countries seeking to formulate a policy response to bubbles and their aftermath.

Richard Koo

Since 1988, I have been writing and researching the Japanese boom and bust cycles. It is perhaps one of the most sensational economic stories of all time: the world has witnessed the rise and fall of a dynamic global economic power. Despite its fall from grace which began in 1990, Japan (as of 2018) is still considered the third largest economic power in the world. The year 1990 should be as comparable in statue and significance in Japanese history as 1929 is to the United States; a significant turning point and the start of one the most devastating bust cycles in world history.

The extraordinary bubble economy of Japan that lasted for decades and reached a super bubble zenith in the late 1980s will go down in the annals of time as one of history's greatest economic triumphs. From 1955 to 1990, stock prices increased 100 times in value, and land prices rose 70 times in value. The Heisei Bubble years (1985-86 to 1990) led to the all-time peak for the Nikkei of 38,957 on December 29, 1989. During the *Meltdown of 2008*, the Nikkei declined to 6,994 in October of that fateful year. It was one of history's great reversals of economic fortunes; for Japan was in the center of one of the most significant bubble economies of all times. In 1990, the island nation witnessed *The Heisei Bubble Collapse* and hit a brick wall, and then fell into a deep recession. It was the end of an astounding bubble era and the start of a long-term bust era of asset-price bubbles.

The descent was devastating as falling land, and stock prices accounted for the loss of 1,500 trillion yen in wealth, an astronomical amount equivalent to three year's Japanese GDP. A major casualty of the meltdown was commercial real estate: From 1989 to 2004, prices fell a whopping 87 percent. Golf club memberships did worse: the collapse from the 1989 peak to the bottom in 2003 was 95 percent. Japan experienced that degree of economic devastation and still remained the second largest economy in the world throughout the 1990s.

CRASH OF 1990

Some observers and analysts were expecting the Nikkei to soar to over 45,000 by the end of 1990. That never happened. As typical in most boom periods, stock prices broke loose from their underlining fundamentals and began to float at unsustainable higher levels. The euphoria was that the bull market was never-ending.

Also typical in most boom periods are the monetary activities of the Central Bank Reserve System. Tight monetary policies by the Bank of Japan (BOJ) was a crucial factor in derailing the boom period. Indeed the intent was not to cause major damage but to slow things down. Regulators were extremely concerned about inflationary pressures and did not want to see *asset prices* keep rising at an extraordinary pace. It was felt that the combination of double-digit stock and real estate gains could spin out of control and ultimately undermine the general price stability in the economy. In short, the Bank of Japan wanted to release some *steam* out of the so-called bubble economy of Japan. However, what started out as a fine-tuning process, turned into a landslide. Like the *Dot-Com Collapse of 2000* prices came tumbling down very quickly. After the market fell in the early 1990s, 90 percent of mutual fund money was withdrawn from stocks.

The descent began on January 5, 1990, as the Nikkei fell 600 points. Newspaper reports blamed the fall on the fear that the Gorbachev reforms would not succeed. On January 16th, the market fell 666.41 points with the Nikkei closing at 36,850.36. At that point, the momentum started to build; a psychology of market retreat began to move investors. By February 26th, $400 billion had been lost in stock value, and investors were shaken. On March 20th, the Bank of Tokyo raised the discount rate one full percentage point to 5.25 percent in a bid to strengthen the yen; but conditions still got worse. The stock value of Nippon Telephone and Telegraph hit a record low of $6,503 per share. This stock at one point sold between $19,000 to $20,000 per share in 1987, so this was a clear sign that the collapse had generated real damage.

It was a three-month descent that shook Japan like a massive earthquake, with many investors fleeing the markets. By the time this first wave was over, $1 trillion in wealth had been lost, resulting in a 28 percent drop in the 225 stock Nikkei index. The market bottomed out at 28,002.07 on April 2, 1990, ending a very turbulent period for Japanese investors and the world community.

At the Group of Seven meeting in April of that year, Japan appealed for greater assistance in curtailing the problems it was having in its markets. Japan was told that the solution could be found by raising domestic interest rates to higher levels. Market interventions in the currency markets were having minimal impact on stabilizing the yen. For the Japanese economy, the easy money party was over.[1]

Time Magazine reported that the total market capitalization of the Tokyo Stock Exchange fell to $2.9 trillion during the great crash.[2] In the wake of this historic event, several analysts and investment strategists were predicting the occurrence of a much more significant collapse during the fall of 1990 or early 1991. Barton M. Biggs, a managing director at Morgan Stanley & Co., indicated in his analysis that the Nikkei could fall to a level of 17,000 or 18,000 in coming periods.[3] One of his basic premises was that, in general, it is not unusual for a super-long bull market to lose 40 to 50 percent of its value in a major crash. It has happened before, and as this analysis reveals, it happened again.

By July, Japan was back to normal, and the Nikkei was managing a rebound - closing at 33,172.28 on July 17th. With their confidence restored, the Japanese people were feeling happy and very excited about their prospects for the future. Consumer spending resumed and the psychology of the boom period was revived. In short, the resilient Japanese had bounced back again.

OIL EMBARGO 1990

The invasion of Kuwait by Iraqi forces during the first week of August in 1990 created a perceived energy crisis for the industrialized world. The American and the United Nations-led worldwide embargo of the importation of Iraqi and Kuwaiti oil placed a heavy burden on Japan. For this island nation with virtually no natural resources, the oil embargo presented a serious threat to the continuation of its boom period. Recuperation from the first quarter collapse was short-lived, and this next crisis was falling upon the Japanese economy at a very critical moment. Investor psychology reversed again as markets began another round of steady declines. From the start of the Mid-East tension in late July to the end of the first week in August (the period after the invasion) the Nikkei dropped over 5,200 points, as fears of a major confrontation grew surrounding the crisis. Uncertainty dominated the markets, regardless of the fact that Japan was prepared to deal with the situation.

Statistics revealed by the Ministry of International Trade and Industry indicated that Japan had two petroleum reserves that could cover the nation's needs for 142 days. Despite the fact that Japan imports nearly 99 percent of its petroleum requirements, the country had become much more energy efficient since the oil shocks of 1973 and 1979. Also, its sources of oil had grown more diversified, even to the point of where 13 percent of the country's needs were linked to strong Japanese equity (ownership) interests in oil producing companies. Kuwait and Iraq accounted for roughly

12 percent of Japan's oil imports, whereas Saudi Arabia and the United Arab Emirates were responsible for 37.5 percent of the 3.8 million barrels of oil imported daily. Additional sources of oil from Indonesia, Mexico, China and elsewhere would undoubtedly help to avert any major collapse in its industries. But the bulk of its oil requirements had been met by the Middle East, with Saudi Arabia as a major supplier.

With rising inflation, the prospect of higher oil prices, and the threat of recession in America, Britain, and Spain; Japan braced itself for operating in a grossly uncertain global economy. The complexity and pervasiveness of oil in the industrialized world signaled that a major crisis was at hand which could produce enormous economic ramifications. With the announcement of the Kuwaiti annexation, the Nikkei fell 893.41 points. This time the Nikkei reacted to problems much more profound than rising interest rates or an unstable currency: a major energy crisis was developing, a crisis that affects currencies, interest rates, inflation, consumer psychology and the prospect of a global recession.

As inflationary pressures continued to rise, the Bank of Japan announced on August 30th that it was raising the discount rate from 5.25 percent to 6 percent, providing further evidence that Japan was taking an aggressive stance against inflation. Volatility in the stock markets generated higher anxiety in the Japanese investor who began to realize that Japan's bubble period was over. The Middle East crisis directly signaled that the party was over. Stock prices fell, and interest rates rose as Japan began a period of tight monetary policies.

The crisis hit large Japanese banks (hard) that held sizable stock portfolios due to falling stock prices. From the start of 1990 to September, the Nikkei had dropped over 14,000 points. More than $1.5 trillion in stock value had vanished. With such a high concentration of wealth under the control of a few institutions and individuals, the Japanese financial world was at the crossroads, with the stage set for a grand collapse in both its real estate and stock markets.

Having made substantial real estate loans during the *Booming 80s*, many large Japanese banks entered 1991 confronted with falling property values throughout Japan. However, the most notable declines would occur in Tokyo where Japanese corporations created the largest speculative real estate bubble in the 20th Century. Global economic forces helped to create this incredible land value in Japan and consequently created the conditions to reverse it. The Iraqi Affair dealt the last major blow to the Japanese bull market. There would be temporary recoveries, but the long-term trend for the early 1990s would be downward.

During 1991, revelations of stock market and political scandals began to surface, causing many small Japanese investors to lose further faith in their system. Reports revealed that some of Tokyo's sizeable institutional brokerage houses had participated in some shady deals that favored wealthy investors and in some cases, mobsters. This was not an unusual characteristic of a system based on extreme speculation. The greed syndrome during a super-long bull market generates this type of activity. It had reached its height during the *Booming 80s* and was still in progress as the world entered the 1990s.

With the start of 1992, it was clear that the Japanese economy was in the beginning phase of a full-blown recession. The boom period had faded, and massive foreign investment had slowed to a trickle. By the end of the first quarter and the start of the new Japanese fiscal period (March 31st), the Nikkei Stock Average stood at approximately 18,560, a clear indication that optimism was not in the air. The collapse of its stock markets and real estate markets, along with a steady progression of a reversal in its export-led economy, brought about a fundamental change in Japan.

During the first half of 1992, many of Japan's major industries had fallen on hard times. Steel companies, auto manufacturers, banks, airlines, brokerage houses and department stores fell into a slump. Real estate prices had dropped 30% in Tokyo and nearly 40% in other parts of Japan. Banks were left holding over $425 billion in real estate loans based on the depreciated values.

By June 1992, the Nikkei had fallen below the 16,000 level; it was in full retreat. In March 1993, *Business Week* magazine reported the following:

> "The crash in stock and land prices has deflated financial asset values by a staggering $8.5 trillion...A huge 8.6% of the banking industry's $6 trillion in outstanding loans now may be...on shaky ground."[4]

To restore some stability to this enormous problem, Japan's Finance Ministry resorted to pouring billions of dollars of government-controlled savings into the stock market; a calculated move to keep stock prices from falling to super critical levels.

In addition to cutting the discount rate to 2.5% in 1993, the Japanese government began making preparations for an enormous economic stimulus package designed to jump-start the sluggish economy. In April, the ruling Liberal Democratic Party (LDP) announced that the package would total 13.2 trillion yen or roughly $117 billion in spending programs. It would be a grand strategy to halt the deepening effects of the three-year recession. However, these measures could not stop the economic fallout of the boom and bust cycle. Pouring money into maintaining high values in real estate and stock prices ultimately lead to nowhere but further losses. The deflationary forces that swept across the entire world had to be allowed to work their will throughout the entire Japanese economy. This basic economic reality would not be understood until years after the fact.

Japan was at the crossroads entering the last decade of the 20th Century. Its mission, at that moment in history, was to adjust to a massive shakeout in its financial markets during the early 1990s. However, this economic cleansing was not undertaken and, instead, the nation went through the 1990s in a state of paralysis. Old-line politics and entrenched interests held the country hostage to strategies that did not work!

Thus, Japan entered the 1990s with many factors moving to bring about a downturn in its markets. It turned out to be a decade of severe economic stagnation with the general economy mired in a host of crippling financial and economic issues. The decade witnessed a state of political paralysis accompanied by a rapid succession of over nine prime ministers struggling to bring about a closure to the crisis. The Nikkei zigzagged throughout the decade in a continuing downward spiral. Consumer and investor confidence remained at an all-time low, while the all-powerful banking system never crawled out of the mountains of debt and bad loans that kept creeping back into the system.

By the end of the 1990s, Japan was still considered the second largest economy in the world (which was a fascinating statement considering the length and degree of its contraction) and the Japanese government had taken on nearly $5.5 trillion in debt. Deflationary forces were clearly on the loose throughout the economy, and Japan was no longer a country *at the crossroads*, but a nation that now had to contend with building a *new road* to navigate the enormous uncertainties and opportunities of the 21st century.

DECLINE OF THE LIBERAL DEMOCRATIC PARTY

By June of 1993, the political landscape in Japan was in turmoil. The Liberal Democratic Party (LDP) the dominant political force in Japan for nearly four decades, began to collapse. A no-confidence vote in the government of Prime Minister Miyazawa signaled the start of a prolonged political crisis that continued throughout the 1990s. The LDP had been in power since 1955 and represented a stable and cohesive force in helping to direct Japan's rise out of the ashes of World War II. But, the season for change had arrived: Japan's economic, financial, and political problems could no longer be managed in total agreement by its rulers.

Revelations of scandals, corruption, links to organized crime and a deepening economic recession shook the foundation of the LDP. The high-flying *Booming 80s* that took Japan to the zenith of financial and economic power collapsed with the start of 1990 when the bubble period began to unravel. Japanese investors lost trillions of dollars in wealth, and a different mood began to slowly penetrate specific segments of the society.

This new wave of thinking was evidenced by the sudden popularity of a book entitled *Honest Poverty* by Koji Nakano. Nakano's book put forth a strong case against materialism and blind acquisitiveness, a concern that Japanese society had become greedy and self-indulgent. Part of his theme was reminiscent of Ravi Batra's (author of *The Great Depression of 1990*) thesis of the age of the acquisitors; a period of history when acquiring wealth is the dominant force in the political and economic life of a nation. By June 1993, more than 600,000 copies of *Honest Poverty* had sold, and Japan was in the beginning stages of a period of massive societal reforms and economic restructuring.

The reform and transformation of Japan's political order was a clear indication that it was not immune to the political crisis sweeping across the entire world since the formal ending of the Cold War. The slow but steady collapse of apartheid in South Africa, the demise of the Soviet Union, the fall of Eastern Europe, governmental turmoil in Italy, Colombia and various governments throughout Africa and elsewhere, were clear signs of a disintegrating world order that had been the dominant force for much of the 20th Century. Japan would be no exception; some very painful adjustments were required to regenerate the fallen juggernaut.

Despite the slowdown that resulted from the *Crash of 1990*, Japan continued at an almost frenzied pace, pressing hard for its place as a technological powerhouse in the next century. In 1990 alone, the Japanese invested nearly $675 billion into fixed investments. Many major multinational Japanese corporations continued their investments in research and development and overseas facilities. Even as adversity derailed the overall economy, many corporations (in various industry sectors) with well-entrenched global strategies and resources, continued on course in building their global empires. For those with strong market shares in America and the European Community, the decade of the 1990s proved to be very profitable.

THE BANKING SYSTEM CRISIS

At the root of the banking crisis stood the *Crash of 1990*, which destroyed the real estate and stock market bubble economy. Banks were sitting in the center of this enormous speculation. By the mid-1980s, they were involved in taking on riskier loan deals, particularly in the commercial real estate and construction industries. As mentioned in an earlier section, at the height of the real estate bubble, Japan's real estate value was higher than all the land value in America. It was a market saturated with extreme valuations. This previously valuable land/property was offered as collateral on loan packages. When property values fell and debtors could no longer make their loan payments, banks were left holding less valuable collateral. Also, small credit associations and unions eventually got caught up in many of these same speculative development deals.

The other major factor that prolonged the banking crisis is the fact that banks were some of Japan's largest shareholders and investors in the markets. In fact, hidden reserve funds of many of these banks were based on the valuation of stock portfolio investments. In some cases, when the crash hit in full force, the hidden reserves of some banks were wiped out.

By the first quarter of 1994, the long-term value of commercial property had fallen by 70 percent from its high in 1989. Billions of dollars of taxpayer's money were spent trying to stabilize prices in the markets, but the deflationary forces continued at a torrid pace.

In Robert Sobel's book, *The Great Bull Market, Wall Street in the 1920s*, he informs us that, "The key to any financial crash is the banking system. If banks can remain solvent and retain public confidence, then recovery may take place." I think Japanese regulators may have missed this point. Old-line politics and old business alliances did not quickly adjust to the new realities of the busted 1990s. It was a slow drawn out affair that witnessed multiple billions of dollars wasted on ill-conceived strategies.

In the 1990s, a tremendous amount of *half-measures* and *tinkering* did not get at the root of the banking crisis. When an economy enters a bust period, swift and direct actions must be taken by regulators to purge the system of maladjustments, miscalculated investments, bad loans and inefficient business models and businesses. These major activities are required to restore confidence in the system. Japanese leaders were unwilling or unable - in the early stages to quickly clean the slate (American-style, brutal and bloody, and accept your losses .i.e. the S&L crisis) and rid their economic system of inefficient banks, bad loans, and unproductive enterprises. Old-line politicians, bureaucrats, and people in business struggled throughout the l990s to hold on to their power and fortunes while Japan wallowed in the mud and became a question mark to the world. Ultimately, shareholders in the fallen banks and enterprises would have to face up to their losses. Fortunately, for Japan and the world, their economy did not fall into a deep depression with soup lines and raging unemployment. But this story is not over, for Japan is still struggling with many of these same problems as of this writing (2018).

REFORM MEASURES

Various stimulus packages and reforms initiated throughout the l990s, illustrate how deeply the crisis had engulfed the Japanese economy. As a lesson for future reference, it's essential to *study* the impact of these measures to understand more clearly what did not work as solutions in this *bust cycle*. The following is a small selection of the leading reforms, stimulus efforts and the significant developments that took place during the l990s:

(1) As mentioned elsewhere, during the early years following the *Crash of 1990*, the government attempted to support prices in the stock and real estate markets by repeated interventions into the system to maintain high valuations and price stability. *The Wall Street Journal* reported in a June 1995 article that the Japanese government used three government-controlled funds to conduct these operations: "a huge postal savings system; a postal life-insurance plan; and the national pension scheme...their funds hold total assets of nearly $4.61 trillion...Since 1992, each national budget allowed for some of these assets to be used to support stocks."[5] From August 1992 to

January 1994, the government spent $300 billion on stimulation efforts. Public money was mainly used to support a bottom in the markets. The government got involved in unsustainable market rallies. This strategy ultimately led to nowhere but further losses. These forays into the markets only made it possible for speculators to *ride* the rally and *sell* at the end of a government buying spree. Smart short-term investors in Japan (or international players) probably employed that strategy.

(2) Bank failures were mostly not allowed during the first five years of the bear market.

(3) New bad loans subsequently replaced multiple billions of dollars of bad loans written off many lender's books. It is one of the main reasons why the banking system could not revive itself in full force: in many cases, weaker borrowers were kept alive to avoid taking the heavier write-offs. This strategy meant that valuable financial assets were not put to the best use.

(4) For the most part, the average Japanese stayed on the sidelines on many fronts throughout the decade. In the age of consumer sovereignty, this strategy by the Japanese consumer certainty played a role in the continuation of the downturn: until consumers start spending, the decline will continue. Analysts repeatedly warned that consumer demand had to be stimulated and confidence restored. Confidence remained low, particularly as deflationary forces began to sweep throughout the system. Spending was low, and by 1998, the Japanese savings rate had shot up to 30 percent of disposable income. Savers were hoarding some $9 trillion in wealth. There was virtually no confidence or faith in Japan's political, economic and financial systems. Many were tired of the scandals and a decade of economic mismanagement. Most people remained risk-averse and stayed on the sidelines.

(5) Lack of consumer demand promoted deflationary forces or *price destruction* (as the Japanese referred to it). As Japanese consumers continued to delay major purchases, with expectations of further reductions in prices, lower prices continued on a downward spiral throughout the decade. Another factor contributing to this phenomenon was the global allocation of Japanese corporate investments in new plant and manufacturing facilities. By 1994, most new ventures went to China (mainland China absorbed close to one-fifth of Japanese high-tech and component plants) North America and other developing economies in Asia. Relocation of these new facilities provided access to cheaper labor costs, allowing multinational corporations to remain competitive in the global arena. Lower cost products produced abroad eventually translated into lower prices in Japan. By the year 2000, domestic wholesale prices had fallen by 9 percent since 1991. Price cuts were evident in several sectors; from 55-cent burgers from McDonald's to $82 suits made in China. Also, the Japanese version of an Ameri-

can *Dollar Store* (the "Only Store") began offering every item in its stores for 99 yen or roughly 82 cents.

(6) While the Japanese economy remained mired in a decade-long recession, some of its major corporations such as Toyota, Honda, Sony and other multinational firms did well and remained profitable and competitive throughout the decade. After the *Crash of 1990*, these firms increased efficiencies across the board in relocation, currency tactics, and other strategies. In the year 2000, Japan imported more from Asia than from North America and Western Europe combined. In response to the crisis in Japanese leadership, Mr. Norio Ohga, CEO of Sony Inc., stated in an April 1998 interview that, "The thinking of political leaders is really domestic thinking only...too insular."[6] To the outside world, Japan was not making the right decisions as the second most significant economic power in the world.

(7) During the boom and bust period of 1995-2000 that was centered in America, a new class of entrepreneurs and business leaders emerged in Japan. Perhaps the most successful businessman in this group, was Masayoshi Son, founder of Softbank Corp. Mr. Son was instrumental in helping Yahoo! get started on the Internet, and at the height of the *Dot-Com Era*, he was estimated to be worth $60 billion on paper. The emergence of this new class of business leaders represented a clear challenge to the old guard.

(8) The so-called *Big Bang Reforms* economic plan was introduced in Japan during the first quarter of 1998. The 10-pound, 2,132-page document spelled out a carefully orchestrated plan to restructure and modernize the Japanese economy. The plan included across the board deregulation of its industries and markets, opening up Japan's financial institutions and commerce to foreigners, a $75-$90 billion stimulus package, $50 billion in tax cuts and additional public works spending.

(9) Interest rates fell throughout the 1990s in a grand effort to ignite a recovery. At some points during the decade, rates fell to zero or near zero levels, to combat the deflationary forces and other economic problems.

(10) By the first quarter of 2001, Japan was still stuck in the mud with the same problems. On March 8, 2001, Finance Minister Kiichi Miyazawa alarmed the public with the statement that, "Japan's public finances are very near collapsing." The currency markets had a field day with that remark, and within days, the Nikkei was falling to very low levels. On March 14, 2001, the Nikkei closed at 12,152.83, its lowest level since the mid-1980s. World talks centered on whether there would be a financial meltdown in Japan. Some of the issues debated were Japan's $5.4 trillion public debt (which was estimated to be 130 percent of gross domestic product), its continuing

deflationary problems, the unsolvable banking system crisis, super-low consumer demand and confidence levels, political stagnation and other related issues. Also, in March 2001, under the direction of Bank of Japan governor Masaaki Shirakawa, Japan began experimenting with quantitative easing (QE). Between 2001 and 2006, this first round of QE was focused on addressing the ongoing banking crisis and the faltering public finance issues.[7]

ECONOMIST RICHARD KOO AND THE BALANCE SHEET RECESSION

In reference to the Japanese bubble economy of the 1980s and the bust period of the 1990s, groundbreaking research by economist Richard Koo (2009) is now providing a new economic analysis of the *Great Depression of the 1930s*.[8] Examination of his theories reveals strong similarities between Japan's so-called *lost decade* of the 1990s and America's *Great Depression* years of the 1930s. According to Koo, the recession that began in the early 1930s was not an ordinary garden-variety recession, but was (what he calls) a *Balance Sheet Recession* where businesses and households were focused on paying down debts and repairing their balance sheets. For 15 to 20 years, Richard Koo had an opportunity to study and observe this phenomenon during the *Great Recession* years in Japan. His final analysis is that Japan of the 1990s and the U.S. of the 1930s endured the same type of economic depression: an extraordinary boom period followed by a drastic reduction in asset prices, aggregate demand, and money supply. When this happens, the private sector is more interested in getting out of debt rather than maximizing profits; which is why monetary policies that provide zero interest rates are not very useful.

As chief economist for the Nomura Research Institute (a Japanese think tank) Koo has spent the past 27 years living in Japan in deep observation and analysis of Japan's lost decades. His book, *The Holy Grail of Macroeconomics: Lessons From Japan's Great Recession*, is the definitive analysis of Japan's deflationary collapse that began in the 1990s. This groundbreaking study has brought to the surface something other economic textbooks have not uncovered, the significance of what he describes as the *Balance Sheet Recession*.[9] When there is a wholesale across the board collapse of asset prices, businesses and households will focus intensely on minimizing debt and repairing balance sheets. When asset values plunge to super low levels, the debt remains and must be dealt with as a first priority. In this type of economic environment, Koo tells us that, "Monetary theory does not work in a Balance-Sheet Recession until fiscal policy has been applied and balance sheets have been repaired."[10]

Not only did Richard Koo live through the Japanese recession, but he was also an active participant in the policy debates over a 15 year period. His eyewitness examination of the events that shaped the crisis, as well as his theory of the balance sheet recession, enables us to understand better the reasoning for his conclusions of why we are looking at a different type of recession. The main assertion in Koo's theory deals with the massive plunge in asset prices: "When a nationwide plunge in asset prices eviscerates asset values, leaving only the debt behind, the private sector begins paying down debt en masse. As a result, the broader economy experiences something economists call a "fallacy of composition." It occurs when behavior that would be right for one person (or company) leads to an undesirable outcome when engaged in by all people (or companies). Japan's economy has suffered from this fallacy often over the past fifteen years."[11]

Many companies went into the *Great Recession* in high leverage financial situations. It is entirely understandable given the steady and consistent price appreciation that occurred on many asset classes over a period of decades. Companies and individuals borrowed against these assets taking out very sizable loans. Thus, when the collapse came, the first order of business was to clean up deplorable balance sheets by paying down debt loads with existing cash flow. Koo reminds us that executives do not want the outside world to know that these problems exist on their balance sheets, so the need for the cleanup process is essential! Companies that were still generating profits targeted these cash flows for debt reduction. With businesses not reinvesting their cash flows, the economy will subsequently lose the vital force of aggregate demand. It is one of the reasons why monetary policies are useless in this type of economic crisis. Koo tell us that from 1991 to 1995 interest rates fell 800 basis points (from 8 percent to 0.5 percent) and this brought about no significant economic impact. On the household side of the spectrum, Japanese workers focused their resources and savings on paying down mortgages and had no appetite for taking on new debt even at zero interest rates. All of this would bring about contraction in aggregate demand which is the central cause of a recession.

THE 1997 ECONOMIC POLICY FAILURE

Similar to what happened during the *Great Depression* in the year 1937, the Hashimoto Administration attempted a program of fiscal consolidation or fiscal tightening (in 1997) with disastrous results. Similar to 1937, when a government begins to reduce fiscal stimulus and introduce austerity measures prematurely in a *Balance Sheet Recession*, the economy will move into a meltdown mode. In response to strong recommendations by the Organization for Economic Cooperation and Development (OECD) and the International Monetary Fund (IMF) for Japan to reduce its spending programs in the face of an aging population and large deficits, the country went on a crash diet to cut spending and raise taxes. The plan in 1997 was to reduce the fiscal deficit by 15 trillion yen, in addition to the introduction of a consumption tax hike from 3 percent to 5 percent, an increase in social security costs (taxpayer's share), the discontinuance of a supplementary budget and other cost-cutting measures. What happened next was not what the doctor ordered: the economy fell into a downward spiral for five straight quarters. These measures initiated a credit crunch and banking system crisis. Thus, a plan that was designed to reduce the deficit and control government spending did the opposite.

By the fiscal year 1999, Koo informs us that the annual deficit increased by 16 trillion yen to 38 trillion yen. The 1997 policy failure (just like in the American policy failure in 1937) was a critical economic history lesson. Richard Koo is correct when he tells us that this was, "a prime example of what happens when a government tries to engineer a fiscal debt reduction plan during a balance sheet recession." Tax revenues fell, deficits increased, and the Japanese economy was thrown off course en route to a sustainable recovery. Corrective action (new stimulus programs) was taken in 1998 by the Hashimoto Administration. However, the measures were too late to quickly reverse a downward course. Much stronger measures were subsequently implemented by Prime Minister Obuchi to correct the failed policies of 1997.

Given the fact that it takes considerable time for companies to repair their balance sheets (something that could not be achieved in a few short years) at the beginning of the recession, it was not surprising to see the minimal effects that fiscal stimulus had on the economy. The economy would reach temporary stabilization, then fall the following year again. In short, policymakers and economists were baffled about the weak response, and this would continue to confound successive government and central bank attempts at solving the massive ongoing economic problem. Thus, even with the lucrative prospect of zero interest rates, Japanese firms - en masse - would spend years paying down existing debts.

Koo's research revealed that Japanese firms stopped taking out new loans in the mid-1990s, and by 2002 to 2003, the debt repayment process hit a record high of over 30 trillion yen per year. A significant decline in the repayment process (by the private sector) began to take root in 2004, and by 2005, the repayment process for most companies was over, and recovery began to take place throughout much of the economy. It represented a significant turning point for Japan and why Richard Koo identifies Japan's *Great Recession* as a 15-year crisis (1990-2005).

The recovery that began in 2005 signaled to the Bank of Japan that it was time to change the monetary policy of zero interest rates (Zero Interest Rate Policy: ZIRP). As borrowers began to return to the market, it was a strong indication that balance sheets had been cleaned up and that the recession was over. By July 2006, the key benchmark rate was raised to 0.25 percent, and by February 2007, the addition of another 25 basis points increased the rate to 0.50 percent. Also, quantitative easing was abandoned in 2006. Koo reminds us that as recovery begins to take shape after a grueling balance sheet recession, the demand for loans by the private sector remains weak due to what he terms as the "debt-rejection syndrome." This initial aversion to debt in the early stages of recovery is understandable, given the fact that for many, enormous debt became a trap and a kind of debt prison for many years. And if a company or individual can move forward and operate without debt, that is a better remedy and path to follow. Enormous debt is a colossal burden, especially in a balance sheet recession.

While most critics will point to Japan's so-called lost decade as an absolute failure, Richard Koo argues that Japan "avoided a major depression because the government decided to apply fiscal stimulus and kept it going over many years." It is the reason why we do not call Japan's nearly two-decade downturn a *Great Depression*: the government succeeded in preventing a catastrophic decline in the nation's standard of living despite the economic crisis. To Richard Koo, this was one of the most successful economic policies in human history. Japan spent 140 trillion yen and avoided a deep economic depression.

However, after two years of a short-lived economic recovery, Japan, like the rest of the world, had to endure the *Meltdown of 2008* in the United States. In a global economy, no nation can escape the impact of a significant slowdown in the world's most influential economy. Japan would weather the storm. However, there would be another crisis that would knock this nation to its knees and begin a new chapter in economic catastrophe.

THE MASSIVE EARTHQUAKE OF 2011

On March 11, 2011, Japan was hit by a roughly 9.0 massive earthquake, tsunami and nuclear disaster that dealt the nation a catastrophe of enormous proportions. The economic impact of this triple blow disaster was felt throughout the world. In an age of instant news and communications, the world witnessed parts of Japan being ripped apart by massive earthquake damage, vast walls of water swallowing coastal areas and a smoldering nuclear disaster in a nation that had experienced the devastating force of the atomic bomb 66 years earlier. The disaster left more than 20,000 people dead or missing and thousands of people homeless. Transportation arteries, energy resources, and several industries were crippled. And in the midst of this epic disaster, the world witnessed the worst nuclear crisis in decades with the Japanese government struggling to contain the fallout. The initial cost of the disaster was estimated to be $300 billion.

As the third largest economy in the world (China became the second largest economy in 2010) Japan's massive disaster had an immediate impact on the global economy. Its export markets were derailed, generating shortages for parts and critical components in the manufacturing sectors. These economic dislocations were particularly damaging to the export markets of U.S. and China. The triple blow disaster forced an already weakened Japan into another recession. By late August 2011, Japan's exports had fallen for five straight months, leaving little doubt that the country had been dealt a severe blow to its economic engine. In Appendix C (Fukushima: An Economic X Factor) a more in-depth analysis and discussion of this extraordinary disaster is presented.

JAPAN AS THE PIONEER OF QUANTITATIVE EASING (QE)

After experiencing a series of setbacks and failures during the so-called *Lost Decade of the 1990s*, by 2001 the Bank of Japan (BOJ) embarked on the path of implementing quantitative easing (QE) as an unconventional economic tool to help stimulate the overall economy and to finally deal a death blow in the battle against deflation. As the first developed economy in the world to experiment with QE, Japan (spearheaded by the BOJ) moved aggressively in deploying the use of the money creation system (of its central bank) to tackle its growing list of economic problems.

The initial target of the BOJ was Japan's ailing banking system. Between March 2001 and December 2004, the BOJ injected 35 trillion yen of monetary liquidity into the system. Also, QE was focused on long-term government bond purchases which led to reducing long-term interest rates. The success of these initial operations made it possible for Japan to exit its QE strategy by March 2006. However, it would not be long before the BOJ was required to reenter the QE arena with even more significant financial firepower.

Successive rounds of QE (2008, 2010, 2013, 2016, etc.) had to be introduced to deal efficiently with the changing dynamics of the international financial community, as well as continuing its battle against deflation and reaching pre-determined inflation targets. By October 2014, the BOJ would announce that it was expanding its QE operations by 80 trillion yen per year, a clear sign that the Japanese economy was still in a fierce battle against its old enemies of deflation and lack of economic growth.

PRIME MINISTER SHINZO ABE AND ABENOMICS

As a long-standing member of the Liberal Democratic Party (LDP), the election of Shinzo Abe in 2012 represented a resurgence of the political power of this party that had lost credibility in the early 1990s. Abe came to power promising to end the deflation that had been a plague in the Japanese economy for decades. Known as *Abenomics*, this new platform of reflationist policies was designed to overhaul the Japanese economy and effectively begin a new era. The BOJ's chief architect and central banker, Haruhiko Kuroda, implemented radical reforms and tactics to catapult the Japanese economy out of the massive stranglehold of deflation.

Abenomics advocated the use of three economic arrows as the driving force of its reforms: (1) Fiscal stimulus (2) monetary expansion and (3) structural reforms. Under the fiscal stimulus arrow, the government would introduce new spending programs to stimulate demand. The monetary expansion arrow would concentrate on printing new money to help generate pre-determined inflation levels and support Japan's export markets. Structural reforms focused on the improvement of various regulations designed to make Japanese industries more competitive.

Despite the massive money printing and the BOJ effectively assuming the role of Japan's bond market, the stagnation and deflationary forces continued to plague the Japanese economy. Abenomics achieved some measure of success with its anti-deflationary policies and was given a vote of confidence by the Japanese people with Shinzo Abe's reelection in 2017. Also, Haruhiko Kuroda was reelected (for another five-year term) in February 2018 to continue his reflationary policies. The ruling elite was fully aware that it would have to continue these unconventional economic policies at all cost. There was no turning back!

These successive rounds of massive money printing managed to lower the value of the yen (which had a positive impact on Japan's export markets) but didn't generate the expected level of inflation that the planners had hoped would occur. This phenomenon provided prima facie evidence that the third largest economy in the world could print massive amounts of new currency and not ignite high levels of inflation or hyperinflation. Devaluation of the currency was taking place, but not on a scale that would cause a major crisis.

By August 2016, the BOJ owned 35% of all Japanese government bonds issued. The central bank also began buying broad market Japanese ETFs, Real Estate Investment Trusts (REITs), as well as publicly traded Japanese companies. The BOJ was steadily moving towards assuming a much more pervasive position in the economic life of the nation. By purchasing stocks, bonds, ETFs, etc., and placing these assets on its books, the BOJ was effectively bringing stability to its markets. The debt to GDP ratio had exploded to over 230 percent and was expected to increase to 300 percent of GDP over the next decade. With little or no economic growth, the BOJ was still planning to move government bonds onto its books at the rate of seven to eight percent per year. With an aging population, persistent deflation and rising debt, Japan was still in a deep struggle to overcome a chronic deflationary crisis.

The year 2016 would also witness the BOJ introducing negative interest rate policy in Japan (NIRP) as another tool to stimulate the economy. Also, a report that surfaced in April 2016 revealed that the government was considering making available gift certificates to low-income young people to help stimulate the economy. As discussed in Chapter Four (The Extraordinary Power of the Federal Reserve System), this would be a form of *Helicopter Money* that would be placed directly into the hands of the people that could effectively stimulate demand. I do not doubt that Japan will probably be the first developed nation in the world to deploy this economic tool and strategy.

SUMMARY/ANALYSIS

After over 40 years of massive progress and building one of the most successful technological and economic societies in world history, Japan hit a massive barrier in 1990 and started a descent into economic chaos.

Based on the ground-breaking research of Richard Koo, we now have a much better understanding of why Japan lingered in its *Great Recession* for 15 years and why this dynamic country did not fall into a deep depression reminiscent of the 1930s *Great Depression* in America.

Despite the massive loss of wealth, after nearly a decade into the economic crisis, Japanese consumers were still hoarding over $9 trillion in wealth. Japan's corporate titans were still globally competitive, the Japanese people were still completely committed to developing new innovative *Information Age* technologies, Japanese corporate titans made serious inroads into mainland China, Japanese money and investments helped to fuel the boom and bust cycle of 1995-2000 in America and a new class of entrepreneurs emerged to challenge the old-guard. Even after losing trillions of dollars during the long bear market, Japan is still rated the third most significant economic power in the world.

However, the road ahead in the 21st century will be very different from the post-World War II era. With an aging population (median age was 45 years old in 2011) low birth rates, immigration restrictions and significant population shrinkage, Japan's future growth will need to focus on productivity, immigration and demography. Japan has had no real population growth in 20 years: births are remaining below the significant replacement rate. By some estimates, Japan is losing a million people every year. Consumer spending is decreasing, with elderly households spending less on communications, transportation, utilities, education and various types of recreation.

It is estimated that by the year 2050, the median age in Japan will be 55 and the total population will be approximately 100 million people, half of whom will be elderly. A significant decrease in a younger workforce in the decades ahead will have an impact on the ability of Japan to maintain its status as one of the most significant dynamic power centers in the world.

As the *Canary in the Coal Mine*, Japan's road ahead is filled with considerable uncertainty. The massive use of unconventional central bank tools may ultimately be a trap leading to the destruction of its currency (the yen) and yen-denominated assets. As of 2018, no one knows any of the possible outcomes of the massive use of central bank money creation out of thin air. The only thing that can be observed thus far is that it has kept Japan functioning and continuing its battle against deflation for nearly three decades. Money printing has kept Japan out of a *Great Depression*!

Japan's government debt of over one quadrillion yen (that's a one followed by 15 zeros), is the largest in the world. And as this nation continues down the path of acquiring more and more debt, the economic dilemma will become much more profound and questionable. What is clear is that this strategy is not the road to recovery; it is a plan to keep the nation alive and kicking for as long as possible. *Japan is at the crossroads, and no one knows how long this can be sustained*!

NOTES

(1) Approximately one year later (final week of April 1991) the Japanese and Germans were called upon to lower interest rates to assist in ending a recession in America. President Bush held an informal meeting with the Group of Seven representatives at the White House in a grand effort to lower world interest rates. As the recession deepened in America, the need for lower domestic interest rates became the Bush Administration's primary focus. However, continued cuts at home without international support placed the U.S. in a precarious situation. Japan's Finance Minister, Ryutaro Hashimoto, stated that pressures at home, specifically in its land prices and a tight labor market had placed Japan in a difficult position; it could not immediately lower its interest rates. Peter Trull, "Bush Pushes G-7 Countries on Reducing Rates but Gets Unenthusiastic Response," *Wall Street Journal*, April 29,1991, pp. A2 and A16.

(2) Barbara Rudolph, "Pop! Goes the Bubble," *Time*, April 2, 1990, pp. 50-52.

(3) Michael R. Sesit and Marcus W. Brauchli, "Tokyo's Market: Was It a Bubble Just Waiting to Burst,"*The Wall Street Journal*, April 3, 1990, pp. C1 and C21.

(4) Larry Holyoke, Neil Gross, Robert Neff and Karen Lowry Miller, "Fixing Japan," *Business Week*, March 29, 1993, pp. 68-74.

(5) Robert Steiner, "Japanese Stocks Tumbling Without a Net,"*The Wall Street Journal*, June 15, 1995, p. A12.

(6) Jon Herskovitz, "Japan's Big Firms Thrive Amid Crisis Plaguing Economy," *San Francisco Chronicle*, April 13, 1998, p. A13.

(7) Mitsuhio Fukao, *Japanese Financial Crisis and Crisis Management* (Japan Center for Economic Research, September 21, 2009)

(8) Richard Koo, *The Holy Grail of Macroeconomics: Lessons From Japan's Great Recession*, (John Wiley & Sons (Asia) Plc. Ltd., 2009) p. 1

(9) IBID, p. 1.

(10) IBID, p. 15.

(11) IBID, pp. 17-18.

CHAPTER EIGHT
EUROPEAN ECONOMIC CRISIS REVISITED

The euro experiment has been fascinating...but it was conceived with a mixture of flawed economics and ideologies...For all the emotions that the euro has brought on, for all the commitments that have been made to preserve it, in the end, the euro is just an artifice, a human creation, another fallible institution created by fallible people.

Joseph Stiglitz

What's happening in Europe is monumental; an ongoing crisis that offers no easy solutions. With the world still reeling (in 2018) from the credit crunch and *Meltdown of 2008*, the question remains if we are very likely looking at a replay of 2008, but this time on a much grander scale. It was the financial sector in 2008 that was on the brink of failure; now it is entire nations. Since the 2008 meltdown, European banks, along with their American partners, continued to pile on enormous mountains of debt, leverage, and risk. As one of the most extraordinary global economic experiments in world history, the European Union (EU) is the epicenter of the next phase of the global financial meltdown.

According to the IMF and other global economic analysts, the EU ranks as the first to the third largest economy in the world (based on specific systems of measurement). When we consider the amount of trade conducted by the EU (both imports and exports), the trading bloc generates more movements of goods and services than the U.S. and China. Thus, the EU is fundamental to a continuation of a fully functioning global economy in the 21st-century context.

Central bankers, particularly in Europe and the United States, have done and will continue to do everything within their power to prevent the collapse of the EU and the euro. Of crucial importance is the prevention of Europe descending into a Japanese style deflationary spiral, which could lead to decades of economic stagnation. After nearly ten years following the great 2008 meltdown, the EU was in a state of political and economic paralysis, questioning its existence and struggling to maintain a semblance of legitimacy and relevance for hundreds of millions of its citizens.

In the event of the downfall of the euro, the fate of eurozone nations and the euro would suffer a similar decline to the time when Richard M. Nixon took the U.S. off the gold standard in 1971. When America came off the gold standard, that event broke the Bretton Woods accord. The dollar was devalued and suffered crippling inflation and stagflation for nearly a decade until Federal Reserve Chairman, Paul Volcker, broke the back of inflation in the early 1980s and re-established confidence in the American currency. A massive euro decline and devaluation - at this time in history - represent the most severe crisis we have seen since the 1970s, and most likely, the 1930s as well.

Created out of the ashes of World War II (with a great deal of persuasion by the United States), the development of the European Union (EEC or EU) initially focused on prevention of any further conflict on the continent. After centuries of war, and in particular, the two world wars of the 20th Century, the Europeans were seeking to establish a new era of lasting peace and prosperity. In World War I, 17 million people died, and over 20 million people were wounded or maimed. Approximately twenty years later, World War II witnessed 60 million dead and the birth of the *nuclear age*: The European landscape was left in complete devastation and ruins, and Hiroshima and Nagasaki were bombed into the dark ages. And we must never forget that when the world embarked on World War II, no nation at that point in history possessed nuclear weapons. If nuclear weapons had been available before that devastating global war, there is absolutely no doubt in my mind that a nuclear holocaust would have engulfed the entire planet and wiped out civilization as we know it today.

So why am I talking about global wars in a book focused on an impending (or imminent) global economic meltdown? The short answer is that it was a prolonged deflationary depression that played a significant role in helping to bring about the second world war and the mad rush to develop nuclear weapons. Let's be clear here; devastating economic times and deep deflationary depressions can, over time, lead to military conflicts, social unrest, revolutions, trade wars, currency wars and significant discontent between nations and within nations. Deep economic distress is a central prerequisite to global conflict and war.

The Great Depression of the 1930s is a prime example of how things can spin completely out of control with the rise of fascism, dictatorships and the dark side of humanity descending into chaos and barbarism. And let us remember that what preceded the 1930s great depression years was the boom period of the *Roaring 20s*, a period characterized by extreme wealth inequality and stock market manipulations coupled with an era of mass economic innovations: one of the greatest *boom and bust cycles* of all time.

In 2018, nearly 78 years since the advent of World War II, we are staring into the abyss of a looming economic crisis more significant than anything ever devised by humanity. When the final big crash comes, we will not witness the advent of a garden-variety recession or even something that we can label a *Great Recession*. The *Great Reckoning* and *Grand Convergence* is expected to be something much greater than that, and this is why we must think much more deeply about the ultimate consequences of this looming crisis and how it might be resolved (if we move in the right direction) to save our civilization. That is what is ultimately at stake here, and what happens in Europe is central to the survival of this current global civilization.

The post-World War II era witnessed the establishment of NATO, a common market, the beginnings of a joint government under the European Union of nation states and a new global currency under a single monetary policy. It was a very ambitious undertaking, and it took decades to arrive at a working model and framework.

The success of a single eurozone market was the foundation that was designed to pave the way for the eventual political union of all participating European nations. With the birth of the euro and its promise of a stable world currency, many skeptics condemned the idea from the start as an unworkable experiment that would not last. However, having gone this far with the development of a new currency, which has become the second leading currency in the world, a possible breakup of the eurozone block is now viewed as the most significant economic threat to the entire world.

SHADES OF THE *MELTDOWN OF 2008*

The *Meltdown of 2008* opened wide the problems and weaknesses of the eurozone, exposing many unresolved issues that prevented compromise and collective action. When there is total systemic collapse and confidence is lost in the banking system, a lot of hidden problems are unveiled. For instance, companies learned that their credit lines were frozen as the banks fought for their financial survival. Global credit could freeze up again (as in 2008) very quickly in a sovereign debt crisis. Credit lines just cannot be relied upon when banks are sucked into a death spiral.

Greece of 2011 was very similar to Lehman of 2008, except on a much grander scale. The contagion factor was very strong, and chaos and mayhem could have spread very quickly. Letting Lehman fail in 2008 had very dire consequences; the resulting meltdown nearly plunged the world into a full-blown depression as events spiraled out of control very quickly. After the experience of Lehman in 2008, no one wanted to risk Greece leaving the euro or defaulting on its debt. Since financial groups and institutions do not disclose what they hold in sovereign debt, global markets could quickly move into a state of panic from the unknowns and uncertainties. Fear and panic would quickly cascade into Italy, Spain, and many other countries. The ultimate risk in this scenario is that the implosion of the euro would have meant the explosion of Europe. Thus, no one wanted a disorderly Greek default. The risks were far too high!

Investors were terrified of a repeat of 2008. In not knowing which institutions were genuinely solvent during that crisis, banks stopped lending to each other. The hidden reality in late 2011 was that banks in America and Europe were still suffering from the fallout of 2008. A sudden default would have forced big banks to absorb massive losses on government bonds and other asset classes.

The EU is America's biggest trading partner, representing 17 percent of total exports; a slowdown there will have a measurable impact on American business and finance: there would be a significant shortfall (in Europe) of spending on American goods and services. U.S. Banks hold about $2 trillion worth of investments (burdened with sovereign debt) in European banks. According to the European Commission, in 2014 European investors and firms made roughly 1.99 trillion euros worth of direct investments in America. A major recession in Europe would quickly spur the onset of a significant slowdown in America; this would not be a de-coupled situation. If the European sovereign debt crisis spirals out of control, it would be hugely detrimental to the American economy. The two regional economic blocks are tightly connected, which is why Fed Chairman Ben Bernanke printed countless trillions of dollars to bailout both the U.S. and European financial systems during the 2008 meltdown. Since the European Central Bank (ECB) had not yet been authorized to print money, issue Eurobonds and conduct quantitative easing (QE) operations, it was necessary for the Fed to step in and bail out (provide lending facilities and funding) European banks during that devastating crisis.

After the Lehman collapse in 2008, China began a massive stimulus program. In the face of a severe slump in its export markets, China implemented a $586 billion (4 trillion yuan) stimulus package to encourage growth and domestic consumption which was instrumental as a stabilizing force in the global economy. These measures provided comprehensive economic support at a critical time. In 2011, the world was again looking to China and other emerging nations (the BRICS member nations: Brazil, Russia, India, China and South Africa) to serve as stabilizing economic forces in the face of the European sovereign debt crisis.

After a half-century of European integration, the response to the sovereign debt crisis was viewed as a severe lack of political will by the EU. Some saw the European leadership response as piecemeal, half-measures and tentative guarantees; dragging their feet over bailouts. The EU was viewed as being behind the curve on the issues and events, struggling to manage a crisis that was driven by the markets which rapidly got out of control. And the continued implementation of half-measures failed to cure the problems.

The European Central Bank's (ECB) financial power to print money and monetize debt was not initially agreed to by Germany and other conservative and economically stable EU members. Germany felt that the more profligate countries would be let off the hook for their bad fiscal conduct. German leaders were extremely fearful of the potential of hyperinflation and a banking system collapse similar to what ripped apart their nation during the 1920s and 1930s, which ultimately gave rise to Hitler and the Third Reich. So to the German mindset, the issue of central banks printing money to solve debt problems was not the right approach; it was a solution that only extended the problem and risked creating a much more significant problem down the road. The rules at the time only allowed the ECB to buy government bonds in the secondary market but on condition that it used an equivalent amount of assets. The Germans had previously stated that they did not want to compromise the ECB for the sake of a collective solution. Thus, it had been a step by step reaction to events, and it would continue to be that way until a significant policy shift required a different approach. At that point, the Germans needed to decide to leave or stick with the euro. Given the choice of risking inflationary ECB lender-of-last-resort policies or walk away, some analysts believed that the Germans would have elected to walk away. However, that did not happen.

Asian countries, the United States and others were hesitant to pump more resources into the sovereign debt crisis until they saw the Europeans investing more of their resources, with much firmer controls instituted and fiscal and economic reforms put in place. As one G20 official stated, "Nobody wants to spend money on something they doubt would work." The more I pondered the problems confronting the eurozone during this time of crisis, the more I began to think that the U.S., by far, was in a much more favorable condition (politically and economically) than the European Union.

THE GREEK TRAGEDY

Greece did not initially qualify for admission into the eurozone in 1999. However, by June 2000, it was deemed that Greece had made the grade and could participate in the new currency by January 1, 2001. The initial attraction to the euro by peripheral countries, such as Greece, was access to cheap funds. However, in joining the eurozone, a nation had to give up its own currency. By doing this, Greece (and every other country in the eurozone) gave up the ability to adjust exchange rates with their own currency whenever a crisis hit; the ability to print money was abdicated, and it could no longer respond flexibly to economic events. But the allure of the euro was strong and offered a weaker nation an opportunity to participate in a promising new global currency.

After adopting the euro, Greece went on a spending spree and borrowed money. During the lending boom of the early 2000s, it was believed that membership in the eurozone made Greece, Portugal, and Spanish bonds safe investments. Thus, foreign investment capital flowed into these nations. The spending spree in Greece (as well as in Portugal and Spain) that allowed these nations to (briefly) live beyond their means. All of this generated inflation: a general rise in wages and prices in these countries compared to the other more stable economies of Germany, Finland, and France.

Then the global financial crisis hit in 2007-2009. The inflow of capital ceased: revenues plunged, and deficits rose sharply. As a result, Greece found that it could not pay its bills or repay the bonds. From that point and moving forward, Greece was forced to accept the remedy of deflation: falling prices and wages; where incomes fall, but the debt burden stays the same. That's what makes deflation a tough pill to swallow. Standard and Poor's, UBS, and other analysts warned that Greece could not grow itself out of this crisis and that this would likely go on for many years.

In early October 2009, Greek bonds were dumped by global investors, driving their market values down and yields up. Portugal's 10-year government bonds also started to plunge in December 2009. By April 2010, Greece's credit rating was reduced to junk status. It was the beginning of a new contagion of fear about sovereign debt. And, as this fear began to spread, the cost of sovereign debt borrowing began to escalate to unsustainable levels. The eurozone treaties initially forbade bailouts; however, as the crisis continued to deepen, this became a necessary evil. EU leaders did not want to rescue Greece for fear that this would create an unwanted precedent.

Without the ability to borrow money in the bond markets due to the extreme cost of borrowing, Greece was effectively shut out of the debt markets. Greece petitioned the EU and the IMF for economic rescue funds. The first bailout package was provided in May 2010 for 110 billion euros ($140 billion). The IMF, Germany, Austria, and Finland were the main creditors for that deal. In 2005, Greece owed 195.4 billion euros; by 2011 the debt burden had grown to 328.6 billion euros: debt to GDP had risen to 143 percent. The founding EU treaty agreement had established the debt to GDP ratio to be 60 percent. Greece was over-extended and exceeded the allowable GDP ratio by a wide margin.

What happened in Greece was a microcosm of what would eventually spread throughout the world as the *sovereign debt contagion* was finally unleashed. It was not hard to imagine other countries in Europe or states and cities in America undergoing the same set of circumstances of protests, riots, looting, suicides and violent confrontations with law enforcement.

Many nations were sitting on fragile recoveries and massive debt overload; Greece was not alone! As of the first quarter of 2012, at least 386 billion euros had been committed to preventing the collapse of Greece, Ireland, and Portugal. It is not a situation that was sustainable in the long term; these were strategic bailouts designed to buy time and ward off the *Day of Reckoning*.

GREEK RESISTANCE TO AUSTERITY: After suffering seven years of deep recession/depression and five years of austerity, many people in Greece were seeking massive change in their country's relationship with the eurozone and the euro. The GDP had fallen 25 percent, and the unemployment rate was in the 25 percent range as well. Thus, in the historic election on January 25, 2015, the Greek population went to the polls and voted into power the far-left Syriza party, giving it the mandate to break the back of eurozone austerity measures imposed by the IMF and the EU. The new

Greek Prime Minister, Alexis Tsipras, and Finance Minister, Yanis Varoufakis, became the hard-line vanguard that would change the calculus and direction of the Greek economic tragedy. The dynamic duo promised the Greek people that they would reject the austerity measures, renegotiate bailout terms, crackdown on corruption and tax evasion, and avoid exiting the eurozone and the euro. It would be the major turning point, the time to rebuild the broken Greek economic system.

In a July 2015 referendum that would decide on how to handle future austerity measures and other harsh EU imposed demands, 61 percent of the Greek population voted no on any actions that would impose stringent economic restrictions on the Greek economy. It added greater strength to the Tsipras government's mandate in its struggle against the Troika of the ECB, the IMF and EUB headed by Germany.

This show of defiance was short-lived and didn't succeed in gaining the upper hand with the titan opposition. Prime Minister Tsipras was forced to back away from his promises to the Greek people and coerced to accept brutal austerity measures to receive Greece's third bailout of 85 billion euro ($96 billion). It was a humiliating defeat for the roughly six-month-old Tsipras government, but near the end of the negotiations, he was slammed to the mat by German Chancellor Angela Merkel, which *The Guardian* described the drama as "extensive mental waterboarding." Merkel's display of massive power destroyed the Greek defiance. She was prepared to keep Greece in the euro, but "not at any cost."

The defeat dealt a severe blow to the Greek population that was fighting for its economic liberation. Greek economist Haralambos Rouliskos described the deal with the Troika as "misery, humiliation, and slavery." Greece was again forced to endure spending limits, pension reforms, tax increases, the sale of state assets and other draconian measures. The fear and concerns by some analysts were that this dramatic defeat would ultimately set the stage for a "fascist takeover" of the Greek government at some point in the near future.

The reality of the Tsipras government was that it was negotiating from a weak position with failing banks, a collapsing economy, food shortages and a nation in dire need of essential medicines. And in a real demonstration of power, the ECB decided not to increase its emergency lending assistance (ELA), and this froze the Greek banking system. Without the deal, the Greek economy would have collapsed entirely, perhaps into anarchy. After seven months in power, both Prime Minister, Alexis Tsipras, and Finance Minister, Yanis Varoufakis were forced to resign. However, before stepping down, the resourceful Tsipras called for a snap election to take place the following month. In September of 2015, he led his party to another victory (winning 145 out of the 300 seats in the Hellenic Parliament) and was reappointed Prime Minister of Greece.

In early April 2016, China Ocean Shipping Company (COSCO) purchased a 67% stake in the most significant port in Greece (Piraeus) for one billion euro, with an allocation of roughly 500 million euro for upgrades and modernization of port facilities. As a critical requirement in most IMF deals, Greece was forced to sell a fixed amount of state assets to receive its bailout funds. It was a golden opportunity for China to establish a logistical hub in the European Union as part of its new "Silk Road" global trading initiative. COSCO also expressed great interest in buying the Greek railway system.

TROIKA POWER OVER GREECE: At the beginning of the Greek sovereign debt crisis in 2009, European and other international banks were the primary creditors and holders of Greek debt. After seven years of deep recessions and three historic bailouts, a significant shift took place in regards to what and who became the chief owners of Greek debt obligations. That transference of creditor status also meant that the potential threat of a Greek default was significantly reduced due to the ECB beginning its official QE operations in 2015. The shift facilitated the move of the private ownership of Greek debt to public ownership, which led to a lower degree of risk in global bond markets.

With the ECB essentially conducting QE operations and absorbing the bad debts of eurozone countries in distress, the threat of a nation leaving the euro was significantly decreased. Losses could henceforth be assumed by the ECB and other European governments rather than the private sector.

Thus, in the early stages of the crisis, bailouts were necessary to avoid the threat of bank failures and contagion that were central factors in the 2008 meltdown. A Greek default was compared to the Lehman collapse of 2008, and there were too many unknowns to risk what could have possibly been a much more massive event. However, by June 2015, the sovereign debt calculus had gone through a fundamental change, and this was the main reason why the Greek defiance carried no real weight in the negotiations with the Troika. Greece could not possibly win a battle against a powerful central bank (ECB) that could create new euros out of thin air. Like central banks in other developed economies in the world, the ECB discovered that it could print money and not generate hyperinflation.

ITALY IN CRISIS

Italy is the third largest national economy in the eurozone and one of the core founding members of the European Union. Long considered part of the PIIGS nations (See Glossary) that are deemed the weaker members of the EU, Italy has been in intensive care for longer than what most EU officials were prepared to admit. The country had experienced no growth for nearly a decade under the euro. Euro membership had been a straight jacket on the Italian economy (fiscal and monetary policies) and far too restrictive.

Italy's real GDP per capita has slumped to a 20-year low. The low economic performance led to a build-up of bad assets on the balance sheets of the nation's banks. Significant declines in the standard of living, particularly in more impoverished regions of the country's southern region, contributed a great deal to the persistent economic decline.

Italy's wealthy north represents the main industrial engine that drives the nation's economy, while the south is considered underdeveloped and weak and much less prosperous. To put this in greater perspective, upwards of 5 million Italians are living in absolute poverty and more than 8 million in relative poverty. All of this was understood before the beginning of a new crisis. The mood in this nation, like that in many other EU nations, was anti-establishment and severe distrust of the political and economic elites. Gross inequality, anti-immigration sentiment, and anti-Brussels domination were widespread.

In 2017, the country's banking system was in deep trouble with the entire banking system on the verge of collapse. Nonperforming loans (NPLs) amounted to 18% of assets, and most banking institutions were undercapitalized (the NPLs in Greece was at 34%; Portugal 12% and Ireland 19%). The urgent need was to prevent bank runs, panic and a meltdown in the overall economy. Additionally, the government was seeking to avoid the bondholder bail-in process which would do irreparable harm to private investors in banking institutions, which in Italy are a lot of mom and pop investors (ordinary Italians held 45 percent of bank debt). To put that in perspective, U.S. banks had a non-performing loan (NPL) ratio of 5% at the height of the 2008 - 2009 financial crisis; so an NPL of 18% was very significant. Since the 2008 meltdown, the bad loan crisis in Italy grew at a pace of 50 billion euro per year for nearly a decade. And similar to the Japanese experience, most of these bad loans were not written off due to expectations of a robust recovery in the national and eurozone economies.

During the first half of 2016, bank shares lost half their values. Headlines were announcing that Italy's banking system could collapse and that the country could elect to leave the euro and the eurozone. UniCredit (over $1 trillion in assets), Monte dei Paschi Siena (had already been bailed out twice), Banco Popolare SC, and Untesa Sanpaolo SpA were among the troubled banks leading the massive declines. Some analysts and regulators reasoned that it would take nearly 52 billion euros to restructure and fix Italy's banking system.

In essence, Italy's banks never really recovered from the 2008 global financial crisis: for the most part, the U.S. recovered from the 2008 meltdown, Europe did not. The use of ZIRP and negative interest rate policies (NIRP) had been economic strategies that failed to produce growth and sustainable recovery.

By some accounts, the euro was the problem. Nobel Prize-winning economist and former chief economist of the World Bank, Joseph Stiglitz, warned that harsh austerity measures and the euro would drive the momentum for people in Europe to want to quit the EU project. According to him, people in Italy "are increasingly disappointed in the euro...Italians are starting to realize that Italy doesn't work in the euro."[1] He firmly believes that Brussels should consider a north euro and south euro as a flexible monetary option to resolve the euro dilemma.

Italy's debt to GDP ratio went from 104 percent in 2008 to 133 percent by early 2015. Not having access to a currency that can be competitively devalued when required had boxed the nation into a corner. Adopting the euro was seen by many people in the country as a bad economic strategy.

From the start of the 2008 financial crisis until late 2016, Italy had appointed three different prime ministers. In a move to shake up the political establishment, Prime Minister Matteo Renzi (the third prime minister and considered a centrist) called for a vote on constitutional reforms that took place in October of 2016. The central goal of the Renzi plan was to usher in a new era in politics with legal changes, disrupting the legislative gridlock of Italy's Senate and the Chamber of Deputies. Analysts viewed the chance for structural reforms and economic modernization as best under a Renzi (Democratic Party) government. Over the previous decade, political stagnation had been a massive problem for the country. Renzi was seeking to increase the executive power of government and decrease the power of the legislative branches.

The referendum was set to piss a lot of people off, especially those who benefitted from a political power system that provided them with favorable arrangements and significant benefits. The Prime Minister placed his political career on the line by promising to resign if the people voted to reject the reforms. When Italians went to the polls in October, 59% of the voters cast their ballots to reject the Renzi political plan. The resounding no vote forced the Prime Minister to resign. After two-and-a-half years in office, Renzi became another political casualty in the ongoing wave of populist sentiment sweeping across the EU. Renzi was up against a barrage of opposition, with the established order in full retreat.

As the premier populist group and the main opposition to the status quo in Italy, Beppe Grillo's 5-Star Movement's main agenda called for a referendum on eurozone membership and for Italy to return to the lira (it's previous currency). It represented a significant threat to the establishment and an unequivocal denouncement of the euro and the eurozone.

The people were sick of Italy's internal system of corruption and the self-interest of politicians. Policies dictated from Brussels, and Berlin added more fuel to the fire, demonstrating high levels of frustration within a broken system. Austerity and the restrictive demands of the euro (seen as a major source of chronic unemployment and stagnant wages), as well as the new bail-in EU banking regulations, had pushed millions of voters to the extremities of the political spectrum.

On May 29, 2018, Italy's bond market began to unravel. The alarm bells went off when the markets became fully aware that Italian 2-year yields had surged from -0.3% to more than 2.5% (up 158 basis points) during a short period of two to three weeks. The rate on ten-year notes rose to 3.44%, up 76 basis points. These were significant moves indicating that investors were seeking greater returns for the perceived greater risks in Italian bonds. Fear and uncertainty regarding Italy's internal politics and economic performance began to cause investors to question the future of

Italy's political system. With the popular 5-Star Movement gaining ground, Italy's future was doubtful. After Brexit of 2016, Italy was now expected to be the next major country in the EU to step forward with a revision of its relationship with the European Union project and the euro.

The European Central Bank (ECB) was in observance mode, ready to step in if the crisis appeared to spin out of control. The ECB was committed to buying 4 billion euros of Italian bonds per month (and more if required) with a schedule that would continue until September 2018. Unlike the Greek crisis of 2010, the ECB is in a much stronger position to rescue EU members that are facing difficult economic and financial challenges.

The next trading day the markets were calm in the U.S., indicating that a major crisis in Italy was not to be feared, at least, not at that point. But again, this was not the end of the story; Italy would have much more to say in the months and years ahead.

FRANCE

France, in partnership with Germany, is a central power broker on the stage in the EU economic drama. Officially the second most influential political power in the EU, France has worked closely with Germany to develop feasible solutions for the nearly decade-long debt crisis.

The aftershocks of the *Meltdown of 2008* witnessed many governments that were swept from power as economic weaknesses rose to the surface. Some of the failed governments are as follows: (1) Spain (Jose Luis Rodriguez Zapatero, November 2011) (2) Portugal (Jose Socrates, June, 2011) (3) Greece (George Papandreou, October 2011) (4) Italy (Silvio Berlusconi, November 2011) (5) the U.K. (Gordon Brown, May 2010) (6) the Netherlands (Mark Rutte and his Cabinet, April 2012) (7) Greece (Prime Minister, Alexis Tsipras and Finance Minister, Yanis Varoufakis, August 2015) (8) Italy (Prime Minister Matteo Renzi, November 2016). All faced the wrath of enraged populations or strong political oppositions in parliaments that disagreed with their leaders and their economic policies.

After the astonishing results of the Brexit vote in June of 2016 (See Chapter Nine) and the election of Donald Trump (in November 2016) as the 45th president of the United States, the global populist movement grew much stronger in the developed world as millions of people became disenchanted entirely with establishment politics and politicians. In the case of France, the far-right National Front, headed by Marine Le Pen, became the most influential opponent against the establishment and the eurozone project. She called the Brexit vote the "biggest political event in Europe since the fall of the Berlin Wall."[2]

The nationalistic fervor in France and elsewhere in the eurozone was rapidly expanding in 2017. France held its presidential election on April 23, 2017, and a runoff was declared for the top two contenders, Emmanuel Macron of En Marchel and

Marine Le Pen of the National Front (FN). On the May 7th run-off, Macron scored a decisive win over Le Pen, presenting clear evidence that the majority of French voters were not prepared (at least not at that point) to go down the path of the populist revolution spearheaded by the National Front. The business friendly vision that Macron presented to the voters promised a continued integration of EU policies and the euro. However, despite Macron's victory, opposition to the EU would continue to remain active in France.

In 2017, nationalism and anti-establishment parties were significant factors voicing political and economic dissent throughout the eurozone. Many people were fed up with Brussels and the EU bureaucrats. In eight of the EU's 28 countries, insurgent and nationalist parties held prominent roles in government. In regards to the refugee crisis, many governments (Hungary and others) refuse to comply with EU plans for relocation of refugees throughout the eurozone. The revolt and populist uprising were building momentum awaiting a catalyst that would tip the scales.

THE CYPRUS AFFAIR: In March 2013, the tiny Mediterranean island nation of Cyprus became another casualty from the fallout of the 2008 meltdown. With its banking system collapsing and its government knee deep in debt, Cyprus was forced to request a bailout from the infamous Troika (the European Union (EU), European Central Bank (ECB) and the International Monetary Fund (IMF)). After some months of negotiations, a bailout deal was presented to the Cypriot government that shocked many people around the world. In what became known as a "bail-in," nearly 6 billion euro of bank depositor money was confiscated as part of the roughly 16 billion euro bailout plan. The bulk of the losses were focused on bondholders and large bank account holders with more than 100,000 euros in their accounts. Reports indicated that nearly a third of all bank deposits in Cyprus were from non-eurozone countries, and much of that was believed to be offshore accounts held by Russian oligarchs and money launderers seeking to avoid taxes and finding ways of moving money to safe haven locations. However, the pain and misery experienced by the 1.1 million people of Cyprus was more pronounced and levied a more substantial burden on the bankrupt society. In the aftermath of this confiscation scheme, the unemployment rate soared, and real estate prices dropped 20 to 25 percent in value. Also, a ban was placed on check cashing, and stringent limits were placed on the amount of cash that could be taken out of the country (a move to prevent large-scale bank runs). And typical in most IMF and EU deals, demands were made for Cyprus to drastically shrink its banking sector, make significant budget cuts, privatize state assets and implement structural reforms. As a major banking institution in this crisis, Cyprus Popular Bank was ordered to be restructured, and all of its bondholders and bank account holders with more than 100,000 euros would ultimately experience significant losses, as confiscated financial resources were converted into equity shares of the failed institutions.

It was a raid on a nation's bank accounts and a robbery performed (in broad daylight with the robbers fully identified) for all the world to see. So if the EU plan was in part motivated by punishing tax dodgers and money launderers, it proved to be a case of overreach, having a more significant damaging impact on the average citizen of Cyprus. It was one of the worst financial decisions made at that time. And as we shall see, it would set the stage for additional versions of this model for future bailouts in other European countries. The Bank of Cyprus and Cyprus Popular Bank established the new European paradigm for bank "bail-ins."

ECB NEW BAIL-IN RULES: Starting in January of 2016, the ECB implemented bold new "bail-in" rules as part of its tools for dealing with bank bailouts. The principle new law is that no bank (in a bailout situation) would be entitled to receive public money until creditors representing at least 8 percent of the institution's liabilities have made contributions towards the rescue plan. The idea here is to make investors (not public money) pay a significant share of a rescue program. Thus, creditor investments in the bank, as well as uninsured depositors (accounts over 100,000 euros), would see the value of their holdings decreased as they are converted into shares in the bankrupt entity. In theory, the promise was that small investors would not be touched in this process.

Another interesting twist in this new European paradigm was that throughout the eurozone national authorities (in each eurozone country) would no longer be responsible for dealing with failed banking institutions; the administration of this task was transferred to a new entity known as the Single Resolution Mechanism.

GERMANY

In the center of the European Union, and at the very core of its existence, sits the powerhouse Germany. It is the most durable economic power in Europe and is in a unique position to orchestrate and complete the grand EU design started over 65 years ago. In short, Germany leads the EU and is the reluctant leader of the EU project. Its dominance will continue to increase throughout the eurozone. However, it's also expected that an anti-German fervor will increase as populist movements continue to grow in strength and widespread popularity.

Germany is the fourth largest economy in the world and a major global exporter. It is Europe's largest economy and third largest exporter to the G-20. In fact, half of Germany's GDP is derived from its exports, with roughly half of its export business conducted in Europe and the other half in the rest of the world.

Given that global demand for goods and services are decelerating, German reliance on strong export markets will ultimately be derailed. This entrenched stagnation in the global economy has witnessed exporters experiencing significant declines, particularly in the oil industry. As of mid-2017, analysts were predicting that Germany would eventually experience major reductions in its GDP and massive export contractions as the global economy continued to weaken.

And similar to Japan, Germany's aging population will continue to play a role in bringing about a slow growth economy. It is also a trend that will impact most of the developed nations in Europe, as structural imbalances and over-capacity remain systemic and deflationary.

As the largest bank in Germany with over $2 trillion (1.8 trillion euros) in assets, a deepening financial crisis at Deutsche Bank (DB) raised further concerns about the stability of Germany's financial institutions. It's a mega-bank with a major global presence, particularly in the EU and the United States.

The public announcement that Deutsche Bank was suffering significant financial and economic losses had many analysts and observers drawing comparisons with Lehman Brothers of 2008, notably as observations declared that the bank had $47 trillion in notional derivatives exposure at the end of 2015. Would this be the next major global financial institution that would constitute the defining moment of our next major crisis? The numbers looked gruesome when observing the collapse of the bank's share price. From its peak in July 2015, to roughly 14 months later, the value of the shares had fallen 65 percent. Hence, the market value of the firm had descended from $50 billion to $16 billion. Net revenues took a beating during the first half of 2016, falling 21 percent. Also, a $14 billion settlement (over the investigation of the bank's sales of mortgage-backed securities) with the U.S. Justice Department was still to be negotiated and restructured to a more favorable outcome.

At the end of the day, like the banking crisis in Italy, there may be a rescue for DB. The ECB will step in with whatever is required to backstop DB.

EUROPEAN CENTRAL BANK (ECB)

The European Central Bank (ECB) has sole responsibility for monetary policy. It is a mandate and a precondition of the creation of the monetary union. The 19-nation eurozone is under a common monetary policy but does not share in the same fiscal policies; each nation manages its own taxing and spending programs, and there are major differences in how each eurozone nation conducts its fiscal plan. That is one of the primary structural defects in the ECB system: healthier better-managed economies are paying for the shortcomings and failures of weaker poorly managed economic systems.

Initially, the ECB did not have similar powers as the Fed in the U.S.: it did not have the authority, the license, or the independence to quickly inject itself in the markets the way the Fed did. As of late 2011, the ECB had not been authorized to issue so-called euro bonds. In fact, Chancellor Angela Merkel made it clear that Europe was "a long way from euro bonds" and that they are "extraordinarily inappropriate." She also indicated that the EU treaty barred the central bank from a role as the lender of last resort. The new ECB president, Mario Draghi, was also opposed to the ECB as lender of last resort and felt that central bank bond buying was inflationary. Germany was firmly against the idea of joint debt issuance of bonds (the euro bond) mainly because it feared that spendthrift nations still did not have the fiscal discipline to participate in this type of offering. Also, German Economic Minister Philipp Roesler stated that the ECB did not have unlimited firepower. The Germans were very cautious about opening wide the spigot for bailout operations which they doubt would be useful in the long run. However, the ECB did participate in the secondary bond markets and was a major purchaser of Spanish and Italian bonds on the open market during the second half of 2011 in a drive to keep borrowing costs down for those nations.

Despite the almost unanimous German opposition to euro bonds, the European Commission presented a study that showed that joint euro bonds are the way to stabilize debt markets. To many analysts observing this unfolding economic drama, to avoid contagion, there would need to be some level of intervention by a central bank. Indeed, there was a chorus of pundits and global institutional investors calling for more intervention by the ECB.

Thus, initially, the ECB could not print money, buy assets from European Union nations and issue euro bonds as defense or rescue measures in the event of extreme market madness. But some observers and analysts believed that in an extraordinary situation, like in the case of Italy needing a bailout, the ECB would have been given temporary powers to print money and monetize debt. Italy was a country that was viewed as too big to bail, and it could not be allowed to collapse or default on its sovereign debt. A sudden collapse in Italy would have torpedoed many large banks in Germany and France. In the over-leveraged global banking system, many institutions could be swallowed in a rapidly moving massive debt implosion.

OFFICIAL QUANTITATIVE EASING

Driven by events, policies and economic Q.E. strategies implemented by other major central bankers around the world (the Fed, BOJ, BOE, etc.), the ECB was forced to reconsider its stance on Quantitative Easing (QE) and public bond purchases. In June and September of 2014, the ECB executed limited versions of QE in response to the external risks to the eurozone. Also, the global struggle against deflation began to intensify in 2014, with falling oil prices taking the air out of global inflation. Like the developed economies in the U.S. and Japan, the eurozone had established the goal of a 2 percent inflation rate as part of its overall economic recovery plan. But, by December 2014, the inflation rate in the EU had fallen to minus 0.2 percent, and this was a clear sign that a new strategic direction was required. The fear that deflation would establish a firm grip on the eurozone (similar to the Japanese crisis) was real and had to be prevented at all costs.

Thus, in January 2015, the ECB made the formal introduction of a 1.1 trillion euro QE program for the eurozone, aiming to achieve price stability, expand the scope of asset purchases to public sector bonds, generate long-term competitiveness for the European economy, and stimulate some measure of structural reforms. The first phase of the operation covered the period from March 2015 to September 2016, with the ECB allocating 60 billion euros per month towards the purchase of private bonds, agency bonds, and member state treasury bonds. If and when the eurozone inflation rate reached 2 percent, the QE operation would be halted. Similar to the BOJ in Japan, the primary focus of this QE project was the struggle against deflation. In addition to QE, negative interest rates (the ECB's key rate was -0.4 percent) and other measures were employed to combat the economic distress of deflation and slow economic growth.

In this dramatic move, the ECB (and by extension, Germany) had joined the global party in collectively printing trillions of dollars in new currencies. It represented the beginning of a series of "money printing press parties!" Either by design or economic necessity, the ECB had become the eurozone's de-facto lender-of-last-resort. However, German Finance Minister Wolfgang Schaeuble was clear in his warning to the ECB architects, that the proposition of using low-interest rates to stimulate an economic recovery could be a trap similar to a "drug addiction." Projections presented by Standard & Poor's indicated that under QE a eurozone recovery would require over 2.4 trillion euros and at least three years to resolve their problems.

The ECB became active in the purchase of government bonds and was also considering the purchase of corporate bonds as part of its stimulus plans.

Over the next two to three years, the ECB followed a path similar to the Fed in implementing its QE programs, beginning at a lower purchase amount and adjusting the monthly purchase amounts higher as market conditions and global events demanded. From March of 2015 to March of 2016, the average monthly purchase allocations were 60 billion euros. Then in April 2016, the average monthly allocation increased to 80 billion euros, and that continued until March 2017. In December 2016, ECB President Mario Draghi announced that the QE program would be continued beyond March 2017 and extend to December 2017 at a reduced pace of 60 billion euros.

QE IS DEBT CANCELLATION: By introducing and injecting the full power of QE into the EU crisis, the ECB was able to effectively cancel 1.3 trillion euros of all European government debt during its first round of QE. As stated elsewhere in this publication, similar debt cancellations were implemented in the U.S., Japan, and the U.K. When a central bank buys government bonds, it effectively cancels those bonds, so long as it never sells them and so long as it rolls them over when they mature (as all central banks do as part of their protocol). What happens is that the government pays interest on its bonds to the central bank and then the central bank returns to the government the profits (less expenses) it earns from that interest income. When the bonds mature and are replaced with a new issue, they have, in effect, been canceled. Richard Duncan reminds us that:

"The ECB is not the only central bank cancelling government debt through Quantitative Easing. The Fed has cancelled $2.5 trillion or 13% of all US government debt. The Bank of England (BOE) has canceled 375 billion pounds or 23% of all UK government debt. And, the Bank of Japan has cancelled Yen 345 trillion or 32% of all Japanese government debt."[3]

Quantitative Easing produces a wealth effect in the developed world as well as creates the opportunity to cancel the equivalent of trillions of dollars of governmental debt. With less debt outstanding, governments in the eurozone (and elsewhere) were placed in a position to borrow and spend more to create jobs, generate economic growth and restructure their economies. What has been off-setting the massive money printing by central bankers in the West, are the critical factors of *globalization and the marginal cost of labor*. Globalization is deflationary, and this prevented high levels of inflation from taking root in the developed world.

EUROZONE DILEMMA

The European sovereign debt crisis is a quagmire of toxic waste, CDS contracts, derivatives, broke governments, collapsing banks and over-indebted entities. A conflagration is in the making that could engulf the entire world. Despite all of the concentrated efforts and documents that were published on this crisis, many analysts think that the euro and the eurozone are doomed.

A stark choice may be that the EU needs to forge deeper macroeconomic integration or risk a total collapse: the eurozone may not last much longer without such a remedy. What has emerged is whether the EU can continue its march towards the grand vision for an economic and political union; will the EU continue to integrate and forge a federal system or disintegrate and collapse? On top of all this is the specter of a demise of the euro igniting an era of chaos, civil war or worse.

With some countries feeling that joining the eurozone was a big mistake and feeling trapped in the euro, discussions have been held suggesting the formation of a new core of eurozone countries that could save the euro; a group of countries that are more committed and economically capable of living within the guidelines of the treaty. Finding a solution to allow a nation to leave the eurozone without grave economic and financial ramifications is a challenge and will require a much longer time frame to arrive at a solution: a creation of a plan and strategy to orchestrate a controlled default of an insolvent government.

For any country to suddenly attempt to quit the euro and the eurozone would create massive problems for the global economy and that is the central dilemma of this crisis.

The economic plight has also brought to the surface design flaws in the EU organization plan that sought to join together incompatible economies in a system that has faltered under the strain of opposing economic systems. On the one hand, you have nations that have overspent and over-borrowed without limit which created an opportunity for abuse. On the other hand, some governments have walked the line and followed the discipline laid out in the treaty, and they have been forced to bail out the weaker economies to prevent contagion. What follows is harsh austerity programs in the weaker member states and resentment on all sides. For most of these nations (Greece, Portugal, and Spain) austerity programs did more harm than good, driving them to the point of economic life support status (bailouts to survive).

When the economic paralysis begins in an uncompetitive country, the course of events is similar; a cycle is set in motion. As a debt expansion swells to a point where credit dries up; a credit crunch leads to a slowing economy and decreased consumption and businesses begin to fail. Banking and other financial institutions will then start to make credit more difficult to acquire to avoid bad credit risks. With less economic activity comes less tax revenues for governments, making it harder to service debt. This set of circumstances leads to huge budget deficits as governments have to borrow more money to continue to function. A debt ceiling is reached, and a government is either forced into bankruptcy and default or a bailout scenario.

In the grand scheme of things, the entire global economy runs on credit. When there is a significant bursting of a debt bubble, things can go completely haywire very fast with bank runs, derivatives unwinding, CDS contract payouts, global money markets freezing up, interbank lending dries up, private and public defaults, and social and political instability. The sovereign debt would be dumped like toxic waste matter, and investors will fly to whatever is perceived as safe investment havens (precious metals, fire sale real estate deals, cash, and other hard assets). In the case of the eurozone, a scenario like this could quickly lead to dissent and a loss of belief in the European Union. Without a quick recovery mechanism, the economic system would grind to a halt, and with it, much of the global economy: dominoes (weak economic and financial entities) will fall all across the globe.

The disintegration of the European Union is something that major global central bankers will struggle to the bitter end to keep from happening. We can be confident that this will be the likely scenario.

BREAKING UP IS HARD TO DO

It's impossible to predict what could ultimately be the economic trigger event that could bring about a euro collapse or massive eurozone crisis. With so much at stake, it is reasonable to assume that the power brokers of the world will do everything within their power to prevent the collapse of the euro. Versus 2008, Europe of 2012 became the epicenter of the global debt crisis with enormous potential for a global meltdown. In 2018 (six years later), the situation had evolved to something far greater.

ECONOMIST OTMAR ISSING: Otmar Issing, an economist who designed the monetary policy of the ECB and is considered by many people to be the father of the euro, began presenting a rather bleak future outlook for the currency. In an interview with Central Banking in October of 2016, Issing tells us that:

> "It will be a case of muddling through, struggling from one crisis to the next one. It is difficult to forecast how long this will continue for, but it cannot go on endlessly. Governments will pile up more debt - and then one day, the house of cards will collapse."[4]

As a leading German economist, Issing was recruited by the EU in 1998 to work on the bold currency project. He knew that such an enterprise would be imperfect. However, it was what everyone wanted at the time, and it was an exciting challenge for a man of his economic skills and abilities. As stated earlier, the use of a common currency was considered a prerequisite for a political union that would take shape at a later time in history. No EU authority was superimposed on the national sovereignty of each nation's fiscal policy; they would only be required to share a common monetary authority under the control and direction of the ECB. And according to Issing, "there is no likelihood of political union in the near future."

In regards to the initial Greek bailouts, Issing reminds us that:

> "What initially took place was that a bail-out occurred that saved the banking system - and mainly stopped French and German banks from incurring losses in Greek bonds. It created a situation with all the wrong incentives. It would have been better to demonstrate a country could leave the euro and rejoin from a much stronger position later. Such an event would have clarified that being a member of the 'euro club' can only come by meeting the club's economic rules. But this opportunity was missed."[5]

According to Issing, the "euro project is unworkable in its current form." The superstate envisioned in Brussels of a "United States of Europe" is something that is unlikely to happen. In 2012, he said the euro could be safe if weak countries like Greece left the EU. In 2017, he was less hopeful about the currency's future.

Issing is well aware that exiting from QE is problematic and will most likely require a globally coordinated effort by the world's major central bankers. Unlike the U.S., the EU's QE exit will be more complicated and problematic.

JOSEPH E. STIGLITZ: Nobel Prize-winning economist Joseph E. Stiglitz came to a conclusion in his book, *The Euro: How a Common Currency Threatens the Future of Europe* (August 2016), that the euro has created a systemic problem for the nations that are tied to it. With significant flaws at birth, the euro was expected to bring the countries of Europe closer together and generate prosperity, but as Stiglitz has observed, the currency has not lived up to this promise. The vast socio-economic differences between the various countries have prevented the euro's effectiveness in accommodating the genuine economic needs and financial requirements of the different European nations. According to Stiglitz, the currency does more to promote divergence rather than convergence, which leads to the development of a series of intractable problems.

In his words, "The 2008 global financial crisis morphed seamlessly into the 2010 euro crisis." He postulates that the euro (in its current form and use) is more of a problem than a solution. He is advocating for a more flexible currency that would allow each participating country to "adopt its own version of the currency." From Stiglitz's perspective, the stringent requirements imposed by the euro on the 19 member nations is the basis for an unhappy marriage. He tells us that:

> "There is a simple answer to this apparent puzzle: a fatal decision, in 1992, to adopt a single currency without providing for the institutions that would make it work. Good currency arrangements cannot ensure prosperity, but flawed currency arrangements can lead to recessions and depressions. And among the kinds of currency arrangements that have long been associated with recessions and depressions are currency pegs, where the value of one country's currency is fixed relative to another or relative to a commodity."[6]

His analogy in this analysis is the gold standard. He compares the euro's inflexible requirements and standards to those imposed on nations that were once tied to the gold standard. His verdict is that *the gold standard didn't work and neither will the euro standard*. To Stiglitz, the euro is a straightjacket that impedes the adjustments in pricing and productivity between and among member nations. It is a big problem, and it is not going away.

For the 19 nations that have had an intimate connection with the euro, many are now voicing grave concerns about the euro's place as a transformative agency in Europe as well as its status in the global economy. A sound economic theory is suggesting that economically and politically similar states or areas work best under a common currency. Given that a *United States of Europe* is unlikely during this current era, it is reasonable to assume that the euro is not likely to survive in its current iteration.

In the event of an EU collapse, each nation would return to their previous currency before 1999. The euro could descend to the 50 cents to 70 cent range in the $4 trillion (daily trading volume) global currency market. Major currency traders will not hesitate in bringing about a rapid decline in the value of the euro; it would represent a prime opportunity to benefit from its collapse. No one should underestimate this process, when blood is in the streets, the jackals, hyenas, vultures, and lions will come for the kill, and the euro will be the feast!

Like an earthquake, this is something that is very likely to happen without warning. A sudden collapse would most likely be followed by a declaration of a European bank holiday to slow the rapid pace of events. History tells us that in 1933, President Roosevelt declared a bank holiday for an entire week, during which time his administration made preparations to pass new legislation, the Emergency Banking Act. The Federal Reserve System also took that valuable time to recapitalize the banks with fresh currency. A similar thing happened after 911, a bank holiday was declared, along with the closure of the stock markets. Thus, one scenario envisions a declaration of a bank holiday with a period of one to two weeks of enormous chaos in the markets while governments, banks, and global central bankers coordinate a recovery effort. In the end, there will probably be massive reforms, sovereign debt defaults, and bankruptcies. And let us not forget the possible introduction of some form of a global digital currency as a replacement for the euro, the dollar or both. We can rest assure that the global elites are working on some new and creative economic plans that will bring about a new era in the event of the collapse of the euro.

So, it is wise to hope for the best, but it is also wise to make preparations for what may become a nightmare scenario of global economic proportion. It is better to be prepared and not have something happen than to be unprepared in the face of a sudden financial time bomb that was triggered by some small out-of-the-blue issue.

SUMMARY/ANALYSIS

Europe never really recovered from the *Great Recession and Meltdown of 2008*; major economic problems were never fully resolved, only managed to prevent systemic collapse and contagion. Moreover, much of the eurozone remained in a depression since the start of the financial crisis. What is interesting in this observation is that the United States was able to achieve a measure of economic recovery, cutting its unemployment rate (at the start of the financial crisis) from roughly 10% to less than 5% seven to eight years later. In many EU nations, unemployment soared into double-digits and stayed there during the same period.

The EU will not survive if significant structural, political and economic changes are not made. The fundamental flaws in the EMU's design are searching for a remedy that accommodates its main participants. Countries with different economic needs and various fiscal policies are desperately struggling under the one currency euro policy. Under the existing regime, there is a more than 90 percent probability that the crisis will deepen. With widely divergent macroeconomic conditions (there is no centralized fiscal policy coordination); problems have merely multiplied after the *Meltdown of 2008*, the defining crisis that exposed the system's weaknesses.

A redesign of the euro monetary system could be the answer. Ideas of a flexible euro or the development of a two-tiered system seem viable and worthy of implementation. EU architects could consider a stronger version of the euro for the original six founding members (representing the core pillars of the EU) and a weaker or more flexible euro version for the less integrated peripheral nations. It would release a lot of tension and friction in the monetary system and provide for better coordination of differing macroeconomic fiscal policies. This could save the union and decrease the need for various nations seeking to leave the EU.

The basic mission of this chapter was to provide a fundamental analysis of the unfolding nature of the eurozone crisis, and to that end, present a likely scenario of future developments. As a collective body of nations, bound by history, culture, and war, the European Union may be on the verge of collapse, and this would represent a much more massive event than the collapse of the Soviet Union in the early 1990s.

For over the past 500 years, Europe has been in the center of many global events and this now appears to be a historic finale, an apex from which the Europeans will either move to consolidate economic power and political will (a federal system of member states) or collapse and revert to nation states with a diminished influence in global affairs. This is what we are witnessing: the birth or collapse of a worldwide empire. After decades of planning and orchestration, the power brokers and architects in the background are trying to figure out how to make this thing work, how to consolidate this massive power base.

This analysis has tried to point out the various complications in this process, some glimmers of hope and the enormous risks that are tied into the super over-leveraged global economy. There are vast political, social, economic, financial and technological complications involved in this unfolding drama. Internal and external forces will drive the EU to the brink of further integration or disintegration. And out of this process will be forged a new global reality.

This chapter also considered the deep economic connections between the EU and the United States. Are the destinies of these economic powers intertwined in a way that a collapse in one power will lead to a direct or indirect decline in the other? In this current crisis, I would argue that there is room for divergence, given what we have witnessed since the 2008 meltdown. The U.S. management of the crisis and its use of Quantitative Easing stopped the decline into the abyss, which set the stage for a stock market and real estate recovery on its shores. However, the European Union had a different outcome, enduring greater economic declines in several nations, and didn't start the official use of QE until January 2015.

Since the late 1980s, the growth and development of the global economy has strengthened the connections and deepened the technological and financial ties of these two economic regions. And since the euro and the eurozone is under enormous pressure, the United States and the dollar has benefitted from the crisis, as investors seek safe havens in *less damaged economies*. International investors are continuing to buy (or park their money) in U.S. dollar-denominated assets (stocks, bonds, real estate, etc.).

A country managing its own currency could pursue competitive devaluation and increase demand for its exports (the Japanese strategy). Leaving the euro was the best case scenario for Greece, but not for the EU! The Troika made it nearly impossible for Greece to leave the euro during that fateful summer of 2015, given the option to either secure its freedom or face a devastating depression. A Grexit at that moment in history would have been an earth-shattering event, setting the stage for other disgruntled EU nations to follow a similar path.

With the official authority of the ECB (in January 2015) to print money and conduct QE operations throughout the eurozone, came the new reality of debt consolidation and cancellation by Europe's central bank. What had worked like a charm in America in the years following the 2008 meltdown, would now be the primary solution for the entire eurozone. The ECB would henceforth be in a position to bail out the Italian banking system if it reached that point. Under QE, this is entirely doable.

The EU architects came to a glaring realization that the breakup of the eurozone and currency block would be a "Lehman event" that would trigger an extraordinary economic crisis. In a region of the world that had been responsible for two global wars in the 20th century, it would be much better to continue holding the EU project together for as long as it is humanly possible. Creating the trading bloc had established peace and security in Europe for nearly 70 years, and no one wanted to disrupt that arrangement, not even the politicians that were campaigning to change the system.

NOTES

(1) Joseph Stiglitg, "the EURO: How A Common Currency Threatens The Future of Europe," W.W. Norton & Company, New York, 2017.
(2) EU Referendum, "Brexit 'most important moment since BerlinWall: Le Pen," BBC Newsnight, June 28, 2016.
(3) Richard Duncan, "Europeans , Rejoice! The ECB Is Cancelling Your Debt! Watch Free Video," Richard Duncan Economics in the Age of Fiat Money, March 2018.
(4) Christopher Jeffery, "Otmar Issing on why the euro 'house of cards' is set to collapse," *Central Banker*, October 12, 2016, (Goldcore Blog online article).
(5) IBID. Otmar Issing.
(6) Joseph E. Stiglitz, *The Euro: How a Common Currency Threatens the Future of Europe*, W.W. Norton & Company, August 16, 2016.

CHAPTER NINE
BREXIT

The force that turned Britain away from the European Union was the greatest mass migration since perhaps the Anglo-Saxon invasion. 630,000 foreign nationals settled in Britain in the single year 2015. Britain's population has grown from 57 million in 1990 to 65 million in 2015, despite a native birth rate that's now below replacement.

Nigel Farage, Leader of the
United Kingdom Independence Party (UKIP)

Brexit is a valuable history lesson that most economists, investors, and traders should find very instructive. It shook up the world but did not cause a Lehman-style meltdown. There was a huge expectation that the UK would remain in the EU.

On June 23, 2016, voters in the UK voted to leave the European Union, and in the midst of that momentous decision, the global economy was thrown into a state of shock, and for most analysts and observers, this was something completely unexpected. Many people didn't anticipate that the majority of Britons would - in fact - vote to leave the EU project.

Most investors expected Britain to remain in the EU, so the result was a devastating wake-up call. The markets reacted violently: within two days of the vote, more than $3 trillion of stock market values went up in smoke. The Dow fell nearly 1,000 points (a 5% decline in the average), and the London FTSE witnessed a drop of 10% on June 23rd, the day of the actual vote. The Dow futures fell almost 700 points on the morning of the vote. According to the *Bloomberg* Billionaires Index, in the massive sell-off, the world's 400 wealthiest investors lost a combined total of $127 billion the day after the historic vote. The two-day carnage went on record as the worst market downturn since the 2008 meltdown.

The following headline speaks to the daily carnage:

"Brexit aftershocks send global markets tumbling"

On Friday, June 24, 2016, the Dow fell 611.00 points, and the Nasdaq was down 202.06 points. Blood was running in the streets as investors were flocking to safe-haven investments (the U.S. dollar, gold, bonds and the yen). Britain's currency, the pound sterling, fell off a cliff, plunging 11% in the overnight trade, the most substantial one day drop in modern currency history: a collapse of nearly 17 U.S. cents. The battered currency was beaten down to its lowest level (in over three decades: since 1985) against the U.S. dollar. The day after the historic vote also witnessed the price of gold soaring by more than $85 an ounce and silver to almost $18.40 an ounce. Moody's, the U.S. rating agency, downgraded the UK's long-term debt from "stable" to "negative." Stocks of some of Europe's major banks took a terrible beating: Barclays, Royal Bank of Scotland, UBS Group, Credit Suisse, Deutsche Bank AG, etc.

REVOLT AGAINST THE ESTABLISHMENT AND THE EU

With more than 30 million people voting, when the results came in the breakdown was as follows: 48.1% (16,141,241) remain; 51.9% (17,410,742) exit. The majority of the lower, middle and working class UK citizens in most parts of England and Wales voted to leave the EU, while residents in London, Scotland and Northern Ireland voted to remain. In the former industrial hubs in the north, residents had suffered from imposed EU immigration policies, job losses and the growing wealth inequalities that had become a global phenomenon. The vote was primarily driven along class lines, with the upper-class elites and their supporters on one side, and the populace working-class groups on the other. The Brexit vote to leave the EU was a demand for change and a revolt against the establishment that favored the wealthy elites and the furtherance of EU domination.

The narrative quickly turned to whether the UK was the first domino to fall in what some EU watchers viewed as the beginning of the end of the European Union. Polls that were taken in France, the Netherlands and Italy revealed a 40% unfavorable rating regarding the euro and the EU. Populace sentiment throughout the EU was applauding the Brexit vote and considered it a victory. If nothing else, the Brexit vote represented a significant turning point in the ongoing EU crisis.

The politicians and the elites did their best to try to convince the Brexit voters that it would be in their best interest to remain in the EU. The threat that the markets or the economy would suffer under an exit vote did little to persuade them to support a pro-EU stance. The general sentiment was, "I don't care. It's already bad, and I'm ready to roll the dice." All the major power brokers joined in the chorus to keep Britain in the EU: European Union officials, the bankers and central bankers here and abroad, heads-of-states throughout the EU continent and overseas, academic scholars and the elites and various other promoters all pushing to maintain the status quo and keep the existing system intact. But for many voters the pain was deep, and the distrust in a global economic system that favored the wealthy elites and the well-connected had finally reached a boiling point. It would not be business as usual; Brexit was the turning point!

With EU officials in Brussels calling the shots on immigration, many Britons were feeling a loss of sovereignty and lack of control over the direction of the nation. The impact that EU dominated immigration policies were having on the working class was severe and detrimental. A sense of powerlessness dominated the narrative for those in favor of leaving the EU. Voters in the UK were fed up with immigration policies, too many regulations, gross economic inequality, and euro-skepticism was running high. For some people, it was a vote for independence, a vote to unveil the xenophobia linked to the refugee crisis, a vote to express the deep distrust of globalization, and a vote against extreme wealth inequality.

Far-right groups in other parts of Europe hailed the Brexit vote a major *victory* for all Europeans who were sick and tired of the EU and the euro. Anti-immigration and Right-wing parties in France, Slovakia, the Netherlands, Denmark, and Sweden were all announcing their goals of holding similar types of referendums in their nations.

Billionaire investor George Soros, economist Nouriel Roubini, and others began voicing their deep concerns that the abrupt UK divorce from the EU could lead to the collapse of the entire 28-nation project.

The original six EU members (Belgium, France, Germany, Italy, Luxembourg and the Netherlands) met on June 25th in Berlin to establish new plans and strategies for moving forward. After the historic vote, a major European Summit was held by the 27 remaining presidents, chancellors and prime ministers in the EU (19 of these nations use the euro) to affirm their commitments and a pledge to continue the unity affecting the lives of nearly 500 million people throughout the European heartland. Central to this unified union is the freed movement of people, goods, finances, and services. As the world's largest trading bloc, it's essential that the free flow of people, products, and capital remain intact for the pan-European project. In a show of unity and common interest, a joint statement by foreign ministers of Germany, France, the Netherlands, Luxembourg, and Belgium was presented after the historic vote:

> "We will continue in our efforts to work for a stronger and more cohesive European Union of 27 based on common values and the rule of law. It is to that end that we shall also recognize different levels of ambition amongst the Member States when it comes to the project of European integration. While not stepping back from what we have achieved, we have to find better ways of dealing with these different levels of ambi-

tion so as to ensure that Europe delivers better on the expectation of all European states..However, we are aware that discontent with the functioning of the EU as it is today is manifest in parts of societies. We take this very seriously and are determined to make the EU work better for all our citizens."[1]

BREXIT WAS NOT A LEHMAN EVENT

Even in the face of the initial brutal collapse, global central bankers (particularly in the U.S. and Europe) sat quietly on the sidelines observing the carnage without providing any interventions. They stood ready to intervene if it became necessary. However, the decision was to take no action. Damage control for the global economy was not required, for like Japan in their great crash of 1990, most of the economic wreckage was contained in Britain and did not spread like a major virus. Despite the fact that London is a major powerhouse in global financial markets, it was interesting that no systemic problems were constricting the monetary flow in credit markets.

Brexit was a massive problem that had the potential to undermine the global economy, but it didn't. The initial phase of the crisis was short-lived, with investors returning to the markets in a show of financial force to continue the bull market, at least in the United States, the flight capital region of the world. Fear that the EU would begin to fall apart after the departure vote in the UK quickly began to dissipate. Confidence was restored, and the blood in the street scenario ceased to exist. The atmosphere settled down, and investors regained their composure. Within less than a month after Brexit, global stocks recovered more than $4.5 trillion in market value, and the Dow and the S&P went on to hit new all-time highs.

The actual fallout from the Brexit vote will extend perhaps over a period of years, with a slow movement of events and issues that accumulate over time. There will be bumps and potential landmines in the road, but the march forward will continue.

The wholesale panic in global markets didn't last long; within three weeks the S&P 500 was setting new highs, fear in the markets had subsided. What this indicated was that the crisis was contained and that this was not a "Lehman Event." Some commentators suggested that there would be more referendums, and in some cases, exit referendums, and they were right.

BRITAIN IS NOT GREECE: No one could deny that the EU project had been beneficial for all Europeans and the world. The motto that, "nations that trade with each other are unlikely to go to war" is something that all Europeans have deeply appreciated since the end of World War II. Peace and security had been a blessing and was something that had to be maintained, particularly in the nuclear age and rapid advances in technologies.

No doubt, Brexit was bad news for the overall spirit of the EU and the euro, and for all of those who continued struggling to hold this project together. The British economy suffered a large negative shock. But Britain and the UK was not Greece in this economic episode; the island nation wields a great deal more economical and financial power in the global arena. The city of London (often called the *City*) is considered by many the major financial center of the world.

The loss of Britain as a member state was to witness an economic powerhouse leaving the union. The island nation was the EU's wealthiest financial market and a dominant global titan, economically and militarily. And since Britain didn't use the euro as its currency (the UK never seriously entertained the notion of giving up the pound), the damage to the euro was minimized.

FALLOUT AND LONG-TERM IMPLICATIONS OF BREXIT

The internal political and economic damage to Britain's economy would take time to work itself out. For instance, the political stance of Scotland requesting and voting to remain in the EU. Analysts immediately began predicting a new referendum in Scotland voting to declare independence from the UK. The UK will have to renegotiate its trading relationship with the EU, a process that was scheduled to extend over a minimum of two years. Within that period, the UK would still be a member of the EU.

The U.K. represents 18% of the EU's aggregate economy, second only to Germany. The UK walked into these negotiations with a strong stance given that this nation is the third largest export market for Germany and the fifth largest in Italy and France. Much of these trade relationships were in place before the advent of the EU. And the fact that British banking titans are major distribution financial arteries that are critical for continental Europe, suggest that what will transpire in these negotiations is an accommodative posture facilitating a smooth transition for the UK's exit to non-member status. The EU will be in no position to punish Britain for leaving the EU. Many of the elites in power will not benefit from a nasty divorce, and that alone assures a favorable outcome for all participating parties. There will most likely be no major disruptions in the trade relationship pipelines.

Since the UK is the first nation to request a formal exit from the EU, the reset of global investment channels will be tedious and complicated. However, the parties are expected find many areas for compromise and agreement to keep the markets flowing.

Britain's Prime Minister, David Cameron, began the process (in 2013) of promising a referendum vote to allow for a political dialogue on the EU issue. He then led an effort to persuade Britons to remain a part of the EU project and subsequently placing his political career on the line by promising to resign if the majority voted to leave the EU. After the voting results were revealed, Cameron went before the cameras and announced that he would resign by October 2016. Thus, David Cameron became another political casualty in the growing resentment against the Brussels' elites and EU mandates.

After Cameron stepped down, the new Prime Minister Theresa May, began the preparations for following through with the voter mandate. The next step in the EU timetable was the invoking of Article 50, which would give the EU formal notification of the UK's intentions to exit its membership in the trading bloc.

On Friday, March 29, 2017, Prime Minister Theresa May triggered the process of Article 50 of the Lisbon Treaty, starting the two-year process of negotiations. Her vision of the complex process is that it would yield new opportunities for the UK and that Brexit was going to be a success for UK nations.

The actual terms of Britain's exit will have to be agreed to by the remaining 27 member national parliaments, a process that may extend well beyond the two-year window. In the meantime, the UK will still be required to follow the EU mandates and abide by all of its laws and treaties until its membership is dissolved.

SUMMARY/ANALYSIS

In mid-2016, BREXIT shook up the world by doing the unthinkable. The majority of UK citizens voted to leave the EU project. The European Union absorbed the shock, but this was just the beginning. Brexit was a historical turning point for the EU project, the wake-up call announcing a change in thinking by a majority of people who have declared their independence. It was the sounding of an alarm that something had changed and that people were no longer willing to accept the status quo of EU domination. Brexit was a battle cry by the opposition, sent out into the world to rally the troops to take the struggle to the next level.

All across the European Union opposition leaders in various countries were embolden to move forward with their strategies and build stronger movements. Brexit proved that it was possible to oppose the elites in Brussels and chart a new direction. Indeed, this was the beginning of a new broad-based movement that will play out over a period of years and will grow stronger especially during the next global economic meltdown. Brexit was the start of an intellectual, political, social and economic revolution.

NOTES

(1) Jake Cordell, "EU referendum: Foreign ministers of EU's six founding members hold crisis meeting in Berlin to discuss Brexit response," City A.M., June 25, 2016.

CHAPTER TEN
PRESIDENT DONALD TRUMP AND THE REPUBLICANS: THE TURNING POINT

We've lost over a fairly short period of time, 60,000 factories in our country. Closed, shuttered, gone. 6 million jobs at least, gone. And now they are starting to come back...The word that I want to use is reciprocal when they charge 25% for a car to go in, and we charge 2% for their car to come into the United States, that's not good. That's how China rebuilt itself.

President Donald Trump

The reason for fearing that the U.S. economy will soon overheat is not simply that it is currently at or very close to full employment and growing at a healthy clip. It is rather that it is also now getting an extraordinary degree of monetary and fiscal policy stimulus at this very late stage of the cycle.

Desmond Lachman

On January 20, 2017, Donald Trump was sworn in as the 45th president of the United States. His ascension to power would also be the year of President Trump's economic honeymoon and *the quiet before the storm*. There was very little in the way of economic and stock market rumblings throughout that entire year: No collapse and no major downturns in U.S. markets. In fact, U.S. markets were unusually calm, which supported the thesis that U.S. markets were the global safe haven for flight capital from various parts of the world. The Dow Jones Industrial Average soared 25% in 2017 with great expectations for continued prosperity. In the year 2017 alone, the Dow closed at all-time highs more than 70 times. This was more record highs reached in any previous years in the history of the markets. In response to that stellar year, President Trump stated (on board Air Force One in early February 2018) that "The reason our stock market is so successful is because of me...I've always been great with money."[1]

However, we cannot dismiss the fact that after eight years of economic recovery promoted by the previous Obama Administration with the strong support of Fed QE policies set the stage for the smooth and orderly transition of power for the new Trump Administration. And we should recall that when former President Obama took office, the *Meltdown of 2008* was a raging inferno, raising hell all over the world. As stated earlier in the chapter on Obama, his administration had to hit the ground running with innovative solutions to stop the devastation of the rapidly escalating economic meltdown. The unemployment rate was at 10%, and Americans were losing 800,000 jobs monthly. At the end of Obama's eight years in office, the economy was in recovery mode.

The extraordinary election of Trump was part of the global backlash against establishment politics, in particular, traditional politicians and their supporters. There was also smothering anger in America regarding the wealthy billionaire class and the banking industry (the one percent) that were bailed out during the *Meltdown of 2008*, and resentment that the 99 percent (everyone else) receive little or no assistance. And it's a firm conviction of this publication that the Democrats fell short when it came to helping millions of people stay in their homes during the meltdown. When Obama took office, the Democrats had control of the Senate, the House of Representatives, and the White House. They had the power to have brought about a much more comprehensive solution to the mortgage crisis but failed to do so.

Thus, when the 2016 elections rolled around, millions of voters (many of whom lost their homes) wanted a different kind of change and were not interested in establishment politicians, either from *the left or the right*. It is my firm belief that if the Obama Administration, Congress, and the Fed had done more to have stopped millions of people from losing their homes, the Republicans would have lost the election in 2016, and certainly, a billionaire with Trump's demeanor would not have been elected president. Spending trillions of dollars bailing out the wealthy and spending far less on everyone else, was a *big mistake*. It set the stage for the Republicans to take control of the White House, the Senate and the House of Representatives, leaving the Democrats fighting for a voice in Congress and with a much more diminished power base.

So, as part of the backlash against establishment politics, the majority of Americans chose billionaire Donald Trump as an anti-establishment president. Even though he is a billionaire, and would ordinarily be considered part of the 1%, Donald Trump is not perceived to be part of the wealthy ruling elites and a proponent of globalism.

But I digress, this chapter was included in this book to bring clarity and objectivity to economic agendas and financial markets no matter which political party controls the White House. After all, the banking industry and Wall Street are so deeply entrenched in Washington D.C. that it doesn't matter which party is in power. The historical record is clear; both parties have accommodated the structural and financial policy objectives of the banking elites and Wall Street. However, it is fair to say that the billionaire power brokers generally get more leverage with the Republicans in office.

So, politics aside, let's take a look at the economic changes that took place within slightly less than two years of Republican power and policies. Also, as we shall see, after the Trump Administration honeymoon in 2017, things began to heat up in early 2018, setting the stage for extreme volatility and economic chaos. With the stock market as a leading indicator and a barometer of the economy, the stage was set in 2018 for the beginning reversal of the ten-year bull run.

THE BULL RUN CONTINUES: January 2018 started with the markets in strong upward momentum, with analysts predicting the possibility of another year of positive growth and smooth sailing. Some optimistic analysts stated that "The stock market is having its best start to a year in more than three decades." And based on this evidence, more gains were expected for the remainder of 2018. Big technology stocks had a banner year in 2017, with such companies as Apple, Microsoft and Facebook up nearly 40 percent. Jeff Bezos (CEO of Amazon.com) became the wealthiest person on the planet ($130 plus billion), as the stock price of Amazon, gained 24.1% at the start of the new year. Record highs for the markets were reached on January 26, 2018: the Dow Jones Industrial Average closed at 26,392.79; the Nasdaq Composite Index closed at 7,415.06, and the S&P 500 settled at 2,839.25. U.S. stock markets were soaring, and optimism was in the air. And by mid-July, Bloomberg's Billionaires Index announced that Jeff Bezos net worth had soared to north of $150 billion, making him the richest man in modern history. Inside of six months, his wealth had increased by roughly $25 billion!

FLASH CRASH OF 2018: Extreme volatility characterized stock market action during February 2018. On Friday, February 2nd, the Dow Jones Industrial Average (the Dow) fell 666 points which was a shock to many investors and completely unexpected. Analysts cited the fear of rising inflation, bond market yields (the ten-year Treasury yield reached a four-year high of 2.85%), wage growth (with a 2.9 percent growth in 2017), rising interest rates (courtesy of the Fed), huge tax cuts, (courtesy of the Republicans), worries about the confrontation between the Trump Administration and the FBI, and the belief that the market was due for a correction. Investors absorbed the analytical commentary over the weekend, and on Monday all hell broke loose.

On Monday, February 5th, the Dow suffered its worst single-day drop in history, falling by almost 1600 points (a decline of 1,597 points) before recovering to close down 1,175 points for the session. It was a flash crash orchestrated by the above key concerns, driven by fear and the rapid speed of program trading. At that point, many people started thinking that the bull run was over. On a global scale, from the record high in January to the flash crash in February, global markets had lost $5.2 trillion. Fear and uncertainty became the dominant psychology of many investors.

The February 5th rollercoaster week was full of fear and greed. On Tuesday, February 6th, the Dow fell 567 points, and on Wednesday the markets calmed down a little, with the Dow falling 19 points. But on Thursday, February 8th, the downward action resumed with the Dow falling a whopping 1,033 points. Friday, February 9th, witnessed another very volatile day, with the Dow falling 500 points, and then rising 500 points to end the session up 330 points. For some analysts, these extreme moments of volatility in the markets were expected to continue periodically for the remainder of 2018, driven by a host of issues converging on the massive superbubble in stocks and other asset prices. *The 2018 Flash Crash* was a "threatening sign" and warning of things to come!

TRUMP AND THE REPUBLICAN TAX CUT

In December 2017, Trump and the Republicans approved a new bill for a massive tax cut, the first significant tax cut and overhaul of the system in 30 years. Overall, the primary focus was on the reduction of tax rates for corporations and business owners: the corporate tax rate was cut from 35% to 21%. The implementation of this tax cut coming at the tail end of a boom period had more to do with keeping a political promise than adding something substantial to the economic recovery. With the economy already in recovery mode, corporations experiencing strong earnings, an unemployment rate at or below 4 percent, and the inequality factor completely out of synch with capitalistic normalization, this tax cut was doomed to create greater imbalances throughout the economic system. Arguably, from a historical perspective, this could very likely be one of the key factors helping to ignite the next global economic crisis.

Similar to the Bush tax cuts in 2001 and 2003 (the *Meltdown of 2008* followed that episode), expected tax revenues would be reduced requiring the Treasury Department to issue a lot more debt to cover the shortfall. President Bush inherited a budget surplus, from the Clinton Administration, and it was squandered. Due to the Dot-Com bubble economy of the late 1990s, the Clinton Administration had budget surpluses in 1999, 2000 and 2001. For the fiscal year 1999, the budget surplus was $1.9 billion, while the fiscal year 2000 (the year of the crash) witnessed a budget surplus of $86.4 billion.[2] The Bush tax cuts, along with financing two wars played a significant role in helping to initiate the *Meltdown of 2008* and the $1 trillion yearly deficits that followed in its aftermath. Should we expect anything different this time around? I don't think so.

The federal budget deficit would increase from the level of $666 billion in 2017 to nearly $1 trillion in 2018. Analysts were predicting that we would probably experience $1 trillion (plus) deficits for several years.

These tax cuts were ill-timed and simply created another factor that would help to burst the superbubble in global asset prices. Trickle-down economics is ingrained in the Republican DNA, with many of their leaders confident that their supply-side tax cut policies can be successful in any economic season (there should always be some recognition of the current stage of business or economic cycles before adopting tax cuts).

Let us take a moment to consider the case of "Boom and Bust Cycles." It would probably be much more beneficial to apply a tax cut (in conjunction with the Fed reducing tax rates) during the inferno of a bust cycle. It makes better economic sense to save this fiscal tool for when the economy needs it. And considering all of the critical issues raised in this publication, adopting an inappropriate policy or pursuing the wrong economic goals will (in the end) prove to be fatal.

When an economy is in recovery mode, and the unemployment rate is low (below five percent), tax cuts are simply not required to improve the economic performance. It is a blatant waste of resources and, in this late stage of a bull run, will only create excessive funding for the wealthy (one analyst called it "a useless giveaway to the rich") and exacerbate the problem of wealth inequality in American society. Writer and analyst, Dion Rabouin, wondered "was it a good idea to hit the accelerator when the economy was already at the speed limit?" The 2017 tax cuts was a monetary drug that would generate a temporary high, then fade away when a massive crisis hits the economy. Economist Richard Duncan puts it this way:

> "The combination of tax cuts and increased government spending - on top of Quantitative Tightening - is set to drain $3 trillion out of the financial markets over the next three years. The United States has never had to endure a Liquidity Drain anywhere near that size before. It's likely to drive interest rates much higher and the price of stocks, property, and commodities (including gold) much lower."[3]

The Chinese credit rating agency, Dagong, voiced its displeasure with the Republican tax cuts by downgrading its U.S. sovereign rating from A- to BBB+. Their main concern was that the U.S. tax cuts would "directly reduce the federal government's sources of debt repayment." Dagong also warned that "The virtual solvency of the federal government would be likely to become the detonator of the next financial crisis."[4]

The reality on Capitol Hill is that when a particular political party is in power, especially when that party controls the White House and Congress, that is the time to fulfill as much of their agenda as possible regardless of any economic conditions that are prevailing at the time and are not perceived as fatal. For the most part, politicians will concentrate on getting as many of their main programs implemented as quickly as possible while they still have the power. For the Republican Party, this means tax cuts for the wealthy and deregulations across the board. By August 2018, Trump and the Republicans began to unveil its plans for a second tax cut (a capital gains taxation cut for the wealthy) of roughly $100 billion. It appears that two major tax cuts was required to complete the Republican agenda.

TRUMP'S TARIFF WAR WITH CHINA AND OTHER NATIONS

On March 22, 2018, President Trump declared that the U.S. would be placing tariffs on $100 billion on steel and aluminum imports from China and lesser amounts on other foreign countries in the belief that this would "safeguard American jobs." As of 2018, China had a $375 billion trade surplus with the U.S. and was also a major purchaser of U.S. Treasuries. Response from the markets was not favorable. On the day of the announcement, the Dow fell 589 points (at the worst point in the day) ending the session down 420 points. On Friday, March 23rd, with fear and tension continuing to spread, the Dow fell 572.46 points, closing at 23,932.76. The markets were spooked with added uncertainty regarding global trade issues with the second largest economy in the world.

No doubt, in the loss of jobs, industries, and businesses, the U.S. has been on the losing end in its trade relations with China. After decades of globalization and global corporate policies strongly supporting this new era, initiating a tariff war in the name of protecting American jobs was viewed by many analysts as an ineffective strategy doomed to fail.

In support of his stance; Trump stated that "Our Steel and Aluminum industries (and many others) have been decimated by decades of unfair trade and bad policy with countries from around the world...We must not let our country, companies, and workers be taken advantage of any longer. We want free, fair and smart trade."[5] Chinese Minister of Commerce Zhong Shan confirmed that China didn't want a trade war, but warned that "There are no winners in a trade war...It will only bring disaster to China and the United States and the world."

In the age of "Globalization," protectionism (particularly by the largest economy in the world) is extremely dangerous and could easily ignite worldwide trade wars. It brings to mind the most famous tariff act of the 20th century: the Smoot-Hawley Tariff Act of 1930. Often cited as one of the main causes of the Great Depression of the 1930s, this act was signed into law by President Herbert Hoover on June 17, 1930, setting off a tidal wave of unintended consequences. As mentioned in Chapter Four, "1,028 American economists urged President Hoover to veto the bill, but he refused." What followed was a chain reaction of retaliation by various nations throughout the world.

There are some important lessons that we must learn from the last most severe tariff act that took place in American history nearly 90 years ago. Senator Reed Smoot and Representative Willis C. Hawley introduced this legislation with the expressed intention of protecting American jobs, farmers, and the agricultural industry. More than 20,000 imported goods were targeted for increased tariffs, and the impact on the rest of the world was severe. The ripple effect through several industries was profound, moving swiftly throughout international commerce resulting in a complete breakdown in world trade.

History tells us that by mid-1932 (two years after the bill passed), imports to the United States had decreased by 40 percent. Exports followed a similar path, moving from a high of $7 billion in 1929 to $2.4 billion by 1932.

The United States abdicated its leadership in the free world; no one was in charge, and each nation had to pursue a course of action for continued survival. And foreign retaliation was a major contributor to accelerating the downward spiral.

On June 16, 1930 (the day President Hoover signed the bill), the stock market witnessed a loss of over $1 billion, which was a vast amount of wealth at that time. The export market for U.S. made automobiles fell by roughly 82 percent on an annual basis, from a high of $541 million in 1929 to $97 million by 1933. There were major bank failures throughout the entire world, and much of this had to do with the breakdown in international trade; there was a significant connection between the severe decline in global trade and the international monetary system collapse.

What we learn from this history lesson is that when the United States initiated its protectionist policies in 1930, this led to angry retaliation from all of its trading partners which ultimately caused the disintegration of world trade. The potential for a replay of that set of events is possible, given the fragile nature and superbubble conditions of the global economy in 2018.

Nobel prize-winning economist Robert Shiller was concerned that the growing trade tensions could spark a global crisis. His remarks regarding the Smoot-Hawley Act provides a valuable history lesson on business expectations and uncertainty:

> "When you ask about the size of the impact on the economy, I think a lot of it is more psychological than direct, unless they really slam on tariffs...the greatest economic damage could be caused by firms adjusting their investment behavior rather than the new tariffs themselves."[6]

As part of his election pledge to bring back blue collar jobs and American manufacturing industries, Trump was drawing a line in the sand with China with the hope of making radical changes in their trade relationship. But it is very unlikely that imposing new tariffs on steel and aluminum would bring back a significant number of jobs for those industries. What Trump was attempting to do is something that should've been done decades ago when American corporations began relocating to other parts of the world to take advantage of cheaper labor costs and lower operating expenses.

The sad reality is that a trade war would ultimately increase the prices of consumer goods to American consumers. As tariffs increase the price of finished products and commodities, end-stage manufacturing producers will pass the increases on to the buyer. Prices will rise for consumers. It will essentially be an added tax on these products that will ultimately lead to a temporary spike of inflation and other unintended consequences. With the increasing prices of imported goods, Americans would be expected to purchase more affordable American made products, which in turn, would generate more American jobs. This strategy at the macro level will most likely not produce the intended results; the net result will witness more American jobs being lost than created. In a report published by economists at Trade Partnership Worldwide (an economic consulting firm in Washington D.C.), the analysis is clear on the impact on American consumers and their subsequent behavior. The economic complexity begins to reveal itself as a ripple effect that reverberates throughout the general economy:

> "...consumers reduce spending when they are hit by higher costs (of a new car, a new washing machine, etc.) and, for many, lost wages from unemployment. As a result, households pull back on spending; services like education, entertainment, and even healthcare are on the front lines of the spending reduction impacts, with additional attendant job losses."[7]

This thoughtful report also brings to the surface what the potential job numbers would look like with the implementation of tariffs and the resulting retaliation from U.S. trading partners. The findings of this group of economists are significant:

> "The tariffs, quotas, and retaliation would increase the annual level of U.S. steel employment and non-ferrous metals (primarily aluminum) employment by 26,280 jobs over the first one-three years, but reduce net employment by 432,747 jobs throughout the rest of the economy, for a total net loss of 400,445 jobs."[8]

According to their analysis, every state would experience a net loss of jobs with more than two-thirds of the impact hitting workers in the low-skill and production areas. The bottom line, for every steel/aluminum job that is gained due to the new tariffs, sixteen jobs would be lost in other fields. And we can safely assume that this economic scenario (at some level of similar dynamics) would repeat itself in other sectors of the economy where tariffs would be applied. In a trade war, the main losers (on both sides of the conflict) are the workers and consumers, which ultimately leads to a failed economy.

In response to Trump's initial threats to impose tariffs, China threatened to impose tariffs of 25% on 106 American products including soybeans airplanes and autos. In response to China's plans for retaliation, Trump informed the U.S. Trade Representative to begin thinking of adding $100 billion of additional tariffs against China. Shortly after that, the Trump Administration began contemplating across the board 25% tariffs on automobiles that were not only being imported from China, but also from other trading partners.

Concerns from Canada, Mexico, Japan and the EU sounded the alarm that the U.S. was starting to drift into dangerous territory advocating its protectionist policies beyond reason. In addition to China, the Trump administration was also actively pursuing policies to make adjustments to The North American Free Trade Agreement (NAFTA). A major threat to the global economy was perceived especially if many U.S. trading partners began implementing retaliatory tariffs.

TRUMPONOMICS AND THE "AMERICA FIRST" AGENDA

The globalists had spent decades setting up and implementing structural initiatives to establish the pervasive reality of globalization. With the support of innovative technologies, the Internet revolution, the robotic and AI revolution, and billions of people around the world willing to work for $5 to $10 per day, this globalization trend and movement will not be derailed by one country in the world trying to reverse the mandates of the overall system. As stated elsewhere in this publication, the American worker (as well as every other worker in developed economies around the world) is exposed to the internationalization of wage competition of the developing nations on the planet.

The reality is that this global labor force has a global reach across borders and is the main source of the deflationary forces driving down the prices for products and services, a system that was implemented by multinational corporations and advanced technologies over a period of several decades.

Globalization and vastly improved technological advances (in production facilities), has been responsible for providing the opportunity for central bankers in Western economies and Japan to print trillions of dollars and not generate hyperinflation. What the United States and other developed economies need to do is to capitalize or benefit from these (once in a lifetime) global arrangements (See Chapter Sixteen). This is an extremely important factor and could provide a much needed to solution to this global dilemma. What is clear, is that the strategy chosen by Trumponomics (in the long run) is doomed to fail.

If we continue on this path of promoting the development of trade wars, it will only add more fuel to a fire that will cause the massive implosion of global asset superbubbles in this current environment. What Trumponomics is attempting to do for the American worker and manufacturer might seem noble, supportive, and even patriotic, but it's five to six decades too late and will bring about unintended consequences. This tariff dispute is like asking the American people to go back to using the eight-track tape in the digital age or we should all start watching black and white TV in the age of color, high-definition and flat screens. The trend and trajectory that we are on cannot be changed, but it can be modified. However, imposing heavy-handed tariffs on the entire world *is not the way*. There are no direct and simple solutions to this problem (implement tariffs), it is a much more complex situation. Trying to roll back decades of globalism with the stroke of a pen is fantasy.

In mid-April 2018, China unveiled its master plan for becoming a major technology power in the 21st century: "Made in China 2025"[9]. Stating that it plans to "seize economic leadership in advanced technology," raised eyebrows and deep concerns all over the world. It was reminiscent of the fear, in the West, regarding Japan's economic and technological ascendency during the mid to late 1980s (See Chapter Seven). Japan was seemingly unstoppable, and its prowess in technology considered a threat to the dominance in the West. Japan also had supportive government subsidies for its high-tech industries and restrictive policies on foreign competition and access to its markets.

In the 1980s, it was President Ronald Reagan targeting large trade deficits with Japan, with a focus on steel, semiconductor technology and autos. The Reagan administration strategy (similar to the Trump administration) was designed to protect specific American industries, save jobs and reduce the trade deficit. Tariffs, quotas and other import restrictions were employed to reverse the strength and growth of Japan's economic and technological ascendancy. The fear of Japan becoming the number one economic power in the world with America serving as its premier marketplace, was a major concern of the Reaganomics and Republican lawmakers.

Similarly, everybody knows that China plays hardball when it comes to allowing foreign companies access to its markets, and the pursuit of other practices (heavy subsidies for local Chinese businesses), etc. China is attempting to build a self-sufficient high-tech society (following a similar trajectory as Japan) and has the people, resources, discipline and political will to make it happen. The communist government has openly announced that it will pump hundreds of billions of dollars into this grand initiative. Some of the industries targeted are as follows: robotics, new materials and biopharmaceuticals, nanotechnology, electric vehicles, electrical equipment, aerospace and aviation equipment, information technology, agricultural machinery, medical devices, wind, solar and other green technologies, and many others. China's expressed intention is to move from a low-cost factory assembler of products to an innovator of advanced technologies.

As of 2018, China production facilities assembled 80 percent of the world's computers and 90 percent of its mobile phones. As a low-cost production intermediary, it has to rely on getting the components and advance technology from the EU, Japan, the United States and elsewhere. The natural evolution is to become (ultimately) a high-tech society with domestic innovative technology centers. Thus, over a period of decades, technology transference has come from the United States, Japan, Taiwan, and European nations. Major multinational corporations from all over the world built this global paradigm as a result of competition, the need for low-cost labor and access to China's consumer markets. And all of this is much more complex than just one nation having dominant control over all of these major industries.

The Trump administration made it part of its goal to stop China's push for technological dominance in the 21st century by disrupting the entire trade relationship between the two countries. Claims by the Trump administration that China "engages in theft of technologies and intellectual property" added more tension to the escalating crisis.[10] To some extent, this issue morphed into a tech war and manufacturing war that would extend far beyond trade tariffs, especially if the focus becomes to stop "Made in China 2025" and the theft of technologies. The dire message sent throughout the world is that this would surely take us into the arms of a global recession. It will get messy and disrupt other more important relationships between the two superpowers, as well as undermine other international power structures, such as the World Trade Organization (WTO).

In the midst of an excruciating recession (the likely forecast for the next major downturn), it is hard to believe that China will not gain access to the technology and research it is seeking to fulfill its mission in the 21st century. We cannot stop "Made in China 2025" no more than we could stop "Made in Japan" in the 1970s and 1980s. Technology transference will happen with or without the consent of Trumponomics.

In the age of the Internet and Information Age Technologies, is it feasible to risk the start of global trade wars (in part) because we want to stop a nation from pursuing its technological goals or fear that they may become the number one superpower in ten years? There are other ways to deal with this matter without resorting to a full-blown trade war especially at a time when the world is already sitting on the precipice of a global collapse (although this is not fully acknowledged by most mainstream analysts and economists). And once this kind of thing gets started, it's hard to stop; it's like a physical fight between two combatants, it doesn't stop until someone is knocked out, driven to submission (one side gives up) or is eliminated.

Thus, as Trumponomics attempts to reverse the deflationary forces of globalization and removes the ability of central bankers in the West to create money without generating hyperinflation, we can expect to move quickly and aggressively (in the opposite direction) into the realm of inflationary forces. Once we start down that path, it will mean higher prices, high unemployment rates, accompanied by a stock market and real estate collapse, as well as other unintended consequences.

The most important thing in a trade war is to be sure that you are not inflicting more damage to yourself than to your opponent. In the deeply entrenched globalization paradigm, it is very difficult to know how much pain will ultimately be inflicted on your country's consumer markets, workers, business owners and corporations. A prime example of an unintended consequence is the following: American companies that had spent decades building market share in foreign markets would be positioned to witness the erosion of their precious consumer market shares in the event of harsh foreign government retaliatory actions. In the case of China, the likely scenaro is that it will reach out to other global corporations to replace American firms, which will decrease their revenues and market shares, as well as increase job losses for American workers. When the sales of U.S. exporters are reduced due to tariffs, the firms that are impacted will begin to curtail hiring and lay off workers. In the industries that China is targeting, American jobs will be lost in the fields of agriculture, chemicals, aerospace, energy, shipping, etc. The Official *China Daily* stated in an editorial that "the United States had failed to understand that the business it does with China supported millions of American jobs and that the U.S. approach was self-defeating."[11]

Another example of unintended consequences is the Mexican Senate strongly considering suspending Mexico's support and cooperation with the United States in combating counterterrorism, international drug trafficking, and management of immigration border issues. The Mexican Congress' Permanent Commission proposed to the executive branch to "consider the possibility of withdrawing from any bilateral cooperation scheme" with the US on any of the above issues.[12]

By mid-May 2018, the potential trade war between China and the U.S. had begun to settle into the arena of negotiations, with both sides searching for a way forward. Perhaps the fact that China owns $1.2 trillion in U.S. Treasuries (which helps finance U.S. debt) brought some calmness to the situation, or that both parties realized the irreparable damage that their economies and the global economy would suffer. If allowed to spin out of control, the ramifications could run wide and deep.

However, by the end of May, Trump had reversed his stance again and was ordering $50 billion of tariffs placed on Chinese imports. Part of the renewed threats was focused on the issue of the theft of American intellectual property and the formal request by the Trump administration for Beijing to commit to specific numbers in purchasing more goods and services from America. Trump was demanding that China reduce its yearly trade surplus with America by $200 billion, something that would be very difficult to achieve even in the best case scenarios.

In reaction to the sudden change of heart in Washington, China stated that it was prepared to defend its interests in the event of a full-blown tariff war. State news agency Xinhua confirmed that "China's attitude, as always, is: we do not want to fight, but we are also not afraid to fight..." *The Global Times*, the Communist Party's official People's Daily, reported "The Chinese Government will have the necessary measures in place to deal with a U.S. withdrawal from any settled agreement. If the U.S. wants to play games, then China would be more than willing to play along and do so until the very end."[13]

Concerns over raising the tariffs on automobiles by 25% were voiced in other parts of the world (Germany, Mexico, and Japan) with tensions rising under the threat of U.S. protectionism. The global trading system was starting to unravel, with no perceivable winners in sight. There would be many losers, especially consumers all over the world.

Then, on May 31, 2018, America and the world was presented with another trade war shock: the U.S. was moving forward with placing tariffs on Canada, the E.U., and Mexico. U.S. Commerce Secretary Wilbur Ross announced that a 25 percent tariff would be placed on steel imports and a 10 percent tariff on aluminum imports from the targeted countries and region. As predicted, retaliation began to move onto center stage with Mexico stating that it would adopt and impose similar tariffs. The initial list of targeted products included grapes, apples, steel, pork legs, and various kinds of cheese.

By the third week of June, US trading partners were threatening retaliation on specific product categories, jobs and companies specifically in American states with core Trump supporters. These tariff threats were strategic and surgical, with the full intent of weakening President Trump and the Republican's voter base before the midterm elections. This represented the first round of anti-Trump and Republican tariffs designed to weakened their power base.

As China responded with a threat of $50 billion worth of tariffs on American imports, Trump ordered the U.S. Trade Representative (Robert Lighthizer) to put together another list of $200 billion worth of Chinese goods to be subject to a 10% tariff. And if China retaliates again, the US would increase the tariff bounty on yet another $200 billion of Chinese products.

By late June, China and the EU began holding meetings to address the aggressive stance and tariffs of Trumponomics. With the policies of the Trump administration considered a major threat to globalization and free trade, Brussels and Beijing began taking action to "form a group inside the World Trade Organization (WTO) dedicated to rewriting the global rules on subsidies and tech policy."[14] An alliance between China and the EU was viewed by some analysts as a major step in a direction that could isolate the United States and its "America First" agenda.

On July 6, 2018 (two days after the Independence Day holiday in America), the trade war between the United States and China became official and began in earnest. Each side was no longer just issuing threats; the largest trade war in history had been launched! A 25% tariff was placed on $34 billion worth of Chinese imports entering America. In response, China vowed swift retaliation on $34 billion worth American exports heading to its shores.

Moving forward into 2018, it is reasonable to assume that every country and region that America plays hardball with on tariffs and protectionist policies, will reciprocate in kind. When the global economy slips into recession, trade wars will simply accelerate the damage just as it did in the early 1930s. In the event that this crisis escalates into a much larger trade war, international trade organizations (like the WTO) will decline and major pillars of global stability will slowly collapse.

The most glaring display of indecisiveness came out of Washington, with the Trump administration moving erratically through the process of establishing and negotiating the proposed trade tariffs. One day Trump is prepared to negotiate, the next day the deal is off. These tactics might work well in the business world but could prove disastrous in the White House. This unpredictableness of Trump is something that increases the level of uncertainty in the global arena and is another serious factor that may likely play a role in igniting the next global collapse.

REPUBLICAN ROLL BACK OF DODD-FRANK

The Dodd-Frank Wall Street Reform and Consumer Protection Act was the first major piece of legislation that emerged after the 2008 meltdown. One critical observation of the new bill is that it did not bring back a version of the Glass-Steagall Banking Act of 1933 nor did it mandate stringent regulations for the OTC derivatives market (Over-The-Counter derivatives), two key factors that played significant roles in the *Meltdown of 2008*. In short, many analysts considered Dodd-Frank ineffective and burdensome in the key areas that were the most vulnerable: OTC derivatives, the separation of commercial banks and investment institutions, and stopping the massive growth of too-big-to-fail banking institutions. Dodd-Frank was already a weak law, but in the Republican and bank lobbyist eyes, it wasn't weak enough.

Ten years after its passage, the Republicans (with a central mandate to deregulate, especially in the financial arena) made it a point to roll back provisions and dismantle as much of the Dodd-Frank legislation as they could. The big story here is the demand by the banking industry to clear away as many regulations that infringe on their day-to-day operations. The big banks scored a legislative victory by getting the following regulations removed or modified:

(1) The reduction of oversight and capital requirements, specifically the increase in the threshold in which banks are considered a threat or critical to the banking system. That threshold moved from $50 billion to $250 billion, placing over two dozens large financial institutions into a new category under much fewer regulations.

(2) The new legislation would no longer require many of the nation's big banks to undergo an annual stress test mandated and required by the Fed. This test is designed to determine if a bank is strong enough (has enough capital) to survive an economic decline and still be in a position to make loans to customers. The large banks did not want to deal with this type of regulation on an annual basis.

(3) The new legislation would also exempt dozens of large institutions from having to execute plans called *living wills* that essentially provides a liquidation design that states how a bank will sell off assets in a way that will not create problems in the financial system or place downward pressure on the economy.

The official tone and rhetoric for the new bill were that it would benefit thousands of community banks and credit unions and "spur lending and economic growth without creating risks to the financial system." Supporters of the new legislation gave the appearance that these adjustments to Dodd-Frank were more for the smaller institutions and not leaning heavily for the Too-Big-To-Fail institutions. Senate Majority Leader Mitch McConnell stated that "Dodd-Frank's enormous regulatory burden has been inefficient and unhelpful for financial institutions of all sizes, but it has hit Main Street lenders especially hard."[15] The top Democrat on the Senate Banking Committee, Senator Sherrod Brown (D-Ohio) stated (as the bill was nearing passage) "We know what happens next. It is hubris to think we can gut the rules on these banks again, but avoid the next crisis."[16] Senator Elizabeth Warren stated that "This bill was written by the big banks to help big banks."[17]

The bill received bi-partisan support in the Senate, with 16 Democrats and one independent Senator joining in to support the Republicans in this legislative process. There was no gridlock; enough Democrats favored the deal based on the perceived support it would give to the thousands of community banks and credit unions. They also leaned heavily on the words of former congressman Barney Frank (D-Mass), who was the co-sponsor and author of the Dodd-Frank 2010 legislation. According to Barney Frank (who is now a banker), "Dodd-Frank overhaul doesn't weaken rules put in place to prevent a financial crisis." Frank also tells us "This bill, as it passed the Senate, does not in any way weaken the rules, the problems against derivatives, which were a major part of the problem... It does not in any way weaken the restrictions against people making mortgage loans and then securitizing them."[18]

In support of the bill, Democratic Senator Heidi Heitkamp (D-N.D.) stated in a speech on the Senate floor that "I think it's really important that we debate the actual merits of this bill and not the boogeyman merits: the statements that this bill will somehow lead to the catastrophic downfall of our financial system...Even Barney Frank disagrees with that evaluation of this bill."[19]

There was a lot of disagreements among those in the Democratic Party, particularly among the Senators and congresspersons that had constituents that felt a heavy burden with the original Dodd-Frank legislation. However, this was just the beginning assault on Dodd-Frank; the attacks will continue until the 2010 legislation is ripped apart.

No doubt, the banks will continue to lobby for the further dismantlement of Dodd-Frank. The 2018 legislation was just the opening round of a 15-round battle. Big banks will use the Fed or Congress to defuse the Volcker Rule that still limits their ability to use proprietary trading as a platform in their investment activities. The Volcker Rule banned this high-risk strategy. According to Ed Mierzwinski, a senior director at the U.S. Public Interest Research Group, "Weakening the Volker Rule means allowing banks to play with other people's money again. That was the casino economy before the crisis."[20] The rule was put in place to help prevent a reoccurrence of the 2008 collapse, yet the deregulators are searching for ways to strip it away. Having absolutely no safeguards protecting our financial system is irresponsible and outright dangerous.

SUMMARY/ANALYSIS

Trump and the Republicans, will drive the credit bubble to its highest peak and then watch in astonishment as it blows up! New tax cuts for the wealthy will lead to a collapse similar to the Bush era, compounding the inequality of wealth issue. If there is a move to slash social programs spending to help pay for the tax cuts along with increased military spending, the social fabric of America will begin to fall apart for the obvious reasons cited throughout this publication. Also, we have to remember that quantitative easing has been taken away and we now have quantitative tightening along with rising interest rates. These are the types of activities that typically precede the start of a major recession.

Tax cuts, unrestricted and unfettered capitalism, and front-loading the majority of the wealth into the hands of the wealthy elites, is certain to bring about a major implosion of the global super bubble at some unsuspecting moment in time. There are no safeguards; when we stumble into the next recession, it will be exacerbated by all of the misguided policies and legislation put in place to assure a period of utter chaos.

President Trump's initiation of the opening rounds of global trade wars may, over time, escalate into a much greater crisis. Since there are a lot of moving parts, characters and interconnections in this drama, the US may find itself in a trade war against the world. The "America First" agenda which aims to protect American industries and workers may end up doing just the opposite. Some analysts believed that much of what Trump was doing in implementing tariffs, renouncing previous trade agreements and making overt economic threats, had more to do with establishing a stronger posture in trade negotiations with U.S. trading partners. The bold attempt to reverse decades of American trade deficits in an era of firmly entrenched globalization was Trump's biggest gamble of his presidency in 2018. If the strategy fails, we will be looking at a replay of the early 1930s or the mid to late 1980s. If his tactics succeed, America will move into a position of leveling the international playing field in regards to saving or gaining a few jobs. But it's a long shot!

Coupled with the devaluation of currencies, trade wars on the scale of the early 1930s will certainly make it much more difficult to avoid a Great Depression.

The Republican push to deregulate and dismantle the Dodd-Frank Banking Act will not stop with the passage of the reform bill signed into law on May 24, 2018, by President Trump. Other aspects of Dodd-Frank (such as the Volcker Rule) are a thorn in the side of large banking institutions, and they want them removed. There is no mistake about this verdict; there will continue to be an all-out assault on Dodd-Frank as long as the Republicans are in power (have control of the White House and Congress) and the Fed is given the green light to defuse the undesirable aspects of the 2010 legislation.

NOTES

(1) Terri Cullen, "Trump boasts: 'The reason our stock market is so successful is because of me'," CNBC, November 6, 2017.
(2) Brooks Jackson, "The Budget and Deficit Under Clinton," FactCheck.org, February 3, 2008.
(3) Richard Duncan, "The Government-induced Liquidity Crisis Could Crush The Markets," Macro Watch, February 2018.
(4) Tyler Durden, "China Downgrades US Credit Rating From A- to BBB+, Warns US Insolvency Would Detonate Next Crisis," ZeroHedge, January 16, 2018.
(5) President Donald Trump, "Donald Trump on Twitter," http://twitter.com/realdonaldtrump/status/969183644756660224?/lang-en, March 1, 2018.
(6) David Scutt, "It's just chaos: Nobel Prize-winning economist Robert Shiller warns that an 'economic crisis' is brewing. ", *Business Insider* Australia, March 26, 2018.
(7) Dr. Joseph Francois, Laura M. Baughman, and Daniel Anthony, "Policy Brief Round 3: 'Trade Discussion' or 'Trade War'? The estimated Impacts of Tariffs on Steel and Aluminum." Trade Partnership Worldwide, LLC/ The Trade Partnership, www.tradepartnership.com, June 5, 2018.
(8) Ibid., Trade Partnership Worldwide.
(9) Joe McDonald, "Made in China 2025 plan irking Beijing's trading partners," *The Associated Press*, April 12, 2018.
(10) Ben Blanchard and David Stanway, "Chinese media says U.S. has 'delusions' as impact of trade war spreads," *Business News (Reuters)*, June 21, 2018.
(11) Brend Goh and Michael Martina, "China slams surprise U.S. trade announcement, says ready to fight," *Reuters* (Shanghai/Beijing), May 30, 2018.
(12) Christopher Woody, "Mexican officials are ready to stop helping the US fight terrorism and drug trafficking to get back at Trump," *Business Insider*, June 24, 2018.
(13) Taisei Hoyama, "US=China trade war is back on as Trump revives 25% tariffs," *Nikkei Asian Review*, May 30, 2018.
(14) Alexandra Ma, "China and the EU are teaming up to fight back against Trump's trade war," *Reuters*, June 26, 2018.
(15) John Crudele, "Senate inches closer to rolling back parts of Dodd-Frank," Associated Press, March 7, 2018.
(16) Ibid., Associated Press.
(17) Ibid., Associated Press.
(18) Kelli Ell, "Bill to rewrite Dodd-Frank post-crisis banking rules is 'mostly' reasonable: Barney Frank," CNBC, March 16, 2018.
(19) CSpan, "U.S. Senate Sen. Heitkamp on Banking Bill," CSpan, March 14, 2018.
(20) Money and Markets Editorial Team, "Fed Looks To Ease Rule That Limits Risky Bank Trading," Money and Markets, May 30, 2018.

PHASE III: THE GRAND CONVERGENCE

CHAPTER ELEVEN
KONDRATIEFF AND THE
K-WAVE THEORY:
SUPER-LONG ECONOMIC CYCLES

The coming boom from 2023 into 2036 and beyond will not be as dynamic in developed countries like United States as the boom from 1983 to 2007 when the Baby Boom generation drove dramatic earning, spending, and borrowing trends, innovation (in the 1970s) of new technologies, and their adoption.

Economist Harry S. Dent

Reality is far more complex and messy than many of the grander themes and explanations would have us believe.

Economist Peter Dicken

The *long wave cycle theory* (K-Waves) was popularized by the Russian agricultural economist Nikolai Dimitriyerick Kondratieff (1892-1938), who began publishing his theories in economic journals during the 1920s. His thesis and main ideas on economic cycles were published in various papers in 1922, 1925, and 1926. His last document entitled *Long Economic Cycles* came out in 1928, which brought together the central hypothesis and critical ideas of his belief in super-long economic cycles. His ideas were hotly debated both inside and outside of Russia. He based his statistical data on the capitalistic free market system which supported the premise that the capitalistic system was cyclical and periodic, moving through stages of prosperity, recession or depression, and recovery. His theories ran counter to communist ideology (particularly under Stalinistic Russia) which promoted the complete collapse of capitalism. After Lenin's death in 1924, Joseph Stalin (the successor of Lenin) pursued economic policies that supported complete government control of the economy. Marxism did not favor the cyclical ideas of Kondratieff (which were also predicting the demise of communism), and this eventually led to his demise.

Kondratieff was arrested in July 1930 and sentenced to eight years in prison. While serving time in Siberia, Kondratieff was actively planning to continue his writings and research (with new publications), but the communist leadership was fearful of the acceptance of his economic ideas supporting the boom and bust nature of capitalism. Thus, in September1938, after another trial that sentenced him to ten additional years, he was instead placed before a firing squad and promptly executed. It was Joseph Stalin who personally gave the order to have Kondratieff executed on September 17, 1938.

Kondratieff's last document was published one year before the October 1929 stock market crash, and his theories indicated that a downward wave was in motion prior to the Great Depression of the 1930s. The beginning of the *Roaring 20s* carried the inflationary spiral to its last peak, and the 1930s produced the last phase (of deflation and depression) of the downward wave.[1] According to Kondratieff's theory, a long wave cycle will last from 45 to 60 years (*K-wave cycle*), with the average being 54 years. The statistical data he compiled covered 140 years which represented two and one-half cycles. Each completed cycle was broken into two phases: a rising wave and a downward wave. Each phase averaged roughly 25 to 27 years and would be characterized by certain economic, political, technological and social events. During the period of a complete cycle, one major depression would occur, and at least thirty years of technical innovations would be possible. Kondratieff based his original theories on data compiled from the United States, Germany, France, and England. The data consisted of a 19th Century price series that included interest rates, cash deposits, foreign trade figures, the average level of commodities, and the production of pig iron, lead, and coal.

K-Wave theories advocate the notion of economic seasons which are the various phases the cycles will pass through: spring, summer, autumn, and winter. During the spring phase, economic prosperity is dominated by new modes of production and rising inflation. Peak economic developments and inflation characterize the summer phase, while the autumn or fall phase will witness a credit boom and a speculative bubble. The winter phase is characterized by deflation, massive debt rejection, and economic depression.

The foundation of the long wave cycle consists of massive investments in long-term capital goods, large plants, railways, bridges, canals, other types of infrastructure developments and the rise of a skilled labor force to work in the new industries created by emerging technologies. Historical evidence indicates that great scientific breakthroughs and discoveries occur during the downward cycle, whereas, the application of new technological inventions and innovations find their greatest support during the upswing cycles. As the world moved into the 1990s, we witnessed one of the most astounding periods of scientific discovery in the history of humanity. Breakthroughs in the areas of digital technology, solar energy, laser technology, superconductivity, hydrogen fusion, semiconductors, robotics, fiber optics, bioengineering, innovative communication systems, satellite systems, the Internet and many others were destined to replace entire industries and restructure the world of the 21st century. Based on Kondratieff's theory these developments indicated that the end of a long wave cycle was in progress during the 1990s.

The actual periods covered by Kondratieff's first two and one-half cycles consisted of the following:

(1) First Cycle: the end of the 1780s to 1844-1851, reaching an inflationary peak between 1810 to 1817.
(2) Second Cycle: from 1844-1851 to 1890-1896, reaching an inflationary peak between 1870-1875.
(3) Third Cycle: began in 1890-1896 and peaked in 1914-1920, and was in its last phase when Kondratieff concluded his analysis.[2]

Modern Kondratieff exponents disagree on the actual years that ended the third cycle and began the fourth. However, it appears that the *third cycle* ended in the years 1940-1948 which would also indicate that the *fourth cycle* began during that period. Based on the dynamics and timetable of the theory, the *fourth wave* should have concluded in the mid-1990s, the key technological transition period leading to the 21st century. Out of the chaos of the massive restructuring process of the *Information Age Revolution*, the *fifth wave* was born, which will carry us to approximately the mid-21st century.

Significant historical evidence supports the thesis that major technological changes are associated with long wave cycles. What we will ultimately witness at some point in the 21st Century, is a powerful "techno-economic paradigm shift" from one mode of operation to another (the transition from the industrial age), with entire economies transformed by information age technologies. The result will be what economist Peter Dicken describes as the "crystallization of a new paradigm, generating a new global economic reality." New modes of production, distribution, marketing and organization will form the core of many of the new revolutionary systems that will drive the global economy of the future.

Combining some of Dicken's analysis with some additional data, several key technological revolutions emerge as the central developments of each *K-wave cycle*. The following summaries of each period list the key techno-events and the primary countries associated with these developments:

(1) First Cycle: the end of the 1780s to 1844-1851; technological forces: steam power, cotton textiles, and iron; leading nations: Britain, France, and Belgium.
(2) Second Cycle: from 1844-1851 to 1890-1896; technological forces: railways, iron, and steel; leading nations: Britain, France, Belgium, Germany and the United States.
(3) Third Cycle: from 1890-1896 to 1940-1948; technological forces: electricity, chemicals, oil, automobiles, airplanes, and cinematic film; leading nations: the United States, Germany, Britain, France, Belgium, Switzerland and the Netherlands.
(4) Fourth Cycle: from 1940-1948 to the 1990s; technological forces: electronics, synthetic materials, pharmaceuticals, petrochemicals, integrated circuits and computer technology and atomic power; leading nations: the United States, Japan, Sweden, Germany, Britain, France, Belgium, the Netherlands, Russia, and Switzerland.
(5) Fifth Cycle: the 1990s to approximately the mid 21st Century (based on the original 45-60 year timetable) technological forces: digital computers, laser technology, robotics, semiconductors, superconductivity, biotechnology, solar energy, nanotechnology and the entire realm of Information Age technologies; leading nations: the United States, Japan, Germany, Britain, France, Belgium, the Netherlands, Switzerland, India, the four Tigers (Hong Kong, Singapore, Taiwan, and South Korea) and mainland China.[3]

There are certain important implications embedded in the above analysis. If Kondratieff's theory holds true, then by the mid-1990s the U.S. and world economy had entered the last phase of a downward wave, which bottomed out and came to a close sometime before the year 2000.[4] This also implies that a fifth wave was born and a new upward trend in economic and technological progress would become a manifestation throughout the world during the early years of the 21st Century. This winter phase of the cycle may have adjusted, given the fact that the United States experienced a significant boom and bust period from 1995 to 2000. However, when we consider the downward wave in the case of Japan (at the time, the second largest economy in the world), then the theory seems relevant. More thoughts on this issue will be discussed in Chapter Fifteen where we explore Harry Dent's thesis on demographics and related cycle theories.

Now here is where the historical information gets really interesting, particularly when we observe what was happening in America at the end of the 19th century. According to the theory, the *third wave* began in the period 1890-96, a time when many of America's major corporations were being born through a series of mergers and acquisitions. According to Gray Emerson Cardiff (editor of *Sound Advice*), in the year 1899 more than 1,200 companies were involved in consolidations. He tells us that, "the result of these frenzied mergers was the modern industrial conglomerate whose emergence was to be the hallmark of twentieth-century American business."[5] During this period such companies as United States Steel, Union Carbide, General Electric, United States Rubber, Standard Oil of New Jersey, DuPont Chemical, Eastman Kodak and others were born. Also, the modern version of the American stock exchange began to emerge in the late 1890s.[6]

Thus, the turn of the century witnessed an explosive period of activity by the major corporations that would dominate a large percentage of American business throughout most of the 20th Century. Shortly after the year 1900, the film, automobile, telecommunication, chemical, and oil industries began major growth periods. A boom and bust period ran from roughly 1896 to 1907, culminating in what market analysts refer to as the *Panic of 1907*.

A similar set of developments and events marked the beginning of the 21st Century. The 1990s witnessed the birth of the *fifth wave*, a merger and acquisition frenzy in America, explosive growth, and development of new technologies (the birth of the Internet Revolution) and the amazing boom and bust cycle of 1995-2000. The major corporations that were successfully formed during the birth of the *Information Age Revolution* may dominate much of the business activity (on a global scale) of the 21st Century. Such companies as Amazon.com, Google, Microsoft, and Apple are a few of the titans that will dominate business development in the 21st century.

I'm aware that all "cycles are not created equal," however, it's very interesting that a boom and bust cycle occurred at the end of the 19th century. Despite the difference of nearly 100 years, I'm fascinated with the fact that a similar boom and bust cycle emerged at the end of the 20th Century.

K-WAVE CYCLE AND INFLATION

It appears that the inflationary peak of the *fourth wave* occurred during the period 1970-77, which was a decade that witnessed extreme inflationary pressures. Long cycle analysis points out that prices have gone up about the same number of years as they have gone down within a given century.

In short, inflation has never been a permanent reality. Periods of inflation and deflation alternate within a complete cycle: when inflation ends deflation begins. In essence, deflation is a gravitational pull on escalating prices that extend beyond the limits of the overall system. What goes up must come down! An examination of Britain's consumer prices in the eighteenth and nineteenth centuries illustrates this point. There were 53 inflationary years and 47 deflationary years during the eighteenth century. For the nineteenth century prices rose 47 years and fell 53 years.[7] When the final tally is completed for the 20th Century, we will most likely find slightly more inflationary years, for the inflationary phase that began since World War II was one of the most intense periods of escalating prices. More paper money is in the system than any previous cyclic period, particularly in America which has been the central driving force in the world economy since the Second World War.

We are further informed by long cycle theorists that over the centuries wars have been inflationary and the cessation of wars have been deflationary. Analysis of the War of 1812, the American Civil War, World War I, World War II, the Vietnam War, and the Cold War of the Bipolar era are clear examples of this basic premise. For instance, America's debt climbed from $65 million to $3 billion during the Civil War. For World War I, the debt was more severe, it went from approximately $1 billion at the beginning of the conflict to $26 billion by the end of the fighting. Continued advancements in science and technology produced an ever-growing number of sophisticated weapons during the following decades. With the invention of these new weapons of destruction came a higher price tag, thus the price of war continued to escalate.

However, with the end of World War II and the advent of the Bi-polar era, the economic impact of the arms race in nuclear and high-tech weaponry was astronomical. The cessation of World War II and the birth of the *atomic age* set the stage for the most extraordinary military buildups in the history of the world. Trillions of dollars were spent during the long forty-five year period of the Cold War. This generated an extreme cycle of continuous inflation. The collapse of the Soviet empire was a clear signal that the struggle had finally ended on economic grounds: the Soviets literally busted their economic system fighting the Cold War.

K-WAVE CYCLE AND JAPAN

Japan's long-term economic and technological rise in the 1950s and its collapse in the early 1990s is consistent with K-wave theory. The *Long-Term Economic Program* adopted in Japan (the *Iwato Boom*) was characterized by massive investments into plants and equipment in heavy industries, railways, and additional infrastructure developments. This major foundation building was accompanied by the rise and development of a skilled labor force to work in the new industries created by emerging technologies. With the exception of a deep recession in the 1960s, the Japanese economic juggernaut stayed on course for over 40 years, building one of 20th Century's most impressive technological and economic societies. Japan became the world's second largest economy and developed one of the leading currencies in world finance. The economic downturn in the 1990s ushered in a period of deflation after a long extended inflationary cycle which developed into a sensational bubble (the tail end of the autumn season) in the 1980s.

The 1990s were the *Busted 90s* and the *lost decade* for Japan, which was consistent with K-wave theory. America was able to escape the economic downturn of

Japan, and in many ways, became a stronger technological world leader as a result of the collapse of the Soviet Union and Japan's decade-long deflationary meltdown. And in keeping with K-wave theory, Japan, the nation that initiated the *Fifth Generation Project* in 1981, rose up out of the ashes of the *Busted 90s* and continued its struggle (fighting deflation) to maintain its statue in the fifth wave during the early years of the 21st Century. With the explosive growth of mainland China, Japan was surpassed by the *China juggernaut*, which became the second largest economy in the world and a major global superpower.

OTHER K-WAVE OBSERVATIONS

I've been fascinated with K-wave theory for nearly three decades. I believe the primary reason I've remained locked into the analysis is the emergence and massive significance of the *Information Age Revolution*. The turn of the 21st Century and the start of a new millennium is a defining moment in historic/universal time; an initiation period of profound technological importance. We have arrived at a point in history where humankind will be able to unveil some of the most powerful secrets in science and the universe: *Future Shock*!

With the start of the new millennium, major corporations are building the foundations and infrastructure of an incredible new technological civilization. Very similar activities were taking place at the beginning of the 20th Century, with major corporations setting the stage for enormous technological development and discoveries throughout the entire 100-year period. K-wave theory has helped me to understand the economic and financial implications of these vast historic developments. As an economic philosophy and long-term strategy, it appears to be useful for long-term analysis.

However, most economists and analysts are not interested in K-wave theory and thus consider it not to be a very useful tool. Through experience, I have grown to understand their position on this matter. It does appear that the theory is not very useful in the short-term and it's inadequate for estimating the timing and emergence of boom and bust cycles. It also appears that significant boom and bust cycles can occur during the time period of the *downward wave* (i.e. both the *Booming 80s* and the *Roaring 20s* occurred during downward cycles), which again supports the premise of not following the theory in the short-term.

For the long-term, the theory is useful for understanding trends and is supportive of long-term directions in a prime mover (nation) in the global economy. For instance, K-wave theory appears to be accurate in its contention that great scientific breakthroughs and discoveries occur during downward cycles, whereas, the application of new inventions and innovations find their greatest support during the upswing cycles. By 2018, it certainly appears that a broad range of new technologies and innovations are destined to move rapidly into commercial applications as we head towards the third decade of the 21st Century. I also feel that we are at the tip of a vast scientific and technological iceberg that is poised to unleash a flurry of new innovative products and exciting new companies throughout this century.

As a civilization, we are imagining the new age through the eyes of Hollywood and science fiction writers, and seriously wondering if a lot of these new technologies can really work. We may soon find out how powerful these new technologies really are: if we can replace the combustion engine and the oil base economy of the *Industrial Age*; if we can produce unlimited sources of energy; and if we can create human-like robotic mechanisms.

Alvin Toffler popularized the term *Future Shock* beginning in the 1970s, and *now* we are ready to move into the realm of the fantastic and the world he envisioned in his writings. And there is no turning back; the genie is out of the bottle and this civilization is prepared to push to the *outer limits* of scientific and technological knowledge.

SUMMARY/ANALYSIS

Whether one believes in K-wave theory or not, the reality is that the *Information Age Revolution* is here, and it's here to stay. This tech revolution is testimony to the K-wave theory of the birth of a new dynamic era. There are still many exciting new technological innovations and scientific discoveries that are yet to hit the scene. Financial and economic resources will be made available to support the rapid growth and development of many of these new technological wonders. Many of these technologies are now ready for the commercial markets. This is a very exciting time for new companies to emerge and for great investment opportunities to hit the markets on a global basis!

I still feel firmly that we are at the tip of the iceberg in reference to the enormous change the world will undergo during much of the *21st Century*. And as the entire world begin to participate fully in the new era of globalism, boom and bust cycles will begin to happen more frequently and in shorter periods of duration. By understanding the true nature of boom and bust cycles, investors and analysts will be able to navigate the peaks and valleys with much greater control and success.

NOTES

(1.) Nikolai Kondratieff, *The Long Wave Cycle*, (New York: Richardson & Snyder, translated by Guy Daniels, 1984) p. 38.
(2.) James B. Shuman and David Rosenau, *The Kondratieff Wave*, (World Publishing, New York, 1972), p. 29.
(3.) Peter Dicken, *Global Shift: The Internationalizaton of Economic Activity*, (The Guilford Press, New York, 1992) pp. 98-102. **NOTE:** Dicken's selected data identifies five key "generic"

technologies that create new technology systems (some of which we mention): (a) information technology; (b) biotechnology; (c) materials technology; (d) energy technology; and (e) space technology. In the "fourth cycle," I included atomic power, which had an enormous economic, military and political impact on the world after World War II. The cessation of the Second World War and the birth of the *atomic age* set the stage for the most extraordinary military buildups in the history of the world. Trillions of dollars were spent during the long 45-year period of the Cold War.

(4.) The date(s) for the ending of the "second cycle" in the 19th Century were 1890-1896. Shortly after the year 1900, the film, automobile and telecommunication industries began major growth periods.

(5.) Gray Emerson Cardiff, *A Millionaire's Guide To Panic-Proof Investing In The Stock Market*, (Danville, California: Sound Advice Press, 1996), p. 13.

(6.) Ibid., *Guide to Panic-Proof Investing In The Stock Market*, p.13."

(7.) James Dale Davidson and Lord William Rees-Mogg, *The Great Reckoning,* (New York: Summit Books, 1991), p. 323.

CHAPTER TWELVE
WEALTH INEQUALITY AND GREAT DEPRESSIONS

First there is the question of why economic activity turned down in 1929. Second, there is the vastly more important question of why, having started down, on this unhappy occasion it went down and down and down and remained low for a full decade.

John Kenneth Galbraith

Unless we embrace radical change ourselves...radical changes will be visited upon our physical world.

Naomi Klein

Extraordinary wealth inequality, where massive levels of corporate, asset and financial wealth are concentrated in the hands of a few people, will ultimately lead to deflation and economic depression. It's an unsustainable system of excessive greed, power, and economic imbalances. With the support of global central banks, super and ultra-wealthy individuals and families are moving into a position of owning nearly half of the world's known wealth. Not only is this detrimental for the proper functioning of the capitalistic model, but is also a threat to the continuation to our global civilization.

The best historical precedence of inequality initiating boom and bust cycles is the Roaring 20s 1929 crash that led to the 1930s Great Depression. The level of inequality in 2008 was similar to levels reached in 1928 and 1929. In 2008, economic imbalances in the global system imploded, resulting in the worst economic collapse in world history.

In the aftermath of the 1929 crash, the Fed did not pull out the economic bazooka - for nearly three years - to stop the banking system from collapsing into total failure. In the aftermath of the *Meltdown of 2008*, Fed Chairman Ben Bernanke initiated the most massive most pervasive bailout in global history, which subsequently restored the wealth and power to the elites and ultra-wealthy. In fact, their wealth (in 2017) surpassed inequality levels achieved in both 1929 and 2008.

As we have seen thus far, since the *Meltdown of 2008*, the Fed's undeclared mandate was to keep the global bubble economy of excessive credit and debt intact. It was not allowed to deflate, because deflation meant the start of the next *great depression*. And if deflation and depression become the dominant reality, wealth, profits, asset valuations and income would become an extreme problem for societies all over the world. This is the Fed mandate, and it is something to be avoided for as long as possible.

The mania of investing, lending and borrowing that preceded the 2007-09 period set the stage for the bust cycle and meltdown. Any time the stock markets began to crash, it was a signal that deflation and a bust cycle was imminent. Each time this occurred, the Fed stepped in and re-inflated the bubble.

Consequently, the rich and powerful were able to successfully recover from the 2008 crisis, courtesy of the Fed providing access to the trillions of dollars created by the central bank to save the commercial banking industry and other private sector corporate entities. This generous bailout was made possible not only in America but also throughout the European Union (EU), with the Fed providing low-interest loans for European banks and the wealthy elites. In 2008, the European Central Bank (ECB) was not allowed to print money, issue euro bonds and conduct quantitative easing (QE). So the Fed provided the intervention for the EU to prevent the onset of the next global deflationary depression.

The evidence is clear, that since 2008, the Fed brought about more enormous disparities between the wealthy elites and everyone else, by focusing its attention almost entirely on bailing out this dominant group. The *Meltdown of 2008* witnessed over $10 trillion of share values erased in the markets; the ten-year recovery period witnessed that wealth and more acquired and soaked up by the global wealthy elites.

In the past, the model was that the inequality phenomenon took root during the boom cycle, while during the bust period the level of inequality would decrease. However, after 2008 and a global economy that was in a mode of slow growth, with economic pockets of recessions and depressions (Greece, Nigeria, Venezuela, Japan, etc.), the wealthy elites continued to grow more prosperous years after the meltdown. The rich were the primary beneficiaries of the massive money printing operations of the Fed; which mainly became a *Fed trickle-down strategy* designed to uplift the wealthy elites. This *trickle-down theory* will come home to roost when the second phase of this party comes to an end.

THE MIDDLE-CLASS DECLINE AND ECONOMIC STAGNATION

Simply put, the vast majority of the population is struggling to stay afloat. When the system finally reaches the breaking point (a significant event or crisis that results in a meltdown), the availability of credit will cease, demand will dry up, prices of goods and services will fall, and unemployment will suddenly rise to high levels. The wealthy elites will flee the markets and move to the sidelines while the next *Great Depression* becomes a reality.

In the case of the U.S., when we examine the elements that are critical to the growth of GDP (consumer spending, government spending, corporate investments, and imports and exports), we see that 70 percent of America's GDP comes from the consumption patterns of its people. Maintaining a healthy and vibrant American consumer population should have been somewhere near the top of the list when the Fed and federal government architects were diligently developing solutions to prevent the 2008 great depression. And the irony of the majority of their *non-supporting middle-class policies* is that in order to jump-start a deadbeat economy, consumers are expected to spend, borrow and consume to create a new cycle of growth and prosperity. This type of recovery cannot happen without a strong middle-class. In fact, democracies are subject to massive failure without the presence of a strong middle-class.

Fed monetary policies gave a significant boost to stock prices and real estate values and generated the wealth effect, but again this benefitted mostly the wealthy. Neither the federal government or the Fed implemented effective bailout policies for the American homeowner during and after the 2008 crisis. Millions of homes were lost, and this had a significant impact on the middle-class. Their wealth got transferred to the banks and the wealthy. It would have been a much wiser decision to have kept millions of people in their homes, and that policy would have gone a long way in helping the U.S. economy to ignite a much stronger recovery. I continue to hammer away at this point (and will continue to do so throughout this publication) because federal reserve policies are not designed to provide direct assistance to the general population during periods of economic collapse. And the reality is that it has the power and capacity to do so.

The backlash and growing dissent in the U.S. and Europe will continue to grow, mainly as the inequality gap increases to dangerous levels beyond containment. Populace movements, class warfare and the rise of extreme organizations will bring about the societal collapse in Western societies that ignore what is taking place in full view: the massive concentration of wealth and power in the hands of a small group of ultra-wealthy individuals and families. And as we shall see, this is a recipe for economic and societal disaster. History has demonstrated this time and time again. However, this time could prove to be massively fatal especially in a world populated with nuclear weapons, highly unstable and defective leaders and excessive greed and fear.

Analysts, writers, and thinkers from all walks of life are sounding the alarms about this growing economic menace that is one of the most significant threats to modern civilization. Writer Mike Roscoe makes a poignant statement as he tells us:

"...the wealth that does exist is increasingly concentrated in the hands of the very rich, to the detriment of society and, in the end, of civilization as a whole. The situation is unsustainable, and I think we might well be seeing the beginnings of the end of our current finance-dominated economic system, a system that depends on growth while at the same time killing the prospects of growth by increasing debt and inequality."[1]

Globalization has been instrumental in fueling the rise of the "billionaire" era and the ultra-rich. An interesting study released in 2014 on wealth inequality presented some startling data. This study was conducted by Gabriel Zucman of the London School of Economics and Emmanuel Saez of U.C. Berkeley. The authors inform us of the following:

(1) "...wealth is ten times more concentrated than income today."
(2) "the rich are getting richer while the middle classes of the developed world get poorer and everyone else - the really poor - struggle along on next to nothing, as they always have done."[2]

As part of their concluding remarks, the authors inform us that, "...wealth inequality appears to have followed a U-shape evolution since 1913, with a marked increase since the 1980s...the increased concentration of wealth at the top seems driven by surging top incomes. The combination of increasing income inequality with increasing saving rate inequality is fueling wealth inequality."[3] My analysis also point to the 1980s as being a pivotal point for extreme wealth accumulation, largely driven by the birth of the fiat currency era of the 1970s.

RISE OF THE GLOBAL BILLIONAIRE CULTURE

The acceleration of the rise of billionaires began during the decade I labeled the *Booming 80s*. This economic movement came into prominence approximately a decade after America abandoned the gold standard in 1971. With the creation of the global dollar standard and the fiat money system, inflation soared during the 1970s and led to Fed Chairman Paul Volcker breaking the back of inflation with high-interest rates during the early 1980s. After 1982, the interest rate trajectory remained on a downward slope for well over 30 years. Credit creation skyrocketed, and boom and bust cycles became more frequent and increasingly more extreme and volatile. This then was the economic environment in which the billionaire evolved.

In the July 1989 issue of *Forbes* magazine, the cover read "**THE WORLD'S BILLIONAIRES**," with a graphic depiction of earth made of gold. *Forbes* chronicled the personal histories and rise to prominence of 89 men, three women and 52 family groups that were worth $1 billion or more. America topped the list with 55 individuals and 27 families identified as billionaires. Japan came in second with 41, followed by 20 billionaires in West Germany. The cover story pointed out that the billionaire had worldwide influence, with vast and widely diffused financial and economic empires.

The *Booming 80s* atmosphere helped to create both a broader base of billionaires with stronger, more dynamic centers of power. Like the 1920s, an enormous amount of wealth and power would be concentrated in a few hands, however, this time the power base was much more global in its design and much more capable of expanding its influence to all corners of the world.

What we have witnessed since the mid-1980s is the exponential rise of wealth inequality in America. The trajectory has been phenomenal, giving rise to what can be appropriately called *the age of the billionaire*. The simple observation is that in the age of the billionaire, the nation's wealth is concentrated in the hands of fewer and fewer people. And in this era, we can observe that the rise of globalization gave rise to a vibrant billionaire class making it possible for them to build business empires that operate throughout the world.

According to *Forbes*, in 1989 the world had 198 billionaires. By 2016, that number had soared to a record number of 1,826 billionaires with total wealth of $6.48 trillion. The almost 90% increase in the number of billionaires over the 27-year period is a testament to the economic power of the *fiat-money and credit expansion* of the new era that came into existence after 1971. In other words, this would not have happened if America had not abandoned the gold standard in 1971. By 2015, the extremes had reached epic proportions: ultra-wealthy families (the wealthiest one-ten-thousandth 0.01%) controlled 14% of the wealth in the United States. By comparison, in 1978 we observe that this group controlled 2.2% of the wealth. The wealthiest 1% of Americans now control more wealth than 90% of the entire American population. And with only four percent of the global population, the U.S. controls 30% of global wealth. This country is also home to 40% of all individuals with $50 million or more in acquired wealth.

Even though the idea of a trillionaire is an absurdity, the reality is that there are nearly 70 Sovereign Wealth Funds that control over $7 trillion worth of wealth. This level of the massive concentration of wealth by such a small group of people had not been seen since 1929. Some other observations are equally startling:

(1) This is not just a U.S. phenomenon: According to the Credit Suisse 2016 *Global Wealth Report*, it appears that only 0.07% of the global population controls nearly half or 50% of the world's wealth.[4] This is neither a recipe for future progress or economic stability. And this trend is expected to get worse as we move forward, producing greater extremes and imbalances.

(2) Oxfam's International 2014 report entitled, *Working for the Few*, provides more incredible evidence of this significant imbalance: (a) the estimated wealth of a mere one percent of the richest people on the planet is an astounding $110 trillion. The entire bottom half of the world's population controls less than 65 times the wealth of this small group of people. Also, it's estimated that just 85 of the world's wealthiest people own the same amount of wealth as the bottom half of the global population. (b) When we examine economic and financial results of the impact of the *Meltdown of 2008* in America, we find that the richest one percent were able to capture 95 percent of the actual financial and assets gains that occurred in the post-crisis recovery. The data also reveals that the bottom 90 percent of Americans witnessed most of their wealth disappear. (c) As this trend of wealth concentration continues, the wealthy will dominant governmental policymaking, which will lead to more and more policies favoring the interest of the rich and powerful, to the detriment of all other citizens. Democracy will be undermined, and deterioration of societal health and economic benefits will become a manifestation in societies all over the world. If the ultimate goal of the wealthy elites (either planned or accidental) is to create a system to control the world and the global economy, then we are currently witnessing the actual formation of that system. (d) Seven out of ten people live in countries where economic inequality has increased in the last 30 years.[5]

To the researchers at Oxfam International, their report disclosed some very shocking revelations. According to Max Lawson of Oxfam, "This huge gap between rich and poor is undermining economies, destabilizing societies and holding back the fight against poverty." In the two years since the 2014 Oxfam report, Lawson states in the 2016 report (*An Economy For The 1%*) that "The richest 1% now have more wealth than the rest of the world combined."[6] The organization recommend that some significant changes must be made if these disturbing trends are to be reversed.

The International Monetary Fund (IMF) joined the chorus of prognosticators sounding the alarm of inequality, particularly in the United States. High levels of poverty and inequality in a rich developed nation that is a central player in our current global civilization, is something that will ultimately undermine the stability of the nation and the global economy. The IMF made the following observation:

> "...the ageing of the US population, with a surge of baby-boomers moving into retirement, is combining with a troubling stall in productivity gains and lack of investment in workers and physical capital to present a new challenge to the economy...46.7 million Americans - one out of seven people - are living in poverty, including 20 percent of all children. Working Americans' share of all income in the country has fallen by five percent in 15 years, and the middle class is the smallest it has been in three decades."[7]

IMF Managing Director, Christine Lagarde, further stated that "Not only does poverty create significant social strains, it also eats into labor force participation, and undermines the ability to invest in education and improve health outcomes...Our assessment is that, if left unchecked, these four forces - participation, productivity, polarization, and poverty - will corrode the underpinnings of growth (both potential and actual) and hold back gains in US living standards."[8] Their final recommendations are for the U.S. to invest in infrastructure, education, tax reforms and higher minimum wages for the lower levels of society. The urgent call is to reverse the negative trends before they lead to further deterioration.

SENATOR BERNIE SANDERS AND THE ISSUE OF INEQUALITY

Senator Bernie Sanders, a prominent Independent/Democrat, who ran for president as a Democratic candidate in the 2016 election, had been a fiercely outspoken opponent against wealth inequality for most of his life. During his populist campaign for president, Sanders delivered a powerful message and economic sermon on wealth inequality in America. He hammered away at how the banking cartel benefitted from the massive bailouts received after the *Meltdown of 2008*, and about a system that is rigged to favor wealth disparity that is so prevalent throughout the American economic system. Sanders championed the economic rights of the middle class and others who have not benefitted from globalization, and he sincerely questioned why the American people were not bailed out after the meltdown.

As an avowed Democratic Socialist, Sanders populist platform was considered by many as a political rebellion and class warfare against the establishment, Wall Street, and the Big Banks. With decades of real wages declining for the average American, CEO salaries experiencing dramatic increases, with American democracy under assault by a wealthy oligarchy and crony capitalism, Sanders political revolution was about a transformation and restoring power and economic fairness to the American people.

In short, Senator Sanders was leading a political revolution in defiance of the billionaire class and Oligarchy that have mostly (and quietly) taken over the American political and economic systems. With a solid backing of 13 million votes in the Democratic primary, Sanders was overwhelmingly supported by young people and millions of others who harbored deep anger and resentment for the status quo and the mainstream establishment that is controlled and directed by the rich and powerful.

The ultimate goal of the Sanders' presidency was to have an American government that functions for the benefit of all Americans not just the 1%. Senator Sanders was keenly aware of the massive corruption in Washington, a political system rigged for special tax loopholes, corporate subsidies, bank bailouts and trade deals favorable to global corporate interests:

"If a bank is too big to fail, it is too big to exist. When it comes to Wall Street reform, that must be our bottom line. The risk of another bailout is too great, and the economic and political power of a handful of huge financial institutions is simply too large," he continued.

"We need a banking system that is part of the productive economy - making loans at affordable rates to small and medium-sized businesses so that we can create decent-paying jobs. Wall Street cannot continue to be an island unto itself, gambling trillions in risky financial instruments, making huge profits, assured that, if their schemes fail, the taxpayers will be there to bail them out."[9]

DR. RAVI BATRA AND THE CENTRAL CAUSE OF GREAT DEPRESSIONS

As stated earlier, enormous wealth inequality ultimately leads to great depressions. This issue of wealth inequality as the central catalyst for significant economic downturns, first came to my attention in the late 1980s while reading Dr. Ravi Batra's thoughts on the *Concentration of Wealth and Depressions*. Vast concentrations of wealth create massive control over various sectors of an economic system. What history has shown is that a massive concentration of wealth on this scale can lead to such enormous imbalances that a *great depression* becomes unavoidable. One of the main lessons I derived from Batra's analysis on this topic, is the central importance of the concentration of enormous wealth during the phase identified as the boom cycle. According to Batra, this is a prerequisite for a final bust cycle collapse. With greater inequality of wealth comes the propensity for the rich to take higher risks in the quest for greater returns.

The last major period in American history when these extremes were most pronounced was the boom and bust cycles of the 1920s and 1930s. During the early 1920s, one percent of America's wealthiest families controlled 31.6 of the nation's wealth, after the five-year boom period (from 1924 to 1929), that number had increased to 36.3 percent. When we examine the late 1920s, 84 percent of the country's wealth was controlled and dominated by the richest 10% of the American population. Bottom line: the boom years of the Roaring 20s gave rise to an excessive concentration of wealth. When this happens, an enormous bust cycle of epic proportions is due to take place. Batra puts it this way:

"However, the speculative fever cannot begin in the absence of wealth disparity, for only the very rich can afford to squander money on investments with a high relatively illusive return. A side effect of the growing wealth disparity is the rise in speculative investments. As a person becomes wealthy, his aversion to risk declines. As wealth inequality grows, the overall riskiness of investments made by the rich also grows...They alone can initiate the fever. In other words, wealth inequality is a prerequisite for manias and bubbles. The greater the inequity, the bigger the bubble and the more painful its eventual bursting...In short, the concentration of wealth has two pernicious effects on the economy. It increases the number of banks with shaky loans, and fuels the speculative frenzy in which even the banking system is caught."[10]

Bubble formations and bubble collapses are initiated and driven by the wealthy elites and the massive expansion and contraction of the bank-controlled credit system. When markets are in free fall, it is the wealthy elites that are doing most of the selling. In the first ten days after the Lehman Bros. bankruptcy filing, wealthy elite investors accounted for roughly $1.7 billion of selling pressure in the markets. With the increase in wealth inequality *comes the ability of fewer and fewer central players to control boom and bust cycles* that target various asset classes.

A significant factor in the acceleration of the growth of inequality, are governmental policies that provide generous tax cuts for the wealthy. The three Republican Administrations during the 1920s were instrumental in delivering this stimulus. This was also on full display during the eight years of the Bush Administration leading up to the *Meltdown of 2008*. Batra reminds us that:

> "The tax cuts of the 1920s generated the sharpest rise ever in wealth concentration in just a matter of seven years. Between 1922 and 1929, the rich became richer as never before. As a consequence, the banking system was the shakiest and the speculative bubble the largest in history. So was the eventual collapse of the economy."[11]

As we have seen over the period of several decades, the stagnation of wages experienced by American middle class workers had reduced their standard of living as well as the aggregate demand in the economy. Decreasing total demand and a decimated middle class, with less wealth and resources, will help to initiate a period of deflation. Batra reminds us that, "...recessions and depressions have been caused by a contraction in aggregate demand." As credit dries up and income declines, a major pillar of the GDP becomes weaker and insufficient in the face of a major economic downturn. This issue of aggregate demand is intensified several-fold when extreme wealth inequality is present. Batra makes the point that:

> "Money supply, aggregate demand, output, and employment then move in a downward spiral, and an ordinary recession turns into a depression. If the speculative bubble is extremely large, then its bursting gives rise to

a great depression. In the aftermath, the concentration of wealth declines, because many fortunes have been wiped out."[12]

And finally, extreme wealth concentration leads to revolution and upheavals. Batra is clear in his assessment of the ultimate consequences of wealth imbalances in a society. His history lesson on this subject is as follows:

> "Time and time again throughout history, enormous concentration of wealth among the few has driven the poverty-ridden masses to rise up and dethrone the affluent from the lofty pedestal of power and prestige in a massive revolution. The wealth and greed of the Bourbon kings of France and their courtiers led to the French Revolution; the czarist regime and the Russian aristocracy were overthrown by the Bolshevik revolution; the shah of Iran was deposed in a bloody uprising. History tells us, in no uncertain terms, that great wealth disparity eventually breeds great upheavals."[13]

THE ART MARKET AS A GLOBAL COLLAPSE INDICATOR

One of the ways to monitor the relationship in the development of extreme wealth and the formation of extreme bubbles is to examine the emergence of art bubbles. When we measure the prices paid for expensive collectibles such as rare paintings, coins, and antique objects, we can observe the extent in which the wealthy will go to acquire rare art pieces, generating extreme inflationary asset price levels in this arena.

During the *Booming 80s*, the Japanese became the second most significant force in the art world, as cash-rich mega-millionaires purchased many valuable art pieces. In one of the world's most notoriously inflated markets of that era, the Japanese investor, in many instances, over-bided the actual value of these artworks and generated an even more enormous inflationary push on prices. Countless millions of dollars were spent on paintings by American and European artists, some of which were painted in the 20th Century!

Perhaps, the deal that most astounded the art world was the purchase by Mr. Ryoei Saito, a Japanese industrialist, who purchased a painting by Renoir called the "Au Moulin de la Galette" for $78.1 million, and a painting by Vincent Van Gogh entitled the "Portrait of Dr. Gachet" for $82.5 million. The grand total, a whopping $160.6 million for two paintings! According to Mr. Saito, this was "no big deal." Perhaps he was right, but I could not help wondering whether he or any other rich Japanese investors would ever pay that much money for any Japanese works of art?[14]

Table 1 presents a list of items that sold for extraordinary prices during 1987 through 1990. Such art houses as Sotheby's and Christie's experienced tremendous growth during this period, receiving large commissions. There was a tremendous increase in surplus wealth in the world during this period. Billions of dollars were spent on paintings, statues, furniture, silverware, and jewelry during 1987, the year of the historic stock market crash. The total 1988 sales by Sotheby's was $1.8 billion, a 27.5 percent increase over their 1987 sales of $1.4 billion. Art simply became another form of high finance and an alternative investment vehicle.

Due to the strength of the yen, Japanese art collectors stretched the limits and sent prices into the stratosphere. Practically all purchases were record-breaking deals and would continue to be so until the end of the cycle and the grand bubble bursting, ending the period of inflationary excesses. When the astounding Japanese Heisei Bubble imploded in 1990, the art bubble also fell into a downward spiral. This rude awakening hit Japan hard, as many wealthy Japanese collectors saw the value of their treasured art pieces fall to record low prices during the early 1990s.

By 1993, many of the paintings that rich Japanese investors had purchased, were down more than 50 percent due to the bursting of the art bubble. As Japan's stock and land values plunged, art prices followed in step, largely because rich Japanese investors had been the heavy speculators during the latter 1980s. When the music stopped, they were the ones left holding the over-inflated merchandise. For many, art was another form of real estate investment, and like real estate, it became another casualty of the *Booming 80s*. The reality of falling collectible prices sent another shock wave through Japan's economy. A critical observation made in January 1993, cited the following:

> "Japan's huge art collection has become just another reminder of the worst excesses of Japan's speculative bubble...banks already suffering from huge inventories of hard-to-sell land are now also saddled with thousands of paintings valued at an estimated $8 billion."[15]

In the early 21st century, Chinese speculators moved into this arena, promoting the same kind of excesses and asset price inflation generated by the Japanese nearly 30 years earlier, and like most global ultra-wealthy investors, they also pursued the path and need to hide and preserve their wealth by the use of high valued collectibles. Getting off the grid and minimizing taxes are additional reasons to move in this direction. In observing Chinese art buyers during the post-2008 period, art dealer, Andrew Kahane, stated that "Chinese buyers want to be seen...spending a lot of money. They want to be seen setting world records."

However, unlike Japanese art collectors in the Booming 80s, most wealthy Chinese art connoisseurs were most interested in artworks painted by Chinese artists. This point is made clear by Thomas Galbraith of Artnet:

"Voracious demand for art in the world's second-largest economy has helped two Chinese artists make it to the top selling list over ten years to 2012...Chinese collectors buy almost exclusively domestic art, and they don't prefer contemporary artists, rather they go for old masters...Sales totaled maybe a couple hundred million in 2002, but by 2011 we were looking at total sales in the region of more than $6.5 billion...Last year [2012], four of the top ten selling artists were Chinese masters, compared to zero in 2002. And over those ten years, two artists, Zhang Daqian and Qi Baishi made it into the top ten, trailing only Picasso and Andy Warhol..."[16]

Consistent with the concentration of wealth into fewer hands is the emergence of outlandish prices for collectibles. Prices paid for several of the collectibles in Table 2 were exceedingly high, particularly for the contemporary art pieces.

For instance, the estimated final price for Jeff Koons' "Balloon Dog" (a brightly colored reflective sculpture that resembles a balloon) was between $35 to $55 million. The final price of $58.4 million went on record as the highest price paid for an artwork produced by a living artist. Seven bidders competed for the right to own "Three Studies of Lucian Freud" by Francis Bacon (1909-1992). The art auctioneer, Christie's, held expectations of an $85 million price tag for this post-war contemporary painting. The final bidder had the privilege of paying $142.4 million for a painting produced in 1969.

When the super-heated auctions at Christie's and Sotheby's begin to experience decreased bidding values and price declines, that's when the art bubble euphoria will start to fade. No doubt, many savvy art collectors have learned how to make millions of dollars riding bubbles during these periods. It is interesting to note that when the painting "Pablo Picasso's Young Lover" sold for $27.6 million in February 2016, that price was 31 percent less than the amount paid by its owner two years earlier. At that same auction, Sotheby's experienced a 54 percent drop (over the previous year) in the sale of its impressionist and modern art pieces. What a difference a year makes.

COMMERCIAL REAL ESTATE AS A GLOBAL COLLAPSE INDICATOR

JAPAN: As stated elsewhere, the Japanese Heisei Bubble experience was reminiscent of the period in America before the 1929 stock market crash. The extreme euphoria, high-flying lifestyle, and the planning of grand enterprises are some of the

BOOMING 80S COLLECTIBLES

ITEM	PRICE	YEAR SOLD
Vincent Van Gogh: "Portrait of Dr. Gachet"	$82.5 million	1990
Renoir: "Au Moulin de la Galette"	$78.1 million	1990
Vincent Van Gogh: "Irises"	$53.9 million	1987
Vincent Van Gogh: "Bridge of Trinquetaille"	$20.2 million	1987
Vincent Van Gogh: "Sun Flowers"	$39.9 million	1987
Picasso: "Acrobat and Young Harlequin"	$38.46 million	1988
Picasso: "Maternite"	$24.75 million	1988
12th Century Book	$11.9 million	1988
1000-Year-old Hebrew Bible	$3.19 million	1989
Mark Hopkins Table	$250,000	1989
Dorothy's Ruby Slippers from "The Wizard of Oz"	$165,000	1988
Rare Drawing of Mickey Mouse by Walt Disney	$110,000	1989
Miniature Stained Glass House by Frank Lloyd Wright	$704,000	1988

TABLE 1

POST-2008 COLLECTIBLES

ITEM	PRICE	SOLD
Francis Bacon: "Three Studies of Lucian Freud"	$142.4 million	Nov. 2013
Jeff Koons: "Balloon Dog"	$58.4 million	May 2013
Picasso: "Pablo Picasso's Young Lover"	$27.6 million	Feb. 2016
Edvard Munch: "The Scream"	$119.9 million	May 2013
Picasso: "Tete de Femme"	$39.9 million	Nov. 2015
Andy Warhol: "Coca-Cola"	$57.2 million	Nov. 2013
Amedeo Modigliani: "Nu Couche"	$170.4 million	Nov. 2013
Roy Lichtenstein "Nurse"	$95.3	Nov. 2013

TABLE 2

characteristics of the speculative mentality. In 1929, the Empire State Building was under construction, a monument designed to become the tallest building in the world. In 1990, Japanese industrialists were in the design stages and planning of a monument that would be the grandest skyscraper ever built in modern civilization: *AEROPOLIS 2001*.

In 2010, the Burj Khalifa was completed (the tallest building in the world), Dubai's monument to its status of wealth and prosperity. Shortly after its completion, Dubai experienced a significant downturn during that year.

CHINA: In response to the *Meltdown of 2008*, China implemented easy money policies to stimulate its economy: the world relied on China as a source of growth during the weak recovery period of 2009-2012. According to a report entitled "Household Registration and Migrant Labor in China," 23 million rural migrant workers lost their jobs in the wake of the 2008-09 meltdown in America. The export industries were hardest hit and suffered immediate economic fallout from America. Trillions of dollars in cheap credit was released by the communist government to help stem the tide of unrest and civil disturbance. However, much of the excess cash flowed into pumping up China's real estate markets. Economic data suggest that real estate investments increased dramatically after 2008, a direct result of the stimulus program initiated by the Chinese government to counter the impact of the global recession. A clear indication of the impact is what occurred in 2009; new construction projects increased across the board throughout China. Large-scale urbanization and rapidly rising incomes were the justification for the extraordinary boom period.

As a result of this great real estate boom period, China became home to the largest number of the tallest skyscrapers in the world. In the year 2015 alone, it was reported that 106 new skyscrapers were built in China, which was the highest number of superstructures ever built in a 12-month period. Half of the top ten skyscrapers in the world are now located in China. Some of the iconic names of these structures are as follows: Shanghai Tower (2,073 feet); Ping An Finance Centre (1821 feet); Golden Finance (1,957 feet); Wuhan Greenland Center (1,988 feet); and Shanghai World Financial Center (1,614 feet). China's real estate building spree is unlike anything that has ever been undertaken by a single country in world history. It is interesting to note that before the year 2000 the tallest buildings in most downtown cities in China were 10-to-30 story structures. This is a sign of the times, with grand commercial real estate ventures signaling an imminent global collapse.

NEW YORK: With wealth inequality soaring during the post-2008 period, the high-end real estate markets in New York and London witnessed extreme transaction deals. On the south side of Central Park sits *billionaire row*, an affluent ultra-wealthy condominium community that, in 2016 and beyond, is expanding to accommodate the demand of more ultra-wealthy clients. With a fabulous view of Central Park and located near the best shopping and restaurants in the area, this prestigious development became a feature attraction for many of the wealthy elite, driving prices to extraordinary levels. In January 2015, a condo sold for $100 million at the One57 building, a 90-story condominium complex. By June 2016, Vornado Realty Trust unveiled its mansion in the sky, a 23,000 square foot penthouse at 220 Central Park South; the price for this trophy property was set at $250 million. Condo fees (alone) per year were scheduled at $520,000, with yearly taxes of $675,000. The total space would include four floors (50th to the 53rd floor, which is part of a 66-floor development scheduled to be completed by 2018), 16 bedrooms, 17 bathrooms and five balconies. The price per square foot would be over $11,000. This is reminiscent of the frenzied speculation that drove the price of the prime real estate in Tokyo to over $10,000 per square foot during the second half of the 1980s before Japan's grand bubble bursting in 1990.

With prices soaring to these lofty levels, several new towers were planned with completion dates scheduled by 2020. One of these new towers is on course to become the tallest residential building in the western hemisphere, 1,550 feet. Also, Chinese investment company, Anbang Insurance Group Company, decided to purchase the Waldorf Astoria Hotel (New York's landmark hotel consisting of 47 floors) in late 2014, as a major condo conversion development project. The price paid was $1.95 billion, and the company plans to spend an additional $1 billion on a major renovation and redevelopment of the property. Of the 1,413 rooms that comprise the Waldorf, 1100 of these rooms will be converted into condos. The plan calls for closing the facility for three years, after which time the property will be reopened with luxury condos and 300 to 500 upgraded hotel rooms.

SUMMARY/ANALYSIS

We are living during the apex of the *Age of the Billionaire*. Gross inequality is expanding in countries throughout the world, and will ultimately lead to the grand bursting of a global super-bubble of debt and credit. When the bubble burst, we can expect a severe collapse into deflation and the onset of economic depression. The Fed and other central bankers around the world will again seek to stop the descent before it becomes too late! All conventional and unconventional tools will be employed during each phase of the next downward spiral: Quantitative Easing (QE), Zero-bound interest rates, Negative interest rates, Helicopter Money, Special Facilities for Debt Forgiveness, etc. The decision will be to either save civilization or let it collapse into barbarism, depression, and chaos.

Thus, the set-up for the next crisis is in place. Since the banks have gotten bigger, it makes their preeminent standing and guaranteed bailout ticket a near certainty in America. And looming on the horizon is the possibility of another credit crunch or a sudden rise in interest rates or oil could be the spark for the onset of an abrupt crisis. *Financial Weapons of Mass Destruction* (derivatives) are in place and again represent a ticking time bomb. The global risk factor has increased since the first phase of the meltdown. *The chess pieces have reassembled; 2008 will happen again, but this time on a much larger scale.* In 2008, it was mortgage-backed securities; at the center of the next significant downturn will be European Sovereign Debt crisis. That debt cesspool is a lot bigger, and there may be enormous obstacles preventing any major bailouts.

The underlining premise of this book is that we have yet to experience the total impact of the *Great Depression of the 21st Century*. We must remain conscious of the fact that economic depressions have the potential of initiating political revolutions, as the world continues to navigate through this period of vast uncertainties. In America (and in other parts of the world), the gap between the extremely wealthy and everyone else (the 1% versus the 99%) is at a level reminiscent or worse than 1928, the year before the crash of 1929 and the advent of the *1930s Great Depression*. History tells us that these types of extremes are not healthy and are unsustainable. I hope that we will not have to wait until everything is broken before we get full consensus on how to realistically deal with this economic crisis of our times.

NOTES

(1) Mike Roscoe, "What Does $200 Trillion of Debt Really Mean for the Global Economy," Published by Positive Money blog on Feb.5, 2015.
(2) Gabriel Zucman and Emmanuel Saez, *Wealth Inequality In The United States Since 1913: Evidence From Capitalized Income Tax Data*, National Bureau of Economic Research, Cambridge, MA, October 2014.
(3) IBID., Zucman and Saez Report.
(4) Anthony Shorrocks, James B. Davies, Rodrigo Lluberas and Antonios Koutsoukis, *Credit Suisse 2016 Global Wealth Report*, Credit Suisse Research Institute, November 2016.
(5) Ricardo Fuentes - Nieva and Nick Galasso et.al, *Working for the Few: Political capture and economic inequality*, Oxfam International (178 Oxfam Briefing Paper - Summary, www.oxfam.org), January 2014.
(6) Max Lawson, An Economy For The 1%: How privilege and power in the economy drive extreme inequality and how this can be stopped, Oxfam International (210 Oxfam Briefing Paper - Summary, www.oxfam.org), January 18, 2016.
(7) Paul Handley, "IMF warns the US over high poverty, inequality", Yahoo News, June 22, 2016.
(8) IBID., IMF
(9) GAO: Senator Bernie Sanders, U.S. Senator from Vermont, "The Veil of Secrecy at the Fed Has Been Lifted, Now It's Time for Change," GAO Audit, www.sanders.senate.gov, November 2011.
(10) Dr. Ravi Batra, T*he Great Depression of 1990*, (New York: Simon & Shuster, 1987) pp. 121-122.
(11) Batra, IBID, pg. 125.
(12) Batra, IBID, pg 123.
(13) Dr. Ravi Batra, *Surviving The Great Depression of 1990*, (New York: Simon & Shuster, 1988) pp. 256-257.
(14) By 1993 the art boom in Japan was over. Japanese investors who had paid extraordinary prices for collectibles during the late 1980s were hit hard by the rapidly falling prices during the deflationary period of the early 1990s. Impressionist art prices had fallen by 50 percent and many American and European dealers traveled to Japan looking to pick up rare paintings for bargain prices. If Mr. Ryoei Saito (who purchased two paintings for $160.6 million during the boom period) had been forced to sell his paintings in 1993, he would have suffered an enormous loss. The boom

and bust cycle works in this manner: whatever had been the subject of the boom period, would depreciate the most during the bust cycle.

(15) Leslie Helm, "Renoirs Stuck in Warehouses," *San Francisco Chronicle*, January 24, 1993, (Sunday Punch) pg. 6.

(16) Agustino Fontevecchia, "China Brings Down Global Art Market In Q1 But U.S. And Europe Feed the Bulls", *Forbes,* 4-24-2013.

CHAPTER THIRTEEN
SINGULARITY OF THE EPIC GLOBAL SUPER BUBBLE

The financial crisis of 2007-2008 converted central bankers into a new class of power brokers...The scope of their activities, and the sheer level of international coordination and its results, was unthinkable before 2008...Never before has money been so cheap - for so long.

Nomi Prins, Author and Journalist

Sustained deflation can be highly destructive to a modern economy and should be strongly resisted.
Former Fed Chairman Ben Bernanke

PARABLE OF A COLOSSAL BUBBLE

It will be a world-class event that people will be talking about for centuries. So this is a historic announcement, an announcement that is more earth-shattering than the development of the nuclear age and the first atom bomb, a statement that is comparable to putting a man on the moon, an announcement that is tantamount to the birth of the Industrial Age. It's a massive development that has been in the making for over a century. It's a development made possible and could only happen as a result of the *age of globalization* and the massive expansion of fiat currencies, credit, and debt. Thus, its birth, in part, is made possible by the *Creature from Jekyll Island* and a series of *boom and bust cycles* spanning decades. We are living in the twilight zone where reality has been placed in suspended animation and time is speeding by like the blink of an eye.

This titanic of economic lore will henceforth be known as the *Singularity of the EPIC Global Super Bubble*. Unlike anything ever devised by man or demigod, it links the world's major bubbles in an inseparable bond in ways that can readily spark or bring unpredictable reactions in the new global financial paradigm. Indeed, this is the most significant *Economic X Factor* ever to set foot on the world stage.

What does the real estate bubble in China, currency wars, commercial real estate bubbles in London, San Francisco and New York, the U.S. stock market bubbles, the global derivatives ticking time bomb, the global ultra-wealthy art bubbles, the U.S. student loan debt bubble all have in common: they are all critical aspects of a worldwide financial paradigm giving birth to a *singularity* with multiple deflationary trigger mechanisms. This vast system of interconnections is preparing the global community for a massive event of contagion and economic mayhem. It is the completion of the *Grand Convergence* which is now set to unleash its deflationary vortex on the world.

Globalization and the world's foremost central banks have created a new *monster*, and perhaps this one will devour us quickly when the time comes for the next major *meltdown*. As this *monster* implodes inward, deflation will strike deep into the core, crushing everything in its path. Global central banks will do battle with the *beast* with massive conventional and unconventional monetary tools, and the monster will respond with a mighty burst and outward explosion of hyperinflation, and the people will scream with horror as the world descends into chaos, war, and disruption.

A WORLD OF BUBBLE MANIA

After the gold standard was abandoned in 1971 and the free-floating global fiat money system was born, the central bank expansion of money creation exploded. Since the late 1970s and early 1980s, we have witnessed boom and bust cycles and bubble creations that have exhibited steeper exponential growth patterns during each major historical crisis: the U.S. boom and bust of 1982 to 1987; the Japan boom and bust from 1985 to 1990; the U.S. boom and bust from 1995 to 2000; and the U.S. and global boom and bust from 2003 to 2008. Some analysts and economists have chosen to identify this entire 24-year period as one great bull market and secular historical boom. This observation is well and good, for I feel that we are indeed talking about the same phenomenon, just breaking it down in a different manner.

However, there was a fundamental change in the paradigm in 2008. Up to that point, the pattern had been for the boom cycles to last for roughly five year periods, with bust cycles and recessions averaging 18 months to three years, except for the extraordinary case of Japan. In regards to the U.S., the Fed became more aggressive with money creation starting with the *Crash of '87*, and building more considerable momentum during the financial crisis of the late 1990s and the year 2000. The bust cycle of 2000 to 2002, which included 911, witnessed larger monetary stimulus plans, igniting the next recovery period. But the 2008 meltdown was the major turning point; it was even given the unique name of *meltdown* to describe the extraordinary events unveiled during the crisis. And with each recovery growing progressively weaker, the stimulus packages had to consist of more firepower, much greater monetary creation by the Fed.

The Fed response to this *meltdown* was mostly unconventional and unprecedented when we examine the historical records of central banking policies. With ultra-low interest rates (near zero from December 2008 to 0.25 percent to December 2015) held in place for seven to eight years, a series of QE stimulus plans (by late 2016 global QE exceeded $13 trillion), and carefully structured coordinated actions with other central bankers around the world, the Fed created an artificial monetary environment that promoted the extension of a bull-run that by 2017, was in its eighth year (known as the *central bank trade*). The pattern had been for the Fed to inflate a new bubble to recover from a previous bear market decline. We had gone three years past the norm (the five-year boom cycle) and everyone was wondering how long could this thing go on?

The standard reality of bubbles is that they all burst, and there are no exceptions. They do not gradually descend back down to earth; they explode with a loud burst shocking the masses and the uninformed, spreading distress and misery across the land. The economic fallout is generally massive, wiping out trillions of dollars of wealth. There are winners and losers in every episode, in many cases, it is a zero-sum gain, with the smartest insiders and professionals walking away with the profits.

The asset price inflation since 2009 had produced massive gains for those in position to reap the benefits. These prices will rise until the magicians pull the plug on the party, then there will come the great fall that generates asset-price deflation. The next economic phase (a bear market) is a brief recession (if we are lucky) or a dramatic push into a deflationary depression if things spin entirely out of control (the worst case scenario).

Meanwhile, the fate of the U.S. and the world is in the hands of the Fed and other major world central bankers. However, this time around (as announced elsewhere in this publication) we are looking at the formal development of a *new paradigm* which economist Richard Duncan identifies as the new era of *Creditism*. In simple language, this new system of expanding credit and debt (two sides of the same coin) is what is keeping our global economy alive and functioning.

The challenges are enormous, particularly in the developed world where aging populations are spending less and planning to retire, where deleveraging of the epic super-debt bubble will continue for years, and where falling commodity prices may persist as a significant catalyst for deflation. However, global central bankers are signaling that this epic bubble will have to continue.

As this new era continues to take shape, fiat money creation is financing yearly U.S. national budget deficits. This process of Fed intervention is defined as monetizing the debt (See Glossary). In the case of Japan, the monetization of national debt became the standard operating procedure by the Bank of Japan (BOJ). The European

Central Bank (ECB) has done the same thing, along with other major central banks around the world. The result in all of these cases is the establishment of higher debt loads and the devaluation of currencies.

SUMMARY/ANALYSIS

Given that central bankers have not used all of their unconventional tools, we can expect additional surprises in the future if they are determined not to allow this historic and unprecedented epic bubble to fully deflate. There are still more options that can be deployed that are much more preferable than a deep deflationary depression. But this will require that central bankers and politicians expand their understanding of the broad fundamental changes that have taken place in the global economy over the past several decades.

With the removal of liquidity from the monetary system under quantitative tightening (QT) in the United States accompanied by rising interest rates, we can expect the systemic collapse of many of the bubbles discussed in this chapter. These are typical events that precede the bursting of real estate and stock market bubbles. Credit contraction and the decline of easy money policies will undoubtedly move the global economy into a downward spiral.

We have reached the zenith of capitalism, and it has evolved into something that very few mainstream economists even recognize. There is this intellectual suspicion that something has changed, but few understand what that is.

CHAPTER FOURTEEN
THE SUPER NOVA OF DEBT/CREDIT AND DEFLATION

The question is not whether we are going to abandon capitalism and replace it with a different kind of economic system. We did that long ago. The question is: Are we going to allow the economic system now in place to collapse.

Economist Richard Duncan

When we have a bear market again, and we are going to have a bear market again, it will be the worst in our lifetime...Debt is everywhere, and it's much, much higher now.

Jim Rogers, Chairman of Rogers Holdings Inc.

We are experiencing a super debt cycle that has been in motion for the past two decades; wherein debt escalation is moving in an upward trend with no end in sight. We are inundated with a massive profusion of debt in all facets of the global economic system. In fact, the worldwide economic system is dependent on debt growth to generate economic growth. In the normal capitalistic sense, there is no solution outside of the continued expansion of this new debt paradigm, what economist Richard Duncan refers to as a new era of *creditism*.

Since the *Meltdown of 2008*, much of the toxic private debt was converted into public debt, expanding the risks in the public sector (taxpayer obligations) at the global level; an expansion that took root in countries all over the world. The entire global economy is now facing a sovereign debt crisis and global deflation, and too much debt ultimately leads to a period of prolonged deflation, similar to what has occurred in Japan. Also, the rapid increase in private-sector debt will eventually lead to a period of severe deleveraging initiating prolonged recessions. Hence, we are in a debt supercycle with no painless standard capitalistic solutions in sight.

Economist Kenneth Rogoff warns that "The problem with high debt levels is that it's very paralyzing."[1] And during the next significant downturn, it will become painfully apparent that much of this debt will not be repaid or serviced, generating a severe crisis for many counterparty creditors, forcing them into bankruptcy.

When the *McKinsey Report* (a publication produced by the McKinsey global Consulting Research firm) came out in February 2015 with a scathing report on massive global debt loads, many analysts immediately understood the global implications of enormous debt expansion in nations throughout the world. The report compiled data on debt owed by governments/countries, corporations, banks, and households (public and private debt) and revealed a world firmly addicted to higher levels of debt. By first quarter 2015, total debt worldwide had risen by $57 trillion since the start of the Great Recession that began in December of 2007.

The numbers are revealing: the total global debt load was around $140 trillion in 2008, and by early 2015, it had climbed to nearly $200 trillion. The Mckinsey report makes the case that the additional $57 trillion in debt gave rise to only $15 trillion in new global GDP, with GDP moving from $55 trillion to $70 trillion over an eight-year period.[2] During that same period, corporate debt soared from $3.5 trillion in late 2007 to nearly $7 trillion in 2015.

Standard & Poor's (S&P: a top U.S. rating agency) did an interesting analysis in 2016 on the borrowing behavior and patterns of corporate America, and discovered that corporate debt was "getting out of control." Their finding indicated that corporate America had borrowed over $10 trillion since the *Meltdown of 2008*. Instead of deleveraging during that period, the low cost of borrowing and a strong bull market encouraged these companies to expand their balance sheets with massive amounts of debt. In 2015 alone, $1.5 trillion was borrowed. After examining the balance sheets of 2,000 U.S. corporations, the S&P gave us this startling revelation:

> "U.S. corporations have a record $1.84 trillion in cash on their books. That's the good news. The bad news is that more than half of this cash belongs to just 25 companies or about 1% of Corporate America. The group includes tech giants like Apple (AAPL) and Microsoft (MSFT)...If you remove the top 25 cash holders, you'll find that for most of Corporate America, cash on hand is declining even as these companies rack up more and more debt at historic rates. The bottom 99% of corporate borrowers have just $900 billion in cash on hand to back up $6 trillion in debt...This resulted in a cash-to-debt ratio of 12% - the lowest recorded over the past decade, including the years preceding the Great Recession...A cash-to-debt ratio compares how much cash a company has compared to debt. The higher the ratio, the better. A cash-to-debt ratio of 12% means companies have just $0.12 of cash for every dollar of debt."[3]

The report also makes the point that the Fed had kept its key interest rates near zero since the advent of the 2008 crisis. The strategy was to encourage borrowing and spending to stimulate the economy. However, what the report reveals is that "Companies didn't borrow to buy machinery, equipment, or anything else that grows a business. Instead, they borrowed to buy other companies and their stock, also known as a "share buyback."[4]

All of this was a clear indication that the vast majority of this new debt was not being channeled into the productive capacity of the global economy, but was misallocated on developmental projects (ghost cities in China) corporate share buybacks (in corporate America) and speculation in the markets. The result is that expanding debt creation was having less and less impact on real economic growth throughout the worldwide economy. This is the kind of stuff that will quickly unravel during the next major downturn, revealing who was indeed scaling the heights of folly. Debt deflation will have a devastating impact on the bottom 99% of corporate borrowers who soaked up the virtually interest-free money offered by the Fed.

Japan tops the list as the country that had fallen deeper in the rabbit hole of debt, which we explored in greater detail in an earlier chapter. Moving along a similar path, China's debt load soared from $2 trillion in the year 2000 to $28 trillion in debt by early 2015. In the years following the *Meltdown of 2008*, China accumulated $21 trillion of debt in a little less than eight years, which was an extraordinary development. In 2014, 5200 emerging-market companies issued a combined total of $1.1 trillion in bonds, much of it to finance commodity-production and manufacturing production capacity. However, in a world already drowning in a sea of excessive supply of most raw materials, as well as finished products, the additional debt expansion by these companies did not bring the added profits in a world experiencing decrease demand.

And there is another more sinister aspect to this debt monster; it's deeply embedded in the foundations of the world economy where write-offs and other expedient solutions will not work. Those in the know are keenly aware that the entire global economic system would collapse if there are too many radical adjustments to this debt pyramid. The debt boom and credit expansion are on hyper-drive and steroids, and it will continue until we stumble or are maneuvered into the next major economic and financial implosion.

This massive debt expansion has generated a *paradigm shift* throughout the global economic system which is now firmly in place. The vast majority of this debt cannot be repaid, and as far as the international banking cartel is concerned, this new paradigm is an ideal situation to continue earning interest payments on all of that wonderful debilitating debt; it is in their best interest if the debt is never repaid. After all, paid off debts do not generate interest payments.

To stimulate and propel the global economic recovery after the *Meltdown of 2008*, global central bankers decreased interest rates by more than 650 times, a clear indication that the massive crisis had produced catastrophic damage. Also, the unconventional central bank tool of negative interest rates (NIRP: something that was not envisioned before 2014) added another layer of risk and debt expansion. By 2016, government bonds with NIRP totaled nearly $13 trillion. It's apparent that the world will need to embrace a new paradigm in economics; a definite indication as to where this is all heading. Let's be clear in this narrative: the worldwide economic system is in a desperate situation!

DEBT AND DEFLATION

The historical record on what happens when there is a massive build-up of debt at the government, business, and household levels is clear: at the point when the debt can no longer be sustained, deleveraging, bankruptcy and other restrictive measures get implemented. In general, during tough times, consumers will be forced to cut back on expenditures, focusing more on necessities such as food, toilet paper, soap, housing, medical care and gasoline for the automobile to get to work. The sale of non-essentials, such as big appliances, clothing, cars, eating out, etc., will decline, leading to a measurable decrease in economic activity.

In the case of the U.S., where consumer spending account for 70% of total GDP, if large segments of the population begin to delay purchases and severely reduce expenditures, this will lead to a downward spiral in the economy. A chain reaction of events will start to unfold, exacerbated by the presence of excessive debt loads.

As consumers cut back, business revenues decline, cash-flow shortages manifest, liquidity problems surface leading to cost-cutting measures and layoffs. Prices will fall because distressed companies will begin to sell off their inventories at low prices to generate revenues. Construction projects will be shut down, and factories will be forced to close their doors. For those remaining employed, salaries may be cut or frozen as companies struggle to stay afloat. Decreased incomes lead to less spending, and in a slow growth economy, it doesn't take much of an economic shock to move to the downside, an event that would undoubtedly move us into negative territory very quickly. This is what happened in 2008, the initiation of an accelerated deflationary collapse.

Recessions that follow a significant financial crisis, associated with massive accumulated debts, tend to be deeper and more uncontrollable. The *debt problems* that caused the crisis shifts from the private sector to the public sector generating a negative impact on government revenue streams (taxes). High unemployment has a major effect on governmental finance and budgets: lost jobs mean government collects less tax revenue; the government has to spend more on unemployment benefits, food stamps, and other social programs. Anemic economic growth makes it difficult to grow your way out of the crisis, and without an intervention, the problem lingers on for many years.

As business and consumer confidence get eroded with collapsing stock markets, business closures and soaring unemployment take center stage. And as business owners and consumers spend and invest less, this will cause more turmoil in the markets. If prices and business revenues stay down for a significant period, wages will decline as well. It generates what some analysts call a "negative feedback loop" that drives an economy into a recession or deeper economic crisis.

When there is a massive debt implosion, deflation is the first economic plague that creates a depression phenomenon. In a deflationary environment, fixed-rate debt becomes more expensive to maintain due to less money in circulation and decreased incomes. Regular monthly payments on mortgages, car notes, etc. are difficult to sustain. And given that deleveraging would dominant consumer psychology during a deflationary debt cycle, it is clear to see why this is considered the worse economic environment imaginable. Every clear thinking politician, economist or central banker should always seek to avoid this monster. And keep in mind, the longer this type of economic crisis continues, the deeper the painful consequences that society will have to endure, and the more difficult it would be to break free of its death grip.

Since the beginning of the *Great Recession*, central bankers and governments around the world have been committed to not letting the most enormous debt bubble in history implode, unleashing what would undoubtedly be a massive demonstration of global deflation and economic chaos, much worse than the *1930s Great Depression*. And once debt deflation is allowed to settle deeply into the fabric of a financial system, it is very difficult to get rid of it. What needs to be fully appreciated and acknowledged, is that a prolonged period of deflation can eventually lead to (in this global era) regional and global wars.

Given the mentality and contentious nature of many global leaders, corporate oligarchs and those who have visions of global domination, the potential to descend into *barbarism* is a real and deadly threat to our global civilization. Once our world moves in that direction, exponential deterioration could take place very quickly. It will not be a slow progression into the deflationary vortex due to the fact that we are in the midst of the most massive debt and credit bubble in the history of the world. The pain, confusion, and chaos that would result from the bursting of this bubble are unimaginable.

Over 60 million people were killed during World War II, and at the start of that war, no nation in the world possessed nuclear weapons. The finale of World War II was the birth of the nuclear age that witnessed the devastating destruction of the atom bombs that were dropped on Hiroshima and Nagasaki. The Great Depression preceded that great war, with fascism, racism, excessive greed (by those in power) and economic distress running rampant throughout the world. The main point here is that WW II began with the world possessing no nuclear weapons.

So why do I raise these issues in a book that should only be discussing such things as interest rates, unemployment, GDP and inflation? Well, the short answer is that economic issues are intimately tied to the social, political, technological and spiritual growth or decline in our global civilization. And given the financial and economic extremes that our world is now experiencing, it is time for deep reflection by those who sincerely understand this narrative and can sense the impending danger.

Some of the nuclear weapons in today's world are 3,000 times more powerful than the atom bomb that was dropped on Hiroshima. Thus, if our leaders start pushing buttons, it would most likely mean the end of our civilization. There would be survivors, but the world would be left in utter chaos and a state of complete barbarism.

Inherent in the threat of the release of debt deflation is the ultimate manifestation of economic devastation and war. For those who favor allowing this bubble to implode to clean the slate of all bad debt, there needs to be a deep reflection on the full nature of the kind of bubble confronting our world. It is the most significant debt and credit bubble ever devised by man, and just cleaning the slate is not the remedy for something this massive.

SUMMARY/ANALYSIS

The big story in this chapter is that our global economy is heading into the next financial crisis with an extraordinary amount of accumulated debt at all levels of society. And since the U.S. and most of the developed world has not experienced a deflationary depression in nearly 90 years, we are most likely overdue for such a crisis. *The Meltdown of 2008* is often compared to the *Great Depression of the 1930s*, for history is telling us that the deflationary impact of both economic events are very similar.

The ball and chain of debt firmly attached around the ankles of millions of people around the world will be the finishing blow that will bring about what could be the worst economic depression in world history. It is a crisis that has been building momentum for over a period of decades, with the Fed and other global central bankers delaying the *Day of Reckoning*.

NOTES

(1) Kenneth Rogoff, "Austerity and debt realism,"*The Guardian*, June 1, 2012.
(2) Richard Dobbs, Susan Lund, Jonathan Woetzel and Mina Mutafchieva, "Debt and (not much) deleveraging," McKinsey Global Institute February 2015 Report, February 2015.
(3) Justin Spittler, "Why 99% of U.S. Corporations Could Go Bankrupt in the Coming Deflationary Depression," Casey Research, May 31, 2016.
(4) Ibid. Justin Spittler.

CHAPTER FIFTEEN
HARRY DENT AND DEMOGRAPHIC TURNING POINTS

No matter what the world conditions are, there are always people and companies all over the world with huge amounts of capital to invest. That capital will always search and flow towards the safest and best returns possible no matter where they are in the world.

Larry Edelson, Global Analyst

In May of 1987, I completed my MBA degree at San Francisco State University and was looking forward to considering my next career move. Little did I know that an event in the fall of that year would change my life forever and start me on a journey towards an in-depth analysis and understanding of boom and bust cycles. The *Crash of '87* struck on October 19th, and that seminal event had a profound impact on my thinking and awareness on what was really happening in financial markets throughout the world.

I can't recall (at all) any significant discussions in any of my classes regarding the nature and significance of *boom and bust cycles* in global economic thought. When I started researching the great crash of 1987, I came to a startling realization that we had gone through a boom period (or cycle) while I was studying for my MBA, *and I didn't know it*. My curriculum did not expose me to any examination or the study of *boom and bust periods*. No doubt, this would have better prepared me for the massive changes that took place in the explosive decade of the 1990s. And perhaps I would have had a much better frame of reference from which to evaluate significant economic events in the global arena.

What was a major topic in several of my classes at that time, was the incredible developments that had taken shape in Japan. Japanese management techniques, technological, scientific and marketing prowess was examined in great detail. There was fear and admiration concerning the strength and resilience of this island nation. One of the books that was required reading in one of my classes was *A Book of Five Rings* by Miyamoto Musashi, the famous Japanese swordsman. Another favorite was *The Art of War* by Sun Tzu. I guess my instructors were preparing American business students for the brutal competitive warfare that takes place in the world of business, especially international business.

In those last few years of the 1980s, Japan had become so powerful that economists and analysts were predicting that it was destined to become the number one economic power in the world. The United States was being overtaken and surpassed by the strength and ingenuity of the *Japanese Juggernaut.*

Deeply influenced by the *Crash of 1987*, and as a novice in the economic arena seeking to become a first-time author, in 1988 I began working on my first book entitled, *World Economic Collapse: The Last Decade and the Global Depression*. It was my first major attempt to understand economic cycles and the underlying reasoning for the existence of boom and bust periods. Little did I know, that this would define my professional development and interests for decades to come.

It was a very critical decision I made at that point because I had initially thought of writing a book about stock market investments, which would have been a much better decision. There is a moral to this story, which is why I've decided to discuss my *economic awakening* in this book.

As I continued to research my chosen topic, the world was going through some profound changes. In 1989, the Soviet Union's global empire began to implode, bringing about an enormous wave of challenges for the decade of the 1990s. The war in Iraq in 1989 was another earth-shaking event that helped to bring about a recession in America during the opening years of the 1990s. And in 1990, Japan began its epic collapse, which was a shock to many observers and analysts. Thus, as a novice rogue economist, I was pulled deeper into my analysis and convinced that the decade of the 1990s would experience a depression. I was mesmerized and fell under the spell of a world descending into chaos.

So let me put this into perspective, like other authors during the early 1990s (Ravi Batra, Lord Rees Mogg, Robert Prechter and others), I was thoroughly convinced that we were in the midst of a massive downward wave. And by the time 1992 came on the scene, the primary drivers of my analysis was not only Japan's bubble collapse in 1990 (the second largest economy in the world), the Soviet Union demise, and the first war in Iraq, but also the collapse of the Savings and Loans industry during the late 1980s, the junk bond market implosion, and the *Crash of 1987* as the initial catalyst for the economic downturn of the 1990s. Despite the fact that these were compelling events that would participate in reshaping the world of the 1990s, they did not derail the critical direction and mission that America was destined to achieve. *And that was a very important and expensive lesson for me to understand*. My first book came out in 1994, and aside from some good narratives and historical data, *it was utterly useless in predicting the outcome of that decade.*

And the irony runs a little deeper. I had worked as a computer operator with mainframe and minicomputers in the late 1970s, and witnessed the adoption and transition to the microcomputer revolution by the mid-1980s; so I had some real appreciation for computer technology. Also, I chose as the topic for my MBA thesis the examination of revolutionary new emerging digital technologies. My master's thesis at San Francisco State University was entitled, *Analysis of the Optical Disk Industry & Business Plan for a Start-Up Company - KMT, Inc.* I had a focus on the developing *Information Age Revolution* and how it was unfolding with innovations. However, the subsequent reality was that my thesis was a mere academic exercise and not positioned as a strategic plan to execute in the marketplace. Fortunately, I was able to revisit my thesis in 1994 by working on a new book project.

I continued my science and technology analysis by coauthoring a book in 1996 entitled, *Black Futurists in the Information Age: Vision of a 21st Century Technological Renaissance*. I have to give credit to my coauthor, Timothy L. Jenkins, for helping me to re-focus my attention on the unfolding *Information Age Revolution* of the mid to late 1990s. I ran into Timothy at a multi-cultural book conference in San Francisco in 1994 where we began to discuss the significance of the Information Age. During his visit to San Francisco, Timothy had the opportunity to read my master's thesis on optical disk technologies and was convinced that we needed to coauthor a book on science and technology as it related to the contributions of African Americans. By 1996, the book was a reality, and to our credit, we had published a book on scientific and technological developments in the early stages of the Dot-Com and Internet revolution of the mid to late 1990s.

Having a coauthor at that point in my career was very important; I have to question if I would have moved in that direction (on my own) in developing a book on the dynamic emergence of the Information Age.

Thus, despite all of the fireworks and doom and gloom of the early 1990s, by 1995 the commercialization of the *Internet Age* was born. And that was a huge phenomenon! Had I remained on the same course as my first book had dictated, it would have lead to a period of wasted years and missed opportunities. I had spent close to seven years working on that book and, by 1994, I still did not have the complete picture and clear understanding of boom and bust cycles.

When I reflect on this period, I have to conclude that I had not completely understood the power and cyclical nature of economic cycles, particularly in regards to the tech revolution of that emerging era. Fortunately, I did ultimately participate as an investor and trader in the Dot-Com bubble but didn't have great timing and recognition of the emergence of its collapse in the year 2000. In other words, the cyclical pattern of economic developments was not a working model in my toolbox that I systematically employed in a full analysis of stock markets and central banker activities. My journey and investigations were still incomplete, and it had been a long and hard period of trial and error.

From my conscious experience of the late 1990s, it became imperative for me to apply this canon of strategic planning for the 21st century: always continue to develop a working knowledge of new technologies, expand my awareness of boom and bust cycles, and maintain a never-ending system of research on the global economic system. The combination of understanding economic cycles and the emergence of technological revolutions generates and stimulates a powerful mindset. For millennials and boomers who may be reading this book, keep in mind how essential it is to have a multidisciplinary approach to the central topics covered throughout this publication.

More than ever, it's very important to have a strong personal vision about the future and what may be expected to be unveiled in this explosive period of *Technological Revolution*. There are many technological disrupters scheduled to be implemented in the not too distant future (and I will have much more to say out that in a separate publication). Thus, the moral of my story is as follows: "*He who fails to see the whole picture is committed to an incomplete vision of the future.*"

HARRY S. DENT AND THE SCIENCE OF DEMOGRAPHICS: THE MISSING LINK

Harry S. Dent is a well-known economist and analyst who has been going strong for over 30 years using demographic trends and other cycle indicators to predict significant shifts in the market. He is not a mainstream economist and is probably considered by most academic scholars as a *rogue economist*. His breakthrough in 1988 was the development of *The Generational Spending Wave*, what he grew to acknowledge as the holy grail in his economic thinking.

As the foundation of his economic thesis, this core discovery was to unveil a powerful link between the science of demographics and generational analysis, and the impact this has on economic performance and what is likely to occur in the markets. In short, Dent managed to elevate demographic analysis to a whole new level, making it a powerful and very useful economic tool.

He discovered a strong correlation between the S&P 500 and demographic trends, which unleashed the recipe to his secret sauce: that "People do predictable things as they age." And in that revelation, he came to understand a series of historical patterns and cycles that were all based on demographic analysis. Also, his analysis is pivotal in understanding the dynamic forces that influence economic growth and key turning points in *boom and bust cycles*.

Whenever I want to examine demographic information in regards to economic performance, I will always consult Dent Research, for he has been consistently accurate about significant turning points in the global economy based primarily on demographic trends. Of particular importance to me is his prediction during the early 1990s, where Dent was forecasting a major boom in the United States. His book, *The Great Boom Ahead (1993)*, was a masterpiece in predicting the economic and market developments for the 1990s, particularly in light of all the doom and gloom that was prevalent during the early recession years of that fabled decade. It's his bold prediction in the early 1990s that will always remind me of the fatal errors I committed to remaining focused on a depression era scenario during the early years of that decade. My misfortune is that I didn't read his book while conducting my research!

Instead of descending into a depression, America became the most exciting market in the world during the 1990s. In fact, the *Daring '90s* (a name I coined for this decade) turned out to be one of the most explosive bubble markets (if not the greatest) in the history of boom and bust cycles. Flight capital migrated to America, the financial capital of the world moved from Tokyo back to New York, the commercial Internet economy was born, and Dot-Com mania was the main "get wealthy" event. Dent's analysis of what the *Baby Boom* generation was expected to do, was astoundingly correct. He was predicting a boom, and it happened far beyond even his estimation. Here is what Dent said in the opening pages of his 1993 *rogue economic classic*:

> "Get ready for an unprecedented economic boom. Forget what some experts are saying about a slow, measured growth of the economy. Forget what doomsayers are saying about a depression...I have some welcome news for you, news of a dramatic upswing in the economy, news of a dawning new era of prosperity in which many of you will actually feel wealthy...This final phase of the 1990 to 1993/1994 recession is just the last nasty dose of medicine to prepare us for the most potent phase of the greatest economic boom in our history...The coming boom will be even more astonishing in its intensity, its length, and in the heights it reaches. So while we are gutting out this severe, temporary slump we should be preparing for the great surprise of our times - a long, unprecedented boom - without inflation!"[1]

So the 1990s was a very significant decade, and Harry Dent and his organization, Dent Research, made a clear assessment of what was to follow the early recession years of 1990 to 1993/1994. The primary reason why Dent was so confident in his analysis, was what the historical demographic data had unveiled. At the root of his explosive revelation is the fundamental fact that "people are the force that drives markets and economic development." What the Dent Methodology unveils is that in "each generation people do predictable things as they age over time." His research brings to light, predictable patterns and behavior in regards to the earning of income, spending and consumption, and the demographic periods of productivity in society. Taken into full consideration, all of these factors can lead to making some compelling predictions.

According to Dent, "a new generation emerges about every 40 years or so, and as this generation goes through its life cycle of earning, spending and productivity, the impact is felt far and wide throughout the economy."[2] Dent's analysis states that, on average, members of each generation will enter the workforce at around age 20; marriage and apartments happen near the age of 26, and the growth of families with children takes shape around ages 28 and 29. In their early 30s, these developing members of society are actively buying their first starter homes. With the growth of families, between the ages of 37 and 41, these members will move on to buy larger homes. The peak spending phase will occur between the ages of 39 and 46, with the more affluent members extending their spending binge to around age 53. This key observation is what solidified Dent's prediction for the 1990s, because the first wave of America's massive *Baby Boom Generation* had entered this phase starting in 1983, with continuing waves through to the year 2007. Within the ages of 46 and 53, the average member will begin to shift his or her focus on preparation for retirement. Thus there will be less consumption and more saving during this phase. In their early to mid-60s, most will begin to retire and will have accumulated their greatest net worth (cash, investments, and assets) at that time. Afterward, the focus will be on vacation homes by age 65 and nursing homes by age 84.

The *Baby Boom Generation*, the largest and most influential generation in the history of demographics, has had a profound impact on the entire world since World War II. The traditional window of time used to evaluate the birth and size of this generation in America has been 1946 to 1964. And when adjusted for immigration, the size of the Baby Boom population is 76 to 80 million people. **Within the first and second decades of the 21st century, the generation of boomers will move into a retirement phase that will span over a 20 year period, with 10,000 boomers expected to retire every day.**

Under the Dent Method, the years and actual total number of Baby Boomers are adjusted to paint a slightly different picture. According to Dent, "The birth trends for Baby Boomers started in 1934 but accelerated in 1937 and peaked in 1961."[3] Adjusted for immigration, the size of this population group came to a total of 109.2 million people. Again, with the peak spending year identified as 46, the long-term boom period from 1983 (1937 plus 46 years) to 2007 (1961 plus 46 years) is substantiated by the "Spending Wave" of the massive Baby Boom generation.

According to Dent the 1990's boom was a readily predictable event once there was a clear understanding of demographic trends and technology innovation cycles. In his prediction of the "great bust" ahead, he tells us that:

> "The 1990s was totally predictable as the greatest boom in U.S. history if you simply looked at projectable demographic trends and cycles of technology innovation and the S-curve projections of progress. But economists don't dirty their hands with such consumer fundamentals. They don't consider

them as important as the intricacies of government policies. That's why they totally missed the greatest boom in history and will miss the greatest bust just ahead."[4]

THE DENT METHODOLOGY AND LONG WAVE CYCLES

In Chapter 11 we discussed the topic of Kondratieff's "Long Wave Cycles" that were indicating a downward wave in progress during the 1990s. Dent was fully aware of the implications of the K-Wave theory when he made his bold predictions for the latter part of that decade. To Dent, something had changed over the decades in the 20th century that altered the 45-60 year cycle analysis presented by Kondratieff. Dent agreed with Kondratieff's four-season analysis (two boom and bust cycles comprising the four-season cycle) but disagreed with the length and widely accepted timeline of the theory. His thoughts on this matter are as follows:

> "The first credible economic cycle I studied in the early 1980s was the Kondratieff Wave...This cycle of inflation and deflation was characterized as having four seasons: a spring boom with mildly rising inflation; a summer recession with inflation rising to a long-term peak with major wars; a fall boom with falling inflation, powerful new technologies moving into the mainstream, and a credit bubble that leads to high speculation and financial bubbles; and then finally the winter season with the bursting of the bubbles, debt deleveraging, deflation in prices, and depression...This cycle seemed to lose its generally predictable pattern decades ago for two reasons: First, after World War II the cycle got very exaggerated, with massively higher inflation trends from the entry of the supersized Baby Boom generation into the workforce, which is inflationary; second, when the next winter season to follow the Great Depression was due in the 1990s on that old sixty-year cycle, we got the greatest boom in history instead.

> At the same time, however, I was studying demographics and the Baby Boom. I understood that there was no way we could have a great depression when the largest generation by far was in its sweet spot for spending and borrowing in the 1990s...I presented my thoughts on a new, four-season economic cycle that spanned approximately eighty years. I saw that the Baby Boom simply exaggerated the cycle in terms of the magnitude of inflation and booms, and life expectancies took a big leap in the last century, extending all human-related cycles, including the length of booms and busts."[5]

Given the massive size of the Baby Boom generation and the shift from an agrarian society (the early 1900s) to the more affluent urban middle-class that dominated much of the 20th century, Dent decided to make some critical adjustments to the four-season model. Instead of a roughly sixty-year long-wave cycle, his analysis arrives at presenting an eighty-year model. The dramatic changes over the past century convinced Dent that the theory had to be adjusted to accommodate the modern era.

Traditional proponents of Kondratieff's theories and ideas will undoubtedly disagree with this approach, however, given Dent's record over the past 30 years for accurately predicting critical turning points in the economic arena; I think it would be hard to disprove this approach.

Dent's Demographic Methodology was an important breakthrough on his part, something that has not been fully appreciated by many economists (both mainstream and rogue), analysts and investors who carefully study economic developments. However, despite the fact that many people are not keenly aware of the significance of demographic science in the realm of economics, the popular discussion is that changes in the demographic arena are having an enormous impact on our world. For instance, many observers are beginning to understand that older people spend less money, pay fewer taxes and invest less, particularly as they move further into the retirement phase of their lives.

And as the demographics in Western societies continue the transition into older population groups and technological advances continue to accelerate over the next ten years, our world will continue to shift in the direction of deflation, not inflation. I agree with Dent that deflation and a downward cycle will dominate the period 2016 to roughly 2023. Dent is firmly predicting that we are now (2018) in the *winter season* of the four-season model, and that means deflation and depression ahead.[6]

SUMMARY

One of the main reasons why I continue to support Harry Dent's demographic thesis and his spending wave analysis is that he was absolutely right about the *great boom ahead* in America and the timing of the *Japanese meltdown* in the early 1990s. He wrote two books identifying these predictions that in large part was based on his convictions on what the demographic data was telling him.

I have a vivid memory of the atmosphere of the late 1980s and early 1990s, and it was doom and gloom, and as a novice economic analyst and writer, I was firmly in the depression camp. A variety of long-wave cycle theorists that promoted some version of the K-wave economic philosophy misunderstood the full picture of what would evolve during that fabled decade. Throughout much of the first half of the 1990s, I was committed to the downward wave and the great depression theme, but it was all an incomplete analysis. Not understanding the power of demographic cycles and trends was a very expensive lesson I had to learn and fully appreciate over time. And the irony of this revelation is the fact that I'm a member of the powerful *Baby Boom generation* that has been the main driver of global economic developments over the past several decades.

The power of the massive *Baby Boom generation* radically changed the forecast from dark and gloomy to a bright and sunny boom atmosphere. And as stated earlier, the 1995-2000 boom cycle was one of the most astounding bubble markets in financial history. Of course, over time, the lessons learned during that decade, has made me a lot better rogue analyst and economic thinker.

Harry Dent provided the right analysis of what would occur during the boom years, and I'm in full agreement with what he is predicting for the *winter season*.

NOTES

(1) Harry S. Dent Jr., *The Great Boom Ahead: Your Comprehensive Guide To Personal and Business Profit in the New Era of Prosperity*, (New York: Hyperion, 1993), pp. 3-5.
(2) Harry S. Dent Jr., *Great Boom Ahead*, p.9
(3) Harry S. Dent Jr., *Great Boom Ahead*, p.36-37
(4) Harry S. Dent, Jr., *The Sale of a Lifetime: How the Great Bubble Burst of 2017 Can Make You Rich*, (Delray Beach, FL: Delray Publishing, 2016), p. 74.
(5) Harry S. Dent, Jr., *The Demographic Cliff: How to Survive and Prosper During The Great Deflation Ahead*, (New York: Portfolio/Penguin, 2015), pp. 27-28.
(6) Given the extraordinary, unconventional power of global central bankers (particularly the Fed), we cannot rule out the possibility of periods of inflationary pressures or even hyperinflation in the West during the winter season. What has transpired since the *Meltdown of 2008* has demonstrated a new level of power that is firmly in the hands of global central bankers and the international banking cartel. They are taking global economics to a whole new level.

CHAPTER SIXTEEN
RICHARD DUNCAN AND CREDITISM

Speculative manias gather speed through expansion of money and credit. Most expansions of money and credit do not lead to a mania; there are many more economic expansions than there are manias. But every mania has been associated with the expansion of credit.

Charles P. Kindleberger

Like many analysts, rogue economists, investors and prognosticators of our current global economic crisis, I've been very adamant about the end result of this gigantic experiment in central bank money creation: that after this extraordinary boom period, we will experience a remarkable bust cycle, one that I have labeled the *Day of Reckoning* and the *Grand Convergence*. History has demonstrated over and over again the cyclical nature of boom and bust cycles, which every boom period of a particular strength has been followed by a bust period of equal or greater force. And what has also been revealed by the historical analysis is that the severity of the bust cycle is determined, to a great extent, by the extreme nature of the boom cycle. There have been no exceptions, so it's not reasonable to expect that things will turn out differently this time around.

Thus, like most astute observers and investors of this crisis, preparing for the bust cycle is the best financial survival strategy, particularly as we stare into the abyss of massive uncertainty in global markets.

In my book entitled, *Global Economic Boom and Bust Cycles*, published in 2012, the central thesis was that the *Meltdown of 2008* that culminated in the serial collapse of some of the most powerful corporations in the world, represented only the tip of the iceberg and was just the first phase of this epic global economic implosion. In 2018, we are still witnessing the systematic unfolding of this giant global financial bubble, kept alive and sustained by the powerful global central banking system.

This enormous meltdown was labeled the *Great Recession* instead of the *Great Depression of the early 2000s*, due to central bank interventions and governmental fiscal policies that prevented the development of a full-blown catastrophe. What we are now witnessing (in 2018) is the largest bubble and credit/debt expansion in modern economic history, and when this entire system finally implodes, it will bring into existence some very harsh economic and financial realities.

The *Meltdown of 2008* (and its aftershocks) was the initial bursting of this bubble and the *first phase* of the *Great Depression of the 21st century*. As this secular bear cycle continues to unfold in the last stage of its journey, the sovereign debt crisis that has a stranglehold on most of the developed world has evolved into the epicenter of a massive credit and money supply expansion bubble that threatens to derail the entire global economic system.

In my analysis, the year 2012 was the pivotal turning point in this unfolding drama. It was clear that governments around the world and their central bankers were conducting a titanic battle to prevent contagion and collapse into deflation and global depression. The universal mantra was to keep the current system in place at all costs. And at that point in history, it was clear to me that the longer our leaders delayed in implementing the full measure of economic and depression-era reforms, the more difficult it would become to stop what was inevitable: *Global economic turmoil and collapse*!

Thus, I was convinced that we needed fiscal policies (for our era) similar in strength and magnitude to those of the *New Deal* policies of the 1930s under President Roosevelt. Also, I'm equally convinced that *Information Age Revolution technologies* will play a pivotal role during the next recovery phase. However, the *Day of Reckoning* has been postponed, and the apparent agency of this colossal feat has been the Federal Reserve System (the Fed) and other central bankers around the world. But there is a much broader theme in this story that I was overlooking, and this is where economist and analyst Richard Duncan brings clarity and focus to some very significant issues. His full analysis is thought-provoking and presents some very novel economic ideas. Also, I think his overall position on this crisis should be given complete examination and consideration by political leaders, central bankers, and planners around the world. Since central bankers are operating outside the box, using unconventional monetary tools, then it stands to reason that they should - at a minimum - consider the views of Richard Duncan.

CAPITALISM VS. CREDITISM

Duncan offers us a critical lesson on this current crisis and how we might arrive at a favorable solution. As the author of *The Dollar Crisis* (2005) and *The New Depression* (2012), he brings to the table a unique understanding of the crisis we are confronted with at the macro level. In a careful and thoughtful reading of his thesis, the reader comes to understand that Duncan seriously reconsiders various aspects of western economic dogma and capitalistic beliefs that have persisted for centuries; that much of what we accept as capitalistic gospel has all been changed right before our eyes. We have grown to accept these beliefs as reality with no further discourse.

For instance, Duncan declares that the global economic system that we now operate under is no longer strictly classical *laissez-faire capitalism*, but is now (what he considers) an economic system of *creditism*. In short, *capitalism* has evolved into this new economic system of *creditism*.

Thus, in this current state of affairs (2018 and beyond), Duncan believes that the classical laissez-faire method will not be our economic salvation, but rather a necessary furthering of this new paradigm of *creditism*, where credit growth drives economic growth. In this new paradigm, credit is the new money and as Duncan affirms, "If credit contracts significantly, globalization will not survive." He alerts us to the fact that "Our society has failed to understand that our economic system has changed. Therefore, it has not yet grasped the possibilities inherent within this new system. Credit can now be deployed by the government on a scale so vast that it can revolutionize the production potential of this planet."[1] This is central to understanding Duncan's economic thesis that we must continue to have credit growth to survive, or the global debt/credit house of cards will collapse!

Duncan talks about a four-decade credit boom that witnessed a massive credit expansion from $1 trillion in 1964 to $52 trillion by 2008. It was an astronomical growth in credit that created this new era of *creditism* and globalization. In his words, "The money supply is no longer the most important factor affecting economic change. It is the credit supply that matters now. Consequently, the quantity theory of money must be adjusted to reflect that fact." His explanation of what trillions of dollars of new credit have generated is clear: "What did a $50 trillion expansion of credit do to the U.S. economy? First, it brought about unprecedented prosperity in the United States by creating wealth, profits, jobs and abundant tax revenues. Moreover, it generated a vast amount of financial capital. But $50 trillion of credit did more than make the United States prosperous; it fundamentally transformed the structure of its economy."[2] In addition, Duncan also makes the point that this explosion of credit and debt transformed the entire world, pulling millions of people out of poverty in various countries around the globe.

Thus, as most analysts continue to operate under the old capitalistic assumptions, they will not consider or give credence to the possibility of a new economic paradigm. Duncan invites us to think outside the box and to explore a much broader or alternative dimension of the capitalistic system/model that now dominates the economic activities of our world.

I have to credit Duncan for bringing a great deal of clarity and sanity to much of my thesis that I've been supporting over a period of decades. Like Duncan, I've been following this story for a long time. My fundamental analysis was clear on a significant part of the global picture (particularly the narratives I have presented regarding boom and bust cycles). However, I was missing a much more complete picture and *unconventional analysis* on the issues of money, credit, the demise of the gold standard, and the globalization of the marginal cost of labor and its impact on the forces of inflation. And most importantly, his theories on *creditism*.

It's important to observe (as Duncan points out) that without globalization, hyperinflation (in America and other developed nations) would have taken root some time ago. I have also advocated that globalization and new technologies, such as robotics and AI, were having a significant impact on the wages of the American worker. However, I underestimated its impact and thought that it would take a much more extended period before this process would play out on a global scale. On the other hand, Duncan, who has been living in Asia over the past 25 years, has a more intimate relationship with the issue of the marginal cost of labor. Workers in Asia are making far less income per hour per day than a comparable employee in the industrialized West, particularly in the United States. We are invited to look deeper into his analysis regarding the fact that "three billion people live on less than $2 to $3 per day." The corporate titans of globalization have penetrated this labor force in a myriad of ways, which ultimately translates into global deflation.

Duncan's analysis helps us to understand a deeper dimension of this problem: that globalization is massively deflationary and that central bankers (particularly the Fed in the U.S.) can print money without generating hyperinflation. This is a very critical observation because it's going to remain a significant factor in what may define economic development for the remainder of the 21st century and beyond. Duncan's simple explanation of this process is that "Globalization has resulted in a 95 percent decline in the marginal cost of labor in a relatively short span of time. Not long ago, blue-collar workers in Michigan were paid a wage of $200 per day to work on an automobile assembly line. Today, the same job can be done in China or India at the cost of $5 per day per worker. That collapse in the price of labor represents one of the greatest upheavals in prices in history."[3]

There are two fundamental facts that Duncan would like his readers to understand:

(1) That the Austrian cycle theory is a correct model.
(2) That governmental policy is to keep this credit bubble alive for as long as possible. The alternative of letting this bubble burst presents a scenario that is sure to lead to a great global depression.

So, what in essence is the "Austrian cycle theory" telling us that is so important? The short explanation that Duncan would like for his readers to appreciate is the theory's connection to the creation of credit. Austrian economists are convinced that the initiation of business cycles is the consequence of the excessive growth in bank credit driven by low-interest rates established by central banks and the fractional reserve system. A low-interest-rate environment stimulates borrowing from the banking system. When this occurs over a significant period, a buildup of excessive credit generates imbalances in the system. Newly issued bank credit generally leads to an increase in capital spending which over time results in widespread unproductive investments. Thus, the credit-fueled boom will lead to the bursting of a credit bubble. After this credit phase has run its full cycle, the correction that follows is a recession (or depression) or bust period. The money supply goes through a contraction as the downturn eventually restores balance again. Mainstream economists do not support this theory on how business cycles evolve. Therefore, we cannot expect that any economic thought leaders will embrace Duncan's approach to remedy our current financial crisis.

The second significant fact that Duncan wants his readers to understand fully and not lose sight of is that government policy (particularly in developed nations) is focused on keeping the current *global credit bubble* alive for as long as possible. This means that they will use every ounce of power they have to sustain this massive credit system, for the alternative of allowing the bubble to deflate or implode borders on complete economic chaos and massive global population disillusionment. The best economic model and example of the scale of the potential of this impending bust cycle is the *Great Depression of the 1930s* and the war that followed in the 1940s! And what is expected to follow this great boom will not be a garden variety recession; it is destined to be something far worse, and the major players know this.

Moreover, in keeping with a belief in the Austrian School of Thought, Duncan further informs us that "Booms do not occur in the absence of credit expansion...the adoption of fiat money in place of commodity money, combined with regulatory changes that reduced banks' liquidity reserves, allowed an unprecedented explosion of credit, which in turn, generated an equally extraordinary economic boom."[4] This transformation has been dramatic and had (over a period of decades) changed the lives of millions of people around the world. The major downside of this new paradigm is that this credit must continue to expand, for when it stops expanding, a new bust period enters the picture. In fact, his analysis reveals that when "credit grows less than 2%, the U.S. economy goes into recession." We are therefore caught in a systemic credit expansion paradigm that must be sustained for as long as possible.

The expansion of credit causes asset prices to rise. If we stop the expansion of credit, we will see that asset prices will begin to fall. The most recent example of this phenomenon is the housing crisis of 2007-2009. And, according to Duncan's thesis, "The New Depression began in 2008 when that credit could not be repaid and, as a result, credit began to contract."

THE HISTORICAL ROOTS OF THIS CRISIS

In Duncan's historical narrative, the current global economic crisis has its roots as far back as World War I when European nations went to war to decide who would control Europe. He tells us that, "...a breakdown of the Gold Standard at the beginning of World War I...caused the Roaring Twenties to roar. All the fiat money and government debt created during the war set off the boom, and the boom ended when the credit could not be repaid in 1930."[5] What's unique about his observations here is the direct connection between the massive fiat money printing that occurred as the various European nations went off the gold standard to finance the war. The key economic factor that fueled the bubble was the fact that "Europe sent a great deal of its gold to the U.S. to pay for war materials, something it could not have afforded to do had it remained on the gold standard."[6]

Duncan reminds us that the gold holdings of the U.S. rose by 64 percent during the 1920s. This influx of highly valued "commodity money" played a significant role in the development of the *Roaring 20s*; it made the rapid growth of the availability of credit possible. Since the Europeans didn't have enough gold to pay for the war, it was necessary to start printing a lot of paper money to finance the government bonds issued to pay for that global conflict. That massive printing of currencies led to the sensational boom of the 1920s in America; it also led to the disastrous hyperinflation in Germany in 1923.

The *Roaring 20s* boom cycle was primarily an American affair. Europe was not booming during the twenties but was mired in a recovery mode struggling to rebuild itself after the devastating war. Saddled with war reparation debts and loan debts, Germany (a crushed economy) was in deep economic turmoil throughout that fabled decade. The destructive force of hyperinflation nearly wiped out its middle class in 1923.

When the crash of 1929 initiated the start of the Great Depression in America, this had grave consequences for European nations, in particular, Germany. The damaging monetary effects of America's economic decline spread to Europe, bringing about more depression on the global level.

Weimar Germany was getting back on its feet when the economic crisis began. Germany had been dependent upon American capital as part of its recovery plan. Then, what occurred after 1929 was one of the worse governmental policy measures initiated during the early stages of the crisis. Under the direction of the Hoover Administration, capital and loans that had been provided to Germany during the 1920s were ordered to be repatriated to the U.S. This repatriated capital severely destabilized Germany and its reconstruction efforts, and quite literally set the nation on a path towards political extremism.

The Weimar Republic had to send $14 billion in gold and currency to the U.S. to meet the demand. Their banking system collapsed, investors were ruined, bankruptcies soared, industrial production collapsed, and the unemployment rate increased to 25 percent. Thus, Germany was the hardest (European nation) hit by the depression with over 6 million people unemployed, hunger and soup lines and widespread disillusionment among broad segments of its population. This was fertile ground for the growth of Nazism and the rise of Hitler. In January 1933, Adolf Hitler became Chancellor of Germany.

Thus, World War I destroyed the Gold Standard in much of Europe during that time. However, there is another piece to this European story which resonates with a part of the narrative of our current crisis. For this critical insight, I draw on the work of John Mauldin and Jonathan Tepper and their book, *Code Red*. Something happened in Europe in 1931 that would have profound ramifications around the globe. Mauldin and Tepper explain:

> "If the 1929 crash had simply ended in 1931, we might be calling it the Almost Great Depression, but it didn't. The second leg down started with the failure of Credit-Anstalt, Austria's biggest bank, in May 1931. The bankruptcy of Credit-Anstalt started a cascade of bank runs in Hungary, Czechoslovakia, Romania, Poland, and Germany. As in the current crisis, in 1931 a European banking crisis was the catalyst for a sovereign debt crisis and currency war. The banking crisis that began in a peripheral European country in 1931 soon spread to all major global economies. Global trade plunged, international capital movements dried up, industrial production slumped, unemployment surged. The parallels with the European crisis today are eerily familiar...When the runs of 1931 happened, Britain was the first to take itself off the gold standard on September 19 of that year. The pound immediately fell 30 percent against the U.S. dollar. At the time, there were about 25 countries with close economic or imperial links to Britain that had tied their currencies to the sterling, so the shock waves of devaluation extended around the world to Australia, New Zealand, South Africa, and even many countries that hadn't been part of the British Empire...Britain's move also set off a chain reaction of devaluations in Japan, the United States, France, Germany, Sweden, and Norway, among others." [7]

As the above analysis reveals, the bankruptcy and collapse of a large European bank began a process of contagion that was not contained. Within one year the damage had spread like a virus, forcing one nation after another to leave the gold standard and to devalue their currencies. This series of events also led to a massive surge in *flight capital* leaving Europe between the years of 1932 to 1937. Rich Europeans deeply concerned about the rise of Hitler and Mussolini, as well as the rapid economic declines in their nations, saw America as a safe haven and a place where their wealth could be preserved and given an opportunity to grow. Money flowed out of government bonds and into American stocks, generating what global analyst Larry Edelson refers to as "one of the greatest bull markets in history." Edelson's analysis reveals that during the depths of the Great Depression, "the Dow Jones rallied from a low of 40.52 in July of 1932 to a high of 195.2 in March of 1937...a gain of 372% during the worst depression in history."[8] So the rich and well-connected prospered in the crisis, while the masses endured unemployment, soup lines, non-access to credit and a host of other debilitating conditions.

However, despite all of these developments, the U.S. did not leave the gold standard during World War I nor during the *Roaring 20s*. It wasn't until 1933, when President Roosevelt took office, that the U.S. was finally taken off the gold standard as part of the *New Deal programs* to stimulate the economy. By leaving the gold standard, the U.S. was able to devalue the dollar, which led to rapid increases in stock and commodity prices. Economic output began rising, reversing the downward GDP trends of the first three years of the 1930s.

As many students of history know, the *Roaring 20s* was one of the most daring boom periods in the history of economics and finance. But as stated earlier, all great boom cycles will eventually lead to great bust cycles. So when the debts accumulated from the great war could not be repaid, this led to the bust cycle known as the *Great Depression of the 1930s*. This collapse was brutal and ultimately led to the meltdown of the international banking system and a 25 percent unemployment rate in America and Germany.

By 1940, after a decade of global depression, the stage was set for World War II that would witness the death and destruction of over 60 million people. Duncan tells us that the U.S. increased its spending on that war by 900 percent and that this effectively brought to an end the *Great Depression*, as the government effectively took over the economy.

This massive military spending on World War II was a significant economic pivotal point in history; the U.S. government took over all major aspects of the economy: production, distribution, wages, prices, and labor. In the words of Duncan, "This war effort completely transformed the structure of the U.S. economy." In his thesis on *creditism*, *capitalism* died as a result of the two major world wars of the 20th Century. After the second world war, the U.S. economy never returned to a normal capitalistic model. After Germany and Japan were defeated, and the birth of the atomic age became the new war paradigm, the U.S. government and the Fed continued to play the central role in the economic life of the nation.

The U.S. was holding nearly 70% of the world's gold at the end of the war. Therefore it was not possible to establish a commodity-based gold standard in the traditional sense. Thus, a new gold standard was created with the U.S. dollar serving as the reserve currency of the world.

In the 1960s, America spent heavily on the Vietnam War and its Great Society Programs which ultimately led to the breakdown of the Bretton Woods agreement and the gold standard. Here Duncan reminds us that in March of 1968, "Congress changed the law so that dollars no longer had to be backed by gold."[9] According to Duncan, "the nature of money changed in 1968, and that fundamental change transformed the American economy. Since that time, credit has become the key economic variable." And by 1971, President Nixon took the U.S. off the gold standard and effectively brought to a close the Bretton Woods international system.

The big change that we need to understand here is that "Once dollars were no longer backed by gold, the nature of money changed. The worth of the currency in circulation was no longer derived from a real asset with intrinsic value...it was no longer a commodity money. It had become fiat money - that is, it was money only because the government said it was money."[10] It's at this point that another significant shift takes place in global economics; *the removal of restraints on how much paper money could be created.*

Another key component to this evolving system of *creditism* is the issue of the expansive growth of trade deficits. During the 1980s, the U.S. (for the first time) began running massive trade deficits with the rest of the world. The global impact was a reduction in inflation in the American economy. Duncan reminds us that, "Those deficits allowed the US to circumvent the domestic US bottlenecks of full employment and limited industrial capacity." This led to the expansion of globalization and a buildup of enormous wealth in such nations as Japan, China, South Korea, and elsewhere. By 2006, the U.S. trade deficit had soared to $800 billion, which represented 6% of GDP. Low labor costs in various foreign nations, was a major contributing factor in decreasing the forces of inflation, particularly in America.

Since the 1980s, America has also benefitted from the foreign capital that flowed into its government bond markets to help finance the "Current Account deficits." This expansion of government bond purchases pushed up the prices of these bonds while driving down their yields. The decrease in these benchmark rates led to the lowering of interest rates in other areas of the economy, i.e., mortgage rates, student loans, etc.

This explosion of credit also initiated the "Age of the Billionaire" and financed the birth of the *Information Age Revolution*. Duncan again drives home the point that "Economic progress was no longer achieved the old-fashioned way through savings and investments, but, rather, by borrowing and consumption. That profound change was reflected in the sharp decline in the national savings rate, which dropped from 12 percent of national income in 1950 to 1.7 percent in 2007..."[11]

In summary, Duncan tells us, "The New Depression and the Great Depression were both caused by credit-fueled economic booms. In both instances, the boom began when the link between money and gold was broken. The earlier episode began in 1914 when World War I destroyed the Gold Standard in Europe. This time the credit boom began when the United States severed the link between dollars and gold in 1968 and then destroyed the Bretton Woods international monetary system in 1971...The 1914-1930 boom ended in worldwide economic collapse when the credit that had fueled it could not be repaid."[12]

QE IS DEBT CANCELLATION

With a clear and concise presentation, Duncan demonstrates that when central bankers (in particular the Fed in his analysis) utilize quantitative easing (QE) as a monetary tool, this effectively leads to government debt cancellation. It is one of those overlooked and seldom talked about issues many analysts don't include in their broader discussion about the overall crisis (it is something that is known but is not widely discussed).

However, Duncan makes it a point to present this factor to the international finance and economic communities. The implications of this central bank policy are profound and have the potential of significantly reducing the impact on much of the dire predictions of an impending global economic collapse. In other words, central bankers in developed economies are in a rare position to do what has never been done before on a scale that is astounding.

So how does this procedure work? Duncan walks us through the process utilizing the following bullet points:

- When a central bank buys the government debt, it is the same thing as cancelling the debt.
- The government pays interest on its bonds to the central bank and then the central bank returns to the government the profits it earns from that interest income. That means the bonds have, in effect, been canceled...unless, the central bank actually sells the bonds back to the public one day - which I don't think they ever will.
- ...this reality of trillions of dollars of "debt with no cost" has enormous implications.
- Governments have much less debt than is generally understood - and that means they could spend more and finally end this global economic crisis.[13]

In reviewing the Board of Governors Federal Reserve System Press Release of January 9, 2015, we are informed of the following:

"The Federal Reserve Board on Friday announced preliminary unaudited results indicating that the Reserve Banks provided for payments of approximately $98.7 billion of their estimated 2014 net income to the U.S. Treasury. Under the Board's policy, the residual earnings of each Federal Reserve Bank are distributed to the U.S. Treasury, after providing for the costs of operations, payment of dividends, and the amount necessary to equate surplus with capital paid-in.[14]

As the Fed press release states, based on the Board of Governors' policies, at the end of each year, the Fed is obligated to transfer most of its profits to the U.S. Treasury. From 2008 to 2014, the Fed paid the U.S. Treasury $506 billion. Roughly $99 billion along was paid in 2014. Based on Duncan's analysis, this 2014 payment represented 20 percent of the budget deficit for that year.

In the aftermath of the *Meltdown of 2008*, most economic observers assumed that Fed money printing and QE, on the trillion-dollar level, would undoubtedly lead to high rates of inflation or even hyperinflation. However, after three rounds of QE and eight years later, we did not experience high rates of inflation. In fact, the reality had been a disinflationary economic environment or real concerns over deflationary global forces.

Duncan makes the point that, what has been off-setting the massive money printing by central bankers, are the critical factors of *globalization and the marginal cost of labor*. As mentioned earlier, he declares that globalization is deflationary, an economic reality that will continually be driven by low-cost labor for decades to come.

DUNCAN OPTIONS FOR THE FUTURE

Rather than being stuck with a scenario that our global economic system is doomed to failure and collapse, Duncan would have our monetary and fiscal leaders to think outside the box concerning the current crisis. The credit bubble that has been installed and sustained over the past four to five decades is a reality that we have to live with. In other words, it has been fully implemented, and there is no way to simply reverse this new era of *creditism*. It is understood that breaking the link between money and gold should not have become the central force in our economic development for this extended period. But here we are, and what are our options moving forward? Duncan's steadfast advice is that we need to take advantage of this crisis and not let it go unused. Of his recommendations, there are two that I consider well worth our attention:

(1) Government to carry on doing what it does now - that is, the status quo, borrowing and spending to support consumption (Option two). This approach would sustain the economy for at least a decade. Then there would be a U.S.

sovereign debt crisis, and the world would collapse into a New Great Depression.

(2) Option three is for the government to borrow and invest in a way that not only supports the economy but actually restructures it to restore its long-term viability. This option, rational investment, is the only one of the three with the potential to result in a happy ending. It differs from option two, the status quo, in a very significant way. In option two, the government continues to borrow and spend in a way that boosts consumption in the economy. Spending in that way creates economic growth, but only once. When the money is spent, it is gone. It yields no long-term return...In option three the government would borrow and invest, and the government's investments would yield a return. In fact, given the magnitude of the resources the government has available to invest, the returns that could be generated would be sufficient to restore the government's finances to health - perhaps even making it possible for the government to repay all of its debt within a relatively short period of time.[15]

The first option presented above is what the U.S. has been doing since the *Meltdown of 2008*. It is also the strategy that Japan has been using for many, many years. The so-called status quo would buy time and keep the world out of what Duncan refers to as the *New Great Depression*, but it only postpones the *Day of Reckoning*. This option will likely be the path chosen by our leaders unless there is an awakening to the dynamic possibilities of Duncan's third option.

Option three is one of the main reasons I became interested in Duncan's economic thesis and strategic ideas. In my book, *Global Economic Boom and Bust Cycles*, I presented an entire chapter on information age technologies and promoted the idea that this *tech revolution* would become the foundation of our recovery in the 21st century. I also presented a chapter announcing the end of the *age of oil and other fossil fuels* that drove the global paradigm of the *industrial era*. It will take trillions of dollars to transition and ultimately transform our world with the full adoption of vast new energy vectors that will present the world with unlimited sources of green energy.

I challenged our leaders to consider not wasting valuable resources and brain power on going to war and other wasteful activities. Since the year 2000 alone, we have spent trillions of dollars on fighting in the Middle East (estimates of $3 trillion or more) and have nothing to show for it. In fact, in 2017, that whole region and parts of North Africa is destabilized and bordering on absolute chaos. Nothing was accomplished except that certain corporate entities and the international banking cartel were able to profit from all of the destruction, death and economic failure. Millions of people were uprooted and forced to flee for their lives.

Duncan's fear, as well as mine, is that if our leaders fail to seize the opportunities available to move in the direction of progress and enlightenment, rather than drift in the direction of endless wars and global conquest, we will be doomed and not discover any real economic salvation!

Ironically, the realization that central bankers are at the root of this massive crisis is where we will need to find our required solutions. Duncan reminds us that, "Those who want to understand what lies ahead must understand this: the Fed's one and only policy has been and will continue to be to perpetuate the boom by ensuring that credit continues to expand."[16] Let's be clear, "this combination of fiat money printing and globalization has never happened before." So, it is indeed a rare historical economic development and a crisis that the U.S., and by extension, the world should not let go to waste. Something can be done; it may not be elegant, but it could ultimately mean the difference between *barbarism or civilization*. In 2018 (and beyond), that is our choice!

WHAT DUNCAN IS RECOMMENDING

Duncan's thesis offers the U.S. a feasible alternative to economic collapse and chaos. And like many of us, he has appreciated the QE operations of the Fed during and what followed the *Great Recession*. These operations kept the world out of the *New Great Depression* and allowed us to live another day (several more years without complete economic disintegration) on government and Fed life support systems. Duncan believes that if a total collapse occurs, it may be decades before the world would be able to recover from the economic fallout. Of course, in that scenario, the world would most likely descend into dystopia, chaos, and war on a scale greater than the 1930s and 40s. Ultimately - at all costs - this must be avoided.

Among all of the nations in the world, it is America that is best positioned to execute a plan for full recovery and initiate a new economic and technological era. And again, this is a rare opportunity presented for the first time in history, where a nation can print a fiat-currency (paper money without a commodity-based backing) and spend without generating massive inflation. However, that window of opportunity is limited, and any significant missteps will mean economic failure.

Given these dire circumstances, we are left to ponder how the world will escape the ultimate trap that has been set for us over a period of decades. Most economic prognosticators that are expecting a significant downturn at some point in the future don't offer a solution outside of allowing the capitalistic model to go through the bust phase and ultimately (after an intense economic downturn) arrive at the door of recovery. The one main point that they are missing, and what Duncan is helping us to understand deeply, is that this is an *extraordinary global bubble* that could usher in a period far worse than the conflagration of the 1940s. Duncan is warning us not to go there; not to allow this terrible thing to happen and take root in our current economic system.

A critical problem, of course, is that many economists and analysts have not bought into his thesis on *creditism*, and therefore don't understand where we are in the economic scheme of things: that *capitalism* has evolved into *creditism*. What Duncan is inviting us to do is to explore his unconventional ideas and theories and to commit trillions of dollars to implement unique investment strategies by the government and private sectors. Duncan is presenting the most practical and expedient measures that will allow us to take advantage of the opportunities inherent in the *creditism system*.

In the U.S., fiscal policy will come back in vogue if President Trump implements his plans for infrastructure development throughout the United States. It is in line with a significant part of Duncan's vision, and as his analysis has demonstrated (in his charts and graphs supporting his theories), there is no limit in the near term of how much the government can borrow and spend.

According to the federal government, the nation's debt to GDP ratio was 104.17 percent in 2015. In Japan, where the central bank's borrow and spend model has been demonstrated to the extreme, the debt to GDP ratio has soared to as high as 250 percent in recent years. As examined in the chapter on Japan, this nation has been battling the forces of deflation for over 25 years, using quantitative easing (QE) and a host of other economic stimulus measures, moving from 60 percent of GDP to the 250 percent level during that period of time. The case that Duncan makes, and I'm in full agreement, is that (given these dire circumstances) the U.S. can expand its debt load to accommodate a fiscal spending and investment model. But as he advocates, we should not just consider infrastructure projects as the only solution; the more aggressive approach would be to borrow and invest in the new technologies of the future.

Duncan is suggesting a joint venture partnership (JV-Partnership) between the U.S. government (public sector) and private sector companies. Under this arrangement, the U.S. would supply the capital and take a 60 percent ownership stake in the new enterprises that are (or would ultimately become) listed companies on stock market exchanges. As the revenues of these companies rise and stock values increase on the open exchanges, the U.S. government, and by extension, the American people would benefit from the enormous increase in wealth. This would allow (over time) for overall debt levels to decrease and to set the stage for a new technological and economic era not only in America but throughout the world.

In his presentations, Duncan advocates that the federal government should invest a trillion dollars over the next ten years in each of the following sectors: Green Energy, Nanotechnology, Biotechnology, Genetic Engineering, in addition to other promising new technology sectors. The rational logic in this approach is that instead of investing trillions of dollars in military spending, wars and other wasteful non-productive areas, consider massive expenditures in the full development and implementation of information age new technologies, thereby ushering in a new technological era. This would be an investment blitz, unlike anything the world has ever witnessed by a government. This new paradigm will even venture beyond what Sovereign Wealth Funds (see Glossary) have demonstrated in recent years, where government revenues are invested in real and financial assets. In a low-interest rate environment (which may persist for some time), it would be feasible for the U.S. government to pursue investment policies on this grand scale.

WHERE I DISAGREE WITH DUNCAN

What Duncan is advocating is to take the final leap into the future; lay the foundation and implement the full measure of information age technologies with QE and fiat money printed by the Fed. One major roadblock, of course, is the entrenched corporations that have dominated and who profit from industrial era technologies: oil, nuclear fission energy, coal, etc. Big Banks and these global corporate titans are reluctant to abdicate their power in favor of this glorious new era that may not leave them as the controlling economic power. There will be a significant power struggle to see what or who will dominate in this new era.

And the place where I think the battle should be fought and won in the early stages of the development of this new paradigm, is the energy sector. It will take multiple trillions of dollars to transform the energy arena to focus almost entirely on new information age green technologies. Instead of spending $5 trillion or more on numerous new technology sectors (what Duncan recommends), I would recommend diving deep into constructing the new green energy vectors for the 21st century and beyond. Concentrate a massive amount of capital over the next ten years to finally develop a new era in clean energy that will not only save our planet but will also avoid the most devastating depression in global history.

Open the *Pandora's Box* of the vast array of new green energy technologies, allowing the U.S. and the entire world to establish this new era and to bring to an end the destructive power of *industrial era* energy technologies. This is the right time for that to happen, which offer immeasurable benefits to billions of people all over this planet. As stated above, the U.S. (in 2018) is in the prime position to make this happen. If it fails to do so, it will be one of the greatest economic blunders in world history.

RICHARD DUNCAN'S MESSAGE TO PRESIDENT TRUMP

On January 20, 2017, President-elect Donald Trump was sworn in as the 45th president of the United States. Richard Duncan prepared a special video presentation for President Trump, outlining some major recommendations that his new administration should strongly consider to avoid economic collapse and failure. In essence, Duncan tells Trump that he can make America great again by dealing effectively with the issues discussed in this chapter.

First and foremost, President Trump may be aware that there is a massive global bubble. However, it is questionable as to whether he knows how to avoid causing an implosion of this ticking time bomb. This is where the implementation of the right policies will be crucial in preventing the next great depression.

In regards to governmental policies, Duncan's message is to make recommendations that will steer the new Trump Administration away from potential minefields. Some of his primary concerns are as follows:

(1) In this era of creditism, it is imperative that the Trump Administration avoid any policies designed to drive up interest rates significantly. Higher interest rates cause credit to contract and asset prices to fall. When these events occur, the U.S. economy will be driven into a depression and the global bubble will pop, initiating the great implosion. The simple explanation on interest rates in this era of creditism is as follows: As interest rates fell in the global economy, there was a massive expansion in credit; when interest rates begin to rise, there will be a considerable contraction in credit. This is the main reason why interest rates will need to remain low during this critical transition period in the creditism cycle.

(2) It's essential to maintain low inflation and not to pursue policies that would bring about significant increases in the inflation rate. It is here where Duncan is adamant in recommending that trade tariffs not be imposed on imported goods. Trade tariffs will push up interest rates and also cause inflation to rise. It must be understood that cheap products made from low-cost labor abroad are what pushed down inflation. And furthermore, low inflation is what makes QE possible, and it is QE that has kept the world out of Duncan's *New Great Depression*. This is what globalization has made possible. Like it or not, this is the reality now confronting our world. Since this is what has been created, we cannot ignore the fact that pursuing policies that were *ineffective* in the past - even in the purely *capitalistic system* - will not work in our current *creditism system*.

(3) Duncan was also recommending that Trump should not cut taxes, especially on the wealthy. This is counter-productive! If taxes are cut, the budget deficit and national debt will need to be increased to pay for the reduced taxes to the large corporations and the wealthy. The old republican theory of *trickle-down economics* simply will not work during the second phase of this current crisis. We have recent history to validate this claim. When President George W.

Bush took office in 2001, he immediately pushed for tax cuts, and Congress approved a $1.35 trillion tax cut package. The second package of $350 billion followed in 2003. Analysts estimate that the tax legislation enacted under President Bush wiped out nearly $6.3 trillion of anticipated revenue. And as stated elsewhere in this publication, this was the main source of the huge yearly deficit numbers leading up to the *Meltdown of 2008*. Duncan makes the point (and I wholeheartedly agree) that cutting taxes for the wealthy will not induce them to spend more; and in my opinion, it will only increase inequality. As for tax reduction for large corporations; they will still seek to expand their operations in low-cost labor countries (markets), or become even more aggressive in buying back their company's stock on the open markets.

Duncan applauds Trump's (stated) plan to implement infrastructure development projects. That's a start, but as he admonishes, "don't stop there." He alerts the new Trump Administration that this is a prime opportunity to invest in the new industries and technologies of the future. In fact, this is a once in history opportunity to do something that has never been done in the known history of the world. The United States government is in a prime position to allocate trillions of investment dollars to transform its economy and initiate a new era of growth and development. Trillions of dollars can be spent without generating high rates of inflation; that was demonstrated during the post-recession period of 2008 to 2016 when the Fed balance sheet increased by $3.6 trillion, and there was no real inflation. QE can be a useful tool as long as there is no significant inflation.

Duncan tells Trump that, "Government investment in 21st Century industries and technologies in the U.S. will lock in another American Century." Either by accident or design, globalization as a system now consists of a labor force numbering in billions of people and production facilities entrenched in nations throughout the world. With two billion people living on less than $3 per day, this system will continue to expand for decades to come. The most important message contained in this new reality is that globalization is deflationary, and this deflationary trend will keep marching forward for some undetermined period of time.

Thus, Trump is in a position to implement fiscal and monetary stimulus plans on a scale unimaginable in any other time in the history of this nation. Here is what Duncan has in mind:

(1) Infrastructure Developments: Duncan considers this strategy as an excellent path to generate jobs and economic growth in the short and medium term. These investments will create profits "for our society indirectly, through job creation and greater efficiency." However, Duncan is quick to point out that, "Better infrastructure alone is not going to make America great again."

(2) Public and Private JV Partnerships: Here is where Duncan makes his strongest pitch for investing and funding the technological revolution of the future. His vision is that the U.S. government becomes the largest venture capital firm in history. As stated earlier, its primary role will be to provide the capital to fund thousands of select companies that are focused on the transformative new age technologies. The government would take a 60% equity stake in these companies, leaving 40% for the private sector to manage and build out their 21st-century innovations. Duncan recommends selecting 10,000 of the most promising companies in the U.S. to participate in this grand venture. According to Duncan, "...government investment in the industries of the future will mean great jobs and strong economic growth for Americans for the rest of the century." This is, therefore, a much stronger plan of action for long-term growth, as well as the enormous benefits that will be derived from the full implementation of a vast array of new technologies.

(3) Duncan's New Technology Sectors: As mentioned in a previous section, Duncan is recommending that Trump considers investing $1 trillion in each of the following industry sectors: Green Energy; Genetic Engineering; Biotechnology; Nanotechnology, and other promising areas. As mentioned earlier, my approach would be to focus massive amounts of capital on green technologies that are destined to transform the energy vectors on our planet. Also, I have other concerns about his other recommendations which I address in *Global Economic Boom and Bust Cycles.*

When we observe what happened in the 1940s when the U.S. government increased its spending on the military by 900% (to participate in World War II), it's clear that this massive influx of capital in the war industry brought to an end the *Great Depression.* The unique historical moment that we are witnessing in the 21st century is the economic opportunity to invest and spend trillions of dollars on non-military industries to avoid the onset of what Duncan has labeled the *New Great Depression* and what I refer to as *The Great Depression of the 21st Century.* Again, this is a rare historic opportunity to participate in an incredible venture. However, the window of this opportunity is limited, and it will require that our leaders in government, the Fed, and private industries make the right decisions to move in the right direction. For instance, when Trump and the Republicans moved forward with a plan (in early 2018) to give the wealthy tax cuts, that was an example of moving in the wrong direction. As Duncan states, "Give the wealthy profits not tax cuts." Appeal to their greed for profits and on improving the so-called bottom line. For a more detail analysis on Duncan's "Open Letter To President-elect Trump," you can watch his free video by clicking on the following link: https://vimeo.com/191592053

AMERICA'S WINDOW OF OPPORTUNITY HAS BEEN RELINQUISHED

Some of the initial economic policy moves taken by the Trump administration and the Republicans in 2018, set America on a path inconsistent with the recommendations of this chapter. Economist Richard Duncan had stated in his video presentation to President Trump that tax cuts, tariffs and any policies that will drive up interest rates would be detrimental to the U.S. economy, especially during this critical phase in the creditism cycle. By August 2018, major tax cut legislation had been implemented, tariffs and a trade war had moved to center stage as a global America agenda, and interest rates were steadily rising. Thus, America began moving in a direction that would not be beneficial to the severe economic crisis the world was facing.

The window of opportunity that was discussed in this chapter was intentionally (or unintentionally) renounced, and we, therefore, will have to face the consequences of these political actions. The ability of central banks in the West to print money and not generate significant inflation or hyperinflation will be lost at some point in the not too distant future. This was the critical factor that made the 10-year (inflationary asset) post-2008 recovery a success story. The creditism paradigm and globalization will be severely disrupted, and this will initiate the next major meltdown. At some point, this process will be irreversible, and the U.S. will completely lose its opportunity to print money and invest in an *information Age Technological future* that was outlined in this chapter.

Neither the Fed or the Trump administration have fully acknowledged the validity of the new economic system of creditism that Richard Duncan has expounded on in his economic thesis. With the Fed steadily hiking interest rates and pursuing its policy of quantitative tightening (QT), only added more fuel to the fire and the all but certain consequences of a major collapse. The unfortunate result of this response will be an awakening during the next major meltdown when the Trump administration, Congress, and the Fed are searching feverishly for solutions to stop the momentum into the deflationary (or an initial hyperinflationary) abyss. The U.S. has given up a powerful initiative that could have provided a much-needed solution to address the next imminent global meltdown.

SUMMARY

According to Richard Duncan, capitalism died in the two world wars of the 20th century. It was a death that few recognized, and to this day, still, do not acknowledge. Capitalism evolved into creditism, and it is this creditism that is responsible for the emergence of globalization, which ultimately lifted millions of people out of poverty in various countries around the world. The new dollar standard ushered in a global boom in paper currencies after 1971. And beginning in the 1980s, massive U.S. trade deficits with the rest of the world was fueled by the enormous expansion of credit or creditism. This new paradigm created the world we have today with over seven billion people now populating the planet. This is a critical moment in history, and we need to think very clearly about how we want to lead this civilization to prosper in the 21st century and beyond.

Many economists and analysts are fervently basing their models and strategies on "free market capitalism." But this model cannot resolve the current crisis without bringing about utter devastation. And so many of these analysts tend to arrive at only one general outcome: boom and bust, and the doom and gloom forecast. I know this because that's all I was considering; it's been that way for centuries.

Despite the fact that financial engineering rather than savings, investments, and innovation, is at the center of economic activity in much of the 21st-century American economy, many thinkers will still not consider a possibility that the world is now operating on a different economic paradigm. The expansion of credit is the primary driver of the U.S. and global economy. In Duncan's analysis, when credit grows less than 2%, the U.S. economy goes into recession. Since the early 1950s, this has happened nine times. Thus, the only policy response that we are left with is to continue to inflate the credit bubble when it falls below the 2% growth rate level.

Deflation is evident throughout the world, with the most significant manifestation in excess capacity in manufacturing facilities, goods and labor. Coupled with new robotic and artificial intelligence (AI) technologies, the globalization movement will continue this deflationary trend for some time in the future. If the initiative is not taken to spearhead the growth and development of this new era that Duncan is suggesting, an implosion of the debt bubble (corporate and sovereign debt, and derivatives) will occur at some unsuspecting time in the near future. If something like this spins entirely out of control, a recovery may be almost impossible to engineer given the fact that the world has never generated a creditism bubble of this size and dimension.

Many prominent thinkers, investors, economists and others have voiced grave concerns about the potential fallout from a devastating collapse similar to the 1930s or 2008. Indeed, this is deadly serious and I hope that those in power will consider the research and thesis of Richard Duncan as we navigate through this period of enormous uncertainty. And let us also remember the words of the economist, Dr. Hyman Minsky: "Economies evolve, and so, too, must economic policy."

NOTES

(1) Richard Duncan, *The New Depression*, John Wiley & Sons, (Singapore: 2012) pg. 146.
(2) Ibid, Richard Duncan, pg. 33
(3) Ibid, Richard Duncan, pg.55.
(4) Ibid, Richard Duncan, pg. 109

(5) Ibid, Richard Duncan, pg. 66
(6) Ibid., Richard Duncan, pg. 134
(7) John Mauldin and Jonathan Tepper, *Code Red: How to Protect Your Savings from the Coming Crisis*, John Wiley & Sons, Inc., (New Jersey: 2014), pg. 36
(8) Larry Edelson, *Real Wealth Report*, Money and Markets, a Division of Weiss Research, Inc., (Florida 2015).
(9) Ibid., Richard Duncan, pg. 1
(10) Ibid., Richard Duncan, pg. 3
(11) Ibid, Richard Duncan, pg. 45
(12) Ibid, Richard Duncan, pg. 121
(13) Richard Duncan Youtube video published April 9, 2015
(14) **PRESS RELEASE**, Board of Governors of the Federal Reserve System, January 9, 2015. The following is additional information on interest income received during Fed operations in 2014: "The Federal Reserve Banks' 2014 estimated net income of $101.5 billion was derived primarily from $115.9 billion in interest income on securities acquired through open market operations (U.S. Treasury securities, federal agency and government-sponsored enterprise (GSE) mortgage-backed securities (MBS), and GSE debt securities. Operating expenses of the Reserve Banks, net of amounts reimbursed by the U.S. Treasury and other entities for services the Reserve Banks provided as fiscal agents, totaled $3.6 billion in 2014. In addition, the Reserve Banks were assessed $711 million for the costs related to producing, issuing, and retiring currency, $590 million for Board expenditures, and $563 million to fund the operations of the Consumer Financial Protection Bureau. The Reserve Banks had interest expense of $6.9 billion associated with reserve balances and term deposits held by depository institutions, and recorded foreign currency translation losses of $2.9 billion that result from the daily revaluation of foreign currency denominated asset holdings at current exchange rates."
(15) Ibid, Richard Duncan, pg. 143
(16) Ibid, Richard Duncan, pg. 63-64

EPILOGUE

Much of the twentieth century belonged to Wall Street. The twenty-first now belongs to the central bankers.

Nomi Prins, Author and Journalist

America and the rest of the world never fully recovered from the *Meltdown of 2008*. What we experienced and witnessed in 10 years post-2008, is an extraordinary Fed induce economic recovery and asset price rally unlike anything in the history of economics. With Stocks insanely overvalued and several other detrimental issues (discussed in this publication) converging on this era, our world is confronting a sea of non-classic super bubble conditions, massive debt, and multiple triggers set to detonate the next global meltdown.

As repeatedly stated throughout this publication, this is the biggest economic and financial bubble in history. When the implosion happens, there will be a price to pay for the extreme recklessness. The next crash will catch many of us off guard and unprepared for the fallout and aftershocks. It's happened before (*Crash of 1929*, *Crash of '87*, *The Heisei Bubble Collapse* (Japan 1990), *Dot-Com Bubble Collapse* (2000), and the *Meltdown of 2008*) and it will happen again. In that respect, *this time is not different.*

The economic journey taken in this publication has brought us to the doorstep of an impending crisis of epic proportions, and this trajectory cannot be changed. Capitalism, like everything else in the universe, operates in cycles, and despite the appearance of a vibrant, booming economy in America, we are still moving through the bowels of a deflationary downward cycle. In the ten years post-2008, our economic trajectory was altered in some extraordinary way with the implementation of extreme unconventional Fed tools and strategies. However, this did not change the direction of the *cyclical winter season*. If the global economy stumbles into the abyss, the rescue operation will have to be massive and swift. There will be no time to tinker with solutions and have long debates on what options are available to save the world.

The Fed was instrumental in creating this problem over a period of decades, so it will be up to this institution (and other global central bankers) to fix it! We have a unique opportunity, born out of the reality of *globalization* and the *Information Age Revolution*. Whether the powers that be choose to move in that direction is *highly debatable*, considering the history of our world over just the past 100 years. If the aftermath of the *Meltdown of 2008* is any indication of what we can expect the Fed, the Big Banks, and the federal government to do in the face of a devastating crisis, then it is clear that wealth inequality (will somehow) find a way to become more extreme. The Fed has the power to move mountains, but the history of this organization has proven over the past century that it is focused on trickle-down economics, bailing out the wealthy elites and the international banking cartel. It is very difficult to imagine or logically assume any other outcomes!

With Baby Boomers trying to retire and cutting back on monthly expenses and the purchase of big-ticket items, the demographics are screaming that the next recession will find many people struggling to survive the economic winter. With the Fed tightening (QT), interest rates going up, and the EU signaling that it will be ending its QE operations by December 2018, these are clear indications that the boom and bull run has to come to an end.

The super extreme wealth inequality that is permeating throughout the world is a bad omen, and will only exacerbate recovery efforts after the bubble burst. And ten years after the *Meltdown of 2008*, a massive accumulation of debt (particularly in America) will initiate the next phase of deleveraging by millions of people, corporations, municipalities, and state governments. There is a huge potential for a corporate and junk-bond collapse, as well as sovereign debt defaults.

Unnecessary and wasteful tax cuts (in America) is another factor that will lead to a collapse similar to the Bush era before 2008. Smart money is already starting to leave the market just as they always do when they know the party is about to come to an end. In America, a decade after the 2008 collapse, the top 1% of the population had more wealth than the collective financial resources of the bottom 90% of the people. These types of extraordinary imbalances make it very convenient for a small group of people to control the direction of the financial markets and the economic destiny of nations and ultimately the world. It's a very dangerous scenario that can lead to gross manipulation and undesirable economic consequences.

When the biggest stock market bubble of all time and the superbubble of debt and credit burst and erupt like the Kilauea Volcano on Hawaii's Big Island (2018), it will be an event unlike anything in the annals of economic history. When the big players take to the sidelines, the party will be over, and the deflation will work its will until global central bankers (with the Fed leading the charge) step in and stop the bloodbath. At that point, the ultimate gameplan and master strategy will be revealed!

AFTERWORD: SURVIVING THE NEXT MELTDOWN

The pervasive reality of major boom and bust cycles is that they will always have you guessing about the beginning of turning points. Most people are always shocked and never prepared for the next phase in the cycles. It is very much like a natural disaster, unpredictable and packing a lot of deadly force.

So the question becomes, how does one prepare for the enormous crisis elaborated on in this book? In general, I plan to address this question in a future publication that will be both entertaining and educational. The next bust cycle is very likely to play out over a period of years, so a plan of action needs to be comprehensive as well as life-changing. So my next book (which will be in the form of a novel) will illustrate how a group of people will develop sophisticated plans and strategies to survive and prosper during the next major meltdown.

However, for this publication, I'm presenting some basic steps you can take to begin taking greater control over your finance and economic well-being. Before the commencement of the next major recession, consider some or all of the following recommendations:

(1) **Get Out of Debt:** Get rid of and pay off as much non-essential debt as possible. If a debt obligation is not required or needed, don't have it in your life. In a deflationary depression, debt is like being in a strait-jacket and will serve as a form of confinement. Due to a debt overload, available opportunities will be missed as the struggle for survival remains the dominant preoccupation and strategy. Anyone who has struggled with deleveraging during the ten years after the 2008 financial crisis will know what this is like from personal experience. You are severely limited and trapped in a debt prison with very little ability to grow or expand in any direction. Strive to be flexible and financially prepared for the abundant opportunities that will become available in the markets during the next major down cycle. And keep in mind that economic liberation will be reserved for those who are prepared and focused on building personal wealth during a time of great national and international economic hardships. The strategy recommendation here is to wait and be prepared.

(2) **Save and Build Financial Reserves:** Before the bust cycle begins, save as much money as you can and build your reserves. During a deep recession or deflationary depression, liquidity is Queen (or King), and those who have it are in very strong positions to not only survive but to also prosper. People who don't have some form of liquid cash they can quickly put their hands on, will be severely restricted in their financial life. This is one of the main reasons why wealth inequality soared in the aftermath of the *Meltdown of 2008*. Those who had ample liquid reserves were able to take full advantage of an enormously bad economic situation. Great fortunes will be lost and made during this next crisis.

(3) **Develop Multiple Streams of Income:** Don't plan to rely on one form of income (for instance, one job) as your only monetary source to pay bills, survive and possibly to invest. Consider additional ways and means to generate income in a world that will be undergoing massive change. If you have additional skills and talents that are marketable, consider putting them to good use. This next crisis is going to require that you dig deep and put all your resources (personal and otherwise) towards surviving and building a dynamic future in the midst of chaos.

(4) **Maintain Good Health:** In good or bad times, having good health will enable you to better withstand the pressures in life. However, I will take this a step further and recommend having good mental, spiritual and physical health as your safeguard and armor, because you are going to need it during the next brutal downturn. Good health is essential; if you don't have it, the crisis and the stress will drain you. Declining health during a major economic crisis will likely lead to greater damage and further mental and physical deterioration. Learn about proper nutrition, good exercise programs and other benefit plans and systems designed to make you a more healthier person. And remember, don't overindulge in alcohol or drugs to temporarily escape reality. This will not work; face the music and the chaos head on, and you will achieve much better results.

(5) **Improve Your Credit Situation:** Position yourself to maintain a high credit score as part of your plan to build wealth and acquire resources. Consider the option of purchasing real estate at bargain prices when quality assets go on sale. Only consider using debt when the benefits outweigh the burden of maintaining a debt load: ensure that you are making more money on the proposition than it costs to service the debt. A top credit score in a bust cycle is like having money in the bank or on reserve; you can take advantage of good opportunities at a lower cost of capital.

(6) **Expand your Awareness:** Maintain a positive attitude and vision of the future beyond the grave (the Great Depression) with expectations of being successful, healthy and wise when the recovery arrives. Don't ever give up, and stay focused on your

goals. Many people may fall by the wayside due to the enormous stress and financial difficulties that will be ever-present during the next global crisis. Make a strategic plan not to be a casualty. Recovery will come, and it will be just as unpredictable as any unforeseen natural disaster. That is why it is extremely important to stay focused and to keep working your on strategy and recovery plan.

(7) **This will not be the End of the World:** At times it will feel like the end-of-the-world scenario, but that will be an illusion in a *mind* that is filled with fear and pessimism concerning the crisis. Along the same line, limit your exposure to negative programming, especially overindulgence in TV programming (or brainwashing). Read more beneficial books and study the situation as if your life depends on it. The stronger you are in your mental preparedness, the better you will be able to withstand the pressures of an economic depression. Don't waste *time*; use as much of your valuable *time* to prepare for this crisis.

(8) **Educate Yourself:** Consistent with number seven (above), continue to educate yourself regarding financial, economic, technological and scientific issues. Study the cycles and the boom and bust cyclic periods, particularly over the last 100 years. Become familiar with such factors as the stages in the cycles, Fed policies, the impact of interest rate changes, quantitative easing (QE), and government stimulus programs.

(9) **Consider the Boom and Bust Investment Strategy:** We know that great fortunes are made by wealthy individuals and families who invest in the markets at the bottom of bust cycles. Study the information presented in Appendix A and Appendix B. It will help to shed some light on this issue I label the "Boom and Bust Investment Strategy." It is consistent with what Warren Buffet has been preaching for decades, "Be fearful when others are greedy, and greedy when others are fearful." People in power, the wealthy elites, and their associates are aggressively planning and preparing sophisticated strategies to survive, profit and prosper during the aftermath of the next great collapse. This will be an opportunity for many in the elite camp to turn their central bank conjured money (paper money created out of thin air) into real assets. In a massive display of wealth transference, trillions of these created dollars will steadily move into a position to acquire various types of hard assets: from gold and silver to residential and commercial properties, to seaports, airports, and railways, entire companies and corporate ownership stakes and more. This is the primary reason why you do not want to be holding a lot of debt. Debt is the trap that is being set for the unsuspecting prey.

Make no mistake about this; this is *D-Day* for all of us. Keep in mind, that the Appendix presentations are not recommendations for particular stocks, but are observations on what happens to markets during these very volatile periods in the cycles. Also be aware that moving forward during the next major downturn, we may experience shorter periods of boom and bust cycles as the entire world attempts to unwind an enormous amount of debt and credit. If you are not interested in just being a bystander, observer or victim of the coming bust cycle, then you will need to make some solid preparations to survive and possibly prosper from the financial calamity that will be unleashed upon our world. If you are a stock market investor (or planning to become one) make sure you do your homework: study the markets, study the companies you have an interest in, develop a good understanding of boom and bust cycles, and never stop researching.

Keep in mind that by the third quarter of 2018, foreign and American investors had begun the process of pouring trillions of dollars into the U.S. stock market. Flight capital from abroad had accelerated due to the worsening conditions in many foreign markets around the world. Investor flight capital was searching for a safe haven and investment vehicles for steady growth and higher returns. This flow of capital may continue uninterrupted for at least another year or two which means that the supernova of debt, credit and asset bubbles will grow much larger. It also means that when the bust cycle and *meltdown* finally arrives, it will be much greater in its size, magnitude and impact.

The next several years are going to be very intense and full of global economic situations that may either wipe you out or present some marvelous opportunities if you have prepared for this crisis.

(10) **Build an Investment War Chest and be Patient**: Consistent with number nine above, consider an investment strategy that consists of saving a boatload of cash (as much as you can manage to put aside) that will be targeted specifically for the next major bust cycle. The goal here is to wait patiently (no matter how long it takes) for the inevitable meltdown event to occur. In the meantime (now) use your valuable time to research and prepare a list of excellent stocks or commodities or other investment vehicles that you would like to purchase once their prices have suffered major declines.

We are at the peak in this boom investment cycle and global credit bubble, and when it burst, panic and fear will spread like wildfire throughout the world dragging global stock markets down into the pits. I label the very bottom of these bust cycles and pits, the *wasteland*; that is where the gold and precious assets will be found at bargain prices. Plan on taking a trip to the *wasteland* once all the air has been sucked out of the global superbubble. This strategy requires an abundance of patience and a strong constitution and confidence that you can achieve success in the midst of widespread fear and chaos. Supreme knowledge of what is happening will be your best defense. Remain firm in your convictions!

As I stated in my 2012 publication (*Global Markets and Boom & Bust Cycles*), as individuals, communities, and organizations, we must be prepared for the onset of a major collapse and downward cycle. Similar to preparing for natural disasters, now is the time to put aside the reserves and circle the wagons. No one knows when the bust cycle will commence or how long the downward phase will last. The superbubble (in 2018) may continue to expand for a few more years in what some observers are referring to as a "Panic Up" scenario. If the Dow Jone Industrial Average soars to 30,000 or 40,000 or more, you will need to question whether it is wise to be fully invested in what will undoubtedly be *irrational exuberance* (Greenspan on the *Crash of 2000*). The global economic system is in deep trouble and is embedded with countless trillions of dollars of d*erivatives, credit and debt bubbles* of enormous proportion. This is what will explode in our faces on some unsuspecting day at *some point in the future*. It is better to be prepared, and nothing happens than to be unprepared, and all hell breaks loose. Make some preparations to survive what is likely to be the greatest economic calamity in world economic history!

APPENDIX A

Analysis of 31 Stocks in Boom and Bust Cycles: Dot-Com and Tech Bubble: 1995 to 2000

This section provides examples of various companies and their stock prices at select points during the boom and bust cycles of 1995 to 2000 (see Table 3). As observed in the analysis, the meltdown devastated stock prices that were mainly associated with the Internet and the technology sector. The collapse did not severely damage non-cyclical corporations (Proctor & Gamble, Johnson & Johnson and others) and the banking sector. However, as to be expected, it's clear to see which industry leaders were the strongest.

In the boom cycle from 1995 to 2000, the U.S. economy was showing strong performance and great numbers: low inflation, low unemployment, low-interest rates, high productivity and strong growth. Between 1997 and 2000, economic growth in the U.S. accounted for 30 percent of the total growth in the global economy. Economist, Paul Samuelson, called it, "a honeymoon economy," as the good times continued with Dot-com fever and the birth of the Internet driving the markets.

The atmosphere was charged to the hilt, with investors growing to expect 20 to 30 percent annual returns (the historic annual return of the Dow had been 9 to 10 percent). Speculation was fueled by the growing phenomenon of online trading, which provided (for the first time) a very convenient Internet/personal computer system to place buy and sell orders for stock transactions. The longer the boom period persisted, the more people gravitated to the markets. Like the 1920s, many people would become investors in the markets for the first time in their lives.

A red-hot dot-com fever developed for any company that had Internet-related potential: the markets were constantly searching for the next Yahoo! or Amazon.com. It was dot-com this and dot-com that, and niche markets were spawning clones as fast as the new territory was established, and the IPOs broke records. Greed became a dominant theme and force in the markets, and it was contagious. Many sound thinking people lost perspective of what was going on, and this was not surprising.

It was an exciting *wealth show*, but this was not TV. There were many trading sessions that featured new IPOs with price increases of 40 to 60 points in a day (and some a lot higher). These were fabulous returns especially if one was fortunate enough to get in on the deal at the opening price ($15 to $20 in many cases). Other exciting moments witnessed a stock shoot up 50 points in one day, and the very next day, fall by 50 points (oh well). And take the case of a penny stock moving from $2.00 a share to over $100 per share in a matter of a couple of months (that was interesting). There was some degree of financial insanity to all of this, but few questioned the market fever, especially if they were making money. It was a real show stopper.

As the Nasdaq and the Dow continued to break records, billions of dollars continued to flow into the markets. At the height of the boom period, nearly 50 percent of American adults (49.2 million American households or 48.2 percent of the total population) were involved directly or indirectly (mutual funds, pension plans, etc.) in the stock market.

The tech-heavy Nasdaq hit a beautiful high of 5,048.62 on March 10, 2000. This date went down in history as the major turning point of the boom and bust cycle of the 1995-2000 era. Like the 1990 collapse of the Nikkei, the descent happened in bits and lumps, leaving great confusion in its wake. The market change was so dramatic and so swift that it caused one observer to compare it to a millennium change of "B.C. to A.D.": *the optimistic climate of the boom period versus the gloom and pessimism of the bust period.* A giant financial plug was pulled, and all of the "financial magic" began to vanish. Many venture capitalists, investment bankers, and others walked away rich, while others got clobbered beyond belief. The steep deceleration was both shocking and unreal.

With many investors accustomed to buying on the dips and witnessing rapid rebounds in share prices, the steady declines that continued throughout March and April were brutal and nerve-racking. In the initial stages of a bust period, it's hard to believe that the boom period has bit the dust. But, as we have seen in other times and places, this stage is the most difficult adjustment, particularly for those that were not prepared for the new psychology that slowly permeates throughout the markets. Like a lover who has to adjust to the reality that a love affair has ended, pumped up investors packed their bags and prepared for another season.

In the period between March 11, 2000, and April 17, 2000 (the main crash period) the Nasdaq composite fell 34.2 percent. Selling pressures bombarded the markets from many sources, which included margin calls, mutual fund redemptions, folks fleeing the markets in panic, and many others needing cash to pay their tax bills. However, some investors (even after witnessing these drops) were still trying to wait it out, hoping for a rebound in prices. But, a major rebound never came, and as the correction continued to carve a deeper descent to lower prices, the weakest Dot-Com companies began falling to the wayside in the true spirit of the "Law of the financial jungle" where only the strong will survive. By the end of 2001, the majority of Dot-Com companies had failed, with investors suffering trillions of dollars in losses.

Market analysts tell us that the bust cycle and the bear market that began in March 2000, continued until October 2002. At its peak of 5,048.62, the Nasdaq index fell to 1,139.90, suffering a total collapse of 76.81% over the two to three-year period. Over $5 to $7 trillion in wealth was lost during the Dot-Com bust cycle. Companies like Pets.com and Webvan were completely wiped out and went out of existence, while other stronger tech corporations, such as Amazon.com, Yahoo!, Priceline, and Cisco, survived the carnage. At one point in late September 2001 (the period after 911), the share price of Amazon was trading in the $5 to $6 range. The data also reveals that Priceline fell to a low of $2.44 per share in December 2000.

Price history of closing price data was selected from various points in the cycle to illustrate peak periods and low points in the markets. The dates selected are January 3, 2000, December 1, 2000, September 24, 2001, and February 22, 2002. The January 3, 2000 date represents a peak in the boom cycle before the actual start of the bust period. The December 2000 date illustrates the price collapse in the aftermath of the bust cycle that began in March/April of that year. The September 24, 2001 date was chosen to observe the impact of the terrorists' attacks that occurred on September 11, 2001 (911). In observing the data, we can see the enormous damage and impact this crisis had on company share prices. After 11 interest rate cuts during 2001, the February 22nd data reveals the markets still struggling to regain their footing.

The historical price data selected presents pre-split prices on January 3, 2000 (for those companies that declared forward stock splits) to show an actual peak share price in the cycle. The split-adjusted price(s) on January 3, 2000, are as follows:

Cisco (csco: 2:1) $54.03; Yahoo (yhoo: 2:1) $237.50; CMGI (cmgi: 2:1) $163.22; Ebay (ebay: 2:1) $70.62; Schwab (sch: 1.5:1) $24.67; Safeguard Scientific (sfe: 3:1) $63.21; Commerce One (cmrc: 2:1) $101.81; Globix Corp. (gbix: 2:1) $30.06; Covad Communications Group, Inc. (covd: 1.5:1) $39.33; and Ariba Inc. (arba: 2:1) $95.87.

It's a good exercise to study this material to examine what happened to share prices at various points in the cycles. For instance, the terrorists' attacks in September 2001, drove many share prices to incredible lows. However, many stocks recovered from the dramatic collapse in less than five months. In the case of Kana Software Inc., the recovery was remarkable (from a low of $0.53 to roughly $12.00). And companies like Amazon and Priceline went on to become major superstars in the world of financial markets.

For others, the story was radically different. In the case of Globix and Enron, the bankruptcy strategy became a necessary option as investors watched in horror as share prices plunged to penny stock levels. But again, we must be mindful that some of the stocks listed in Table 3 (and many others not illustrated in this example) came back strong during the next major upswing in the markets.

As investors and analysts, we need to continually expand our knowledge of the markets and new global developments. We should also have good systems and strategies to manage and guide our market decisions. This section is not about providing instructions on how to be a good stock market trader or investor (that training and advice can be received by professional offline organizations and some online trading platforms). The one central theme presented in this Appendix is the power and devastation inherent in boom and bust cycles. Thus as a boom and bust cycle analyst, here are some of the basic factors to consider when observing this phenomenon: (1) Stay focused and aware of when interest rates are rising or falling (2) Be aware of when stocks in various sectors are selling at super high prices or have extraordinary P/E ratios (3) Be watchful for the emergence of speculative bubbles in real estate, stocks, and commodities (4) carefully observe Fed and global central banking activities, especially QE operations and other unconventional tactics and (5) take note of new developments that start to reshape an entire industry. These events and other factors will serve as important signs and warning alerts that a boom or bust period is in progress.

To get a firm grip on the material presented in this publication, it's a good idea to periodically review some of the major issues, and topics discussed regarding the factors and agents initiating boom periods, and the remedies and central bank activities that are likely to be undertaken during the bust cycles. It's also an important exercise to monitor the explosive progress of the Information Age Revolution, for we are likely to witness some extraordinary developments as we proceed through the third and fourth decades of the 21st century.

Having a strategic plan for boom and bust cycles can be a very useful tool to keep polished and ready, for we are likely to experience some very turbulent and volatile periods over the next decade or so. The unwinding of the ten-year Fed-induced boom cycle following the *Meltdown of 2008* is very likely to produce some wild swings in stock markets throughout the world. Those who understand the inner workings of the markets and the massive influence of boom and bust cycles, tend to benefit the most from the various stages in the cyclical patterns. By understanding and fully appreciating the cyclical resolve of boom and bust periods, investors and analysts will be able to navigate the peaks and valleys with much greater control and success. Continue to look for those companies and industries that are strong and dominant leaders, and patiently wait for the *time when they go on sale*.

BOOM & BUST HISTORIC SHARE PRICES: TECH BUBBLE COLLAPSE OF 2000

Company/S	Jan. 2000	Dec. 2000	Sept. 2001	Feb. 2002
Microsoft/msft	$116.56	$56.62	$52.01	$57.99
AOL/aol	$82.87	$41.51	$32.50	$23.75
Cisco/csco	$108.06	$47.88	$24.50	$15.50
CMGI/cmgi	$326.43	$10.50	$1.18	$1.35
ICGE/icge	$200.00	$6.00	$0.50	$0.77
Ebay/ebay	$141.25	$34.31	$46.78	$52.50
Yahoo/yhoo	$475.00	$39.63	$9.25	$14.46
Lucent/lu	$77.25	$15.68	$5.80	$5.49
Kana/kana	$198.00	$12.50	$0.53	$11.78
Silicon Gr./sgi	$9.68	$4.12	$0.51	$2.91
Amazon/amzn	$89.37	$24.62	$7.46	$13.07
Hartford Fin/hig	$45.23	$73.25	$53.96	$65.90
Priceline/pcln	$51.25	$2.44	$2.52	$4.27
Adobe Systems/adbe	$16.39	$33.66	$12.65	$17.57
Citigroup/c	$397.50	$489.38	$390.00	$424.00
Delta Airlines/dal	$50.00	$48.25	$23.99	$32.77
General Electric/ge	$50.00	$51.00	$35.20	$38.09
American Exp./axp	$45.88	$47.49	$40.48	$29.45
Proctor & Gamb./pg	$53.59	$36.97	$34.73	$42.80
Goldman Sachs/gs	$88.31	$82.00	$70.51	$79.00
Bank of Amer./bac	$24.22	$19.88	$26.68	$30.66
Ariba/arba	$191.75	$60.93	$2.04	$3.79
China/china	$94.00	$7.12	$2.03	$2.90
McAfee/mcaf	$46.00	$6.25	$10.05	$11.63
Globix/gbix	$60.12	$3.87	$0.63	$0.04
Safeguard/sfc	$189.62	$8.43	$2.17	$2.92
Commerce/cmrc	$203.62	$28.87	$2.57	$1.82
Covad/covd	$59.00	$2.09	$0.42	$1.63
Schwab/sch	$37.00	$27.31	$10.20	$13.20
Intel/intc	$87.00	$34.12	$21.31	$29.53
JDS/Uni/jdsu	$188.00	$56.18	$6.39	$4.90

Table 3

APPENDIX B
Analysis of 30 Stocks in Boom and Bust Cycles: The *Meltdown of 2008*

This section provides examples of various companies and their stock prices at select points during the boom and bust cycles of 2003 to 2008 (see Table 4). In general, the collapse devastated stock prices across the board. However, as was the case with the Dot-Com *Tech Bubble* era, it's clear to see which industry leaders were the strongest.

Many stocks were beaten down to painfully new lows during the brutal bust cycle. Some of these companies and industries were driven to the edge of the cliff. However, unconventional Fed tools and central bank actions saved the day unlike anything ever implemented before in economic history. Like similar bust cycles, many of the stronger companies and industries were beaten down by the sagging economy and the deepening recession. The 18-month Great Recession was a devastating meltdown (particularly the last eight to ten months), but the massive central bank interventions and government stimulus programs created the economic environment (especially in the United States) for the next bull run in the markets and accelerated asset bubbles in various areas in the economy.

Price history of closing price data was selected from various points in the cycle to illustrate peak periods and low points in the markets. The dates selected are January 3, 2008, December 1, 2008, March 9, 2009, June 1, 2009, and December 4, 2012. The January 1, 2008 date represents a peak point in the boom cycle before the actual start of the bust period in late October of that year. The December 1, 2008 date illustrates the price declines in the aftermath of the stock market collapse and the start of the bust cycle. March 9, 2009, illustrates the lowest point in the bear market when the Dow Jones Industrial Average (DJIA) reached a low of 6,547.05. It was that significant moment in time that witnessed investor capitulation. I refer to this bottom as the *wasteland*; it's a dramatic moment in the historic bust cycle where investors have capitulated, allowing share prices to fall to their lowest levels. The June 1, 2009 date was chosen to observe the impact of the bust cycle and the bottom of the *Great Recession*. In observing the data, we can see the enormous damage and impact the meltdown had on company share prices. And the December 4, 2012 date illustrates the recovery phase for the majority of the stocks presented in this sample.

The *Meltdown of 2008* witnessed the DJIA losing 54% of its value, $6.9 trillion in shareholder wealth, and $3.3 trillion in homeowner equity (according to MortgageWire). The total financial damage on the U.S. economy was $10.2 trillion. The Dot-Com collapse witnessed shareholder losses of $5 to $7 trillion. Thus the 2008 meltdown generated a much greater destruction of wealth.

After several interest rate cuts during 2008 and early 2009, the initiation of the Troubled Asset Relief Program (TARP) in late 2008, the start of quantitative easing (QE) during the fourth quarter of 2008, and the implementation of the Obama Administration's "American Recovery and Reinvestment Act of 2009," the stage was finally set to begin the recovery phase and the next bull market. What we came to understand during this bust cycle, was that much greater financial resources were required (multiple trillions of dollars) to prevent the onset of a *Great Depression*. We can expect that during the next major crisis (the bust cycle I refer to as *The Day of Reckoning*), the Fed and other central banks in the West will be called upon to conduct global bailout operations that will far exceed their actions in 2008.

It is a good exercise to study this material to examine what happened to share prices at various points in the cycles. The *Meltdown of 2008* was a very vicious bust period which drove many share prices to incredible lows. However, given the extraordinary response of the Fed and the federal government stimulus programs, many stocks were able to manage incredible recoveries by the end of 2009 and beyond. In the case of Bank of America, the recovery was remarkable. As stated earlier in the book, by March 2009, the company's shares were trading in the $3.00 range; 85 percent of its stock market value had been wiped out! By mid-2018, the price per share of Bank of America was roughly $30.00. As can be seen in Table 4, many stocks came back strong during the next major upswing in the markets.

For the most part, a devastating market collapse will spread fear and panic among many investors, especially if they are invested in companies that are experiencing a free fall in their stock prices. Check out Las Vegas Sands (LVS) with a share price of $95.37 in January 2008. By March 2009, the price had fallen to a low of $1.42, then (during the bull run) climbed to a high of $45.46 by December 2012. General Motors (GM) presents a similar story, moving from a low of $0.75 in June of 2009 back to a high of $25.41 by December 2012. In one scenario investors in these companies suffered great losses if they were forced to sell their holdings; on the other hand, for investors prepared to purchase strong companies at the bottom of a bust cycle (*the wasteland*), these rare buying opportunities are ideal for those who possess the knowledge and fortitude to battle through these periods of enormous uncertainty. The most important thing is to pick the best-performing companies (in their industries) and to carefully observe which corporations and industries are receiving special assistance and bailout money (corporate welfare and socialistic funding).

As investors and analysts, we need to continually expand our knowledge of the markets and new global developments. We should also have good systems and strategies to manage and guide our market decisions. This section is not about providing instructions on how to be a good stock market trader or investor (that training and advice can be received by professional offline organizations and some online trading platforms). The one central theme presented in this Appendix is the power and devastation inherent in boom and bust cycles. Thus as a boom and bust cycle analyst, here are some of the basic factors to consider when observing this phenomenon: (1) Stay focused and aware of when interest rates are rising or falling (2) Be aware of when stocks in various sectors are selling at super high prices or have extraordinary P/E ratios (3) Be watchful for the emergence of speculative bubbles in real estate, stocks, and commodities (4) carefully observe Fed and global central banking activities, especially QE operations and other unconventional tactics and (5) take note of new developments that start to reshape an entire industry. These events and other factors will serve as important signs and warning alerts that a boom or bust period is in progress or may be positioning to change direction. A prime example of this theory was the sudden one day collapse of Facebook in late July 2018.

As another potent sign of the times and a demonstration of the massive power of the U.S. stock market bubble, Facebook's stock hit a brick wall and fell 24 percent on July 26, 2018. At one point in the trading session, the company's market capitalization had fallen by $151 billion, the largest loss of value by a publicly traded company in a single day. By the end of the trading day, total shareholder wealth had declined $120 billion. Disappointed investors were expecting higher numbers in sales and user growth, but Facebook fell short of expectations. What happened to Facebook was just a preview of what will likely take place with many high flying tech stocks supported by extremely high PE ratios, massive speculation, and nervous investors gambling on additional stock market gains before the bull run comes to an end. We have seen this movie before!

As further evidence that the boom was reaching all-time highs and breaking records, another milestone was reached on August 2, 2018 when Apple Inc. ascended to a market capitalization of $1 trillion. With the price per share reaching $207.05 (the critical number required for the number of outstanding shares), the company became the first U.S. corporation to achieve the $1 trillion status on a public stock market exchange. On the one hand it was a clear demonstration of the strength and vibrancy of the boom period, however, it was also a clear indication that the system was moving closer to a dramatic climax in a volatile and uncertain global economic terrain.

BOOM & BUST HISTORIC STOCK PRICES: MELTDOWN OF 2008

Ticker	Jan. 2008	Dec. 2008	Mar. 2009	June 2009	Dec. 2012
MSFT	$35.37	$18.61	$15.15	$21.40	$26.37
AMZN	$95.21	$40.47	$60.49	$83.05	$252.49
AAPL	$27.85	$12.70	$11.87	$19.91	$82.26
NFLX	$3.72	$3.15	$5.50	$5.85	$12.38
PG	$72.31	$60.49	$44.18	$53.36	$69.31
BAC	$40.30	$12.85	$3.75	$11.21	$9.91
HIG	$84.67	$6.61	$4.10	$15.18	$20.93
LVS	$95.37	$4.00	$1.42	$10.77	$45.46
PCLN	$111.40	$62.73	$78.36	$114.30	$663.81
GM	$23.92	$4.59	$1.68	$0.75	$25.41
CSCO	$26.75	$14.96	$13.62	$19.50	$19.17
F	$6.45	$2.55	$1.74	$6.13	$11.31
DLR	$37.24	$23.48	$27.68	$37.29	$65.83
EBAY	$13.82	$5.15	$4.32	$7.68	$21.88
ADBE	$41.79	$21.00	$16.78	$29.36	$35.30
YHOO	$23.84	$10.74	$12.16	$16.58	$18.93
C	$289.30	$64.50	$10.50	$36.90	$34.29
AAL	$12.72	$5.12	$2.01	$2.95	$12.38
DAL	$13.65	$7.96	$4.19	$6.43	$9.73
AA	$108.57	$27.93	$16.17	$29.49	$25.26
MS	$50.94	$11.35	$16.48	$29.89	$16.61
S	$12.97	$2.11	$3.12	$5.00	$5.68
SCHW	$24.78	$15.55	$11.36	$18.38	$12.88
INTC	$24.67	$12.56	$12.55	$16.50	$19.97
UVE	$7.05	$2.38	$3.45	$5.11	$4.61
GE	$36.80	$15.50	$7.41	$13.86	$20.86
GFI	$13.98	$5.82	$9.52	$11.53	$10.09
BRKB	$93.00	$65.60	$46.20	$59.69	$87.27
AXP	$50.41	$19.64	$10.64	$25.99	$55.84
JNJ	$65.93	$55.33	$46.60	$55.78	$69.86

Table 4

To get a firm grip on the material presented in this book, it's a good idea to periodically review some of the major issues, and topics discussed in this publication. It's also an important exercise to monitor the explosive progress of the *Information*

Age Revolution, for we are likely to witness some extraordinary developments as we proceed through the third and fourth decades of the 21st century.

Having a strategic plan for boom and bust cycles can be a very useful tool to keep polished and ready, for we are likely to experience some very turbulent and volatile periods over the next decade or so. The unwinding of the Fed-induced boom cycle following the *Meltdown of 2008* is very likely to produce some wild swings in stock markets throughout the world. Those who understand the inner workings of the markets and the massive influence of boom and bust cycles, tend to benefit the most from the various stages in the cyclical patterns. By understanding and fully appreciating the cyclical resolve of boom and bust periods, investors and analysts will be able to navigate the peaks and valleys with much greater control and success. Continue to look for those companies and industries that are strong and dominant leaders, and patiently wait for the *time when they go on sale*.

APPENDIX C
FUKUSHIMA: AN ECONOMIC X FACTOR EVENT

The 9.0 quake that hit Japan on March 11 was powerful enough to shift the earth on its axis and make it spin a little faster, shortening the day by 1.8 millionths of a second. It shoved the island nation one parking space to the east. But what felt like the end was just the beginning.

Time Magazine, March 28, 2011

JAPAN - March 11, 2011 (3/11): A 9.0-magnitude super devastating (megathrust) earthquake struck Japan and initiated a triple disaster: earthquake, tsunami, and nuclear power meltdown. According to U.S. Geological Survey, this earthquake lifted a span of the ocean floor 50 feet over a span of 180 miles, setting in motion a massive tsunami that hit the shores of Japan shortly after the initial quake with over 10 billion tons of ocean water. The earthquake lasted an unprecedented five (5) minutes! During the week following this devastating disaster, there were more than 500 aftershocks, with many of them the size of significant earthquakes (one measuring 6.1-magnitude on the Richter scale). Centered off the coast of Honshu at a depth of 17 miles below the earth's surface, this quake generated a biblical-scale disaster with the tsunami attacking Japan's northeastern coastal areas. This quake was so powerful it caused Japan's coastline to subside by one meter. More than 19,000 people were killed, thousands were missing, and millions of people were left living in shelters, with little food and water near-freezing temperatures. Japan's government was entirely overwhelmed by the triple impact of the disaster. For the world and Japan, this became known as 3/11, a massive unpredictable and unexpected event: *An Economic X Factor*.

As the third largest economy in the world and one of the most developed nations on the planet, Japan's moment of extreme catastrophe captured the attention of the collective consciousness of the world as a whole in a way that other disasters didn't, shaping the economic policies, philosophies and technological and energy mandates in nations around the world. The images were profound and reached every corner of the earth with astounding speed. As reporter James Nachtwey stated:

> "First there is shock - disbelief at what you are witnessing...Huge man-made structures were swept away like toys...Houses, cars, ships and locomotives funneled up river channels, smashed against the sides of hills and swept back again as the raging waters receded, left in grotesque positions, as if by a sculptor gone mad."[1]

In Germany, the reactions to the nuclear catastrophe lead to a pronouncement that the nation would be phasing out its nuclear energy sites over a scheduled period of time. Other countries also began to re-think their atomic policies. Many Japanese citizens started to strongly denounce the use of nuclear energy as a power source. Major magazine covers began to announce the uncertain future of nuclear energy:

> **"Nuclear energy: The dream that failed"**
> *The Economist* (March 2012)

> **"Fukushima, March 12: 15:36: The End of the Nuclear Age"**
> *Der Spiegel magazine* (March 2011)

THE NUCLEAR CRISIS

Considered as the worse nuclear crisis since the atomic bombing of Hiroshima and Nagasaki during World War II, the Fukushima Daiichi nuclear power plant became ground zero for 3/11. It was reported that a 46-foot tsunami wave broke through the protective wall of the complex located just meters away from the coastline. The defensive flood walls developed to protect the facility were 16 feet in height (5 meters), while the tsunami wave was higher than 20 feet (or 6 meters) in height. Backup generators were behind the walls, but they were not on higher grounds. Explosions and fires broke out as the nuclear reactors overheated, spilling radiation into the Pacific Ocean, air, and the surrounding land mass. Owned and operated by the Tokyo Electric Power Co. (TEPCO), the rapidly moving tsunami stormed the protective walls of the nuclear plant drowning the backup generators, knocking out cooling systems and causing the complex to leak radiation. Four significant reactors were severely damaged in the catastrophe (three reactors went into the meltdown phase). The initial estimate was that it would take six to nine months to bring the crisis under control. Nearly 90,000 people were evacuated from the surrounding areas (within a 12-mile radius of the nuclear complex).

In a sign that the radiation had seeped into the food chain, officials began to discover radiation contamination in spinach, milk and even tap water. Small amounts of cesium-137 (which is cancerous and has a half-life of 30 years) and iodine-131 were detected in milk. Three months after the disaster, scientists detected radioactive contamination from the plant 400 miles off Japan in the Pacific Ocean. They reported that the levels of concentration were not harmful to humans. Workers in the contaminated facility had to work in protected suits and masks, struggle against explosions, fires, aftershocks, leaks of contaminated water and equipment breakdowns; this would be an ongoing struggle for months to contain the complex nature of the meltdown.

In mid-December, Japan's Prime Minister Yoshihiko Noda stated that "the Fukushima nuclear reactors have been brought to a state of cold shutdown."[2] Many nuclear scientists disputed that claim; however, the government was attempting to move forward to the next stage, to bring to a closure a significant part of the crisis.

In a *New York Times* report, a global team of experts led by Hitachi estimated that it would take three decades to return the site to a "green field" state (a condition safe for human habitation within legal limits of radiation). One of the leading producers of nuclear reactors, Toshiba, stated that it would take approximately ten years.

However, by December 2011, Japan was ready to execute a nuke cleanup operation of the areas evacuated during the crisis. The decontamination process (to deal with the radiation fallout) contemplated consisted of: (1) scrubbing down thousands of buildings and the topsoil of the area of radioactive particles. (2) clean-cutting and scraping forested mountainous areas. The evacuated areas covered about 5,200 square miles, about 3 percent of the land mass of Japan. Thus this land (as far as the Japanese are concern) cannot be abandoned. After the Chernobyl nuclear crisis in 1986, the Soviet Union relocated 300,000 people and abandoned the land affected by the crisis, and as of 2018, that land was still uninhabitable.

In a crisis of this massive scale, the threat of nuclear radiation is severe and can become fatal very quickly. For people near or around the affected areas, the government advice was to "Please do not go outside. Please stay indoors. Please close windows and make your homes airtight...Don't turn on ventilators. Please hang your laundry indoors." I agree with Eugene Robinson, writing in the *Washington Post,* that "Nuclear fission is an inherently and uniquely toxic technology."

In January 2012, almost a year after the nuclear meltdown, detection of radiation in Japan's food supply illustrated the continued struggle of this nation to contain the deadly atomic fallout. In the small town of Onami, located about 35 miles northwest of the Fukushima Daiichi nuclear plant, unsafe levels of radioactive cesium were detected in samples taken from rice farms. As one reporter observed:

> "An ensuing panic forced the Japanese government to intervene, with promises to test more than 25,000 rice farms in eastern Fukushima prefecture,

where the plant is located. The uproar underscores how, almost a year after a huge earthquake and tsunami...Japan is still struggling to protect its food supply from radioactive contamination."[3]

About 160,000 people were evacuated from homes near the plant, an area that may be uninhabitable for many years or even decades. The meltdown released a great deal of radiation into the environment.

The abandoned communities (towns and villages where families had lived for centuries) are a testimony to the enormous losses suffered by the people: large rice fields, large businesses, well-built schools and ancient connections to the land. Tepco's primary focus was to stabilize the reactors. The company was on course to lose 570 billion yen in the fiscal year ending in 2011.

By December 2011, the fear of nuclear power had captured the minds of many people in Japan: the anti-nuclear movement grew larger and stronger as a result of the crisis. As nuclear power operators suspended the operations of their nuclear energy plants for routine maintenance, very few were allowed to resume operations after 3/11. Throughout Japan, concern for public safety prevented the majority of Japan's 54 nuclear reactors from going back online. Only eight plants were in service as of December 2011.[4] Kansai Electric (KEPCO), a utility that covers the cities of Osaka and Kyoto, had only one of its 11 reactors up and running during December 2011. By March 2012, *The Economist* reported that "52 of the country's 54 nuclear reactors were off-line - their power replaced by old thermal plants working at full capacity."[5]

TSUNAMI

As stated earlier, the mega-thrust earthquake displaced over 10 billion tons of ocean water and sent giant waves as high as 46 feet (or higher) traveling at 500 miles per hour to the northern coastline of Japan. The first waves of the tsunami hit Ofunato, Japan just 20 minutes after the massive earthquake. There was very little time for the people of that city to escape to safety. The tsunami and flood waters generated an immense amount of damage, especially in the destruction of towns and villages, and the creation of the nuclear disaster. The massive destructive force of the tsunami just tore through, ripped apart and carried away entire coastal towns and villages creating millions of tons of debris.

One year after the disaster, the wreckage and debris of the tsunami littered the landscape: as reported by *The Economist* "an estimated 22.5m tons of debris scattered across Japan's northeast coast - the equivalent of possibly 20 years of municipal waste...Only 6% of it has been permanently disposed of...Much of the farmland is contaminated with sea water; it will take several years for the salt to be washed out."[6] Approximately 1.5 to 2 million tons of debris (dispersed over an area of 2000 miles by 1000 miles, roughly the size of California) was swept into the Pacific Ocean and began floating towards the North American West Coast. On March 20, 2012, an empty Japanese fishing vessel (the 164-foot Ryou-Un Maru, which the Press labeled the *Ghost Ship*) was spotted drifting off of the coast of western Canada and represented part of the first wave of debris generated by the Japanese tsunami of 2011.

ECONOMIC IMPACT

The disaster caused at least $220 billion in damages in the destruction of towns, villages, infrastructure, and assets; however, that would represent only the first wave of estimated costs and losses. The crisis crippled several industries and left many international firms and investors unwilling to invest in Japan. Before the disaster, Japan already had been wrestling with a decade-long battle with deflation and enormous public debt. And with an aging population, this crisis only exacerbated the core weaknesses of the nation. There was an immediate plunge in stock market values.

As the third largest economy in the world and the fourth largest trading partner with the United States, Japan's natural disaster crisis quickly spiraled into an economic quagmire: stock and commodity prices took an immediate hit as the crisis began to unfold. The prices of oil, natural gas, coffee, lumber, and sugar fell on economic concerns that demand would suffer as Japan was knocked flat on its back. With Japanese manufacturing deeply tied to and integrated with the world's two largest economies (America and China), there was a grave concern of how long it would take for things to get back to normal. Economic dislocations were of significant importance in this scenario. By November 2011, signs of the economic slowdown were evident as the unemployment rate had increased and as the yen rose against the dollar amidst a global economic slowdown. Japan's manufacturers laid off 210,000 workers in October 2011.

AN EARTHQUAKE-PRONE NATION WITH VAST NUCLEAR POWER

Japan is located at the juncture of four tectonic plates, and as a result of this critical geological location, experiences about 20 percent of the most significant earthquakes recorded each year. These are scientific facts that are well known in Japan and throughout the international community. One has to wonder why this nation would have 54 nuclear reactors operating in an active seismic region. Given the potential risks of nuclear fission and radioactive fallout, what motivated the political and business establishment to saturate the geographically small land mass of Japan with nuclear power. It's clear that energy independence was a key factor, especially since Japan has little or no natural resources. However, given Japan's scientific and technological achievements over the past half-century, I expected this nation to become the leading powerhouse and voice in renewable energy technologies. Observations from *The Economist* help us to understand what happened to create this trust and belief in nuclear energy power in Japan:

> "Indeed, much of society, excluding an anti-nuclear fringe, happily accepted the "safety myth" that enabled Japan to cram 54 nuclear reactors on one of the world's most earthquake-prone archipelagos...But if people bought the myth, it was because successive LDP governments, ministries, big-business, lobbies, media barons and university professors sold it to them. Accidents such as Three Mile Island in Pennsylvania in 1979 and Chernobyl in 1986 caused barely a flicker of hesitation over the building of more nuclear plants in Japan."[7]

In nuclear power, especially in the scientific process of nuclear fission, there is no such thing as a *fail-safe system*. Even in the newer designs and other enhancements that scientists and technocrats will state as assurances that another Fukushima Daiichi will not happen, *this is not technology we should support as an energy vector in the 21st century and beyond.* Also, all nuclear power plants produce nuclear waste that has to be buried somewhere on our planet, nuclear waste disposal of radioactive byproducts. The consequences of failure are too enormous, and as a civilization, we need to move in other directions that favor the green revolution. The nuclear crisis in Japan was the final wakeup call to the entire world. *Nuclear fission is a fool's paradise, and we do not ever want to see the worst case scenario.*

In writing for the *Washington Post*, Eugene Robinson presented a very concise analysis of the nuclear power issue shortly after 3/11. In his article entitled "Nuclear power now looks more like a bargain with the devil," Robinson reminds us of some very important realities in dealing with nuclear fission produced energy:

> "The problem with nuclear fission is that the stakes are unimaginably high. We can engineer nuclear power plants so that the chance of a Chernobyl-style disaster is almost nil. But we can't eliminate it completely - nor can we envision every other kind of potential disaster. And where fission reactors are concerned, the worst-case scenario is so dreadful as to be unthinkable...In the Chernobyl incident, a cloud of radioactive smoke and steam spread contamination across hundreds of square miles; even after 25 years, a 20-mile radius around the ruined plant remains off-limits and uninhabitable."[8]

It appears that enlightenment on this issue will occur when the world is forced to experience something worse than Fukushima Daiichi. I hope that the German initiative to phase out its nuclear power plants will have a measurable impact on other nations around the world to abandon this potentially deadly technology. The risks associated with this technology are not worth the so-called benefits that are derived from the use of nuclear power. When it comes to nuclear power, *nuclear fusion* should be the only potential use of this type of energy source in the future. Splitting the atom is an unholy scientific alliance with the devil (the opposite of *good*)!

This analysis of Japan and 3/11 is designed to highlight the potential and real connection between natural disasters and their destructive power to destroy nuclear power facilities and to support the decommissioning of nuclear fission power on our planet. World governments cannot predict nor protect their populations from the unexpected chaos and destruction of natural disasters. And no matter how well-designed and newly constructed (with the latest technologies) nuclear power plants are built; there are NO *fail-safe systems* that we can rely on given the unpredictable nature of natural disasters. This civilization has to factor in the explosive, destructive power of natural disasters when considering the use and operation of such potentially harmful technology as nuclear fission. The risks of widespread radioactive fallout in a densely populated region are just too high to keep such technology in operation. The first year-long struggle in Japan to contain the crisis was an eye-opener, and should have been a valuable wake-up call to the entire world civilization to abandon *Nuclear Fission Technology*.

NUCLEAR POWER ADDICTION

There are 104 nuclear fission reactors in the United States: 22 of these reactors are identical to the nuclear power facilities that failed in Fukushima. The Nuclear Regulatory Commission (NRC) voted 4-1 in December 2011 to approve the building of two new nuclear reactors in the U.S. After over 30 years of a de-facto ban on building nuclear energy reactors, the U.S. finally threw in the towel to restart the building of new systems. It was approved after this country, and the world had had a full opportunity to view the enormous catastrophe of the Fukushima Dai-ichi meltdown. Allison Fisher, an energy expert for the consumer advocacy group Public Citizen, stated that "It is inexplicable that we've chosen this moment in history to expand the use of a failed and dangerous technology." Considering Germany's decision to abandon nuclear fission power, it appears that the U.S. was not thinking clearly. Allison further commented that "the U.S. is approving new reactors before the full suite of lessons from Japan has been learned and before new safety regulations that were recommended by a task force established after the meltdown crisis at Fukushima have been implemented."[9]

According to Michael Golay, a professor at the USA Massachusetts Institute of Technology (MIT) the economic argument for gas-fueled power plants is a lot stronger than investing in risky nuclear reactors: "New nuclear plants are more questionable because there are economic factors right now which favor gas-fueled power plants and the fact that the economy is only growing slowly means that nationally the need for new generation is lower than people were expecting in 2007." Golay also makes the point that a "1,000-megawatt (Mw) natural gas plant takes a few years to permit and build, and costs up to $1 billion for the most efficient, combined-cycle model. A similar-sized nuclear reactor, however, could take five to 10 years to develop and build, and cost well in excess of $5 billion."[10] It is also important to understand that uranium (a finite mineral resource) is a critical ingredient in the development of the nuclear fission power, and like oil is a rapidly depleting resource. Nuclear fission power is another relic/dinosaur of the industrial era and like the combustion engine is on a path to extinction. Why is the U.S. committing five to 10 years and billions of dollars to a failed technology? Golay's analysis was examined by Mexico, and that nation chose to abandon a plan to build ten new nuclear reactors. In recognizing its abundance of natural gas, Mexico decided to pursue a course of building natural gas power plants.[11]

However, as part of the pledge to expand nuclear power, the Obama administration offered the Vogtle nuclear project $8.3 billion in federal loan guarantees.[12] The only conclusion I could arrive at was that this was a *wrong decision* especially in the wake of the meltdown in Japan. When significant disasters like these occur, we as human beings must learn the valuable lessons from the errors and failures in the technology. It makes no sense just to ignore and sweep aside the event and assume that it will not happen on our shores because we think that we will have better safeguards.

As Allison Fisher stated, this is "a failed and dangerous technology," and it needs to be abandoned. The decision to move forward with new nuclear plants is flawed, and resources would be better spent on renewable technologies and other options. World governments just cannot predict nor protect their populations from the unexpected chaos and destruction of natural disasters. Nuclear power plants are also vulnerable to terrorists' attacks, and there is also the issue of nuclear waste that has to be buried safely in the ground. Nuclear fission is old industrial era technology that should be retired along with the use of oil.

A report that surfaced in early May 2016, further solidified a strong opposition against the use of nuclear fission power. The Hanford Nuclear Reservation, located on the plains of eastern Washington at a point where the state meets Idaho and Oregon, was a primary nuclear facility that stored America's atomic arsenal for four decades during and after World War II. Up to nine nuclear reactors operated at this facility, which over time, generated upwards to 56 million gallons of radioactive waste. Similar to the Fukushima storage plan, 177 underground tanks were employed as storage vessels for the radioactive waste materials. The report indicated that the nuclear waste was starting to leak from some of the containers. To fix this problem and establish a long-term permanent storage solution, the federal government estimated that it would cost nearly $110 billion and take almost five decades to complete the remediation project.[13]

When it comes to nuclear power, the focus should be nuclear fusion research. After five decades of research, scientists should be getting closer to a practical solution in nuclear fusion technology. However, even if we are decades away from a working model, this should remain the central thrust in this energy sector. Nuclear fusion would be a renewable and non-polluting technology.

THE FAILED POLICIES AND REMEDIES AT FUKUSHIMA

The ongoing crisis and nuclear disaster of Fukushima continued for years after the initial nuclear meltdown. However, the world was mainly kept in the dark concerning the enormous (actual and potential) radioactive fallout that continued non-stop year after year. Six years after 3/11, the deadly problems at Fukushima Dai-ichi nuclear power plant had gotten worse. The meltdown of the three nuclear reactors on 3/11 continued the meltdown process throughout the period between 2011 and mid-2017. Radiation levels increased, and the situation was entirely out of control. No one knew what was causing the intensity of the radiation output. However, a possible explanation presented by Mike Adams (an independent researcher) suggests that "more fuel rods being exposed or fuel rods coming into closer contact with each other, amplifying and accelerating the mass-to-energy conversion".[14] Remote-controlled robotic measurements taken on Unit reactor 2 in early 2017, recorded extremely high levels of 530 sieverts per hour (levels as high as 650 sieverts have also been detected). By comparison, the meltdown at the 1986 Chernobyl nuclear disaster produced 300 sieverts per hour. To put this measurement in context; a human being exposed to 10 sieverts could lead to death in a few weeks. Exposure to 530 sieverts would lead to instant death. In essence, the Fukushima nuclear meltdown site is what writer Vicki Batts describes as a "Nuclear explosion that doesn't end." It is a continuing ongoing explosion with no definitive end in sight. The following were some of the drastic and unprecedented measures undertaken by TEPCO and the Japanese government to contain this horrific disaster:

(1) Years of groundwater flowing into the reactor buildings became contaminated, and the question was what to do with this water. TEPCO's solution was to began storing this contaminated water in huge bolted tanks, eventually collecting and storing nearly a million tons of this water in over 1500 tanks situated throughout the site. This water is to be stored for up to 20 years. However, some of the tanks began leaking water into the sea and ocean. In May 2018, it was reported that TEPCO was running out of space to store the contaminated water. With the storage space equivalent of nearly 32

soccer fields, the company declared that it was running out of available space and was working on options to resolve their crisis. Reportedly, the site was generating 160 tons of contaminated water every single day since the start of the catastrophe in March 2011.

(2) TEPCO attempted to build an ice wall to prevent groundwater contamination, but that plan failed. Thus, the problem could not be contained and nearly 300 tons (per day) of contaminated water continued spilling into the ocean and nearby sea.

(3) A massive cleanup of radioactive soil in and around the Fukushima plant witnessed another significant effort to collect and store radioactive materials. Over 9 million bags of this stuff was collected, stored in black plastic bags and stacked in fields in rows of pyramid-shaped hills. One estimate stated that this was enough nuclear waste to fill up 800 Olympic-size swimming pools.

(4) In June of 2016, Kendra Ulrich, senior global energy campaigner at Greenpeace Japan, released this disturbing statement regarding future policies on nuclear power: "Japan's nuclear regulator continues to look the other way on major safety issues. The government continues to press ahead with nuclear restarts despite unresolved safety problems that put the public at risk. It's time to break free from nuclear and embrace the only safe and clean technology that can meet Japan's needs - renewable energy."[15] Prime Minister Shinzo Abe and the Liberal Democratic Party (LDP) are pro-nuclear, so Japan, and by extension, the Japanese people are stuck in a nuclear quagmire of incredibly misguided policies.

(5) The release of hundreds of thousands of tons of radioactive contamination into the Pacific Ocean over a period of five to six years (non-stop) represents an enormous environmental catastrophe. Kendra Ulrich makes the case that "The sheer size of the Pacific Ocean combined with powerful, complex currents means the largest single release of radioactivity into the marine environment led to the widespread dispersal of contamination."[16]

(6) Some of the radioactive isotopes released into our air and water are (1) Cesium-137 which poses a severe threat to human health and the environment: it's particularly damaging to our bodies. Scientists tell us that soluble Cesium-137 dissolves in water and can quickly enter our plant, water, animal and food supplies. Its half-life is 30 years. Cesium-134 has a half-life of two years. The half-life measurement is significant because it allows us to understand how long radioactive elements can exist in the environment. The range of these measurements can run from seconds to millions of years. (2) plutonium-239: a toxic radioactive manmade element with a half-life of 24,200 years. (3) uranium-238: another deadly radioactive element has a half-life of

4,460,000,000 years. (4) Strontium-90: Is a radioactive isotope that poses a serious threat to sea life and human beings. Strontium-90 has a half-life, of about 28 years. According to researchers, strontium-90 is potentially more dangerous than cesium due to its ability to mimic calcium that is absorbed into human bones and teeth, and when ingested, it will accumulate in the bones of animals and fish that humans are likely to eat. Strontium can potentially remain in bone tissue for many years. According to the CDC's Agency for Toxic Substances and Disease Registry: "Children are likely to be more vulnerable than adults to the effects of radioactive strontium because relatively more goes into bone when it is growing. Also, children are potentially more vulnerable than adults to radiation damage because they keep radioactive strontium in bone for a longer time."[17] Also, the CDC warns that "thousands of tons of strontium...is still in tanks at the nuclear power plant. It has accumulated in buildings and soils, and some of it is still pouring into the ocean."[18]

(7) Removing the nuclear fuel from the plant itself is a highly dangerous and complicated operation. The latest estimates provided in 2016 by scientists, is that it may take decades before this fuel can be removed safely. What is known is that the fuel that melted down "remains in containment vessels in its reactors...highly radioactive cores of the reactors themselves, each filled with melted uranium fuel." The environment in this part of the plant is so radioactive that exposure to human beings would mean instant death. Remote controlled robots have been sent in to investigate and make observations of the problems. However, the circuit boards of several of these robotic systems were destroyed, rendering the robots inoperable. Bottom line, there is no clear solution here and no technology capable of removing the melted fuel. TEPCO don't know how they are going to solve this problem. Ultimately, robots will represent a significant part of the solution of sealing the molten cores in concrete containers, but Takafumi Anegawa (TEPCO's chief nuclear officer) is clear that this may take several decades to complete. So it is reasonable to say at this point that the Fukushima disaster will be an ongoing world crisis for decades to come.

(8) Melted fuel rods in Unit reactor 2 generated intense radiation over a six-year period that resulted in the creation of a burned hole in the floor of the containment vessel. Since TEPCO could not determine the full extent of the damage, scientists have concluded that the rods and radiation had possibly made contact with the ground and ocean water. According to Fairewinds Energy Education, "there are no easy solutions because groundwater is in direct contact with the nuclear corium (melted fuel) at Fukushima Daiichi."

(9) Nuclear Fuel Criticality: At some point in the continuing processing of melting fuel rods, a critical point could be reached that brings about an explosion that would release deadly radioactive elements into the global atmosphere.

(10) The Fukushima disaster is a global nightmare! Perhaps, Dr. Mark Sircus describes it best as he writes, "The accident is enormous in its medical implications. Through future years, too long to contemplate, we will witness an epidemic of cancer as people inhale the radioactive elements, eat radioactive vegetables, rice and meat, drink radioactive milk and teas...Most of the radiation is being washed out to sea, and it is quite quickly destroying the Pacific Ocean and much of the life in it. We have no idea how much of the radiation is escaping into the atmosphere, but we do know that during the first few weeks of the nuclear accident, because of the explosions, huge amounts of radiation were released into the atmosphere and it circled the globe especially in the northern hemisphere."[19]

(11) Most of the news that surfaced in early 2017 focused on reactor 2, and all of the nuclear complications associated with its immediate environment. TEPCO and other agencies presented very little or no information on reactors 1 and 3. There was no understanding presented about the melted cores in those two reactors.

SUMMARY ANALYSIS

What is the ultimate message to the world regarding the Fukushima disaster of 3/11? It is a message that is prophetically coming from the only nation in the world that has ever experienced the destructive power of an atomic explosion. That message clearly states that we have no future with nuclear fission power, with its deadly procedure of splitting the atom. In essence, it represents death and destruction, yet various nations around the world in their desperation to secure energy resources, are still planning to bring online new nuclear power facilities. It is yet another example of a civilization that has lost its collective mind. It's also a clear sign that we have reached the end of an era, the final demise of technologies that were given birth during the industrial age.

Fukushima's ongoing disaster is a historical testimony that will continue to remind humanity that the toxic nuclear waste and fallout of nuclear power generation is a bargain with the devil. We are living in a fool's paradise, with government officials bending to the will of irresponsible and *greedy corporations* that will do anything to make a profit. There are no limits to this insanity except those that nature will ultimately place on an out-of-control human species. We will eventually be judged and we will probably not like the verdict!

NOTES

(1) James Nachtwey, "Dispatch from Japan: James Natchtwey's Impressions in Words and Pictures," Time Magazine, March 20, 2011.

(2) Briefing Natural disasters, "Counting the cost of calamities," *The Economist,* January 14, 2012, p. 60.
(3) Martin Fackler, "Radiation still a threat to Japan's food supply," *The Sacramento Bee*, January 22, 2012, p. A5.
(4) Tokyo: Japan's energy crisis, "Nuclear winter," *The Economist*, December 10, 2011, p. 47.
(5) Koriyama, Rikuzentakata, and Tokyo, Briefing Japan after the 3/11 disaster, "The death of trust," *The Economist*, March 10, 2012, p.38.
(6) IBID., p. 36.
(7) IBID., p. 36.
(8) Eugene Robinson, "Nuclear power now looks more like a bargain with the devil," *The Sacramento Bee*, March 15, 2011, p. A13.
(9) Steven Mufson, "Why is the Obama administration using taxpayer money to back a nuclear plant already being built?," *The Washington Post*, 02-21-14
(10) Edward Oliver Gonzalez, "USA Nuclear Regulatory Commision still Hogtied and Impotent - Part 4," www. energymaters.com, February 9, 2012.
(11) Ibid. (energymaters.com).
(12) Matthew Daly, "NRC approves first new nuclear plant in 3 decades," Associated Press, December 2011.
(13)Alexander Nazaryan, "Nuclear Waste Leaking at 'American Fukushima' in Northwest," *Newsweek*, May 3, 2016.
(14) Mike Adams, "Media blackout over "unimaginable" radiation levels detected at Fukushima...MOX fuel melts through reactor floor...half life 24,000 years," *Natural News*, February 6, 2017.
(15) Kendra Ulrich, "A Lesson from Fukushima: A safe Clean Energy Future Will Be Nuclear-Free," Common Dreams, March 11, 2015.
(16) IBID. Common Dreams.
(17) Vicki Batts, "Fukushima: Radiation now reported in West Coast Tuna," FukushimaWatch.com, February 16, 2017.
(18) IBID. FukushimaWatch.com.
(19)Dr. Mark Sircus, "Hell Hole on Earth Discovered at Fukushima," Dr. Sircus.com, February 13, 2017.

GLOSSARY

This section includes economic, financial, and other relevant terms used in this book. Some of these terms are unconventional and are given definitions which explain their meaning and usage within a given context. Other terms are in common usage and are broadly defined.

ADAM SMITH (1723-90): As founder and originator of the classical school of thought in economics, Adam Smith paved the way for the modern evolution of capitalism that overcame the "mercantilist" societies of the 15th and 16th centuries of early Europe. In his book, *The Wealth of Nations*, published in 1776, Smith presented the first systematic analysis of economic data and the underlining philosophies that have been significant guides for the economic behaviors of human societies. His analysis advocated a limited role for government, free market systems, and the significance of individual self-interest. The notions of *Laissez Faire* (let them do) and the *Invisible Hand* are popular concepts associated with his writings. To Smith and other classical thinkers that would follow, the free enterprise system was a self-adjusting, competitive environment tending towards full employment with minimal government intervention. Smith's analysis provided little or no understanding of depressions, capitalistic greed, or an adequate picture of the business cycle.

AGE OF LIGHT: Refers to the era in which information and the rate of data transmission are traveling at or near the speed of light. It is the 21st century new age orchestrated by the *Information Age Revolution*. After the year 2000, scientific and technological developments began to accelerate, expanding the power and reach of our intellectual universe. The *Age of Light* has the potential to enable unpredictable scientific breakthroughs and elevated levels of consciousness.

ARTIFICIAL INTELLIGENCE (AI): Refers to the ability of a computer to perform intelligent thinking and make intelligent decisions. It involves the combination of complex and simple software elements to bring about a simulated form of applied logic. AI is the ability of a device to perform various functions similar to human intelligence, variously called reasoning, planning, learning, problem-solving and pattern recognition.

ARBITRAGE: An investment strategy that seeks to take advantage of price differences between two or more markets concerning the purchase or sale of securities, commodities or currencies. The object for the arbitrageur is to profit from the existing or prevalent price differentials.

BALANCE SHEET RECESSION: During a bust cycle or economic downturn, businesses and consumers are focused on deleveraging from balance sheet excesses and reducing their debt loads. A severe decrease in aggregate demand occurs when large segments of the population participate in deleveraging at the same time, prolonging the detrimental impact of the crisis. This was the case during the 1930s *Great Depression* years and Japan's economic downturn that began in 1990.

BIOMASS: A rapidly evolving field of energy development that focuses on converting rotting organic matter, such as plant life, animal waste, commercial and residential garbage and other forms of organisms (present in particular habitats), into various forms of energy. In a sense, it is a system of recycling of living matter that may normally be discarded, never fully utilized. In a process known as "anaerobic digestion," where the free air is non-existent, microorganisms of biomass are converted into methane and other gases.

BI-POLAR: Refers to two opposing views, political systems, economic philosophies, etc. The bi-polar era as mentioned in this text refers to the dominant spheres of influence of the United States and the Soviet Union - the two chief hegemonies of the post World War II period - which strongly influenced and controlled international politics, economics and military competitions throughout the period 1943 through 1991. That era came to an end with the collapse of the Soviet "Command economic system." Communism versus capitalism was one of the central themes of the bipolar era, with the two large continental empires dominating the international arena.

BOOMING 80S: The 1980s was an exhilarating period of Reaganomics and Republican Administrations; a period of massive U.S. budget deficits, the rise of the Pacific Rim, and the emergence of a relatively large number of billionaires. It was also a period of rampant speculation, merger mania, and the rise of billionaire drug empires worldwide.

BRETTON WOODS: The twenty years that elapsed between the two Great World Wars (1919-1939) were marked by boom and bust cycles that shook the foundation of the entire world. The developments in this period eventually led to the establishment of the Bretton Woods agreements, which was the first successful attempt by a large group of nations to control their economic relations. After the First World War, reparations and war debts had been a serious and continuous problem between the quarreling European nations. Hyperinflation knocked Germany to its knees in 1923, and in the aftermath of the stock market crash of 1929, the entire world was confronted with a major economic depression. All over the world, millions of people lost their jobs, their savings and their standard of living. Confronted by these difficult realities, governments resorted to various methods of economic warfare. To prevent a repeat of the aftermath of the First World War and subsequent events, the victorious Western Allies decided to put in place global economic and monetary systems that would address the pressing problems of the post-WW II era. Representatives from 44 nations gathered at Bretton Woods, New Hampshire in 1944-45 and established the blueprint and working models of the International Monetary Fund (IMF) and the International Bank for Reconstruction and Development (IBRD, the World Bank). In conjunction with other international programs, such as the Marshall Plan, these organizations would henceforth be at the center of major short-term currency stabilization problems, and long-term economic developmental projects for nations requiring substantial aid over long periods of time.

BRICS: An acronym that identifies five emerging market economic countries: Brazil, Russia, India, China and South Africa. This group rose to prominence during the first two decades of the 21st century. As an alternative to the World Bank, the BRICS nation established "The New Development Bank" to ensure their continued pace of growth and economic stability in the event of a weakening of global dollar standard. The group also created the Asian Infrastructure Investment Bank (AIIB), an inter-governmental regional development institution, with an operating agenda similar to the World Bank. And similar to the IMF, the BRIC nations created the Contingent Reserve Arrangement (CRA), a multinational currency stabilization fund. More than 21 countries support the AIIB.

BUSINESS CYCLE: A business cycle is defined as the fluctuation in economic activity that an economy experiences as it completes a cyclical journey through time. Normal business cycles are characterized by periods of expansion and contraction, i.e., periods of growth and decline (recession or depression). During expansions, the economy is growing in real terms, as evidenced by increases in economic measures such as employment, industrial production, and sales. During recessions, the economy is contracting, as measured by decreases in the above economic indicators.

CAPE/Shiller P/E Ratio: The CAPE P/E ratio extends the analysis of a company's price and earnings. The standard P/E ratio evaluates the value of a company by examining its share price relative to earnings generated per share. Under the CAPE model, the ratio is adjusted for consideration of inflation with the price divided by the average of ten years of earnings.

CAPITAL FLIGHT: This term refers to massive outflows of a nation's domestic capital that proves to be counter-productive to the overall economy. Such factors as an unstable political situation, hyperinflation, overvalued exchange rates, higher interest rates and greater economic and investment opportunities abroad, have contributed to this phenomenon over the centuries. During the 1980s and early 1990s, capital flight was most prevalent in Latin American countries.

CASHLESS SOCIETY: As the digital revolution in the 1990s continued to evolve, the use of paper currencies as a means of economic and financial exchange also began to be considered for replacement by more sophisticated credit/debit cards, and other forms of "digital-cash and cyber money." According to author Joel Kurtzman, we may transition from a "gold to a megabyte standard," monetary systems based on microchips, computer memory, and high-speed transmission systems. Whether we use free-floating exchange rates or a gold standard, the underlying power of the system will be dependent on massive computer systems. Sometime in the 21st century, we will probably witness the conversion to a completely cashless society dominated by mega-global banking and financial systems. Bitcoin and other permutations of this system are the leading candidates as we head towards the year 2020.

COLD WAR: The post-World War II world of 1945 resulted in a superpower struggle between the Soviet Union and the United States. On economic and political fronts, it was the struggle (on a global basis) of democracy and capitalism versus communism and its command economic plan. A former Allied power during World War II, the Soviet Union, began to pursue expansionist policies, globally, that were at variance with America's economic and political philosophies. By mid-1990, the Cold War was abandoned, particularly by the Soviet Union whose economy was rapidly falling into a depression.

COLLATERALIZED DEBT OBLIGATIONS (CDO): Investment Bankers used Collateralized Debt Obligations (CDOs) as the vehicle of choice to sell to global investors. These debt obligations came in different varieties and would change over time. Some CDOs not only gave investors a claim to the principal and interest payments on residential mortgages, but also to a host of other debt obligations such as student loans, car loans, credit card debt, corporate buyout debt, commercial mortgage payments, and in some cases, monthly leasing payments for aircraft, cars and mobile homes. Others concentrated strictly on mortgage-backed securities. A mortgage CDO featured the claim on a hundred or so mortgage-backed bonds, each of which was a claim on thousands of individual mortgages. The CDO was then sliced and organized into tranches in order to provide payments to specific investor risk categories, from low risk to high risk offerings.

COMMAND SYSTEM: An economic system wherein the state owns and controls the primary means of production and capital. The state decides what the essential priorities of the economy will be and puts in place a plan to carry out those objectives. For instance, in the Soviet Union, the overwhelming emphasis placed on its economy during the period 1945 to 1991, was the development of the military-industrial complex. Faced with an imminent collapse of their economy and hyperinflation, the Soviets were forced to revise their overall economy and seek admission into the global economic order of market economics and free enterprise systems.

CREDIT DEFAULT SWAPS (CDS): As deregulated OTC Derivatives, Credit Default Swap (CDS) contracts were essentially the principle vehicles used to bet against the raging bull housing bubble. In one sense these vehicles were a kind of insurance against failure, but on another front they were used as vehicles to speculate on the demise of the housing bubble. Similar to stock market investors shorting the market or buying put options, the CDS contract was an investment against the downside of a mortgage and housing industry that had exceeded the limits. Hundreds of millions of dollars were invested in CDS contracts for this specific purpose.

CURRENCY SWAPS: These are special agreements allowing countries (A and B) to conduct trade with each other without having to swap for dollars in the process. The active use of currency swaps by various nations throughout the world deemphasize the use of the dollar as the reserve currency of the world.

DARING 90S: The period from 1995 to the year 2000 witnessed the birth of the Dot-Com era and the Internet revolution. This technological revolution generated a great deal of speculation in U.S. stock markets which lead to one of the greatest boom and bust periods of the 20th century.

DEFLATION: In general terms, deflation refers to an overall decline in the prices of goods and services. For most long-wave cycle theorists, the ultimate climax of a boom/bust cycle is a deflationary collapse.

DEPRESSION: In an economic depression, such as the one that occurred in the 1930s, an economy experiences a severe business contraction, rising unemployment, deflation, reduction in consumer purchasing power, public insecurity and a buildup of inventories. For the majority of people, basic necessities dominate their economic planning, which wipes out many consumer demands and services that cater to nonessential needs.

DERIVATIVES: These investment securities derive their value based on the underlying values of other asset groups such as stocks, bonds, real estate, futures contracts, etc. The daily fluctuations that occur in the value of the underlying asset will determine the real-time value of the derivative contract. Two or more parties will come together to execute a contract on a particular asset class. Derivatives are traded on regulated exchange platforms and in over-the-counter (OTC) unregulated environments.

DEVALUATION OF A CURRENCY: It is the result of a nation's currency declining in value in comparison with other national currencies and gold. Devaluations are sometimes engineered or planned, as in the case of the U.S. leaving the gold standard in 1933 and 1971.

DEREGULATION: Deregulation occurs when a government moves to reduce certain regulatory restrictions on an industry significantly. Periods of deregulation, as in the Booming 80s, can sometimes lead to excessive abuse and economic disaster. Deregulation of the S & L and Banking industries in the U.S. during the 1980s is an example of this type of problem.

DINOSAUR SYNDROME: As used in this publication, this term refers to the imminent extinction of various systems, technologies, organizational designs and infrastructures during the evolutionary phase of the *Information Age Revolution*. As the old system designs complete their historical cycles, new information age technologies will move in as replacements for the new era.

DISINFLATION: This process is essentially the slowing down of the pace of inflation. Prices are increasing at a slower rate.

Glossary

DISCOUNT RATE: This could be considered the Fed foundation rate, for the Discount Rate is the interest rate Federal Reserve Banks charge its member banks and other depository institutions (typically overnight) for collateralized loans. The collateral used for such loans are government securities and qualified commercial paper. Commercial banking rates are generally established at levels above this Fed foundation rate.

ECONOMETRICS: A form of computer analysis that describes in mathematical terms, economic relationships between various factors. Relational models will examine economic forces such as interest rates, housing starts, labor, inflation, the money supply and other economic entities. By examining these factors, econometrics strives to present an accurate mathematical understanding of the relationship between these factors.

ECONOMIC MULTIPLIER EFFECT: This economic event occurs as success on one level of business activity ripples throughout an entire economic region or local economy. It allows successful businesses to generate huge profits, pay better salaries and bonuses, allowing employees to purchase more goods and services in the local economy. Local firms will supply products and services for other firms in the region, furthering the recycling of dollars and raising the standard of living for the entire region.

EURODOLLAR: Refers to U.S. dollars held in banks outside of its borders. The principal place of deposit is European banks.

EXCHANGE RATE: The rate of exchange of one currency for another.

FEDERAL DEPOSIT INSURANCE CORPORATION (FDIC): This is the federal agency that insures deposits (within prescribed limits) that are held in member banks and savings and loan institutions. This agency was established in 1933, in the wake of the collapse of the American banking system. Hundreds of thousands of depositors lost their entire savings due to the enormous number of bank failures. The FDIC was put in place to restore confidence and safety in the system.

FEDERAL DEFICIT: When the U.S. Government spends more money in a fiscal year than it brings in, a deficit or monetary shortfall is created. Budget deficits have been a consistent reality for several decades and are likely to continue to escalate for most of the 21st century.

FEDERAL FUNDS RATE: This is the rate that banks charge other banks to borrow funds on an overnight basis to meet Federal Reserve requirements. It is a market sensitive rate and is followed closely by analysts who are charting the direction of interest rate changes.

FEDERAL RESERVE SYSTEM: The "Fed," as it is commonly known, came into being as a result of the Federal Reserve Act of 1913. It is an independent, hybrid organization that coordinates and manages the monetary and banking activities in America; it is the nation's central bank. Through 12 regional Reserve Banks, the system establishes a controlling influence over the economic life of the nation and is responsible for regulating the flow of credit and money.

FISCAL POLICY: The macroeconomic activities and conditions of a nation are influenced by the fiscal policy initiatives of a government. This policy is primarily implemented through the use of tax policies and government spending programs. Some of the fiscal policy objectives include a focus on employment, aggregate demand, economic growth and inflation or deflation.

FLATTENING THE YIELD CURVE: In this yield curve environment, bonds of the same credit quality will show minor difference between short-term and long-term interest rates. The risk assumed by an investor for holding a long-term bond or invetsment would essentially be the same risk in holding a short-term bond. In a normal yield (interest rate) environment, investors are provided greater compensation (yield) for holding longer-term investments (mortgages, bonds, etc.).

FREE FLOATING EXCHANGE RATE SYSTEM: This system came into existence after the 1971 Nixon shock that took the United States off the gold standard. A currency's price or value is determined (by comparison with other currencies) by the supply and demand forces in the foreign exchange market (FOREX). Each day that FOREX is open for business, currency values are adjusted based on a number global factors, leading to an increase or decrease in the value of a currency.

FUNDAMENTAL ANALYSIS: Under this form of analysis, financial and economic statistics are examined as a means for determining the viability of an investment opportunity. A company's balance sheet and income statement would be examined in addition to industry data and the quality and abilities of the management team. A number of both quantitative and qualitative factors are brought together to form a final opinion of a company's future prospects.

G-20: Established in December 1999, Finance Ministers and Central Bank Governors from industrial and emerging-market countries from all regions of the world (20 nations representing 90 percent of global gross national product) met to coordinate and discuss important issues related to global economic stability. The organization helps to promote and support economic development and growth throughout the world. The G-20 is composed of the following countries: Argentina, Australia, Brazil, Canada, China, the European Union, France, Germany, India, Indonesia, Italy, the United States, United Kingdom, Turkey, Republic of Korea, South Africa, Saudi Arabia, Russia, Mexico, and Japan.

G-7: Is an international group made up of seven major industrialized countries in the world. This group assembled for the first time in 1982 with a focus on global economic and financial events. The interrelationship of these seven economic powers and their impact and influence on the global economy represent a key operational forum from which to orchestrate economic stability throughout the world. This group consists of the following countries: Canada, Germany, France, Italy, Japan, the United States and Great Britain. Since the *Meltdown of 2008*, the G-20 has become a much relevant organization for maintaining global economic stability.

GLASS-STEAGALL ACT: The Glass-Steagall Act of 1933 established the division between Commercial Banks and Investment Banks, setting up a Firewall between these entities. In the wake of the 1929 stock market crash and the subsequent collapse of the banking industry by 1933, New Deal politics enacted legislation that would prevent a repeat of the *Roaring 20s* speculative frenzy. Glass-Steagall was one of the main banking laws that came out of the 1930s Depression Era. The act separated investment and commercial banking activities, preventing banks from using depositor money in stock market transactions. It was discovered that during the boom of the 1920s, banks took on too much risk with depositors' money which involved stock market activities and investments.

GLOBAL ECONOMY: Refers to the globalization of the free movement of goods and services. The world is considered one big marketplace, with free market institutions operating on every shore. With the collapse of many communist regimes worldwide, the free market concept won the battle to expand throughout what was previously the Soviet Union.

GENERAL AGREEMENT ON TARIFFS AND TRADE (GATT): This is an agreement put in place and signed in 1947 by 22 nations. The basic mission of this organization is the reduction of worldwide tariffs and the fostering and promotion of free trade throughout the world. In over sixty years of existence, GATT has managed to maintain a semblance of balance and fair play in the international trade arena. However, like so many programs began 40 to 60 years ago, it has been strained to a point where reform is mandatory. In the 1990s, GATT needed to meet the challenge of the ever-growing complexity of international trade problems. The Uruguay Round of GATT talks in 1990 highlighted the issues of intellectual property rights (copyrights and trademarks), agriculture and financial services. With the advent of regional trading blocs in the 1990s, the issues of quotas, subsidies and hi-tech property rights grew more intense, which lead to trade wars by 2018.

GRAND CONVERGENCE THEORY: As defined in this publication, this theory is the confluence of a diversity of economic forces that brings about a manifestation of creative destruction and global economic revision. This interdisciplinary approach seeks to arrive at the truth embedded in several factors that combine in epic proportion at a given moment in time. In our current era (2018), very powerful economic forces will collide to bring about a massive change in our modern civilization. We will witness the rise and fall of nations, technologies, and economic systems and models that are part of the destructive creative nature of capitalism.

GROSS NATIONAL PRODUCT (GNP): The total value of goods and services produced by the U.S. economy within a fiscal year.

GOLD STANDARD: A standard monetary system whereby a nation's currency is assigned a given weight in gold. The currency is officially backed by gold, which is considered a "hard currency."

HARD CURRENCY: In the absence of a gold standard, hard currencies are those that are issued by governmental systems and economies that are stable, enjoy high standards of living, and are perceived in the international community as valuable. At present, the U.S. dollar is the world's foremost hard currency. This championship status will be seriously challenged at some point in the 21st century.

HYPERINFLATION: A rapid increase in the prices of goods and services within a given economy. Prices accelerate daily, sometimes hourly, in a runaway situation. A given currency in this situation is rapidly devalued as more and more dollars, yen or rubles buy fewer goods and services. It is a panic environment which was best illustrated (during the 1980s) by the chaotic conditions of Latin American economies. A more recent example in 2018 is the collapse of Venezuela's currency (the bolivar). As of May 2018, the annual hyperinflation rate was 24,600% with an official exchange rate of 49,478 bolivars for one dollar.

INFLATION: A basic rise in the price of goods and services. During an upward trend in a business cycle, there is a steady increase in inflationary pressure, particularly as the money supply increases relative to the available stock of goods and services.

INVERTED YIELD CURVE: A rare economic event in the capitalist system when short-term interest rates on investments such as U.S. Treasury Bills and Money Market funds are higher than long-term rates. During normal periods, investors are expecting to receive higher rates on long-term investments due to the longer holding periods. According to some analysts, an inverted yield curve is a warning of an impending recession.

INSTITUTIONAL INVESTORS: These are generally large, well-financed organizations that buy and sell large blocks of securities. This category of investor includes insurance companies, mutual funds, pension funds, hedge funds, banks, religious and educational endowment funds and other types of well-financed institutional investment groups.

INDUSTRIAL REVOLUTION: This period marks the beginning of the machine age, a major turning point in the history of man that witnessed rapid advancements in the rate at which things could be done. Centered in Europe (with Britain as the central driving force), it brought the 18th and 19th centuries new concepts like the assembly line system, steam engines, rapid advancements in communication systems, rapid firing guns and much more. Productivity increases in the newly industrialized nations generated the need for more raw materials, machines, factories, and labor. The colonization movement was sped up, as the more powerful nations scrambled for natural resources, land, and wealth.

INFORMATION AGE REVOLUTION: According to Harvard sociologist Daniel Bell, it is the "post-industrial society," the next evolutionary step from the industrial age. It is the brain-intensive age of knowledge and hi-technology, characterized by the creation, production, and distribution of information (John Naisbitt, Megatrends, 1982). This new era includes the development of the thinking machine, knowledge-intensive industries and the synergistic use of information and electronic systems to generate new creations.

JANUARY EFFECT: This is the rise in prices of many small capitalization stocks during January each year. According to *Barron's Finance & Investment Handbook*, "The January Effect is attributed to year-end selling to create tax losses, recognize capital gains, effect portfolio window dressing, or raise holiday cash; since such selling depresses the stocks but has nothing to do with their fundamental worth, bargain hunters quickly buy in, causing the January rally." (John Downes and Jordan Elliot Goodman, *Barron's Finance & Investment Handbook*, third edition, 1990).

LEVEL III ASSETS: These assets appearing on a balance sheet cannot readily be evaluated based on normal measurements of market prices, model numbers, and other indicators of value. In the world of finance, these assets are typically considered illiquid and require a more risk-adjusted structure of valuation. In short, Level III Assets fall in the category of high risk and are problematic especially in a situation where a company's balance sheet is evaluated to determine the worthiness of an investment

MACROECONOMICS: An examination of a nation's economy as a whole. Such major economic forces as unemployment, interest rates, money supply, price levels, inflation and a nation's productive output of goods and services are brought together to formulate an overall analysis of the economy.

MERCANTILISM: Established economic policies of a nation that protects home industries through high tariffs, monopolistic foreign trade practices, and the promotion of greater wealth for the nation by increasing measurably the level of exports over imports. In a book entitled *A History of the Western World*, we are informed that mercantilism, "...was represented by the English Navigation Acts of 1651 and 1662...Mercantilist policies were designed to impede or prevent Dutch imports by the imposition of high tariffs, by outright bans on the shipments of goods by ships of any country except one's own or the producer's, and by subsidies to one's own shippers and manufacturers." (Lyon, Rowen, Hamerow, *A History of the Western World*, Rand McNally & Company, 1970, p443).

MONETARY POLICY: Essentially a set of procedures and tools the Federal Reserve Board has at its disposal to control the U.S. money supply. The Fed tools most commonly used are the discount rate, the federal funds rate, open market operations and the lowering or raising member bank reserve requirements. The central bank is essentially controlling the price of money and credit.

MONETARISM: Advocates that the money supply is the most important driver for economic growth. It is a monetary theory and system popularized by economist Milton Friedman. The basic premise of the theory is that as the money supply expands in the system, greater demand for good and services increase. In the long run, inflation is driven higher as demand grows stronger for fewer goods.

MONETIZE DEBT: In the field of economics, this term refers to the ability to take a non-generating asset and convert it into a new source of revenue. Examples of monetization include the Federal Reserve System (the Fed) and the U.S. Federal Government monetizing debt. When the Fed monetizes U.S. government debt, it will purchase Treasuries (notes, bills, or bonds) issued by the U.S. Treasury. The Federal government then receives a form of monetary credit that can be used in monetary transactions (payment of government bills and expenses), and the Fed records and will place the debt on its books. The U.S. government can monetize debt by issuing bonds directly to the public offering to pay a specific coupon rate (interest rate) on the debt obligation(s). The money received from the sale of the bonds is revenue that the government will use for its monetary operations.

MIXED ECONOMY: An economic system that is composed of both the socialist and capitalistic models. Mainland China is probably the best example of a major world superpower utilizing both systems to its advantage. This economic design will most likely be the wave of the future for the majority of nations. During this era, communism as an economic system has failed, and undiluted capitalism is likely to meet the same fate if an unprecedented level of wealth and power is concentrated in the hands of a few people worldwide. Free enterprise and socialism, as humanistic developments are not likely to go down the drain with capitalism and communism. The new era will call on the best economic factors of both of these major systems and fashion a new economic plan for an entire new world order. The mixed economy is the evolving model for a prospective newly developed future system.

MORAL HAZARD: As presented in this book and according to economic theory, moral hazard is a situation whereby a party has a tendency to take risks but is aware that the risk taker will not assume any negative fallout from the risks. One party takes on the enormous risks while another party or entity bears the burden of any negative consequences. The prime example in this book is the behavior of Big Banks during the *Meltdown of 2008*. Many of these large institutions took on enormous risks, lost billions of dollars but were ultimately bailed out by the U.S. federal government and the Federal Reserve System (FED). Banks engaged in excessive risk-taking with borrowed funds assuming that the FED would be there when and if a bailout was required: big brother will be there no matter what. Rewarding bad behavior is the essence of moral hazard.

MULTI-DIMENSIONAL CORPORATION: This term refers to the emergence of a new corporate entity that fully adapts itself to the multimedia wave of the Digital Age. These new corporate entities will ultimately operate simultaneously on many platforms and in many business environments, providing (in some instances) a complete line of products and services to a highly varied global consumer base.

MULTI-POLAR WORLD ORDER: The bi-polar era that was dominated by the Soviet Union and the United States following WW II through 1991, paved the way for a new type of world order by the mid-1990s. This new multi-polar world order witnessed the rise of several economic power blocks. The most prominent of the newly structured political and economic systems was the European Economic Community, the rise of Mainland China, India, Brazil, an Islamic/ Middle Eastern centered economic community, and a Southern African economic trading community. As these new power centers came into being, major adjustments on the worldwide political and economic landscape have followed.

NATIONALIZATION: Government takeover of a private enterprise as a matter of state policy (as in communist societies) or in the interest of national self-preservation (i.e., to save jobs, prevent exploitation of the nation's natural resources, or to save a collapsing industry). During the opening years of the 1990s, many countries in South America and elsewhere were abandoning nationalization policies and opening up fully to free enterprise.

NOMINAL GDP: This is the calculated version of GDP that does not consider inflation. Inflation is factored out providing a real GDP actual growth without considering the impact of the rate of inflation.

NOTATIONAL VALUE: Notational Value of "over the counter" derivatives represents the underlying market value or amount of derivative contracts. It reflects the value of the trades in the system; however, it is not an accurate value of the amount of money at risk among the participants. That number is determined by the actual performance of the assets underlying the contracts: stocks, bonds, currencies, commodities, stock indices, etc. The creditworthiness of the trading counterparties is also considered in the valuation process.

ORGANIZATION OF PETROLEUM EXPORTING COUNTRIES (OPEC): In September 1960, the Organization of Petroleum Exporting Countries (OPEC) was started by Iran, Iraq, Saudi Arabia, Kuwait, and Venezuela. It was a significant event and the development of a major trading block, which in time, would amass enormous power in global economics and politics. The initial five OPEC nations were later joined by Qatar, Indonesia, Libya, the United Arab Emirates, Algeria, Nigeria, and Ecuador.

OVER THE COUNTER DERIVATIVES (OTC): The value of a derivative contract or security is based upon or derived from the value of specific underlying assets. Examples of underlying assets are currencies, commodities, interest rates, bonds, stocks and market indexes. Generally used as instruments to hedge risks or to speculate in the markets, these contracts often represent high leverage financial transactions. Examples of derivatives are option contracts, futures contracts, forward contracts, swaps and various types of instruments related to the mortgage industry. In general, derivatives are traded through an organized exchange in the market; whereas over the counter derivatives are contracts that are negotiated between two parties.

PETRODOLLARS: Refers to the large quantity of U.S. dollars paid to oil producers during the 1970s. Most of this money was deposited in Western banks, which in turn made billion dollar sovereign loans to many Third World countries during that period. The petrodollar glut of the 1970s was largely responsible for the enormous Third World debt load of the 1980s and 90s.

PIIGS Nations: In the EU, Portugal, Ireland, Italy, Greece and Spain are known as the PIIGS nations. These countries are considered the weaker members of the EU and have been the focus (since the *Meltdown of 2008*) of many of the required bailout operations.

PONZI SCHEME: As a notoriously fraudulent investing scam, a Ponzi scheme will present an investor with a promise of high returns (with minimal risk) on his or her investment. Similar to a pyramid scheme, initial or older investors in the system are provided the high returns with the funding received from the new investors entering the scheme. Eventually, the deception runs out of cash and the whole system begins to collapse exposing the fraud and major losses incurred by the deceived investors.

PRIME RATE: This is the interest rate banks charge their most creditworthy customers; it's the best rate available in a given period. Other rates are built upon the prime rate, based upon economic and financial principles of risk and return.

PARADIGM SHIFT: Represents a period in history when broad, interrelated changes are made in the way societies function, conduct transactions and organize the production and distribution of products and services. Its effects alter existing frameworks and require significant infrastructure developments to accommodate new system designs and technologies. Prime examples of paradigm shifts in global affairs are the *Industrial Revolution* and the emergence of the *Information Age Revolution*.

PHASE I EDICT: This term refers to the historic Federal Court Consent Decree in January 1982, that gave AT&T a two year period to prepare for the complete breakup of its operations. D-Day came on January 1, 1984, which established the era of the Regional Bell Operating Companies (sometimes called the seven Baby Bells) as well as AT&T reorganization in the long distance arena.

PHASE II EDICT: This term refers to the continued deregulation of the telecommunication industry in the 1990s (in the U.S.), which culminated in the implementation of the Telecommunication Competition and Deregulation Act of 1996. President Clinton signed the new legislation on February 8, 1996, marking the end of an era.

PRICE EARNINGS RATIO (P/E): This represents a financial calculation that provides an investor with an estimate of how much they are paying for a company's earning power. The ratio is calculated by dividing a stock's price by its earnings per share.

PROGRAM TRADING: Computer-driven, buy and sell programs utilized by mainly large institutional investors, to take advantage of arbitrage and similar profit opportunities on various markets. Program traders are a major force on large automated exchanges, and are generally cited as responsible for major up and down moves in the markets.

QUANTITATIVE EASING (QE): A form of monetary policy employed by a central bank to stimulate and increase the supply of money in an economy in a super low-interest rate environment. The general notion is that the central bank is printing money to support an economic strategy. However, the reality is that money is created by electronically adding numbers to an account. With the money in circulation, since the *Meltdown of 2008*, the Fed implemented two main strategies: (1) it deployed billions of dollars to purchase Treasury bonds in order to lower the overall rates in the U.S. economy; and (2) the Fed deployed funds to purchase mortgage bonds (mortgage-back securities) to lower home mortgage rates. The overall result was the prevention of a complete collapse in the U.S. economic system.

REPOS (REPURCHASE AGREEMENTS): These instruments are contracts (typically overnight loans) for the sale and repurchase of financial assets. Upon the termination of the stated period, the seller repurchases the asset for the same price in which it was sold plus an agreed upon interest payment for the use of the funds. In essence, Repos are short-term interest-bearing loans against collateral.

RECESSION: In a typical recession an economic system will experience a business cycle contraction and a basic slowdown in economic activity. Economists will declare a recession after specific macroeconomic indicators (such as GDP, employment, business profits, household income, etc.) decline for two consecutive quarters. In recessions, the unemployment rate will rise, bankruptcies will accelerate, inventories will rise, and businesses and households are cutting back on expenditures. A prolonged period of recession and contraction will lead to an economic depression (or Great Depression), which is a much more severe event.

RING OF FIRE: The Pacific Ring of Fire is a 25,000 mile (40,000 km) horseshoe shape seismic belt or arc, home to 452 volcanoes and is an area where large numbers of earthquakes and volcanic eruptions occur each year. The belt expands from New Zealand, through the eastern edge of Asia, swings north across the Aleutian Islands of Alaska, and then moves south along the coast of North and South America. The earth crust is divided into giant rafts of rock called tectonic plates. The theory of plate tectonics indicates that the Ring of Fire is located at the borders of the Pacific Plate and other major tectonic plates.

SECULAR BEAR MARKET CYCLE: A Secular bear market trend as opposed to a cyclical or seasonal period, is a long-term movement in an economy, lasting from five to upwards to 25 years. Within the trend, short periods of bull markets and longer periods of bear markets may occur. In this publication, the period of 2018 to the early 2020s is considered the tail end of a secular bear market trend.

SECULAR STAGNATION (SS): Refers to an era of economic development that is defined by a long-term period of slow growth with low-interest rates and low productivity. During this period, an economy can't maintain an adequate level of demand. A major shift in demographics, significant technological advances, a dramatic rise in economic inequality, a slowdown in population growth, and declining investments in infrastructure, training, and education are some of the contributing factors promoting this phenomenon. The economy is in a slump and may linger there for some time. Due to a significant crisis in the supply and demand paradigm, robust economic growth is postponed. Most people are not interested in borrowing and spending money; conserving wealth and survival are the main economic objectives. A prime example of this economic phenomenon is Japan and its nearly three-decade battle with deflation.

SECURITY AND EXCHANGE COMMISSION (SEC): This federal commission came into being in 1934 as a federal agency designed to protect the investing public against any wrong practices by the securities markets. Security registration and full disclosure by a company issuing investment certificates such as stocks or bonds became part of a new set of regulations that would close the chapter on the abuses and corruptions of the *Roaring 20s*. The de-regulated 1920s led to the New Deal regulations of the 1930s.

SELLING SHORT: A technique used by an investor to make a profit in a declining market. An investor sells a security or commodity futures contract that he or she does not own. In the case of securities, the seller will borrow the securities through his or her broker, make the sale, and cover this position at a later date at a lower purchase price (assuming the price went down). The basic idea is to sell at a high price and buy the stock back at a lower price, covering the borrowed position. If the price of the stock declined in the interim, a profit is made; if the price increased, the short seller incurs a loss.

SHADOW BANKING SECTOR: Another area of the economic system that facilitates lending which includes brokerages, hedge funds, money market funds and structured investment vehicles.

SOVEREIGN WEALTH FUND (SWT): These investment vehicles are large state-owned investment funds that are focused primarily on global investment opportunities. The assets that make up the bulk of these funds are as follows; precious metals, bonds, stocks, property and various other types of financial assets.

SPECULATIVE FRENZY: A wild, uncontrollable period of speculation in stock prices, land, precious metals, etc. It is a time when prices are driven to unreasonable heights due to the frenzied activities of large numbers of investors hoping to make substantial profits in a fast-moving market. The result is a "bubble bursting," generating heavy losses for those unfortunate investors who got in at the tail end of the action or who did not bail out in time.

STAGFLATION: The combination of a steady increase in prices or inflation, and continued slow economic growth and unemployment.

TROUBLED ASSET RELIEF PROGRAM (TARP): Implemented during the enormous turbulence of the *Meltdown in 2008*, TARP was brought into existence to help avert a complete collapse in the U.S. economic system. With the passage of H.R. 1424 enacting the Emergency Economic Stabilization Act of 2008, TARP gave the U.S. Treasury $700 billion to buy up mortgage-backed securities (and other instruments) from banks throughout the land to generate liquidity and un-freeze money markets.

TRADE DEFICIT: Refers to economic statistics indicating that a nation is importing more than it is exporting. A trade surplus is an exact opposite.

TRICKLE-DOWN ECONOMICS: An economic plan or policy wherein the wealthy receive tax breaks, investment tax credits, and other special incentives to encourage greater investment activity in the economy. According to the theory, the economic benefits and profits should "trickle down" to the other levels of society. It was one of the main theories behind Reaganomics and supply-side economics.

WORLD TRADE ORGANIZATION (WTO): This is the global multilateral trade organization that helps to facilitate the flow of international trade between developed, developing and least-developed countries throughout the world. The organization seeks to manage trade disputes, tariff issues and other essential area of international trade relationships. The WTO's main goal is to ensure that global trade flows smoothly and unobstructed with trade restrictions or trade wars. Global rules of trade have been established to facilitate a free flow of goods and services throughout the world benefiting all the nations that are a part of the system.

BIBLIOGRAPHY

Aganbegyan, Abel; *Inside Perestroika: The Future of the Soviet Economy*, New York: Harper & Row, 1989.
Beasley, W.G.; *The Rise of Modern Japan*, (New York: St Martin's Press, 1990), pp. 224-226.
Bonnifield, Matthew Paul; *The Dust Bowl*, (Albuquerque: University of New Mexico Press, 1979).
Browne, Harry; *The Economic Time Bomb*, New York: St. Martin's Press, 1989.
Bruner, Robert F. and Carr, Sean D.; *The Panic of 1907: Lessons Learned from the Market's Perfect Storm*, New Jersey, John Wiley & Sons, Inc., 2007.
Brynjolfsson, Erik; McAfee, Andrew; *Race Against The Machine: How the Digital Revolution is Accelerating Innovation, Driving Productivity, and Irreversibly Transforming Employment and the Economy*, (Kindle Location 16). Digital Frontier Press. Kindle Edition (2011-10-17).
Burstein, Daniel; *YEN!*, New York: Fawcett Columbine, 1988.
Cardiff, Gray Emerson; *A Millionaire's Guide to Panic-Proof Investing ing the Stock Market*; Danville, Sound Advice Press, 1996
Casey, Douglas R.; *Crisis Investing*, New York: Stratford Press, 1980.
Davidson, James B. and Lord William Rees-Mogg; *The Great Reckoning*, New York: Summit Books, 1991.
Dicken, Peter; *Global Shift: The Internationalization of Economic Activity*, (The Guilford Press, New York, 1992).
Dent, Harry S. Jr.: *The Great Boom Ahead*, New York, Hyperion, 1993.
Dent, Harry S. Jr.: *The Demographic Cliff*, New York, Portfolio/Penguin, 2014.
Dent, Harry S. Jr.: *The Sale of a Lifetime*, Delray Beach, FL, Delray Publishing, 2016.
Diop, Cheikh Anta; *Black Africa*, Westport Connecticut: Lawrence Hill & Company, 1978.
Dodd, Paul Manning; *Hirohito: The War Years*, New York: Mead & Company, Inc., 1986.
Duncan, Richard; *The New Depression: The Breakdown of the Paper Money Economy*, Singapore, John Wiley & Sons, 2012.
Erdman, Paul; *What's Next*, New York: Doubleday, 1988.

Erdman, Paul; *Paul Erdman's Money Book*, New York: Random House, 1984.
Financial Crisis Inquiry Commission, *The Financial Crisis Inquiry Report*, January 2011.
Galbraith, John Kenneth; *Economics In Perspective*, Boston: Houghton Mifflin Company, 1987.
Garraty, John A.; *The Great Depression*, New York: Bruce Jovanovich Publishers, 1986.
Goyette, Charles; *The Dollar Meltdown*, New York: Penguin Group, 2009.
Griffin G. Edward; *The Creature from Jekyll Island: A Second Look at the Federal Reserve*, Westlake Village, CA, American Media, 2010.
Grunwald, Michael, *The NEW NEW DEAL*, New York: Simon & Schuster, 2012.
Ishihara, Shintaro; *The Japan That Can Say No*, New York: Simon & Schuster (English Translation), 1989.
Jackson, John G.; *Ages of Gold and Silver*, Texas: American Atheist Press, 1990.
Jenkins, Richard A.; *Supercomputers of Today and Tomorrow: The Parallel Processing Revolution*, Blue Ridge Summit, PA.: Tab Books Inc., 1986.
Johnson, Simon and Kwak, James; *13 Bankers: The Wall Takeover and the Next Financial Meltdown*, Vintage Books (A Division of Random House, Inc.), New York, January 2011.
Kennedy, Paul; *The Rise and Fall of The Great Powers*, New York: Vintage Books, 1989 Ed.
Kindleberger, Charles P.; T*he World In Depression 1929-1939*, Berkeley: University of California Press, 1986.
Kindleberger, Charles P.; *Manias, Panics, and Crashes*, New York: Basic Books Inc. Publishers, 1978.
Kindleberger, Charles P.; *Marshall Plan Days*, Boston: Allen & Unwire, 1987.
Kondratieff, Nikolai; *The Long Wave Cycle*, New York: Richardson & Snyder, 1984.
Koo, Richard; *The Holy Grail of Macro Economics: Lessons From Japan's Great Recession*, (John Wiley & Sons (Asia) Plc. Ltd., 2009).
Kotkin, Joel and Kishimoto, Yoriko; *The Third Century*, New York: Ivy Books, 1988.
Leeb, Stephen and Leeb, Donna; *The Oil Factor*, Time Warner Book Group, 2005.
Lefevre, Edwin; *Reminiscences of a Stock Operator*, John Wiley & Sons, Inc., New York, 1993.
Malabre, Alfred Jr.; *Beyond Our Means*, New York: Vintage Books, 1988.
Malkin, Lawrence; *The National Debt*, New York: Mentor, 1987.
Musashi, Miyamoto; *A Book Of Five Rings*, New York: The Overlook Press, 1974.
Naisbitt, John; *Megatrends*, New York: Warner Books, Inc., 1982.
Negroponte, Nicholas; *being digital*, New York: Vintage Books, 1995.

North, Gary Dr.; *12 Deadly Nega-trends*, Fort Worth Texas: American Bureau of Economic Research, Revised Ed., 1989.

Om-Ra-Seti, Khafra K, *World Economic Collapse: The Last Decade and the Global Depression*, KMT Publications, San Francisco, 1994.

Om-Ra-Seti, Khafra K, *Bubble Markets and Boom & Bust Cycles: Paradigm Revolutions in the Information Age*, KMT Publications, San Francisco, 2002.

Om-Ra-Seti, Khafra K, *Global Economic Boom & Bust Cycles: The Great Depression and Recovery of the 21st Century*, KMT Publications, Sacramento, CA, 2012.

Peebles, Melvin Van; *Bold Money*, New York: Warner Books, 1986.

Prestowitz, Clyde; *Three Billion New Capitalists: The Great Shift of Wealth and Power to the East*, Basic Books, 2005.

Prins, Nomi, *Collusion, How Central Bankers Rigged The World*, Nation Books, New York, 2018.

Rifkin, Jeremy ; *The END of WORK: The Decline of the Global Labor Force and the Dawn of the Post-Market Era*, G.P. Putnam's Sons, 1995.

Rosenau, David and Shuman, James B.; *The Kondratieff Wave*, New York: World Publishing, 1972.

Shelton, Judy; *The Coming Soviet Crash*, New York: The Free Press, 1989.

Sertima, Van Ivan; *Golden Age of the Moor*, (editor: Transaction Publications, New Brunswick, 1993).

Smith, Adam; T*he Roaring '80s*, New York: Summit Books, 1988.

Sobel, Robert; *The Great Bull Market*, New York: W.W. Norton & Company Inc., 1968.

Sutton, Anthony C.; *Western Technology and Soviet Economic Development 1930 to 1945*, Stanford, California: Hoover Institution Press, 1971.

Toffler, Alvin; *POWERSHIFT*, (New York: Bantam Books, 1990).

Wessel, David, *In Fed We Trust: Ben Bernanke's War On the Great Panic*, New York, Three Rivers Press, 2009.

Zuckerman, Gregory, *The Greatest Trade Ever*, Broadway Books, New York, 2009.

ABOUT THE AUTHOR

Khafra K Om-Ra-Seti has worked as a professional stockbroker and institutional trader for the Charles Schwab Corporation for eight years in the 1990s; for six years he was a lead instructor for the BA Completion Program at New College of California; and is currently an active investor in real estate and the stock market. As an author and self-publisher for nearly two decades and a rogue economist and futurist, Khafra continues to expand his research and knowledge in global scientific and technological developments. He has become more focused on the clean energy revolution that is now destined to completely change our way of life in the 21st century. Consistent with this worldview, Khafra is concerned that the global community is moving too slow to declare the end of the *Age of Oil*. His keen interest in computer systems and Information Age technologies evolves from his work with mainframe computers that began in the latter 1970s and early 1980s. His Master Thesis, *Analysis of the Optical Disk Indus-*

try & Busines Plan for a Start-Up Company - KMT, Inc., written in 1987, was a first in predicting the revolutionary power and potentials of laser technology in PC applications and storage systems. He obtained his education from San Francisco State University, earning BA and MBA degrees in finance. In this current book, Khafra continues his thesis on the Grand Convergence Theory leading to the development of the final phase of the Great Depression of the 21st Century. In his analysis, the *Meltdown of 2008* was the first phase of a much greater meltdown that will engulf the entire world.

INDEX

A

A Book of Five Rings 229
AAA credit rating 41
Abe, Shinzo 140, 141, 283
Adams, Mike 282
AEROPOLIS 2001 213
Africa 132
African Americans 230
African-American 33
   first African American president 33
Age of oil and other fossil fuels 35, 248
Age of the Billionaire 204, 215, 245
aggregate demand 96, 137
aging populations 391
AI 24, 181, 200, 201, 202, 203, 204, 205, 206, 207, 208, 209, 210, 211, 212, 214, 215, 216
AIG 20, 30, 56, 64, 88, 109
Air Force One 173
Ally Financial 50, 53
alternative energies 45
Amazon.com 175, 195
America 14, 15, 94, 129, 132, 258, 259
"America First" agenda 181, 185, 188
American Civil War 196
American consumer base 23
American dollar 78, 79
American factories closed 25
American people upside down on mort. 22
American recession in 1973 80, 197
American recession of 1981-82 80
American Recovery and Reinvestment Act of 2009 36
American workers 20, 23, 25
Americans for Tax Reform 44
Analysis of the Optical Disk Industry & Business P 230
Anbang Insurance Group Company 215
Anegawa, Takafumi 284

Appelbaum, Binyamin 87
Apple 175, 195, 223
Arizona 48
art bubbles 209, 210, 389
Artnet 211
Asia 135
atomic age 196, 244
attorney generals 50
Au Moulin de la Galette 209
Augustus, F. Heinze 63
Australia 243
Austria 243
Austrian cycle theory 240, 241

B

Babson, Roger 68
Baby Boom Generation 16, 48, 49, 232, 233, 234, 235, 236, 259
   student loans and the 28
Bacon, Francis 211
Bail Out the American People 53
Baishi, Qi 211
Balance Sheet Recession 136, 137, 138
Ball, Laurence 21
   Lehman Bankruptcy and 21
Balloon Dog 211
bank cartel 6
Bank for International Settlements (BIS) 12, 93, 94
Bank Holding Company 23
Bank of Ameria 19, 30, 50, 52, 53, 56, 57, 103, 121
Bank of England (BOE) 26, 90, 94
Bank for International Settlements (BIS) 93, 94
bank holding companies 23
Bank of America
   19, 30, 50, 52, 53, 56, 57, 103, 121

Index

Bank of England 26, 90
Bank of England (BOE) 94
Bank of International Settlements 120
Bank of Japan (BOJ) 91, 94, 127, 129, 138, 140, 392
Bank of the United States 62
Bank of Tokyo 127
Bank Panic of 1907 63
Bank runs 66
Banking and Currency and The Money Trust 66
banking cartel 64, 72, 86, 99, 206, 224
banking crisis 243
banking industry 50, 174, 186
banking system 45, 46
banking system collapse 70
bankruptcy 28, 48, 53, 66, 114, 116, 225
Banks
   Too Big to Fail" banks xi
barbarism or civilization xii, 249
Barclays, Royal Bank of Scotland 121, 168
Bartiromo, Maria 87
Basel, Switzerland 93
Batra, Ravi 131, 207, 208, 229
Batts, Vicki 282
bear market 17, 391
Bear Stearns x, 20, 22, 30, 109
   the bailout of 21
Beijing 184, 185
Belgium 169, 194
Berlin 169
Bernanke Ben 38, 42, 47, 49, 53, 54, 60, 62, 73, 86, 87, 89, 94, 95, 97, 98, 99, 100, 102, 200, 388
   reappointed Fed Chairman in 2009 38
Bezos, Jeff 175
Biden, Beau 52
Biden, Joe 52
   Big Banks 35, 47, 49, 52, 54, 55, 56, 58, 98, 106, 113, 118, 121, 124, 206, 187, 251
   Megabanks 40
Biggs, Barton 128
billionaire row 214
Biotechnology 193, 250, 254
bipolar era 81
Black Box 116
Black Futurists in the Information Age: Vision of 230

Blackrock 57
Bloomberg 101, 102, 107
Bloomberg Billionaires Index 167
Bloomberg Television 58
Board of Governors Federal Reserve System 246
Board of Governors of the Federal Reserve Bank sys 72
BOJ 141
Boockvar, Peter 388
boom and bust 68
boom and bust cycle of 1995-2000 142
Boom and Bust Cycles 177, 237, 248, 254
boom and bust cycles 17, 30, 63, 70, 78, 87, 119, 126, 197, 198, 200, 203, 207, 208, 228, 389, 390, 228, 230, 231, 232, 234, 237, 240
boom and bust period of 1995-2000 135
Booming 80s 81, 129, 130, 197, 203, 204, 209, 210, 211
Born, Brooksley 99, 116, 117, 119
Brazil 17
Bretton Woods agreement 78, 79, 80, 245, 246
Brexit 16, 92, 167, 168, 169, 170, 171, 172
   British referendum and 26
   European Summit on 169
   Far-right groups and 169
   globalization and 169
   immigration policies and 169
   referendums and 169
   revolt against the establishment and 168
   the working class and 169
   wealth inequality and 169
   wealthy elites and 168
BRITAIN 170
Britain 74, 129, 167, 169, 170, 171, 194, 195, 243
British Empire 243
Brown, Sherrod 187
Brussels 169, 172, 185
budget deficits 96, 392
Buffett, Warren 113
Bull market 127, 128, 129, 133, 170, 390, 223
Burach, Bernard 68
Bureau of Internal Revenue 65
Burj Khalifa 214
Bush Administration 33, 34, 35, 42
Bush era 35, 188, 259

Bush, George 42
Bush tax cuts 176
Bush-era tax cuts 40
Business Week 130
bust cycle 126, 237
Buying stock on margin 67

C

California 48, 50, 51, 277
California Attorney General 52
California's congressional delegation 53
Canada 180, 184, 278
capitalism 222, 238, 239, 244, 250, 255, 256
   unrestricted capitalism 20, 21, 29
capitalistic free market system 77, 191
Capitol Hill 42, 177
Cardiff, Gray 195
Carney, Mark 26
Carter, Jimmy 80
CDC's Agency for Toxic Substances and Disease Regi 284
Central Bank 30, 111, 127, 138, 140, 141, 142, 390
Central Bank Liquidity Swap Lines (CBLS) 108
central bank trade 391
Central Bankers 100, x, xii, 29, 30, 63, 94, 95, 121, 170, 181, 215, 238, 240, 246, 247, 249, 259
   negative interest rates x
   unconventional economic tools x
   zero interest rates x
Cesium-134 283
Cesium-137 283
cesium-137 276
Chambers, John 44
Chernobyl in 1986 279
Chernobyl nuclear crisis in 1986 276
Chernobyl nuclear disaster 282
China xi, 14, 17, 26, 42, 129, 173, 178, 179, 180, 181, 182, 183, 185, 189, 197, 214, 217, 389, 224, 240, 245
   China's real estate markets in 214
   Chinese art buyers and 210
   ghost cities in China and 224
   Golden Finance and 214
   Household Registration and Migrant Labor in China 214
   Mainland China 20, 23, 24, 25
   Ping An Finance Centre in 214
   second largest economy 2010 and 139
   Shanghai Tower and 214
   Shanghai World Financial Center and 214
   tallest skyscrapers in the world and 214
   Wuhan Greenland Center and 214
China Daily 184
Chinese Minister of Commerce 178
Christie's 210, 211
Citigroup 19, 39, 50, 53, 103
class warfare 206
clean energy revolution 37, 45
clean technology revolution 45
climate change 45
Clinton Administration 34, 116, 118, 176
CNBC 87
Coakley, Martha 52
Code Red 243
Cohn, Lawrence 118
Cold War 81, 132, 196
collapse of the entire banking system 74
Colombia 132
Commerce Department 85
commercial real estate bubbles 389
Commodity Futures Modernization Act of 2000 119
Commodity Futures Trading Commission (CFTC) 99, 116, 119
commodity money 242
communist ideology 191
Comptroller of Currency 120
Concentration of Wealth and Depressions 207
Confidence Men: Wall Street, Washington and the Ed 39
Congress 34, 36, 41, 43, 49, 54, 64, 65, 67, 70, 77, 83, 84, 85, 89, 90, 93, 97, 98, 99, 100, 107, 117, 121, 174,
Congressman Lindbergh 66
consumer base, represent 70% of GDP 49
consumers 70 percent of the nation's GDP 22
Coolidge, Calvin 67
CoreLogic 39, 56
Council of Economic Advisors (CEA) 37
counterterrorism 184
Crash of 1929 68, 258
Crash of 1987 229
Crash of 1990 133, 135

Crash of 2011 44
Crash of '29: October 29, 1929 68, 69
Crash of '87 390, 228, 258
Creature from Jekyll Island 389
credit bubble 239, 241
credit creation 240
Credit Default Swap contracts 30
Credit Suisse 168, 204
Credit-Anstalt 243
Creditism 222, 237, 238, 240, 244, 245, 247, 250, 255, 256, 391
Cummings, Elijah 54, 104
currency devaluation 74
currency wars 29, 94, 243, 389
Current Account deficits 245
Czechoslovakia 243

D

Dagong 177
Daqian, Zhang 211
Daring '90s 232
Davis, Ned 392
Day of Reckoning 237, 248
de-leveraging 46, 49
debt and credit 16, 95, 226, 227
   super debt cycle and 222
Debt Ceiling War of 2011 41, 42, 61-68
Debt deflation 224
Debt forgiveness 50, 55
Debt Jubilee 95
deficits 176
deflation 24, 71, 74, 86, 87, 90, 92, 94, 95, 96, 98, 140, 141, 142, 192, 195, 196, 197, 200, 201, 208, 215, 216, 222, 224, 225, 226, 227, 234, 235, 238, 240, 247, 250, 253, 256, 259, 388, 389, 391, 392, 393
deflationary depression x, 46, 47
deflationary forces 181, 183
deflationary impact 26, 27, 29, 30
Delaware 51
deleveraging 223, 225, 259, 391
deleveraging balance sheet excesses 24
deleveraging consumer debt 29
DeMarco, Edward 53, 54
Democrats 20, 27, 40, 45, 46, 53, 54, 55, 74, 99, 174, 187
demographic analysis 231
demographic trends and cycles 16

Denmark 169
Dent Harry 16, 191, 194, 232, 235, 236,
   demographic analysis and 228, 231
   demographic trends and cycles and 16
   Dent Research and 231
   Spending Wave and 233
Dent Methodology 232
Der Spiegel magazine 275
deregulate 186
deregulated 1920s 76
deregulated banking system 58
deregulation 34, 35, 38, 87, 116, 118, 177
Derivatives 15, 29, 31, 99, 105, 113, 114, 115, 116, 117, 118, 119, 120, 121, 122, 123, 124, 186, 187, 215, 256, 389,
Financial weapons of mass destruct and 30
Deutsche Bank AG 121, 168
devaluation of currencies 94, 243
devalue the dollar 244
Dicken, Peter 191, 193
Dimitriyerick, Nikolai Kondratieff 68
discount rate 67, 68, 82
Dodd, Christopher 105
Dodd-Frank 104, 105, 122
Dodd-Frank Reform and Consumer Protection Act 40, 102, 106, 123, 186, 187
dollar 168
dollar liquidity swaps 108
dollar standard 203
Dollar Store 135
dollar was backed and redeemable in gold 75
Donovan, Shaun 54
Dot-Com bubble 116, 135, 176, 258
Dot-Com Collapse of 2000 127
Dow Jones Average 173, 174, 175, 176, 177, 178, 179, 181, 183, 186, 187, 200, 201, 203, 201, 203, 205, 206, 207, 208, 210, 214, 215, 389, 390, 391, 222, 223, 224, 225, 226, 227, 229, 233, 234, 235, 237, 238, 241, 242, 243, 244, 245, 247, 248, 249, 252, 253, 254
   worst single-day drop and the 175
Dow futures 167
downward cycle 192, 229, 235, 258
Dubai 214
Duncan Richard 17, 65, 91, 113, 120, 177, 222, 237, 238, 249, 251, 255, 256, 257, 391
   Creditism. 17
   joint venture partnership and 250
   New Depression and 245

Index

Dupont 68
DuPont Chemical 195

E

Eastern Europe 132
eastern Washington state 281
Eastman Kodak 195
easy money 69
easy money policies 67
Edelson, Larry 228, 244
electric vehicles 182
Emergency Economic Stabilization Act of 2008 90
Empire State Building 213
employment 81
England 168, 192
Erdman, Paul 79
establishment politics 174
EU 14, 15, 17, 23, 96, 167, 168, 169, 170 171, 172, 180, 82, 185, 189, 201, 259 24, 182, 201, 202, 209, 215, 216, 217, 392, 242, 243, 246, 182, 189, 201, 211, 213, 224
euro 59, 95, 168, 169, 170, 171
Eurodollar 79
Europe 23, 24, 29, 43, 168, 182, 201, 202, 209, 215, 216, 217, 392, 242, 243, 246
   middle class in 94
   World War I and 65
European 92
European Bank (ECB) 94, 109, 201, 392
European Community 132
European crisis 120
European sovereign debt 31
European Sovereign Debt crisis 215
European Union xi, 16, 167, 168, 169, 172
   euro and 16
   Sovereign Debt Crisis and 16
Eurozone 96
excess reserves (IOER) 90
Executive Oder 6102 (on April 5, 1933) 75
Executive Order 6260 (on August 28, 1933) 75
expansion of credit 237

F

Facebook 97, 175
factional reserve banking 83
Fairewinds Energy Education 284
Fannie Mae 20, 21, 30, 49, 52, 53, 54, 55, 56, 57, 60, 61
Farage, Nigel 167
fascism 226
FCIC 77, 114, 119
FED 62, 69, 81, 84, 89
Fed vi, vii, x, xi, 15, 17, 62, 63, 64, 65, 66, 67, 68, 69, 70, 71, 72, 73, 74, 75, 76, 77, 78, 80, 81, 82, 83, 84, 85, 86, 87, 88, 89, 90, 91, 92, 93, 94, 95, 96, 97, 98, 99, 100, 101, 102, 103, 104, 106, 107, 108, 109, 110, 111, 112, 115, 116, 117, 123, 173, 174, 175, 177, 186, 187, 188, 189, 200, 201, 202, 203, 215, 388, 390, 391, 392, 224, 227, 238, 240, 244, 246, 247, 249, 251, 253, 254, 257, 258, 259, 63, 64, 65, 66, 69, 77, 80, 81, 82, 84, 85, 88, 99, 100, 119, 176, 177, 186, 202, 250, 257, 259
Federal Board of Governors 85
federal budget deficit 176
federal funds rate 82
federal government 202, 250
Federal Housing Finance Agency (FHFA) 53
federal income tax 65
Federal Open Market Committee (FOMC) 83, 86
Federal Reserve Bank of Minneapolis 122
Federal Reserve 35, 38, 40, 47, 54, 108, 122
   1937 and 46
Federal Reserve Act of 1913 64
Federal Reserve Bank of New York 82, 86, 109
Federal Reserve Banking System 64, 81
Federal Reserve governors 83
Federal Reserve Notes 75
Federal Reserve Regional Bank president 122
Federal Reserve System x, xi, 15, 31, 49, 54, 55, 62, 63, 67, 70, 83, 84, 98, 106, 107, 112
   12 Federal Reserve Banks and 84
   Board of Governors 84
   District Federal Reserve banks and 85
   monetary policies 20, 21, 24, 30
   the mortgage crisis and the 40
   unconventional economic tools 27
Federal Savings and Loan Insurance Corporation (FS 77
Fed's balance sheet 82, 88
Feldstein, Martin 54
Felkerson, James 101, 107, 108, 109
fiat currencies 65, 79, 204, 388

314 Index

fiat monetary system x, 203, 241, 242, 249, 251, 390
fiat-money creation 98
financial capital of the world 232
Financial Crisis Inquiry Commission report 105
Financial Services Regulatory Relief Act 90
financial trusts 67
Financial Weapons of Mass Destruction 113, 215
First National Bank 71
Fiscal Cliff 2013 44
Fiscal policies 29, 35, 42, 44, 96, 136, 250
Fisher, Allison 280, 281
Fisher, Irving 68
Fitch 43
five-year boom cycle 390, 391
Flash Crash 175, 176
Flight capital 232, 243
Florida 48
FOMC 67, 89
    release of Full transcripts and 86
Food stamp 24
Forbes 25, 57, 203
Ford Foundation grant 107
Ford, Gerald 76
foreclosure crisis 20, 50, 54, 55, 99, 104
fractional reserve system 241
France 168, 169, 171, 192, 194, 243
Frank, Barney 105, 187
FRBNY 109
Freddie 30
Freddie Mac 20
    bailout of 21
free-floating exchange rate system 79, 390
Freedom of Information Act (FOIA) 102
Friedman, Milton 73, 95
Fukushima and a Global Nuclear Decision 139, 264-276, 276, 280
Future Shock 197, 198

G

Galbraith, John 200
Galbraith, Thomas 211
Galli, Jordi 96
GAO audit 104
GAO Report 107
garden variety reces. 29, 31, 47, 69, 136, 241

gas-fueled power plants 280
Geithner, Timothy 38, 39, 53, 55, 57, 86, 99, 117
General Electric 68, 195
General Motors 68
General Motors (GM) 20
Genetic Engineering 250, 254
Germany 26, 36, 169, 171, 184, 192, 194, 242 243, 244, 275, 279
    bankruptcies in 243
    clean energy revolution and 38
    hyperinflation in 1923 and 242
    Nazism and the rise of Hitler 243
    nuclear power and 280
    unemployment rate 243
    Weimar Germany and 242
    Weimar Republic and 243
Glass-Steagall Act of 1933 41, 45, 77, 104, 105, 118, 119, 186
global central banking system 237
global debt xi
global deflation 94
global deflationary depression 201
Global Economic Boom and Bust Cycles: The Great x, 20, 237, 248, 254
global trade wars 183
global warming and climate change 35
Global Wealth Report 204
Globalization 24, 26, 29, 178, 181, 203, 389, 240, 124, 91, 97, 178, 181, 183, 185, 188, 198, 204, 206, 388, 239, 240, 245, 247, 249, 253, 255, 256, 258
Gogh, Vincent Van 209
Golay, Michael 280
Gold Reserve Act 75
Gold Standard 65, 66, 69, 74, 78, 79, 80, 168, 203, 240, 242, 243, 244, 245, 246, 390
    free-floating exchange rate system x
    gold-backed currency x
Goldman Sachs 23, 103, 114, 121
Google 195
Gorbachev 127
Gorsuch, Neil 47
Government Accountability Office (GAO) 101, 106
government-sponsored enterprises (GSE Debt) 88
Gramm-Leach-Bliley Act 118
Grand Convergence 22, 389, 237

Index

Great Depression 105
Great Depression in the year 1937 137
Great Depression of 1920 65
Great Depression of 1930s 17, 19, 31, 34, 35, 69, 73, 54, 58, 78, 86, 87, 136, 137, 142, 178, 192, 200, 216, 227, 241, 244
Great Depression of the 21st Century x, 26, 35, 89, 216, 238, 254
    Second Phase xi
Great Recession 14, 15, 19, 21, 31, 37, 48, 55, 56, 80, 89, 136, 137, 138, 142, 143, 223, 226, 238, 249
Great Society Programs 79, 245
Greece 49, 170, 171, 201
Green Energy 16, 250, 254
green technologies 251
Greenpeace Japan 283
Greenspan, Alan 74, 80, 86, 115, 117
Griffin, G. Edward 63, 73, 83, 85
Gross Domestic Product (GDP) 82
Group of Seven 128
Grunwald, Michael 36, 37

H

H.R. 24 2008 42
Hanford Nuclear Reservation 281
Harding, Warren 67
Harris, Kamala 51, 52, 54
Harrison, George 69
Harry Dent 16
Harvard University 34, 104
Hashimoto Administration 137
Hawaii's Big Island 259
Hawley, Willis 178
Helicopter Ben 99
Helicopter Money 95, 96, 141, 215
    quantitative easing (QE) and 95
Hiroshima 226, 275
Hitachi 276
Hitler, Adolf 243, 244
Hollywood 198
Honda 135
Hong Kong 194
Hoover Administration 74, 242
Hoover, Herbert 67, 72, 74, 178
Hoovervilles 48
House Banking and Currency Committee 71
House of Representatives 42, 53, 71, 174
House Oversight & Govn. Reform Com. 104
Housing and Economic Recovery Act of 2008 42
housing bubble 87, 106
HSBC 121
Hubert, Mark 392
HUD 57
Hughes, Chris 97
Hungary 243
hydrogen fusion 193
hyperinflation 141, 181, 183, 389, 240, 242, 247
hyperinflation in Germany 1923 78

I

Iceland 20, 58, 91-93
    megabanks and 59
    economic justice and recovery in 58
Idaho 281
IMF 26, 29, 104, 205, 206
immigration 184
India 23, 24, 194, 240
Indonesia 129
Industrial Age 36, 38, 193, 198, 388
inequality of wealth 94
inflation 59, 62, 63, 64, 66, 77, 79, 80, 81, 83, 89, 90, 91, 93, 94, 96, 97, 192, 193, 195, 196, 203, 209, 210, 389, 391, 226, 232, 234, 235, 240, 242, 245, 247, 249, 252, 253
    hyperinflation and 90
inflationary recessions of the 1970s 80
Information Age xii, 34, 35, 37, 45, 46, 193, 195, 197, 198, 230, 238, 245, 248, 250, 251, 258
    technological advances and 26, 182, 183
infrastructure development 29, 38, 97, 253
interest rates 91, 93, 226
Internal Revenue Service (IRS) 65
International Affairs of the United States Departm 117
International Bank for Reconstruction and Developm 78
international banking cartel 83, 248, 259
international banking system 27
international drug trafficking 184
International Monetary Fund (IMF) 78, 93, 137
international trade 179

internationalization of labor costs 24
internationalization of wage competition 34, 38, 181
Internet 25, 33, 38, 135, 181, 183, 193, 195, 230, 232
investment banking industries 22, 29
iodine-131 276
Iraq 42, 128, 129, 229
Italy 14, 132, 168, 169, 171
Ivry, Bob 104
Iwato Boom 196

J

J.P. Morgan 109
Jackson, Andrew 63
Japan xii, 14, 15, 17, 23, 46, 90, 170, 180, 181, 182, 183, 184, 194, 196, 197, 201, 204, 209, 210, 211, 213, 215, 216, 390, 392, 222, 224, 228, 229, 235, 243, 244, 245, 248, 250, 255, 256, 280
   1500 storage tanks for contaminated water 282
   3/11 and 274
   54 nuclear reactors in 278
   a massive earthquake, tsunami, nuclear disaster 274
   abandon Nuclear Fission Technology 280
   Abenomics and 140
   Abenomics in 141
   aging population and 141, 278
   America and China 3/11 278
   another recession and 139
   anti-nuclear movement and 277
   Balance Sheet Recession and 136
   Bank failures in 134
   banking crisis in 132
   banking system crisis in 138
   battle against deflation and 140
   Big Bang Reforms in 135
   boom and bust cycle in 130, 390
   bubble economy and 126
   busted 1990s 133
   commercial real estate collapse and 127
   commercial real estate collapse in 132
   Consumer and investor confidence collapse in 131
   consumer sovereignty in 134
   Consumer spending in 128, 142
   Crash of 1990 in 132
   debt to GDP ratio in 141
   debt-rejection syndrome in 138
   deflation and 130, 131, 134, 135, 141, 196
   deflation and enormous public debt 87, 278
   economic stimulus package and 130
   end the deflation in 140
   fallacy of composition in 137
   Fifth Generation Project and 197
   Finance Ministry in 130
   Fiscal stimulus in 140
   Fukushima disaster of 3/11 275, 285
   fukushima earthquake and 274
   Fukushima nuclear catastrophe and 15
   Fukushima's ongoing disaster 285
   full-blown recession in 130
   government support prices 133
   grand collapse and 129
   Great Recession in 136, 137, 138, 142
   Hashimoto Administration and 137, 138
   Heisei Bubble and 126, 210, 211
   Hiroshima and Nagasaki and 275
   Honest Poverty (new book) 131, 132
   Honshu and 274
   inflationary pressures and 127
   Information Age technologies 142
   interest rates declines in 137
   Japanese corporate investments 134
   Japan's inflationary cycle and 196
   Kansai Electric (KEPCO) 277
   Liberal Democratic Party (LDP) 283
   long bear market in 142
   Lost Decade of the 1990s 136, 140, 196
   Mainland China investments and 134
   massive earthquake, tsunami and nuclear disaster a 139
   McDonald's in 134
   mega-thrust earthquake and 277
   Mid-East tension and 128
   middle class in 94
   Ministry of International Trade and Industry 128
   monetary expansion in 140
   monetary policies in 136
   multinational corporation outsourcing and 134
   national pension scheme 133
   negative interest rate policy in Japan

Index

(NIRP) 141
no natural resources 278
North American West Coast 278
nuclear catastrophe in 139, 275
nuclear disaster of Fukushima years later 282
nuclear final wakeup call and 279
Nuclear fission and 276
Nuclear Fuel Criticality and 284
nuke cleanup operation in 276
oil embargo impact on 128
Onami 276
Only Store in 135
Pacific Ocean contamination and 283
post-World War II era and 142
postal life-insurance plan 133
postal savings system 133
price destruction 134
Prime Minister Miyazawa 131
Prime Minister Obuchi and 138
Prime Minister Shinzo Abe and 3/11 283
Prime Minister Yoshihiko Noda and 276
purchasing stocks, bonds, ETFs 141
radiation contamination and 276
radioactive cesium and 276
radioactive soil and 3/11 283
real estate and stock market bubble economy 132
reduction in aggregate demand, 136
reform and transformation of 132
reform measures in 133
Remote controlled robots and 3/11 284
Ryou-Un Maru and 278
second largest economy and 131
stock and commodity prices 278
structural reforms 140
super-long bull market and 129
TEPCO 277, 282, 284, 285
the banking system crisis in 132
The Heisei Bubble Collapse and 258
The Liberal Democratic Party (LDP) 131
third largest economy and 139
Tokyo real estate collapse 129, 130
unconventional central bank tools 142
Unit reactor 2 in Fukushima 284
yen and the currency markets 128
Zero Interest Rate Policy: ZIRP 138
quantitative easing (QE) and 140
Jefferson, Thomas 98

Jekyll Island, Georgia 63
Jenkins, Timothy 230
Johnson, Simon 40
JPMorgan Chase 50, 52, 53, 103, 121
Judge Napolitano 107
junk bond market in the 1980s 229
junk bonds 103, 114, 259

K

K-Wave Cycels 192, 193, 195, 196, 197, 234
  upswing cycles and 197
  deflation and 195
  downward cycle and 192
  downward wave and 197
  fifth wave and 193, 195
  fourth cycle and 193
  fourth wave and 195
  inflation and 195
  infrastructure developments and s 192
  Japan's infrastructure developments and 196
  third cycle and 193
  upswing cycles and 192
Kahane, Andrew 210
Kashkari, Neel 122
Kavanaugh, Brett 47
Kennedy, Anthony M. 47
Kennedy, Joseph 68
Kentucky 51
Keynes, John Maynard 77
Keynesian economic principles 76, 91, 95
Kilauea Volcano 259
Kindleberger, Charles 70
Klein, Naomi 200
Kondratieff, Nikolai 68, 191, 192, 193, 194, 198, 234, 235
Koo, Richard 126, 136, 138, 139, 142
Koons, Jeff 211
krona 59
Kuhn-Loeb 64
Kuroda, Haruhiko 140, 141
Kuwait 128, 129
Kwak, James 40
Kyoto 277

L

Labor unions in America 25
Lachman, Desmond 173

Lagarde, Christine 206
laissez-faire economic theories 27, 30
Laurence M. Ball 21
Lawson, Max 205
lean technology revolution 45
Lehman Brothers 20, 21, 22, 30, 32, 87, 114, 167, 170
Lenin 191
Levitt, Arthur 117
Levy Economics Institute 101, 108-110
Lighthizer, Robert 185
Lincoln, Abraham 34
Lindbergh, Charles 64
Lindbergh Charles A. 66, 73
liquidationist policy 74
Livermore, Jesse 68
living wills 186
loan modifications 22, 49, 50, 55, 56, 57, 60, 104
lobbyists 35
Lodge, Henry 62
Lofgren, Zoe 53
London 67, 167, 168, 170, 171, 214, 389
London FTSE 167
London Interbank Offered Rate (LIBOR) 121
London School of Economics 203
Long Economic Cycles 68, 191-193, 198, 234
Long-Term Capital Management (LTCM) 114, 115, 117
Long-Term Economic Program 196
long-term interest rates 49
Low-interest rates 67, 69, 74
Luxembourg 169

M

Made in China 2025 182, 183, 189
Magnetar 30
Maiden Lane II, LLC (ML II - SPV) 109
Maiden Lane III, LLC 109
Main Street 95, 97
mainland China 142
mainstream economists 27
margin calls 67
marginal cost of labor 14, 26, 240, 247
Marshall Plan 78
Marxism 192
Massachusetts 51
Massachusetts Attorney General 52

Matthews, Nicola 107
Mauldin, John 243
MBA thesis 230
McConnell, Mitch 47, 187
McFadden Louis 71, 72, 75
McKinsey global Consulting Research firm 223
McKinsey Report 223
Medicare 41
Mellon, Andrew 74
Meltdown of 2008 iii, vii, x, xi, 14, 15, 16, 17, 19, 23, 24, 29, 30, 33, 35, 38, 40, 54, 59, 60, 74, 99, 101, 102, 104, 105, 110, 111, 113, 115, 118, 119, 120, 121, 122, 123, 126, 139, 174, 176, 186, 206, 214, 222, 224, 227, 237, 238, 247, 248, 253, 258, 259
Merrill Lynch 20, 30, 114
Mexican Congress' Permanent Commission 184
Mexican drug cartels 121
Mexico 24, 81, 129, 180, 184, 185, 281
Michigan 240
microcomputer revolution 230
Microsoft 175, 195, 223
mid-term elections 185
middle class in America 24, 25, 91, 201, 202, 206, 235, 242,
Middle East 129, 248
Mierzwinski, Ed 187
Minneapolis Federal Reserve 123
Minnesota 51
Minsky, Hyman 256
Mitchell, Charles 67
Miyazawa, Kiichi 135
Mogg, Rees 229
monetarist 95
Monetarist economic theory 95
monetary easing 106-108 69
monetary policy 81, 84, 138
monetary system 66, 92
monetary tools
 unconventional monetary tools 20
monetizing the debt 392
Money laundering 121
money printing operations
 QE and 91
money supply 67, 83, 93, 241
Money Trust 63

Index

Moody's 43, 168
moral hazard 47, 106
Morgan, J. P. 63, 64
Morgan Stanley & Co. 22, 23, 103, 114, 121, 128
mortgage crisis 46, 47, 48, 49, 52, 56, 174
Mortgage Electronic Registration System (MERS) 50, 52
mortgage rates 245
Mortgage-back Securities 31, 52, 82, 92, 95, 88, 89, 104, 110,
MoveOn.org 54
multinational corporations 182
Musashi, Miyamoto 229
Mussolini 244
mutual funds 67

N

NAFTA 181
Nagasaki 226, 275
Nakano, Koji 131
Nanotechnology 182, 250, 254
Nasdaq 44, 168, 175
National City Bank 67
National Community Reinvestment Corporation 55
National Economists Club 95
negative feedback loop 226
negative interest rate policy (NIRP) 27, 95
Netherlands 168, 169
Nevada 48, 51
New Deal of the 21st Century 36
New Deal policies 35, 76, 241
New Great Depression 241, 248, 249, 252, 254
New York 51, 63, 67, 214, 215, 216, 232, 389
   Central Park in 214
New York Attorney General 52
New York Federal Reserve Bank 69
New York State Supreme Court 52
New York Times 26, 276
New Zealand 243
Nigeria 201
Nikkei index 126, 127, 128, 129, 130, 131, 135
Nippon Telephone and Telegraph 127
NIRP 91, 92, 94, 215, 225
Nixon Shock 80

Noda, Yoshihiko 276
Nomura Research Institute 136
Norquist, Grover 44
North Africa 248
North America 135
Northern Ireland 168
Norway 243
notional value of derivatives 119, 120
nuclear age 226
Nuclear fission 16, 275, 276, 279, 281, 285
nuclear fusion 280, 282
Nuclear Regulatory Commission (NRC) 280
nuclear waste 279

O

Obama Administration 38, 39, 40, 46, 50, 54, 56, 57, 173, 174, 281
Obama, Barack 33, 34, 74
   21st century New Deal and 46
   21st Century New Deal policy and 45
   New Deal and 45
October 1929 crash. 67
Off-shoring 24, 25
Ofunato, Japan 277
Ohga, Norio 135
oil 281
oil crisis of the 1970s 79
One57 building 214
OPEC 80
Open Market Investment Company 69
Open Market Operations 67, 82
Operation Twist 49, 88
Options Clearing Corporation (OCC) 120
Orange County debacle in 1994 116
Oregon 281
Organization for Economic Cooperation and Developm 137
Osaka 277
OTC derivatives xi, 29, 31, 41, 99, 104, 105, 113, 116, 117, 119, 123, 186
over-the-counter derivatives (OTC) 45
Oxfam International 205

P

Pablo Picasso's Young Lover 211
Pacific Ocean 275, 276, 285
Panic of 1907 63, 195
Patrick, Kathy 57

Paulson, Henry 122
Paulson, John 30
Pennsylvania 71
Pew Fiscal Analysis Initiative 34
Pimco 57
plutonium-239 283
Poland 243
political gridlock in Washington 44
Ponzi Scheme 113
Populace movements 202, 206
Portrait of Dr. Gachet 209
Prechter, Robert 229
President Abraham Lincoln 34
President Andrew Jackson 62
President Barack Obama 15, 35, 36, 38, 41, 44, 45, 52, 53, 58, 104
　clean energy revolution and 37
　Obama's birthday 43
President Bill Clinton 116-118
President Bush 176
President Franklin Delano Roosevelt (FDR) 34, 35
President George W. Bush 34, 252
President Gerald R. Ford 76
President Harry S. Truman 34
President Herbert Hoover 69, 70, 72, 74, 178, 179
President Jimmy Carter 80
President Nixon 80, 245
President Ronald Reagan 54, 80
President Roosevelt 238, 244
President Trump 16, 173, 178, 185, 188, 250
President William Taft 64
President Woodrow Wilson 64
Presidential Executive Order (11825) 76
Preska, Loretta 102
Primary Dealer Credit Facility (PDCF) 109
Princeton University 73
principal forgiveness 53
principal reduction 49, 53, 54, 55, 57

program trading 175
protectionism 178, 184
protectionist 185
Public Citizen 280

Q

quantitative easing (QE) 27, 83, 85, 87, 91, 92, 93, 94, 104, 110, 140, 173, 201, 215, 247, 249, 247, 249, 250, 251, 252, 253, 259, 390
QE 1 88
QE 2 88
QE 3 89
Quantitative Tightening (QT) 92, 177, 259

R

Rabouin, Dion 177
racism 226
Radio Corporation of America (RCA) 67
Reagan, Ronald 80
Reaganomics era 80, 81
real estate markets 89, 91
Recovery Act of 2009 36, 38
referendums 170
renewable energy technologies 278
Renoir 209
Rental Conversion plan 58
Report on the Economic Well-Being of U.S. House 24
repos 109
Representative Willis C. Hawley 178
Republican Party 15, 16, 20, 27, 33, 41, 44, 67, 69, 71, 72, 174, 175, 176, 186, 187, 188, 254
Republican Administrations 67, 173, 177, 208
required reserves (IORR) 90
Reserve Banks 85
reserve currency of the world 78, 245
Reserve, Federal Banking System 64
Reserve requirements 82
Revolving Credit Facility (RCF) 109
Ricardo, David 77
Rickards, James 115, 116
Rickards, Jim 93
Roaring 20s 65, 66, 192, 197, 200, 207, 242, 244
Robinson, Eugene 41, 276, 279
robo-signing 50, 51
robotic manufacturing 25
robotics 38, 181, 193, 240
Rockefeller 64
Rogers, Jim 222
Rogoff, Kenneth 104, 223
rogue economist 229, 231, 237
Romania 243

Roosevelt Administration 46, 75
Roosevelt, Franklin 34, 48, 74, 75
Roscoe, Mike 202
Ross, Wilbur 184
Rothschild 64
Roubini, Nouriel 169, 392
Rubin, Robert 117
Russia 191, 194
Russia sovereign debt default 114
Ryan, Beck & Co. 118

S

S&L crisis 133
S&P 500 44, 170, 175, 231
Saez, Emmanuel 203
Saito, Ryoei 209
San Francisco 389, 230
San Francisco State University 228, 230
Sandel, Michael 35
Sanders, Bernie 23, 27, 106, 107, 123, 206
Saudi Arabia 129
Savings and Loans industry 229
Say, J.B. 77
Schauble, Wolfgang 26
Schneiderman, Eric 51, 52
Schwenninger, Sherle 25
Scotland 168, 171
SEC 99, 117
Secretary of Housing and Urban Development 54
Secretary of Treasury 99
Secretary of United States Treasury 72
Section 13(3) of the FRA 109
Section 14 of the FRA 110
securities borrowing facility (SBF) 109
Securities and Exchange Commission 119
securitization process 51, 52
semiconductors 193
Senate 174, 184, 187
Senate Banking Committee 187
Senate Majority Leader 187
Senator Reed Smoot 178
Series of Term Repurchase Transactions (STOMO) 110
Shan, Zhong 178
Shanghai Tower 214
share buyback 224
Shiller, Robert 179, 189

short sales 53
Siberia 192
silver 168
Singapore 194
Sircus, Mark 285
Sixteenth Amendment (Amendment XVI) to the United States Constitution 65
Slovakia 169
Smith, Adam 77
Smoot, Reed 178
Smoot-Hawley Tariff Act of 1930 70, 178
Sobel, Robert 69, 133
Social Security Act in 1935 77
Social Security benefits 41
Softbank Corp. 135
solar energy 193
Son, Masayoshi 135
Sony 135
Soros, George 45, 169
Sotheby's 210, 211
Sound Advice 195
South Africa 132, 243
South Korea 194, 245
sovereign and government debt xi
sovereign debt crisis 222, 243, 259
sovereign debt loans 49
sovereign funds 29
Sovereign Wealth Funds 204, 251
Soviet Union 68, 81, 132, 196, 229, 276
Spain 96, 129
Special Economic Advisor 38
Special Facilities for Debt Forgiveness 215
special purpose facilities 107
Stalin, Joseph 191
Standard and Poor's Credit Agency (S&P) 43, 44, 223
Standard Oil of New Jersey 195
state attorney generals 50, 51, 54
State of the Union Address in January 2012 51
steel imports and a 10 percent tariff on aluminum 184
stock manipulation schemes in the 1920s 68
Strontium-90 283
student loan crisis 28, 45, 245, 389
Subprime Mortgage Crisis 15, 48
Summers, Larry 38, 117
super bubble 16, 29, 126, 176, 179, 181, 215, 388, 389

super-long economic cycles 68
supply and demand 77, 80
supply-side economics 80, 176
Supreme Court 102
Suskind, Ron 39
Sweden 169, 243
Switzerland 194

T

Taft, William 64
Taiwan 194
tariffs
   25% tariffs on automobiles 180
   steel and aluminum imports 178
TARP 35, 102
tax cuts 67, 93, 97, 208, 252, 254, 259
Taylor, John 56
Tea Party landslide victories 40
Tea Party-aligned Republicans 41
Tepper, Jonathan 243
Term Auction Facility (TAF) 108
Term Securities Lending Facility (TSLF) 110
The 1933 Banking Act 77
The Art of War 229
The Boock Report 388
The Commodity Futures Modernization Act of 2000 118
The Comptroller of the Currency 72
The Creature from Jekyll Island: A Second Look at 63, 85
The Dodd-Frank Reform and Consumer Protection Act 104
The Dollar Crisis (2005) 238
The Economic Security Project 96
The Economist 275, 277, 278
The Fed and Lehman Brothers 21
The Financial Crisis Inquiry Report 101
The General Theory of Employment, Interest and Mon 77
The Generational Spending Wave 231
The Global Times 184
The Great Boom Ahead (1993) 232
The Great Bull Market, Wall Street in the 1920s 69, 133
The Great Depression of 1990 131
The Great Depression of the 21st Century Greatest Economic Depression and 17
The Holy Grail of Macroeconomics: Lessons From Jap 136
The Making Home Affordable Modification Program 39
The American Middle Class Under Stress and Sherle Schwenninger 25
The Minneapolis Plan To End Too Big To Fail 122
The New New Deal: The Hidden Story of Change in th 36
The North American Free Trade Agreement (NAFTA) 181
The Times 51
Three Mile Island in Pennsylvania 279
Three Studies of Lucian Freud 211
Time Magazine 119, 128, 274
Toffler, Alvin 198
Tokyo 215, 232
Tokyo Electric Power Co. (TEPCO) 275
Tokyo Stock Exchange 128
Too Big To Fail 29, 56, 99, 88, 105, 106, 107, 113, 121, 122, 123 107, 113, 122, 123, 186, 187, 207
Toshiba 276
Toyota 135
trade deficits 245
Trade Partnership Worldwide 180
trade surplus 184
trade wars 26, 29, 178, 181, 183, 185, 188
Treasury bonds 67
Treasury Debt 43
Treasury Department 30, 39, 57, 117, 176
Treasury Secretary 38, 55
Treasury securities 89
Tricadia 30
trickle-down economics 44, 46, 96, 176, 201, 252, 259
Troubled Asset Relief Program (TARP) 87, 122
Truman, Harry 34
Trump Administration 27, 93, 173, 174, 174, 175, 180, 181, 182, 183, 184, 185, 189, 250, 251, 252
Trumponomics 181
trust companies 63
TSLF Options Program (TOP) 110
Tzu, Sun 229

Index

U

U.C. Berkeley 203
U.S. and global boom and bust from 2003 to 2008 390
U.S. boom and bust from 1995 to 2000 390
U.S. boom and bust of 1982 to 1987 390
U.S. Commerce Secretary 184
U.S. Court of Appeals in Manhattan 102
U.S. Freedom of Information Act (FOIA) 102
U.S. Geological Survey 274
U.S. government x, 170
U.S. Public Interest Research Group 187
U.S. Trade Representative 180, 185
U.S. Treasuries 92, 110, 114, 178, 184
U.S. Treasury 85, 95, 98, 99, 247
U.S. Treasury Department 117, 122
UBS 121
UBS Group 168
UK 16, 167, 168, 169, 170, 171, 172
Ulrich, Kendra 283
unconventional economic tools 140, 258
   negative interest rates 27
unconventional monetary policies 96
unconventional monetary tools 92, 94, 95, 111, 389, 238
unemployment 66, 74, 183, 225, 226
unemployment rate 174
Union Carbide 195
Unit on Mortgage Origination and Securitization Ab 52
United Arab Emirates 129
United Copper 63
United Kingdom (UK) 16
United Kingdom Independence Party (UKIP) 167
United Nations 128
United States 23, 26, 31, 33, 36, 42, 69, 170, 173, 177, 178, 179, 181, 182, 184, 185, 191, 192, 194, 195, 196, 204, 205, 229, 232, 239, 240, 246, 247, 248, 249, 250, 251, 252, 253, 254, 255, 256, 257, 278, 389, 390, 391, 392, 223, 225, 227, 233, 239, 240, 241, 242, 243, 244, 245,
   104 nuclear fission reactors in 280
   flight capital region and 170
   print a fiat-currency without inflation 249
United States Rubber 195
United States Steel 195

universal basic income (UBI) 96
University of Missouri-Kansas City 107
unrestricted capitalism 116
unrestricted free markets 87
uranium 281
uranium fuel 284
uranium-238 283
USA Massachusetts Institute of Technology (MIT) 280

V

Venezuela 14, 17, 27, 201
Vietnam War 79, 196, 245
Vogtle nuclear project 281
Volcker, Paul 80, 203
Volcker Rule (Title VI of the Act) 105, 187-188
Vornado Realty Trust 214
Vulture funds 57

W

Waldorf Astoria Hotel 215
Wales 168
Wall Street 21, 22, 29, 31, 35, 38, 39, 40, 47, 58, 63, 67, 69, 82, 95, 96, 107, 116, 117, 118, 119, 124, 133, 143, 174 186, 206, 207
Wall Street Journal 117, 133
Wall Street team 39
War of 1812 196
War on Terror 34
Warburg 64
Warhol, Andy 211
Warren, Elizabeth 39, 187
Washington D.C. 21, 22, 26, 27, 34, 35, 39, 40, 41, 43, 44, 49, 54, 55, 69, 76, 84, 85, 98, 99, 116, 118, 206, 281
Washington Post 41, 276, 279
wealth inequalities xi, 168, 200
wealth inequality 16, 23, 24, 26, 27, 97, 169, 177, 188, 200, 203, 204, 206, 207, 208, 214, 259
wealthy elites 26, 63, 259
Wells Fargo 50, 52, 53, 103, 121
West Germany 204
Western Europe 135
White House 35, 38, 44, 45, 49, 89, 121, 143, 174, 177, 185, 188
Willkie Farr & Gallagher LLP 102

Wilson, Woodrow 64
World Bank 42
World Economic Collapse: The Last Decade and the G 229
World Trade Organization 25, 183, 185
World War I 65, 78, 196, 199, 226, 233, 234, 242, 243, 244, 246, 254, 392
World War II 76, 78, 79, 81, 99, 117, 131, 170, 183, 185, 196, 199, 392, 226, 233, 234 244, 254, 275, 281,
WTO 183, 185

X

Xinhua 184

Y

Yahoo! 135
Yellen, Janet 95
yen 95, 142, 210, 278
yuan 95

Z

zenith of capitalism 393
Zero Hedge 121
Zero-bound interest rates 215
ZIRP 91, 92, 94, 215
Zoellick, Robert 42
Zucman, Gabriel 203

www.ingramcontent.com/pod-product-compliance
Lightning Source LLC
Chambersburg PA
CBHW080904170526
45158CB00008B/1988